FORMAL LANGUAGE THEORY

Perspectives and Open Problems

FORMAL LANGUAGE THEORY

Perspectives and Open Problems

Edited by

RONALD V. BOOK

DEPARTMENT OF MATHEMATICS
UNIVERSITY OF CALIFORNIA AT SANTA BARBARA
SANTA BARBARA, CALIFORNIA

ACADEMIC PRESS
A Subsidiary of Harcourt Brace Jovanovich, Publishers
New York London Toronto Sydney San Francisco 1980

ACADEMIC PRESS, INC.
111 Fifth Avenue, New York, New York 10003

United Kingdom Edition published by
ACADEMIC PRESS, INC. (LONDON) LTD.
24/28 Oval Road, London NW1 7DX

Library of Congress Cataloging in Publication Data
Main entry under title:

Formal language theory.

  Proceedings of a conference held Dec. 10-14, 1979,
in Santa Barbara, Calif.
  Includes bibliographical references.
  1. Formal languages—Congresses. I. Book,
Ronald V.
QA267.3.F6   511.3   80-22435
ISBN 0-12-115350-9

PRINTED IN THE UNITED STATES OF AMERICA

80 81 82 83   9 8 7 6 5 4 3 2 1

CONTENTS

LIST OF CONTRIBUTORS

Numbers in parentheses indicate the pages on which authors' contributions begin.

ALFRED V. AHO (325), Bell Laboratories, 600 Mountain Avenue, Murray Hill, New Jersey 07974

JEAN-MICHEL AUTEBERT (49, 89), Université Paris VII, Paris, France

JOFFROY BEAUQUIER (89, 407), Université de Picardie, Amiens, France

LUC BOASSON (49, 89), Université Paris VII, Paris, France

JANUSZ BRZOZOWSKI (23), Department of Computer Science, University of Waterloo, Waterloo, Ontario, Canada

KAREL CULIK II (167), Department of Computer Science, University of Waterloo, Waterloo, Ontario, Canada

JOOST ENGELFRIET (241), Department of Applied Mathematics, Twente University of Technology, Enschede, The Netherlands

SEYMOUR GINSBURG (1), Computer Science Department, University of Southern California, Los Angeles, California 90007

JONATHAN GOLDSTINE (109), Computer Science Department, The Pennsylvania State University, University Park, Pennsylvania 16802

GÉRARD HUET (349), IRIA-Laboria, Rocquencourt, France, and SRI International, Menlo Park, California

MICHEL LATTEUX (89), Université de Lille I, Villeneuve-d'Ascq, France

BURKHARD MONIEN (287), Gesamthochschule Paderborn, Paderborn, West Germany

MAURICE NIVAT (407), Université Paris VII, Paris, France

DEREK C. OPPEN (349), Department of Computer Science, Stanford University, Stanford, California 94305

GRZEGORZ ROZENBERG (195), University of Leiden, Leiden, The Netherlands

ARTO SALOMAA (141), Mathematics Department, University of Turku, Turku, Finland

*IVAN HAL SUDBOROUGH (287), Department of Computer Science, Gesamthochschule Paderborn, Paderborn, West Germany

---

*Present Address: Department of Computer Science, Northwestern University, Evanston, Illinois 60201

PREFACE

A symposium on Formal Language Theory was held in Santa Barbara, California, December 10–14, 1979. The symposium was organized in order to focus on the major open problems of the field, to put recent results into perspective, and to assess current trends. Sixteen invited lectures and 14 contributed research announcements were presented at the symposium. Most of the research announcements will appear in professional journals. The texts of 13 of the 16 lectures are contained in this volume.

The opening chapter is by Seymour Ginsburg, who surveys some of the various methods used to specify languages and classes of languages. One class of languages that arises in many parts of theoretical computer science is the class of regular sets. Although many researchers believe that everything is known about the class of regular sets, there are still many unanswered questions. Janusz Brzozowski outlines the current state of knowledge of six open questions concerning regular sets.

The class of context-free languages plays an extremely important role in formal language theory, and there are many open questions about this class. The class of context-free grammars provides an extremely simple model for the notion of recursion, and therefore many properties of context-free grammars and languages find application elsewhere. Jean-Michel Autebert and Luc Boasson present a number of results that help in understanding the structure of this class. In the following chapter, Autebert and Boasson collaborated with Joffroy Beauquier and Michel Latteux to describe algebraic (i.e., context-free) languages that are "nearly" rational (i.e., regular), leading to some results about minimal cones.

It is well known that there are important connections between the study of formal languages and the study of abstract automata. Jonathan Goldstine believes that there is much more to that connection than meets the eye, and in his chapter, he suggests a method for the specification of automata that would make clear the effect that operations on acceptors have on their external behavior.

One of the most active areas in language theory today stems neither from the study of natural languages nor the study of programming languages but rather from the study of developmental biology. L systems are generative structures that provide a simple model for the notion of parallelism. Investigation of L systems has led to new studies of the combinatorial properties of strings, sequences, and morphisms. Arto Salomaa presents some of the basic questions about morphisms on languages, their equality sets, and the use of these notions in studying grammar forms. Karel

Culik describes research concerning test sets of pairs of morphisms and decidability of questions about equality sets. Grzegorz Rozenberg surveys a large number of the results and open questions about the mathematical theory of L systems.

Trees play an important role in the study of such topics as formal grammars and languages and data structures. Tree-manipulating systems, such as tree grammars and tree automata, arise in the theory of computation and in logic as well as in language theory. Joost Engelfriet brings together a number of results and open questions about trees, tree languages, and tree-manipulating systems. Topics include tree transducers, attribute grammars, alternating automata, L systems, and equivalence problems. One conclusion he draws is that the study of tree languages may be quite useful in developing a unifying structure for more advanced theories of computation.

Determining the complexity of specific questions about formal languages is a productive source of problems. In recent years it has become clear that there is another major connection between the study of computational complexity and that of formal language theory: the similarity of the structure theories of the two fields. Not only do the questions of determinism versus nondeterminism and time versus space arise in both fields, but also the study of classes represented by individual languages (i.e., by complete sets or by generators) is very important in both fields. Burkhard Monien and Hal Sudborough describe many of these topics in their study of the interface between language theory and complexity theory.

Being able to specify and match patterns of strings is an essential part of various information-processing activities. Alfred Aho believes that knowledge of automata and formal language theory can be extremely helpful in developing algorithms for string pattern matching problems that arise in areas such as text editing and lexical analysis. In his chapter, Aho provides evidence of this by examining some basic classes of string patterns that are useful in these activities and analyzes some of the time–space trade-offs that are inherent in these problems.

Rewriting systems are not just formal grammars of the Chomsky variety or L systems. Term rewriting systems arise in the study of logic, programming language specification, abstract data types, and other areas. The study of computation by means of term rewriting systems and of computation by means of equations can be developed in the framework of traditional abstract algebra. Gérard Huet and Derek Oppen survey recent work on computation by equations and rewriting systems.

The fact that formal language theory can arise in areas apparently unrelated to it is well illustrated in the chapter by Joffroy Beauquier and Maurice Nivat. They give formal models for two problems—security and synchronization. By modeling information systems in terms of automata theoretic notions, one may study the set of all behaviors of such a system, and this set is best described as a language. Beauquier and Nivat show how knowledge of the class of regular sets and the class of context-free languages can be quite useful in such a study.

ACKNOWLEDGMENTS

In organizing the symposium on Formal Language Theory, I received many helpful comments and much encouragement from Maurice Nivat and Arto Salomaa. I would like to thank Franz Brandenburg, John Doner, Matthias Jantzen, and Eljas Soisalon-Soininen for their help during the symposium. Jodi Hammond provided a great deal of administrative support. None of this activity could have taken place without the aid and support of Leslie Wilson and Celia Wrathall.

The symposium received financial support from the National Science Foundation under grant MCS79-04012 and from the Department of Mathematics and the College of Letters and Science, University of California at Santa Barbara. The preparation of this volume was supported in part by the National Science Foundation under grant MCS77-11360.

FORMAL LANGUAGE THEORY

METHODS FOR SPECIFYING FAMILIES OF FORMAL LANGUAGES — PAST-PRESENT-FUTURE

Seymour Ginsburg[1]

Computer Science Department
University of Southern California
Los Angeles, California

I. INTRODUCTION

Good morning ladies and gentlemen. It is indeed a privilege and honor to provide the keynote address to this international formal language symposium here at Santa Barbara. It is very seldom that a scientist has the opportunity, as afforded me this day, to speak to such a large group of his peers on some general subject. For me it is a first. As such, I have given considerable thought to an appropriate topic. And its resolution has not been easy. I finally chose the subject "Methods for specifying families of formal languages" for several reasons:

(1) it relates a number of seemingly diverse activities. Knowingly or otherwise, many of you have been involved in at least one method.

(2) it should be of interest to a large segment of the audience. This follows from (1).

(3) it deals with truly basic matters. This is important

---

[1]The author was supported in part by the National Science Foundation under Grant MCS-77-22323. Preparation of this paper was supported in part by the National Science Foundation under Grant No. MCS-79-04012.

to me because of the very strong personal belief, namely "that what language theory needs nowadays is a return to fundamental issues — both old and new.[2] For when all is said and done, the real growth of this field will only continue as long as there are primitive questions of deep-seated significance to resolve.

(4) It indicates at least one direction for future re-search. This will become clear as the discussion progresses.

(5) It involves ideas of concern — either past or present — to me. Indeed, the preparation of this manuscript has given me a unified perspective of a number of themes I had hitherto regarded as different and which have occupied my attention over the years.

As the title indicates, my talk today deals with different ways to describe families of languages (of interest to compu-ter scientists). Specifically, I shall focus attention on three major methods and briefly mention a number of minor ones. Because of the vagueness of problems associated with the topic at hand, e.g., what is a computer-science family of languages, the presentation will frequently be philosophical or specula-tive in nature. And, in deference to the limited time avail-able, it will usually be given at an informal, rather than pre-cise or technical, level. The reader desirous of specific de-tails will have to seek them elsewhere, such as in the cited references.

---

[2] I am not advocating the abandonment of studies of either special language families or technical improvements of es-tablished results. Rather, I am urging a greater effort in seeking out basic language-theory problems.

II. ORIGINS

Let us begin by examining the roots of the field. What were the circumstances leading to the founding of formal language theory as a discipline within computer science? This is actually a combination of two questions. How did formal language theory begin? And how did it manage to become a part of theoretical computer science instead of mathematics or logic or linguistics or philosophy or ...? In the process of reviewing the early history we will see the embryonic development of three major methods of specifying families of formal languages.

It is common knowledge that formal languages arose from the study of natural languages. But specifically, it was the work of the linguist Noam Chomsky (8) in 1956 which is regarded as the starting point. In that pioneering paper, a language is regarded as consisting of (i) a finite alphabet Σ and (ii) a subset $L \subseteq \Sigma^*$. To this day almost all language-theory activity has operated under those two assumptions. [There have been occasional studies (34;33;12) concerned with infinite strings, most recently the work of Nivat and his associates (39;4). But as far as I am aware, sets of words over an _infinite_ alphabet, such as the set $\{a_n^n a_{n+1}^n / n \geq 1\}$, over the infinite alphabet $\{a_i / i \geq 1\}$, have not been seriously examined.] In that same 1956 paper, Chomsky also essentially presented the concept of a general phrase structure grammar.[3] However, it wasn't until three years later, i.e., 1959, that Chomsky (9) delineated the major subtypes now called context sensitive, context free, and right linear. Even though the birth of formal language theory

---

[3]This is the model of a generative device against which all other models are invariably compared.

is usually attributed to the earlier paper, it was the later
one which placed formal languages in a mathematically attractive light and began to draw theoretically oriented adherents.
But both papers indicated that one way to define a family of
languages is by generative mechanisms, i.e., by grammars.

Besides Chomsky, there were others during that time period,
1951-1960, who played a significant role in launching this
field. In 1951 the logician Stephen Kleene spent the summer
at the Rand Corporation in Santa Monica studying neural nets —
in the sense of McCulloch-Pitts. However, the major result of
his research (31), published in 1956, was the characterization
of regular sets in terms of union, concatenation, and Kleene
closure. Subsequent papers by Myhill (35) in 1957 and Nerode
(37) in 1958 expounded further on regular sets. Of particular
note, furthermore, was that Myhill spoke explicitly of associ-
ating a regular set with a simplified type of computing device —
in modern terminology, a finite-state acceptor. These results
on regular sets, and many new ones, were presented in a thor-
ough, unified manner by Rabin and Scott in their famous 1959
article[4] (40).

It is interesting to observe that none of the last three
cited papers seemed to be cognizant of Chomsky's research.
This in spite of the fact that it dealt not only with sets of
words but with "finite-state languages" (8). On the other
hand, Chomsky and Miller (11) in 1958 wrote a lengthy manuscript on finite-state languages but either were unaware of, or
did not realize, their connection with regular sets. The phrase

---

[4]It was here also that the basic notion of nondeterminism
appears for the first time.

"finite state languages" actually appears in the 1956 and 1958 papers. In other words, neither school of thought really understood the other's work. So where was the equivalence between Kleene's regular sets and Chomsky's finite-state languages first noted? It was in Chomsky's 1959 paper (9). In addition, Chomsky's 1959 document mentioned the equivalence between right-linear languages and regular sets. Thus the two streams of activity finally merged. One by-product of this joining was to suggest that acceptors could be fruitfully used to define formal languages.

In spite of the realization in Chomsky's 1959 article that regular sets coincided with right-linear languages, a true appreciation of the importance bf regular sets for formal language theory had to wait until the appearance of the paper by Bar-Hillel, Perles and Shamir[5] (3). It was there that a number of connections were established between regular sets and context-free languages. The premier one was the theorem stating that the intersection of a context-free language and a regular set was context free. The subtlety, influence, and ramifications of that result for language theory, and even the present topic cannot be overstated. Its numerous applications to context-free languages are found in every current textbook. [My favorite: without using the aforementioned result, try to prove that removing a single word from a context-free language still leaves a context-free language.] But its extension to

---

[5]While the paper formally appeared in 1961 the results were widely known in 1960. For example, Bar-Hillel spoke about them in 1960 at various institutions in the United States. And I vividly remember a personal conversation with Bar-Hillel in December 1960 in which he related the findings. This exchange of information, in turn, influenced a manuscript I was then writing (21).

other families of languages is fundamental. A modern version
of that theorm would be: "a finite mask on the finite control
of a particular type of device leads to a device of the same
type," or "a good family of computer science-formal languages
is closed under intersection with regular sets." [I shall refer to any of the three formulations as the Intersection Theorem.] My own thoughts on the latter extension, based on personal experience, is on the extreme side. I believe that a
family of languages which is not closed under intersection with
regular sets should not be studied for its own right but only
for other purposes. In this category of not-really-worth examining, I would place the family of sequential context-free
languages (21). Thus the Intersection Theorem, albeit in a
negative way, is a clue toward determining appropriate families of languages to study.

There is still one link missing between formal language
theory a la Chomsky and computer science. And that was a solid
connection between formal languages and programming languages.
That link was discovered in 1960. In the late fifties, an international committee of scientists constructed a higher level
programming language appropriate for that time. Their product,
which appeared in the May 1960 issue of CACM, was ALGOL-60 (36).
For language theorists,the importance of ALGOL-60 was its description in terms of BNF formalism. For the first time, the
syntax of a programming language was specified in a formal way!
Several months after ALGOL-60 was published, Gordon Rice and
the present speaker noticed (21) that BNF was essentially
equivalent to context-free grammars. That observation opened
the flood gates for formal language theory. Instead of being

of concern to a scattering of linguists, logicians, and mathematicians, formal languages now became an object of study to
that large group of individuals interested in the rapidly developing field of computers. And that connection between BNF
and context-free grammars is, by far, the single most important reason formal language theory is regarded as a part of
computer science and not some other discipline. It is a historical fact that shortly after the connection was established,
formal languages quickly became one of the most active and extensive areas of theoretical computer science. The initial attention went to context-free languages, but soon spread to
other families. Nevertheless, it seems to be as true today as
it was 19 years ago. The almost exclusive interest of "practical" computer scientists in formal languages is with the
context-free languages, especially various subfamilies. My own
dictum here is, "We live or die on the context-free languages."

    Just how useful and important are context-free languages
to computer science? The answer to that question is best left
to the practitioners of our discipline, e.g., the compiler
writers. It is no secret that context-free grammars are only
a first order approximation to the various mechanisms used for
specifying the syntax of modern programming languages. We have
been aware of this since 1961 (17). And during this time span,
many models have been suggested as either more appropriate or
a better approximation. One of recent vintage is the two-level
grammars of van Wijngaarden (42). The fact remains that no
matter what theorists or pseudo-theorists propose as a step
forward for programming-language grammars: if the laboratory
and computer room people refuse to acknowledge and use that
model, then it is just a theoretical construct of marginal

utility. This in spite of how many beautiful theorems emerge
and how many assistant professors get tenure studying its ramifications. Nevertheless, the challenge is still there. Find
a better theoretical model for programming-language grammars
which is accepted by the practicing computer fraternity and
you have made a huge contribution to the field! Also, such a
model might very well change our conception of the nature of a
grammar! Any takers in the audience?

In summary, this early period suggested two methods of specifying formal languages, one by grammars and the other by acceptors. And, as will be seen shortly, the Intersection Theorem played a role in suggesting a third method.

III. SPECIFICATION FORMALISM

Let us now turn to an overview of various methods of specification.

The early sixties witnessed a tremendous growth of language
theory — especially the Chomsky hierarchy. Most of the basic
results of context-free languages were developed, as well as
much of our current knowledge of context-sensitive languages.
Of particular importance was the discovery of acceptor types
for the context-free (10;15) and the context-sensitive languages (32), that is, pushdown acceptors and linear-bounded
acceptors. This, combined with the already known acceptor
types for the regular and the r.e. sets, suggested that there
was an excellent chance many interesting families could be described by acceptors. In other words, it was reasonable to expect "languages to be defined by their recognizers." In view

of the obvious importance of acceptors for computer science and
the ability to define many families by acceptors, specifying
families by devices quickly became the paramount method of description — and has remained so to this day. (Examples of families described that way are the various multicounter languages, the stack languages, and the nexted stack langauges.)
Naturally, one has to resolve the problem of what is a family
of acceptors and how does an acceptor accept, i.e., define, a
language.

Starting from the mid sixties and continuing up to the
present, there have been scores of special families of languages introduced for one reason or another. (Can you really regard yourself as a serious language theorist if you are not a
parent of at least one new family?) Of course, many of these
families were examined for special properties. Nevertheless,
irrespective of their original motivation and irrespective of
their method of definition, these new families were invariably
investigated for their closure properties. Closure under union,
quotient, intersection, intersection with regular sets, gsm,
complementation, word reversal, substitution, etc. You all
know where I'm heading. Many of these families were found to
have common closure properties. As a result, in 1966 Sheila
Greibach and I began a systematic study of families of languages by their closure properties (20). A family closed under
ε-free homomorphism, inverse homomorphism, intersection with
regular sets, union, concatenation, and Kleene closure was
called an AFL. The details aren't important. It is now history that AFL theory quickly developed a vast literature (19)
and still has numerous aficionados. The original structure of

an AFL has since been joined by others. By removing some of
the closure properties, we soon had such structures as trios,
semi-AFL, and cylinders. In the years ahead there will surely
be additional structures defined by closure operations. After
all, there are always hungry doctoral students seeking a thesis
topic. [The situation here is akin to starting with groups,
then going to semi-groups, and finally the various "oids."] If
the trend keeps up, we may need the counterpart to universal
algebras for closure-property structures.

Well, what do closure properties have to do with specifications of formal languages? Plenty! An integral part of
closure-property studies deals with the "smallest family containing some given family of languages and closed under ... ."
An instance of that is the Kleene Theorem for regular sets,
i.e., the family of regular sets is the smallest family containing the finite sets and closed under union, concatenation,
and Kleene closure. Another example is the description of the
context-free languages as the smallest family containing the
Dyck set over two letters and closed under ε-free homomorphism,
inverse homomorphism, and intersection with regular sets. This
approach allows us to define families of languages almost at
will. Pick a family $\mathcal{L}$ and consider the smallest family containing $\mathcal{L}$ and closed under ... . To illustrate, consider the
smallest family containing the linear context-free languages
and closed under substitution. This, of course, is the family
of derivation-bounded (also known as the quasi-rational) languages and has been studied extensively (45;38;22). (In case
$\mathcal{L}$ consists of a single language L, the resultant family is said
to be principal, with respect to those closure properties, and

L is called a _generator_. Thus, in view of the above example,
the context-free language is a principal AFL, more strongly, a
principal trio, and the Dyck set over two letters is a generator.)

Simultaneous with the development of AFL theory, i.e.,
closure-property theory, the notion of a "family of acceptors"
was examined. In (20) the concept of an AFA, standing for abstract family of acceptors, was introduced and studied.[6] The
heart of the definition of an AFA is a universal read function
and a universal write function, both defined over the set of
all possible auxiliary storages. For the purposes of the present discussion, the input tape is assumed to be one-way nondeterministic. Not only did AFA seem to capture the intuitive
idea of reading, writing, moving, and accepting, but it also
yielded many one-way nondeterministic types of acceptors as
special instances. Thus AFA provided a very reasonable model
for families of acceptors. Earlier we noted that acceptors
were obviously computer-science oriented and were the paramount
(but not the only) way of defining families of languages.
Therefore AFA-defined families of languages were important to
study. And then a surprising theory happened. It turned out
that one could characterize both AFL (20) and semiAFL (19) by
AFA. Thus AFL and semiAFL became important families to study,
in the abstract. Because of the decidedly different methods
of definition, i.e., via closure properties and via AFA-accept-
ance, these families of languages had to be "natural" objects
in some aesthetic-mathematical sense. And, of course, "the

----

[6]An alternative approach to a family of acceptors was proposed by Hopcroft and Ullman in their paper on balloon
automata (27).

smallest family containing a given family and closed under
semiAFL or AFL closure properties" now had to be regarded as
an important specification method.

One additional comment on the preceding. All our experience seems to suggest that families of programming languages
are subfamilies of the recursively enumerable sets.[7] Neither
of the above methods of description yields that conclusion. If
only subfamilies of the r.e. sets are permitted, then the closure-property definition would have to be limited to r.e. sets
and the read and write functions of an AFA would have to be
partial recursive functions. Other methods of description
would require similar "recursive" restrictions.

At this point the audience may have a feeling that something is missing. Well, there is. Remember — our initial
discussion centered about the Chomsky hierarchy, and thus included acceptors and grammars. Suddenly we were talking about
describing families of languages by acceptors and closure properties. What in the world ever happened to grammars? Why
were they shunted aside? For an excellent reason — indeed,
just about the best reason there is. And this brings me to
what I regard as the most important open question in language
theory. No — it is not P versus NP; and no — it is not lba
languages versus deterministic languages. The question is
philosophical in nature. Simply stated it is:

what is a grammar?

For our purposes, the question should be modified to:

what is a family of grammars?

---

[7]Subfamilies of the recursive sets, if the recognition
problem is to be decidable.

The answer to the above should have the basic characteristic that families of grammars yield exactly what families of acceptors yield, presumably AFL (or semiAFL). Otherwise, grammars and acceptors could not be viewed as alternative descriptions of the same objects. I shall return to the subject of grammars in a few minutes.

The preceding discourse has focussed attention on three methods of describing families of (computer-science) languages: closure properties, acceptors, and grammars. Are there other ways? Yes — but none that have gained the appeal and widespread popularity of the above three. Several will now be briefly mentioned. Undoubtedly others could be added to the list.

(1) The first is the use of predicates to define language families. Neil Jones did some research on this method. In (28;29) he characterized Turing machines, linear-bounded acceptors, and two-way multitape nonwriting acceptors in terms of certain predicates. The papers by Celia Wrathall (43;44) may also be regarded as work in the same spirit.

(2) A second possible approach involves a familiar tool to computer scientists, namely programs. In the late sixties, Dana Scott (41) tried to gain support for describing acceptors (which are essentially nondeterministic in nature) by programs (which are essentially deterministic in nature). If the idea could be upgraded to include our current view of acceptors, then programs should be capable of defining families of languages. References (25) and (26) by Henke relate to this.

(3) Another method is due to Peter Downey. In his thesis (14) he undertook to provide characterizations of vastly dif-

ferent families of languages, for example, the context-free, the indexed, the ETOL, and the EDTOL languages, in terms of recursion schemes, these being certain systems of equations. His approach seems fruitful and I'm surprised it hasn't received more attention than it has.

(4)   The final way is due to Ronald Book. In (5) he described several families of languages (e.g., the r.e. sets, the arithmetic sets, the rudimentary languages, and the NP languages) in terms of the regular sets and sundry closure operations. The closure operations consist of the Boolean ones and certain "space restrictions," i.e., linear erasing and polynomial erasing, of homomorphic replication. There are, of course, an infinite number of possible space restrictions. In (6) he added the operation of "weakly transitive closure" to obtain the context-sensitive and the PSPACE languages.

Each of the above methods has been used to describe certain families of languages. Whether or not any of these ways can be refined in such a manner as to yield exactly those families described by acceptors is another matter. Those which can would certainly grow in importance, and most likely lead to new insights. Indeed, the more the merrier.

We may abstract the discussion about ways of specifying families of languages as follows. For each method M for specifying families of languages, computer-science oriented or not, let $\mathcal{U}(M)$ be the collection of all such families defined by M. If M_1 is a particular specification mechanism which, for some reason, is "linked" with computers, then $\mathcal{U}(M_1)$ is regarded as a collection of computer-science families.

[There may be many such mechanisms, say $M_2, M_3, \ldots$, with corresponding collections of families, $\mathcal{U}(M_2), \mathcal{U}(M_3) \ldots$.] Suppose M is some specification mechanism. Two possibilities arise between $\mathcal{U}(M)$ and $\mathcal{U}(M_1)$.

(a) $\mathcal{U}(M) = \mathcal{U}(M_1)$. This is the desired situation and suggests that $\mathcal{U}(M_1)$ is a "natural" collection of families, in addition to being of computer science interest. (The more different ways there are to describe $\mathcal{U}(M_1)$ the more $\mathcal{U}(M_1)$ would be regarded as a "natural" collection.) In addition, the importance of M is elevated since it is now a vehicle for describing $\mathcal{U}(M_1)$.

(b) $\mathcal{U}(M) \neq \mathcal{U}(M_1)$. This is what usually happens. After all, how lucky can you be. In this case one either discards M or seeks to slightly modify it so that it becomes a method M' satisfying $\mathcal{U}(M') = \mathcal{U}(M_1)$.

IV. GRAMMARS

Let us return to the fundamental philosophical problems of what is a grammar, i.e., what is a generative system, and what is a family of grammars? The situation now becomes less factual and more speculative. What follows represents my own views on the subject. For a while, I entertained the notion that a grammar was just a one-state acceptor. The underlying rationale was that the change of auxiliary storage in an acceptor was essentially the rewriting in a grammar. However, I ultimately discarded that idea although I suspect there is probably considerable similarity between a grammar and an acceptor. When I look around and see the wide variety of different generative systems — for example, phrase structure, scattered context (23), state (30), indexed (1), two-type bracketed (24), macro (16), and the van Wijngaarden grammars (42) — there is nothing I can visualize as a unifying concept, either technically or aesthetically, except some general sort of "rewriting," i.e., mathematical transformation, process. (Obviously, this type of model can only capture a few superficial aspects of the generative systems. The heart of the model — the nature or essence of the rewriting schemes — will be missing.)

What would such a rewriting process consist of? My intuition says that it should be approximately a 4-tuple $G = (V, \Sigma, P, \sigma)$, where V is the total alphabet, Σ the terminal alphabet, P the productions, i.e., P is a finite subset of $(V-\Sigma)^+ \times V^*$ and σ is in $V-\Sigma$. Naturally $V-\Sigma$ would contain a variety of different-purpose symbols such as variables, intermediate variables, flags, separators, functions symbols, etc. A crucial point arises. What does $x \underset{G}{\Longrightarrow} y$ mean? In other words, what does it mean mathematically for x to be rewritten as y? As indicated above, we can only expect to describe this in broad generalities because of the wide spread of different "rewriting mechanisms" in use. The discussion that follows pertains to having x "combine" with one production to get y, independent of how x was obtained and independent of the remaining productions. We are thus ostensibly employing sequential usage instead of parallel. And what does "combine" mean? To me, that signifies a relation specified in advance in a uniform way (just like the movement of an acceptor de-

pends on the original read and write functions). The phrase
"uniform way" makes more sense in the framework of a family
of grammars. So let us address the modified question of what
is an abstract family of grammars.

By an <u>abstract family of grammars</u> I mean a 4-tuple $(V_\infty,$
$\Sigma_\infty, \rho, \mathscr{G})$. Here V_∞ is a universal total alphabet, $\Sigma_\infty \subseteq V_\infty$ is an
infinite universal terminal alphabet, with $V_\infty - \Sigma_\infty$ infinite, ρ
is a universal rewrite relation on[8] $(V_\infty - \Sigma_\infty)^+ \times V_\infty^* \times V_\infty^* \times V_\infty^*$, and
$\mathscr{G}$ is the set of all 4-tuples $G = (V, \Sigma, P, \sigma)$, where V and Σ are
finite subsets of V_∞ and Σ_∞ respectively, P is a finite subset
of $(V - \Sigma)^+ \times V^*$, and σ is in $V - \Sigma$. For G in $\mathscr{G}$ write $x \xRightarrow[G]{} y$ if
there exists $u \rightarrow v$ in P such that (u, v, x, y) is in ρ. [Thus
the production $u \rightarrow v$, no matter in which grammar of $\mathscr{G}$ it appears, will yield y when applied to x.] Let $L(G) = \{w$ in $\Sigma^* /$
$\sigma \xRightarrow[G]{*} w\}$ and $\mathscr{L}(\mathscr{G}) = \{L(G) / G$ in $\mathscr{G}\}$. Without further conditions
on ρ, the relation $\xRightarrow[G]{}$ and the family $\mathscr{L}(\mathscr{G})$ can be rather
wild. For example, our notion of rewriting allows coding of
a finite set of productions into one production. Specifically,
if $(u_1, v_1), \ldots, (u_r, v_r)$ are r productions, then $(u_1 \# u_2 \# \cdots \# u_r,$
$v_1 \# v_2 \# \cdots \# v_r)$, where $\#$ is a new symbol, may be viewed as a
production in a new ρ representing the r initial ones in the
old ρ. Thus, without additional conditions on ρ, we actually
have not distinguished sequential usage from parallel! As
another example, for each countable family $\mathscr{L}$ of languages
over Σ_∞, there is a ρ such that $\mathscr{L}(\mathscr{G}) = \mathscr{L}$. For let σ_L be a
distinct symbol in $V_\infty - \Sigma_\infty$ for each L in $\mathscr{L}$. Then $\rho = \bigcup_{\sigma_L} \{\sigma_L, a\sigma_L,$
$u\sigma_L, ua\sigma_L)/a$ in Σ_∞, u in $\Sigma_\infty^*\} \cup \bigcup_{\sigma_L} \{(\sigma_L, \varepsilon, u\sigma_L, u)/u$ in $L\}$ has the

---

[8] That is, ρ is a subset of $(V_\infty - \Sigma_\infty)^+ \times V_\infty^* \times V_\infty^* \times V_\infty^*$.

requisite property. Now we have agreed, for the purposes of
the present discussion, that the language families of concern
to us are either AFL or semiAFL. And so we come to the key
question.

(ρ) What are reasonable, nice, necessary and sufficient
conditions on ρ in order for $\mathcal{L}(\mathcal{J})$ to be an AFL (or semiAFL)?
Unfortunately, I only have the question and not the answer.
And remember, the conditions on ρ should be of such a nature
as to allow most of the current grammars to be special instances. Of course, even if the ρ question is resolved, there
still remains the problem of obtaining a more detailed version
of the rewriting process than described in the above model.

Let me comment briefly on the ρ question. In an attempt
to gain some insight into the ρ question, Armen Gabrielian and
I attacked a weaker problem (18). We tried to present a procedure which produced, for each trio $\mathcal{L}$ of r.e. sets, a "family
of phrase structure grammars" defining $\mathcal{L}$. A key factor in our
thinking was how to guarantee closure under intersection with
regular sets. Our approach was to emulate the construction
given in (3) of the Intersection Theorem. In effect, each
variable was a triple, with two of the coordinates being states.
Clearly not very elegant. But desperate people will resort to
desperate measures. Ultimately we managed to describe a procedure, but the rules and families of grammars obtained were
highly artificial and mathematically intractable. Because of
the unsatisfactory nature of the families of grammars, a year
or so later Armin Cremers and I tried to simplify the rules
and the families of grammars determined. We succeeded in that
effort, obtaining what is now called a grammar form (13). How-

semiAFL, but those by (3) and (4) are not. But then, who
ys that semiAFL and AFL are the only reasonable closure-
operty structures to consider in connection with computer-
iented families of languages? The reader might also find it
structive to see for which i, $1 \leq i \leq 4$, there exists $\rho_i \subseteq$
$_\infty - \Sigma_\infty) \times V_\infty^* \times V_\infty^* \times V_\infty^*$ which would realize the legitimate deriva-
ions in (i) above. In any case, it is not clear (to me at
east) how one should distinguish between a type of grammar
nd a type of grammar satisfying some property. Hopefully,
ike art we may be uncertain a priori what we want, but we will
ecognize it if we see it.

V. CONCLUSIONS

Most of the discussion in the preceding two sections has
revolved around methods of specification yielding the families
defined by AFA operating in a one-way nondeterministic manner,
call it method M_1. One can certainly make reasonable cases to
justify that AFA operating one-way deterministically two-way
deterministically, and two-way nondeterministically, call these
methods M_2, M_3, and M_4 respectively, are also appropriate for
describing computer-science oriented families of languages.
[What is so sacred about one-way nondeterministic?] The clo-
sure property structures characterizing $\mathcal{U}(M_2)$ and $\mathcal{U}(M_3)$ are
known (7;2). That for $\mathcal{U}(M_4)$ is not. Whether the remaining
specification methods mentioned earlier, especially families
of gramars, can be modified to yield $\mathcal{U}(M_2)$, $\mathcal{U}(M_3)$, and $\mathcal{U}(M_4)$
respectively, are open.

ever, the simplification was achieved at the exp

the desired generality, i.e., the presentation o

grammars for each trio of r.e. sets. The new moc

ed certain principal semiAFL of the context-free

The emphasis of the research here subsequently ch.

studying abstract families of grammars to examinir

of grammars based on the notion of "looks like" a

mar.[9] The phrase "looks like" is employed since tl

each rule in each grammar of such a family is deter

the shape of the rules in the master grammar. The

of these two attempts was to gain familiarity with ｜

and questions about families of grammar, but to make

in the basic grammar problems.[10]

The discussion so far has been conducted under t.

tion that we all agree, more or less, on which genera

tems fit an intuitive concept of what is a type of gr

But that assumption may be false! Given $k \geq 2$, which

following would you consider a "bona fide" type of gr

(1) Derivation-bounded grammars of bound k.

(2) Nonterminal-bounded grammars of bound k.

(3) k-ambiguous context-free grammars.

(4) LR(k) grammars.

Certainly there is no shortage of literature on each of

especially (4). Note that the languages defined by (1)

---

[9]Technically called an _interpretation_.

[10]Grammar forms itself has moved in an unforseen and
tirely different direction. It has given rise to a
area of activity now referred to as "form theory,"
is the classification and study of computer-science
graphlike structures through the notion of "looks 1.

In conclusion, the study of methods of description of computer-science language families, far from being resolved,seems
to be in its infancy. Many philosophical, as well a technical,
problems remain. All we need are some answers.

REFERENCES

(1)   Aho, A.V. (1968). JACM, 15:647.
(2)   Aho, A.V. and Ullman, J.D. (1974). JCSS 4:523.
(3)   Bar-Hillel, Y., Perles, M., and Shamir, E. (1961),
      Zeitschrift fur Phonetik, Sprachwissenschaft und
      Kommunikationsforschung, 14:143.
(4)   Boasson, L. and Nivat, M. (1979), submitted for publi-
      cation.
(5)   Book, R.V. (1968). JACM, 25:23.
(6)   Book, R.V. (1979). SIAM J.on Computing, 8:434.
(7)   Chandler, W.J. (1969), Proc. 1st ACM Symp.on Theory of
      Computing, 21.
(8)   Chomsky, N. (1956). IRE Trans. on Information Theory,
      113.
(9)   Chomsky, N. (1959). Information and Control, 2:137.
(10) Chomsky, N. (1962). MIT Res.Lab.Electron.Quart.Prog.
      Rept. 65.
(11) Chomsky, N. and Miller, G.A. (1958). Information and
      Control, 1:91.
(12) Cohen, R.S. and Gold, A.Y. (1977). JCSS, 15:169.
(13) Cremers, A. and Ginsburg, S. (1975), JCSS, 11:86.
(14) Downey, P.J. (1974). Ph.D. Thesis, Harvard University.
(15) Evey, R.J. (1963). Ph.D. Thesis, Harvard University.
(16) Fischer, M.J. (1968). Ph.D. Thesis, Harvard University.
(17) Floyd, R.W. (1962). CACM, 5:483.
(18) Gabrielian, A. and Ginsburg, S. (1974). JACM, 21:213.
(19) Ginsburg, S. (1975). "Algebraic and Automata-Theoretic
      Properties of Formal Languages." North-Holland,
      Amsterdam.
(20) Ginsburg, S. and Greibach, S. (1969). In "Studies in
      Abstract Families of Languages." Memoirs of the
      American Math. Soc. 87:1.
(21) Ginsburg, S. and Rice, H.G. (1962). JACM, 9:350.
(22) Ginsburg, S. and Spanier, E.H. (1968). JCSS, 2:228.
(23) Greibach, S. and Hopcroft, J. (1969). JCSS, 3:233.
(24) Harrison, M.A. and Schkolnick, M. (1971). JACM, 18:148.
(25) Henke, F.W. (1971). Report of the GMD, Bonn, Germany.
(26) Henke, F.W. (1972). Report of the GMD, Bonn, Germany.
(27) Hopcroft, J.E. and Ullman, J.D. (1967). Bell Sys. Tech.
      Journ., XLVI:1793.
(28) Jones, N. (1967). Ph.D. Thesis, University of Western
      Ontario, London, Ontario, Canada.
(29) Jones, N.D. (1968). Information and Control, 13:207.

(30) Kasai, T. (1970). JCSS, 4:492.
(31) Kleene, S.C. (1956). In "Automata Studies" (C.E. Shannon
        and J. McCarthy, eds.), Princeton University Press,
        Princeton, New Jersey.
(32) Kuroda, S.Y. (1964). Information and Control, 7:207.
(33) McNaughton, R. (1966). Information and Control, 9:521.
(34) Muller, D.E. (1963). Proc. 4th Annual Symp., Inst. of
        Electrical and Electronic Engineers, 3.
(35) Myhill, J. (1957). Wright Air Force Development Command
        Technical Report WADC TR 57-624, 112.
(36) Naur, P. (ed.) (1960). CACM, 3:299.
(37) Nerode, A. (1958). Proc. Amer. Math. Soc., 9:541.
(38) Nivat, M. (1967). Ph.D. Thesis, University of Paris.
(39) Nivat, M. (1977). Informatique Theorique, 11:311.
(40) Rabin, M. and Scott, D. (1959). IBM J. Res. and Dev.,
        3:114.
(41) Scott, D. (1967). JCSS, 1:187.
(42) van Wijngaarden, A. (ed.) (1969). Numerische Mathematik,
        14:79.
(43) Wrathall, C. (1975). Ph.D. Thesis, Harvard University.
(44) Wrathall, C. (1978). SIAM J. on Computing, 7:194.
(45) Yntema, M.K. (1967). Information and Control, 10:572.

OPEN PROBLEMS ABOUT REGULAR LANGUAGES[1]

Janusz Brzozowski

Department of Computer Science
University of Waterloo
Waterloo, Ontario, Canada

I. INTRODUCTION

The theory of regular languages and finite automata was
developed in the early 1950's, and is therefore one of the
oldest branches of theoretical computer science. Regular languages constitute the best known family of formal languages,
and finite automata constitute the best known family of abstract machine models. The concepts of regular languages and
finite automata appear very frequently in theoretical computer
science, and have several important applications. There is a
vast literature on these subjects.

In spite of the fact that many researchers have worked in
this field there remain several difficult open problems. Six
of these problems are discussed in this paper. There are more
than six open problems about regular languages; the choice of
these six represents the personal prejudices of the author.
It is not our intention here to imply that other open problems
are not significant. However, the problems chosen do appear

[1]Research supported in part by the Natural Sciences and
Engineering Research Council of Canada under Grant No. A-1617.
Preparation of this paper was supported in part by the National
Science Foundation under Grant No. MCS79-04012.

23

to be of fundamental importance and considerable difficulty. Most of them are intimately involved with the fundamental property of finite automata, namely finiteness.

For the most part we have adopted the terminology and notation of Eilenberg [13,14].

II. STAR HEIGHT

In a monograph [21] published in 1971, McNaughton and Papert include a collection of open problems concerning regular languages. Their list is headed by the star height problem. To illustrate their uncertainty about the problem, I quote their final paragraph:

> At this moment we are unwilling to conjecture even that there exist events of general loop complexity two or more. The entire question of events whose general loop complexity exceeds one is wide open. Only one of our conjectures remains credible: that if there exist regular events of loop complexity n, for n > 2, then there exist regular events of loop complexity n whose syntactic monoids are groups. We suspect that someone might prove this hypothetical statement without answering the main question.

After eight years not much has changed. I find it surprising that no progress had been made on such an intriguing question. The interest in the theory of finite automata and regular languages as a research topic for computer scientists has decreased significantly over the last 15 years. This is understandable since the problems that are left are quite difficult and perhaps unfair as Ph.D. thesis topics. However, the number of people that were actively involved in the area was very large indeed, and I would expect that a handful of them would retain an active interest in this problem, as a hobby. Yet there appear to be no new results.

Let Σ be a finite alphabet and Σ^* the free monoid generated by Σ with unit element 1. <u>Regular</u> <u>expressions</u> over Σ are
defined inductively:

   (a) ϕ, 1 and σ for each $\sigma \in \Sigma$ are regular expressions;

   (b) if E and F are regular expressions, then so are

$$\overline{E}, \quad E \cup F, \quad E \cap F, \quad EF \quad \text{and} \quad E^*.$$

In this definition ϕ denotes the empty language and $\overline{E} = \Sigma^* - E$.
The remaining operators are union, intersection, concatena-
tion and star.

   The (<u>star</u>) <u>height</u> Eh of a regular expression E is defined
inductively as

   (a) $\phi h = 1h = 0$,   and $\sigma h = 0$ for all $\sigma \in \Sigma$;

   (b) if E and F are regular expressions, then

      $\overline{E}h = Eh$,

      $(E \cup F)h = (E \cap F)h = (EF)h = \max\{Eh, Fh\}$,

      $E^*h = 1 + Eh$.

In other words, Eh is the maximum number of nested stars in E.
For example, if $E = (\sigma \cup \tau\tau^*\sigma)^*$, then $Eh = 2$.

   If $A \subseteq \Sigma^*$ is a regular language, the height Ah of A is the
least height of a regular expression denoting A. If E is a
regular expression let $|E|$ be the language denoted by E. In
the example above, $|E|$ is of height zero because

   $$|E| = |1 \cup \overline{\phi}\sigma|$$

and $(1 \cup \overline{\phi}\sigma)h = 0$.

   The family of languages of height zero was characterized
in 1965 by Schützenberger [26] who showed that $Ah = 0$ iff the
syntactic monoid M of A is aperiodic, i.e., has only trivial
subgroups. This family of star-free languages is relatively

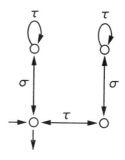

Fig. 1.   Automaton A_1.

well known.   Apart from this, we know that if M contains a
nontrivial group then Ah > 0, but it is not known whether
there are any languages of height two!

As McNaughton and Papert reported [21], for many years
before 1971 the language $|A_1|$ accepted by the automaton A_1 of
Figure 1 was thought to be of height two.   Henneman [18]
showed that it is of height one.   In fact an expression of
height one for $A_1 = |A_1|$ is

$$A_1 = [E \cap F] \cup [(\tau \cup \sigma\tau^*\sigma)E \cap (\tau^*\sigma)^2 F],$$

where $E = ((\tau \cup \sigma\tau^*\sigma)^2)^*$, and $F = (\tau \cup (\tau^*\sigma)^4)^*$.   A natural
height-two expression for A_1 is:

$$(\sigma\tau^*\sigma \cup \tau(\sigma\tau^*\sigma)^*\tau)^*,$$

where $\tau^* = (\overline{\phi\sigma\phi})$.   Informally, one can view A_1 as counting σ's
modulo 2 and counting τ's modulo 2, but only those τ's that
occur after an even number of σ's.   A more complicated example
suggested by Thérien [29] is

$$A_2 = (\sigma\tau^*\sigma \cup \tau\sigma^*\tau(\sigma\tau^*\sigma)^*\tau\sigma^*\tau)^*,$$

accepted by the six-state automaton of Figure 2.   This language is suspected of being a height-two language.

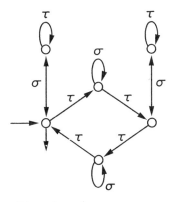

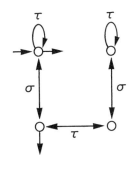

Fig. 2. A_2.   Fig. 3. A_3.

The language A_1 of Figure 1 is very closely related to A_3 accepted by A_3 of Figure 3. This language has a very natural description as follows.

Let $u, w \in \Sigma^*$ with $u = \sigma_1 \ldots \sigma_n$, where $\sigma_1, \ldots, \sigma_n \in \Sigma$. The <u>binomial</u> <u>coefficient</u> $\binom{w}{u}$ is the number of factorizations

$$w = v_0 \sigma_1 v_1 \sigma_2 \cdots v_{n-1} \sigma_n v_n$$

with $v_0, \ldots, v_n \in \Sigma^*$. One can verify that

$$A_3 = \{w \mid w \in \{\sigma, \tau\}^* \quad \text{and} \quad \binom{w}{\sigma\tau} \equiv 0 \bmod 2\}.$$

In other words, A_3 counts modulo 2 the number of ways in which $\sigma\tau$ is a subword of w. A height-one expression is easily obtainable for A_3 from A_1. In fact

$$A_3 = \tau^* \cup \tau^* \sigma A_1 (1 \cup \sigma\tau^*).$$

A natural generalization of A_3 is

$$A_4 = \{w \mid w \in \{\sigma, \tau, \eta\}^* \quad \text{and} \quad \binom{w}{\sigma\tau\eta} \equiv 0 \bmod 2\}.$$

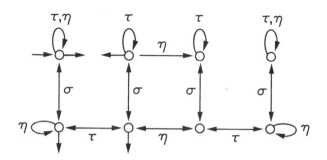

Fig. 4. A_4.

The reduced automaton accepting A_4 is shown in Figure 4. At
the present time A_4 is another candidate for height two. To
the best of our knowledge, the only published work on the star
height problem (other than Schützenberger's paper on star-free
languages) is that of Henneman [18]. His main results are
summarized below. Let G be the syntactic monoid of the language A, and let the order of G by n. Then

    if G is a group,   Ah $\leq$ n;

    if G is a solvable group,   Ah $\leq$ log n;

    if G is a supersolvable group,   Ah $\leq$ 2 + log log n;

    if G is an abelian group,   Ah $\leq$ 1.

Henneman defines the height A_h of a complete (deterministic) automaton $A = (Q,i,T)$ to be the height of the language
$|A|$ accepted by A. The height S_h of a semiautomaton S (automaton without initial state and final states) is the maximum
height of any automaton associated with S. Let $S(q,q') =$
$\{w \mid w \in \Sigma^* $ and $qw = q'\}$ in the semiautomaton S. One easily
verifies that the height of S is equal to the maximum height
of the languages $S(q,q')$ over all $q,q' \in Q$.

Given a semiautomaton S with state set Q and input alphabet Σ, let M be the transformation monoid associated with S.

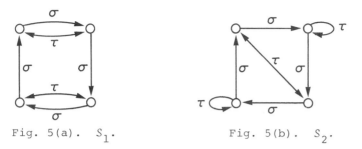

Fig. 5(a). S_1.   Fig. 5(b). S_2.

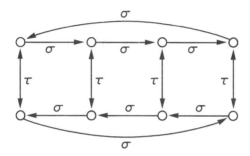

Fig. 5(c). S_M.

Then the monoid semiautomaton of S is a semiautomaton S_M with state set M and input alphabet Σ. Henneman shows that $Sh =$ $S_M h$. To illustrate an application of this result consider Figure 5. One verifies that S_M is isomorphic to the monoid semiautomaton of both S_1 and S_2. Hence $S_1 h = S_M h = S_2 h$. It is easy to verify that $S_2 h = 1$; we can then conclude also that $S_1 h = 1$.

The bounds on star height that were mentioned above apply only to languages whose syntactic monoids are groups. In that case the corresponding semiautomata are permutation semiautomata. Henneman observes that, for a permutation semiautomaton S, $Sh = (S(q,q))h$ where q is any state of S. Hence one needs to consider only one language associated with any semiautomaton.

In the general case, if it is known only that the syntactic monoid of a language A is a group G of order n, then the
monoid automaton has n states. It is easy to find expressions
of height $\leq$ n for any n-state automaton, using for example the
McNaughton-Yamada algorithm [22]. If the reduced automaton
for A has m states and m < n, then of course the bound can be
lowered to m.

In case G is abelian, it is not difficult to write a
height-one expression which is a finite union of expressions
of the form

$$\bigcap_{\sigma \in \Sigma} A_\sigma^{p_\sigma} (A_\sigma^{q_\sigma}) *,$$

where $A_\sigma = (\overline{\phi \sigma \phi}) \sigma (\overline{\phi \sigma \phi})$ is the set of all words over Σ containing exactly one σ, and p_σ, $q_\sigma \geq 0$.

The results concerning solvable and supersolvable groups
are deduced from some classical results from group theory and
the following theorem of Henneman:

Theorem. Let G be a group and N a normal abelian subgroup
of G. Then

Gh $\leq$ (G/N)h + 1.

(The height of a group G is the height of the monoid semiautomaton with state set G, input alphabet G, and multiplication in G as the transition function.)

Henneman's thesis closes with some techniques for proving
that certain two-input semiautomata are of star height one,
and with a list of open problems.

The fundamental question remains: Is the star height hierarchy finite or infinite? Our ignorance about this problem is well illustrated by the fact that we are not even able to answer a much simpler question: Is there a language of height two?

Henneman's results lead one to believe that the star height of a language is a property that can be characterized in its syntactic monoid. Also, almost all known characterizations of subclasses of the class of regular languages can be done in the framework of Eilenberg's variety theory [14]. The following observation shows that this approach can work only if all languages are of height ≤ 1. Let H_i be the class of all languages of height $\leq i$, for $i \geq 0$.

Proposition. H_1 is a *-variety iff every regular language is of height ≤ 1.

Proof. Suppose $A \in H_i$ for $i > 1$, and let M_A be the syntactic monoid of A. By a recent theorm of Pin [24], there exists a finite language B such that M_A divides M_{B*}. However, $B* \in H_1$. If H_1 is a *-variety, it follows by Eilenberg's theorem that also $A \in H_1$. Hence all regular languages are of height ≤ 1, if H_1 is a *-variety. The converse holds since the class of all regular languages is a *-variety.

Note that membership in H_0 is a property determined by the syntactic monoid. Also, H_0 is a *-variety.

III. RESTRICTED STAR HEIGHT

A restricted regular expression is a regular expression without intersections and complements. The restricted star height of a regular language A is the minimum height of a

restricted regular expression E denoting A. Our knowledge of
the restricted star height problem is considerably better than
it is for the problem of the last section. It is known that
the restricted height hierarchy is infinite, and algorithms
for finding the restricted height exist for several families
of languages. However, the general case is still open; i.e.,
given an arbitrary regular language, it is not known how to
find its restricted height. Throughout this section height
means restricted height.

The restricted star height problem was introduced by
Eggan [12] in 1963. He showed that for each $h \geq 0$ there exists a language A_h over alphabet Σ_h which has height h; the
size of the alphabet Σ_h grows with h. Eggan raised the question whether there exist languages of arbitrary height over
the two-letter alphabet. (Languages over a one-letter alphabet are all of height 0 or 1.) The question was answered
positively by McNaughton (unpublished notes) and later by
Dejean and Schützenberger [11] in 1966. Let $A_h = (Q,i,\{i\})$ be
the automaton over the alphabet $\Sigma = \{\sigma,\tau\}$, where $Q =$
$\{0, 1, \ldots, 2^h-1\}$, $q\sigma = q+1 \underline{\mod} 2^h$ and $q\tau = q-1 \underline{\mod} 2^h$ for all
$q \in Q$. Dejean and Schützenberger showed that $|A_h|$ is of
height h.

Eggan related star height of a language to the notion of
cycle rank of a graph representing the language. The rank of
a graph is a measure of the loop complexity of the graph; the
precise definition is somewhat involved. Eggan showed that
for every regular language A there exists a transition graph
(a finite-automaton-like object which permits empty word transitions) whose rank is Ah. Cohen [6,9] showed that the search

can be limited to nondeterministic automata, namely that for each regular language A there exists a nondeterministic automaton whose rank is Ah. We will briefly describe one of Cohen's approaches.

In what follows we need to have an explicit notation for the transitions in a finite automaton. Thus we will use the notation $A = (Q,I,T,E)$ where $E \subseteq Q \times \Sigma \times Q$. For any set S, $\hat{S}$ denotes the set of all subsets of S.

Let $A = (Q,i,T,E)$ be a minimal deterministic Σ-automaton. Let $\tilde{A} = (\tilde{Q},\tilde{I},\tilde{T},\tilde{E})$ be the nondeterministic <u>subset</u> <u>automaton</u> derived from A as follows:

$$\tilde{Q} = \hat{Q} - \phi$$

$$\tilde{I} = \{X \mid X \in \hat{Q}, i \in X\}$$

$$\tilde{T} = \{X \mid X \in \hat{T} - \phi\}$$

$$\tilde{E} = \{(X,\sigma,X') \mid X\sigma \subseteq X'\}$$

where $X\sigma = \{q' \in Q \mid (q,\sigma,q') \in E \text{ for some } q \in X\}$, as usual. One verifies that if $X \xrightarrow{s} X'$ is a path in $\tilde{A}$ for some $s \in \Sigma^*$, then $Xs \subseteq X'$. It follows that $s \in |\tilde{A}|$ implies $Xs \subseteq X'$ for some X such that $i \in X$ and $X' \subseteq T$. In particular, is $\in T$ or $s \in |A|$. Hence $|\tilde{A}| \subseteq |A|$. It is easily seen that $|A| \subseteq |\tilde{A}|$; thus $|\tilde{A}| = |A|$.

Next let $k > 0$ and let $\tilde{A}_k = (\tilde{Q} \times \mathbf{k}, \tilde{I} \times \mathbf{k}, \tilde{T} \times \mathbf{k}, \tilde{E}_k)$, where $\mathbf{k} = \{0, 1, \ldots, k-1\}$, be the nondeterministic <u>k-subset</u> <u>automaton</u> with

$$\tilde{E}_k = \{((X,j), \sigma, (X',j')) \mid (X,\sigma,X') \in \tilde{E}\}.$$

One easily verifies that $|\tilde{A}_k| = |A|$. Note that $\tilde{A}_1$ is isomorphic to $\tilde{A}$.

Let $A_k = (Q_k, I_k, T_k, E_k)$ be a nondeterministic automaton, where $Q_k \subset \tilde{Q} \times \mathbf{k}$, $I_k \subset \tilde{I} \times \mathbf{k}$, $T_k \subset \tilde{T} \times \mathbf{k}$ and $E_k \subset \tilde{E}_k$. In other words, the graph of A_k is a subgraph of the graph of $\tilde{A}_k$. We will say that any A_k satisfying the conditions above is a k-graph of A. Clearly $|A_k| \subset |A|$. Without loss of generality we can assume that A_k is trim (i.e., every state appears in some successful path).

Cohen showed that any nondeterministic automaton recognizing a given language A can be viewed as a k-graph of A, where A is the minimal deterministic automaton recognizing A. For let $B = (P, I_B, T_B, E_B)$ be any trim nondeterministic automaton for A. Let

$$B_p = \{s \mid s \in \Sigma^*, p \in I_B s\}$$

for any $p \in P$. Define the function $f : P \to \hat{Q}$ by

$$pf = iB_p.$$

One can verify that

$p \in P$ implies $pf \neq \phi$;

$p \in I_B$ implies $i \in pf$;

$p \in T_B$ implies $pf \subset T$;

$(p, \sigma, p') \in E_B$ implies $(pf)\sigma \subset p'f$.

Thus all the conditions are satisfied for B to be isomorphic to a k-graph of A.

As an example, consider the minimal deterministic automaton A of Figure 6(a) over $\Sigma = \{\sigma, \tau, \eta\}$, and the nondeterministic automaton B of Figure 6(b). The set of states of A associated with each node of B is shown in Figure 6(b). Note that $\{q\}$ appears twice; hence B is a 2-graph of A. The cycle rank of B is 1 and, if A is the language of A, we conclude

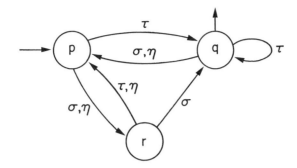

Fig. 6(a). A.

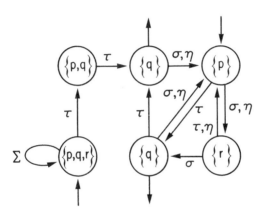

Fig. 6(b). B.

that Ah = 1. One can verify that there does not exist any
1-graph of A that is of rank 1; i.e., it is necessary to use a
2-graph in order to display the height of A. In fact, for
each k $\geq$ 1 an example can be produced where it is necessary
to go to a k-graph. The question is whether k can be bounded.
The following conjecture of Cohen is still open:

Conjecture. If A has m states then there exists a (2^m-1)-
graph of A whose rank is equal to the height of A.

The interested reader is referred to the literature [1,
6-12,17-20] for further results about star height.

IV.   GROUP COMPLEXITY

In the first two problems we have considered two rather
direct measures of complexity of a regular language. It is by
now a well-established fact that many properties of languages
are reflected in the properties of the corresponding semigroups. The problem discussed here deals with the complexity
of semigroups.

A transformation semigroup $X = (Q,S)$, abbreviated ts, consists of a finite set Q and a subsemigroup S of $PF(Q)$, where
$PF(Q)$ is the monoid of all partial functions $Q \to Q$ with composition as multiplication. If X and Y are ts's, then $X < Y$
denotes the relation X <u>divides</u> Y and $X \circ Y$ is the wreath product of X and Y. It is well known that any ts $X = (Q,S)$ has a
decomposition

$$X < A_{n+1} \circ G_n \circ \ldots \circ G_1 \circ A_1. \tag{1}$$

where A_i is an aperiodic (group-free) ts for $i = 1, \ldots, n+1$,
and G_i is a group for $i = 1, \ldots, n$. The (<u>group</u>) <u>complexity</u>
Xc of X is the smallest integer n over all decompositions of
type (1). The Krohn-Rhodes Decomposition Theorem guarantees
the existence of such a decomposition for each ts X. Moreover,
G_i can be chosen to be a simple group such that $G_i < S$. However, in the definition of complexity, these conditions are
not imposed; any finite group may be used in (1).

The open problem is: Does there exist an algorithm for
finding the complexity of a given ts? Intuitively one would
expect that, given the cardinality m of S, one should be able

to eliminate those groups that are "too large" for S and limit the search to groups of cardinality $\leq$ some bound depending on m.   However, no such bound has been found.

Notice that a ts has group complexity zero iff it is a-periodic.   Every ts that is a nontrivial group has complexity one.   The group complexity hierarchy is infinite because it can be shown that for $n \geq 1$ the ts $X_n = (\mathbf{n}, F_n)$, where F_n is the monoid of all functions $\mathbf{n} \to \mathbf{n}$, has complexity n-1.

The complexity problem was introduced by Krohn and Rhodes in 1965.   A rather detailed account of the problem is given by Tilson in a chapter of Eilenberg's Vol. B [14].

An interesting connection between a related complexity measure and a certain hierarchy of languages has been recently made by Straubing [28].   He showed that any transformation monoid X containing only solvable groups has a decomposition

$$X < K_n \circ K_{n-1} \circ \ldots \circ K_1, \tag{2}$$

where for each i, K_i is either aperiodic or an abelian group. Let Xa be the <u>abelian group complexity</u> of X, i.e., the small-est number of abelian groups over all decompositions of type (2).

Let $\mathcal{D}_j$ be the family of all languages that can be con-structed from the letters of the alphabet using boolean oper-ations, concatenation, and $\leq$ j levels of a certain counting operation [28].   Straubing shows that a language A is in $\mathcal{D}_j$ iff its syntactic monoid has abelian complexity $\leq$ j.

V.   STAR REMOVAL

In 1965 Paz and Peleg [23] asked whether every regular language can be decomposed as a product of a finite number of stars and primes, where a subset A of Σ^* is prime iff A = BC implies B = 1 or C = 1, and it is a star iff A = A*.   A positive answer to this question was given by Brzozowski and Cohen [2] in 1967.   The decomposition procedure described in [2] does not lead to a unique factorization as shown by the following example:

$$A = (1 \cup \sigma_0) [\sigma_1 \sigma_0 \cup (\sigma_3 \cup \sigma_2 \sigma_1)(\sigma_2 \sigma_1)^*(\sigma_1 \sigma_0 \cup \sigma_0)]^*$$
$$(1 \cup \sigma_3 \cup \sigma_2 \sigma_1)(\sigma_2 \sigma_1)^* \sigma_1$$

$$= (1 \cup \sigma_3) [\sigma_2 \sigma_1 \cup (\sigma_0 \cup \sigma_1 \sigma_0)(\sigma_1 \sigma_0)^*(\sigma_2 \sigma_1 \cup \sigma_3)]^*$$
$$(1 \cup \sigma_0 \cup \sigma_1 \sigma_0)(\sigma_1 \sigma_0)^* \sigma_1.$$

In both cases all the factors are either stars or primes.

In contrast to this, the ideas of [2] and [23] suggest a natural procedure leading to a unique decomposition as described below.

Let $A = (Q,i,T)$ be a deterministic Σ-automaton and let $A = |A|$.   Consider the Σ-automaton $B = (Q,i,T')$ where the transition function of B is the same as that of A and

$$T' = \{q \mid qA \subseteq T\}.$$

We will show that $B = |B|$ is the maximal left star factorable from A.   Since iA $\subseteq$ T, we have i $\in$ T' and 1 $\in$ B.   If s, t $\in$ B then is, it $\in$ T' and isA, itA $\subseteq$ T.   The last condition is equivalent to tA $\subseteq$ A.   Thus istA $\subseteq$ isA $\subseteq$ T, ist $\in$ T' and st $\in$ B.   Altogether B is a star.   It is also easy to check that A = BA. Now suppose A = B'C for some star B'; then

A = B'B'C = B'A. If s ∈ B', then sA ⊂ A, isA ⊂ T, is ∈ T' and

s ∈ B. It follows that B' ⊂ B, i.e., that B is maximal.

One easily verifies that, given any decomposition A = BD

where B is a star, there is a unique minimal tail C of A with

respect to B (such that A = BC), namely

C = A - (B - 1)A.

The following procedure then suggests itself. Given a regular

language A, find its maximal left star B_1 and its minimal tail

C_1 with respect to B_1. Repeat, replacing A by C_1, etc. After

n steps we have A = $B_1 \ldots B_n C_n$, where C_n is the minimal tail of

$B_n C_n$ with respect to B_n. The process terminates if the max-

imal left star of C_n is 1. The question is: Does this pro-

cess always terminate?

VI. REGULARITY OF NONCOUNTING CLASSES

A language A ⊂ Σ* is <u>noncounting</u> of order n, n ≥ 1 iff for

all u, v ∈ Σ*

$us^n v \in A \longleftrightarrow us^{n+1} v \in A.$

It is well known that every star-free language is noncounting,

but the converse is false in general.

Let $\sim_n$ (or simply $\sim$ if n is understood) be the smallest

congruence on Σ* satisfying $s^n \sim s^{n+1}$ for all s ∈ Σ*. Let

M = Σ*/$\sim$ and let μ : Σ* → M be the natural morphism mapping

each element s ∈ Σ* into the equivalence class [s] of $\sim$ con-

taining s. Then $m\mu^{-1}$ is the set of all words of Σ* that are

in the same equivalence class. The question is: Is $m\mu^{-1}$ a

regular set for all m ∈ M?

In case $\Sigma = \{\sigma\}$, we find:

$$[1] = 1, \quad [\sigma] = \sigma, \quad \ldots, \quad [\sigma^{n-1}] = \sigma^{n-1}, \quad [\sigma^n] = \sigma^n \sigma*.$$

From now on assume therefore that Σ has at least two elements. The case $n = 1$, i.e., the case where M is idempotent, has been characterized by Green and Rees [15]. They have shown that $\sim_1$ is of finite index, i.e., that $M = \Sigma*/\sim_1$ is a finite monoid. It follows that all the classes for $n = 1$ are regular, in fact star-free [3]. Thus every noncounting language of order 1 is star-free.

It is easy to show that $\sim_2$ is of infinite index in case card $\Sigma \geq 3$ using a result of Thue [30]. He has shown that there is an infinite set of "squareless" words, i.e., words s such that $s = ut^2v$ implies $t = 1$. This set of words is clearly noncounting of order 2, and each word constitutes a distinct equivalence class. The same argument shows that $\sim_n$ is of infinite index for all $n \geq 2$ and card $\Sigma \geq 3$. In the case $n \geq 3$ one can use another result of Thue to show that $\sim_n$ is of infinite index for card $\Sigma \geq 2$. Thue has shown that there is an infinite number of "cubeless" words (words s such that $s = ut^3v$ implies $t = 1$) for card $\Sigma \geq 2$. This leaves only the case card $\Sigma = 2$ and $n = 2$, which was settled by Brzozowski, Culik and Gabrielian [3]. Let $\Sigma = \{\sigma, \tau\}$ and let $f : \Sigma* \to \Sigma*$ be the monoid morphism defined by

$$\sigma f = \sigma\sigma\tau \quad \text{and} \quad \tau f = \sigma\tau\tau.$$

One can show that $\sigma f^i \sim_2 \sigma f^j$ iff $i = j$. Hence $\{[\sigma], [\sigma f], \ldots, [\sigma f^i], \ldots\}$ is an infinite set of equivalence classes, and so $\sim_2$ is of infinite index. It was shown in [3] that $[\sigma f^i]$ is regular for all $i \geq 0$. This supports the conjecture that all classes are regular.

This problem was considered by Simon in 1970. The following is a reworking of his unpublished observations.

Let $M = \Sigma*/\sim$ and let $r \in M$. Define the set

$$N_r = \{m \in M \mid r \notin MmM\}.$$

It is easily seen that N_r is an ideal of M, i.e., that $MN_rM = N_r$. We can construct the Rees quotient monoid [5] $M/N_r = Q_r$ of M with respect to N_r as follows. First, the Rees congruence $\longleftrightarrow$ induced by N_r is defined by

$$m \longleftrightarrow m' \quad \text{iff} \quad m \in N_r \quad \text{and} \quad m' \in N_r, \quad \text{or} \quad m = m'.$$

Then $Q_r = M/N_r = M/\longleftrightarrow$. Identify each congruence class of $\longleftrightarrow$ containing a single element m with that element, and let 0 be a new element not in $M - N_r$ that corresponds to the class of all elements of N_r. Then we can view Q_r as consisting of $(M - N_r) \cup 0$, and having the multiplication $\circ$ defined by

$$m \circ m' = \begin{cases} mm', & \text{if} \quad mm' \notin N_r \\ 0, & \text{otherwise.} \end{cases}$$

Note that 0 is indeed the zero element of Q_r. Let ν be the natural morphism $\nu : M \to Q_r$ mapping each element $m \in M$ into the equivalence class of $\longleftrightarrow$ containing m. Let θ be the composition of μ and ν; i.e., we have

$$\Sigma* \xrightarrow{\mu} M \xrightarrow{\nu} Q_r$$

and

$$\Sigma* \xrightarrow{\theta = \mu\nu} Q_r.$$

We are interested in $r\mu^{-1}$. Since $r \notin N_r$, $r\nu^{-1} = r$. Thus $r\mu^{-1} = r\nu^{-1}\mu^{-1} = r(\mu\nu)^{-1} = r\theta^{-1}$, and we conclude that if Q_r is finite, then $r\mu^{-1} = r\theta^{-1}$ is regular. However, it is not known whether $\longleftrightarrow$ on M is of finite index.

A second approach is as follows. Define on any monoid M the following relations:

$m L m'$ iff $m \in Mm'$ and $m' \in Mm$;

$m R m'$ iff $m \in m'M$ and $m' \in mM$;

$m H m'$ iff $m L m'$ and $m R m'$.

These are the well-known Green equivalence relations. Let L_m, R_m and H_m denote the corresponding classes containing m. Then

$$R_m = \{m' \in M \mid m \in m'M \text{ and } m' \in mM\},$$
$$L_m = \{m' \in M \mid m \in Mm' \text{ and } m' \in Mm'\},$$
$$H_m = R_m \cap L_m.$$

If $M = \Sigma*/\sim$ then it satisfies $m^n = m^{n+1}$ for all $m \in M$; hence M is H-trivial; i.e., each H-class consists of a single element. For suppose $m_1 H m_2$. Then there exist $u, v \in M$ such that

$$m_1 = um_2 \text{ and } m_2 = m_1 v.$$

Thus $m_1 = um_2 = um_1 v = u^n m_1 v^n = u^n m_1 v^{n+1} = m_1 v = m_2$. Hence we have

$$m = H_m = R_m \cap L_m.$$

and

$$m\mu^{-1} = R_m\mu^{-1} \cap L_m\mu^{-1}.$$

Thus if one could prove that R_m and L_m are regular for each $m \in M$, one would have the result that $m\mu^{-1}$ is regular.

VII. OPTIMALITY OF PREFIX CODES

Our final problem is a conjecture by Schützenberger [25].

Let Σ be a finite alphabet. A <u>code</u> C over Σ is a subset of $\Sigma*$ such that for all s_i, $t_i \in C$,

$$s_1 \cdots s_n = t_1 \cdots t_m$$

implies $n = m$ and $s_i = t_i$ for $i = 1, \ldots, n$. If C is a code
and $s \in C^*$ we will say that s is a message. Thus every message is uniquely decipherable. For example, $\{a, ab, ba\}$ is not
a code for $a(ba) = (ab)a$. A code C is prefix iff no word of
C is a prefix of any other word of C.

Two words $s, t \in \Sigma^*$ are commutatively equivalent, $s \sim t$,
iff they differ only in the order of their letters, i.e., iff
for each $\sigma \in \Sigma$

$$\binom{s}{\sigma} = \binom{t}{\sigma}.$$

Two languages $A, B \subset \Sigma^*$ are commutatively equivalent, $A \sim B$,
iff there is a bijection θ from A to B such that $s \in A$ and
$s\theta \in B$ are commutatively equivalent. Thus $A \sim B$ iff one can
write $A = \{s_1, s_2, \ldots, s_i, \ldots\}$ and $B = \{t_1, t_2, \ldots, t_i, \ldots\}$ where $s_i \sim t_i$ for all i. For example, let

$$C_0 = \{\sigma, \tau\sigma, \tau\tau\sigma, \tau\tau\tau\sigma, \tau\tau\tau\tau\}$$

and

$$C_1 = \{\sigma, \tau\sigma, \sigma\tau\tau, \tau\sigma\tau\tau, \tau\tau\tau\tau\}.$$

Clearly $C_0 \sim C_1$. Note that C_0 is prefix while C_1 is not.

Conjecture. Every code is commutatively equivalent to a
prefix code.

The conjecture is supported by a theorem of Perrin and
Schützenberger about a restricted class of codes.

Let $C \subset \Sigma^*$ be a code and $s, t \in \Sigma^*$. The pair (s,t) is
synchronizing for C iff for any message w, if $w = ustv$ for

some u, v ∈ Σ* then us and tv are also messages. In other
words the appearance of st in any message w permits us to cut
w into two shorter messages. For example, let

$$C_2 = \{\sigma\sigma, \ \sigma\tau, \ \tau\sigma, \ \tau\tau\sigma, \ \tau\tau\tau\}.$$

The pair $(\sigma\tau,\sigma\tau)$ is not synchronizing for C_2 because the mes-
sage $\tau(\sigma\tau)(\sigma\tau)\sigma$ contains the pair but neither $\tau\sigma\tau$ nor $\sigma\tau\sigma$ is
a message. However, the pair $(\sigma\tau\tau\sigma,\tau\sigma)$ can be verified to be
synchronizing.

    A code C has <u>bounded</u> <u>synchronization</u> <u>delay</u> if there exists
an integer n such that each pair (s,t) satisfying

$$s = s_1 \ldots s_n \quad \text{and} \quad t = t_1 \ldots t_n,$$

with s_i, $t_i \in C$ for i = 1, ..., n, is synchronizing. Codes
with bounded delay have been studied in several papers; see
[25]. One can verify that code C_1 does not have bounded delay
because (τ^{4n},τ^{4n}) is not synchronizing for any n. The code
$C_4 = \{\sigma, \ \sigma\tau\tau, \ \tau\sigma, \ \tau\sigma\tau\tau\}$ has delay bound 1.

    The main result of [25] shows that every code with bounded
synchronization delay is commutatively equivalent to a prefix
code. However, the general case remains open, even for regular codes.

VIII. CONCLUDING REMARKS

    The problems described above do not appear to have any
immediate direct applications to computer science. However,
if one accepts the premise that mathematics should form the
foundation of theoretical computer science, then the questions
are quite relevant. They demonstrate our lack of proper understanding of the basic mathematical objects involved.

To end on a more positive note, I would like to mention two difficult problems that were recently solved. Since 1967 the following question was open: Given a regular language A, can one decide whether there exists an integer n such that $A^n = A*$? The problem was solved in 1978 by Hashiguchi [16] and Simon [27]; the two solutions are independent and use different techniques.

The second problem concerns the dot-depth hierarchy. Let B_0 be the family of finite or cofinite languages. For any family F of languages let FM and FB denote the closure of F under concatenation and boolean operations respectively. Let

$$B_n = B_0 (MB)^n.$$

Then B_n is the family of languages that can be expressed with n or fewer levels of concatenation, and languages in $B_n - B_{n-1}$ are said to be of <u>dot depth</u> n. The question whether the dot-depth hierarchy

$$B_0 \subset B_1 \subset \ldots \subset B_n \subset \ldots$$

is infinite (i.e., whether $B_{n+1} \neq B_n$ for all n) was open since 1967. It was settled by Brzozowski and Knast in 1977 [4]; the hierarchy is infinite.

ACKNOWLEDGMENT

The author wishes to thank D. Thérien for useful comments on this paper.

REFERENCES

1. Backhouse, R.C., Closure algorithms and the star height problem of regular languages. Ph.D. thesis, Imperial College (1974).

2. Brzozowski, J.A., and Cohen, R., On decompositions of
   regular events. JACM 16, 132-144 (1969).
3. Brzozowski, J.A., Culik II, K., and Gabrielian, A.,
   Classification of noncounting events. J. Comput. Syst.
   Sci. 5, 41-53 (1971).
4. Brzozowski, J.A., and Knast, R., The dot-depth hierarchy
   of star-free languages is infinite. J. Comput. Syst. Sci.
   16, 37-55 (1978).
5. Clifford, A.H., and Preston, G.B., "The Algebraic Theory
   of Semigroups," vol. 1. Math. Surveys 7, Amer. Math. Soc.,
   Providence, R.I. (1961).
6. Cohen, R.S., Cycle rank of transition graphs and the star
   height of regular events. Ph.D. dissertation, University
   of Ottawa (1968).
7. Cohen, R.S., Star height of certain families of regular
   events. J. Comp. Syst. Sci. 4, 281-297 (1970).
8. Cohen, R.S., Techniques for establishing star height of
   regular sets. Math. Syst. Theory 5, 97-114 (1971).
9. Cohen, R.S., Rank-non-increasing transformations on transition graphs. Info. and Control 20, 93-113 (1972).
10. Cohen, R.S., and Brzozowski, J.A., General properties of
    star height of regular events. J. Comput. Syst. Sci. 4,
    260-280 (1970).
11. Dejean, F., and Schützenberger, M.P., On a question of
    Eggan. Info. and Control 9, 23-25 (1966).
12. Eggan, L.C., Transition graphs and the star height of
    regular events. Michigan Math. J. 10, 385-397 (1963).
13. Eilenberg, S., "Automata, Languages, and Machines," vol. A.
    Academic Press, New York (1974).
14. Eilenberg, S., "Automata, Languages, and Machines," vol. B.
    Academic Press, New York (1976).
15. Green, J.A., and Rees, D., On semigroups in which $x^r = x$.
    Proc. Cambridge Philos. Soc. 48, 35-40 (1952).
16. Hashiguchi, K., A decision procedure for the order of
    regular events. Theoret. Comp. Sci. 8, 69-72 (1979).
17. Hashiguchi, K., and Honda, N., Homomorphisms that preserve
    star height. Info. and Control 30, 247-266 (1976).
18. Henneman, W.H., Algebraic theory of automata. Ph.D. dis-
    sertation, Massachusetts Institute of Technology (1971).
19. McNaughton, R., The loop complexity of pure-group events.
    Info. and Control 11, 167-176 (1967).
20. McNaughton, R., The loop complexity of regular events.
    Info. Sci. 1, 305-328 (1969).
21. McNaughton, R., and Papert, S.,"Counter-Free Automata."
    Research Monograph No. 65, MIT Press, Cambridge, Mass.
    (1971).
22. McNaughton, R., and Yamada, H., Regular expressions and
    state graphs for automata. IRE Trans. Electronic Com-
    puters EC-9, 39-57 (1960).
23. Paz, A., and Peleg, B., On concatenative decompositions
    of regular events. IEEE Trans. Electronic Computers EC-17,
    229-237 (1968).
24. Pin, J.E., Sur le monoide syntactique de L* lorsque L est
    un langage fini. Theoret. Comp. Sci. 7, 211-215 (1978).
25. Perrin, D., and Schützenberger, M.P., Un problème élémen-
    taire de la théorie de l'information. Colloques Inter-
    nationaux du C.N.R.S., no. 276, Théorie de l'Information,
    249-260 (1977).

26. Schützenberger, M.P., On finite monoids having only tri-
    vial sub-groups. Info. and Control 8, 190-194 (1965).
27. Simon, I., Limited subsets of a free monoid. Proc. 19th
    Annual Symp. on Foundations of Computer Science, 143-150
    (1978).
28. Straubing, H., Families of recognizable sets correspond-
    ing to certain varieties of finite monoids. J. Pure and
    Appl. Algebra 15, 305-318 (1979).
29. Thérien, D., Classification of regular languages by con-
    gruence. Ph.D. thesis, University of Waterloo (1980).
30. Thue,'A., Über die gegenseitige lage gleicher teile ge-
    wisser zeichenreihen. Videnskabsselskabets Skrifter 1,
    Mat.-Nat. Kl, Chrisiania (1912).

GENERATORS OF CONES AND CYLINDERS[1]

Jean-Michel Autebert
Luc Boasson

LA 248 "Informatique Théorique et Programmation"
Universités Paris VI et Paris VII
Paris, France

This short text is devoted to a presentation of some results and questions about algebraic languages. The study of
this particular family can be justified by two main reasons.
The first one is that these languages have a lot of applications (some of them will surely appear throughout this book);
this is essentially because they involve the fundamental mechanism of recursion as a finite description for infinite objects. The second major reason is that, as illustrated here,
this family has a lot of mathematical properties.

After some general preliminaries explaining why various
notions were defined and how they are related, this text will
concentrate on some more specific problems. These have been
chosen in such a way that they give the opportunity of showing
how the recent work is performed as well as of giving some
ideas about the main open questions still unsolved. Two chap-
ters give a rather detailed description of what has been done
about these problems. They are completed by a very short

[1]Preparation of this paper was supported in part by the
National Science Foundation under Grant No. MCS79-04012.

49

conclusion which outlines how all this work takes place in a
more general frame, giving in fact guides for what should be
done in the near future.

I. PRELIMINARIES

Operations on languages have been considered since the
very beginning of the theory of languages. The most obvious
operations are union, morphism, inverse morphism.

A large variety of operations have been defined as output
functions of various kinds of finite automata. Let us describe
some of them which we shall use later:

· a finite automaton which outputs a letter each time it
reads is a sequential machine, and its output function is a
sequential mapping [25];

· the same machine outputting a (possibly empty) word each
time it reads a letter is a generalized sequential machine
(gsm) and the corresponding function a generalized sequential
mapping; these mappings were studied extensively [25];

· we call a-gsm a generalized sequential machine with accepting states and a-gsm mapping the corresponding function:
it is equal to the gsm mapping on the set of words which bring
the automaton from the initial state into one accepting state,
and it is equal to $\emptyset$ (the empty set) on the complement (one
can see easily that an a-gsm mapping is the composition product of a gsm mapping and an interesection with a regular set);

· the nondeterministic version of an a-gsm is an a-transducer [22] and the corresponding mapping (which is multivalued) is an a-transducer mapping.

This list does not exhaust the set of machine-defined operations on languages, not even the set of operations defined by finite-state machines: for example, Schützenberger's transducers [32] and Choffrut's subsequential functions [19] do not appear in our list.

Another point of view, first used by Elgot and Mezei [20], provides a powerful way of dealing with all the above-mentioned operations: instead of describing a machine which outputs $\tau(f)$ for all f and a given τ one describes a two-tape machine which reads a pair of words (f,g) and recognizes whether it lies in the graph $\hat{\tau}$ of τ defined as

$$\hat{\tau} = \{(f,g) \mid g = \tau(f)\}.$$

This has the advantage that a multivalued function τ is treated exactly in the same way as a single valued if $\hat{\tau}$ is given as $\{(f,g) \mid g \in \tau(f)\}$. It happens that the transductions τ of X* into Y* defined in [20] by means of a two-tape finite automaton are exactly the a-transducer mappings of [22]: they are also as was first proved in [31] the transductions whose graph $\hat{\tau}$ is a rational subset of X* × Y*, that is, $\hat{\tau}$ belongs to the least family of subsets of X* × Y* which contains the finite subsets and is closed under union, component-wise product and the corresponding star. From there it is easy to derive the following characterization of a-transducer mappings.

Nivat's Theorem [31]. A transduction τ from X* into Y* is an a-transducer mapping iff there exists an alphabet Z (finite), a rational (regular) set R in Z* and two morphisms h and g of Z* into X* and Y* respectively such that for all u ∈ X*, $\tau(u) = g(h^{-1}(u) \cap R)$.

From the characterization of these transductions in terms
of a two-tape machine one gets the important

Elgot and Mezei's Theorem [20]. The composition $\sigma\tau$ of
two a-transducer mappings, naturally defined as $\sigma\tau(u) =$
$\cup\{\sigma(v) \mid v \in \tau(u)\}$, is an a-transducer mapping.

Now on we shall call rational transduction our a-transducer
mapping. We shall see that rational transductions are the main
tool to study families of languages and that the bimorphism
characterization of them is undoubtedly the most helpful characterization among the three we have given. The study of
families of languages was initiated by Greibach and Ginsburg
[24]: their initial definition of an abstract family of languages (AFL) is the following:

Definition [24]. A family of languages L is an AFL iff
it is closed under union, product, ε-free star (or plus),
intersection with a regular set, ε-free morphism and arbitrary
inverse morphism.

Naturally the morphism h of X* into Y* is said to be
ε-free iff $h(X) \subset YY^*$, i.e., $h(u) = \varepsilon$ implies $u = \varepsilon$ and
the ε-free star denoted + is defined by

$$A^+ = A \cup A^2 \cup \ldots \cup A^k \cup \ldots \; .$$

This definition is completed by the

Definition [24]. The AFL L is full iff it is closed
under star and arbitrary morphism.

These original definitions are equivalent to the following
new set of definitions which we shall use in the sequel, all
the proofs being given in [9].

Definition. The rational transduction τ is said to be faithful iff for all $v \in Y^*$ the set $\tau^{-1}(v) = \{u \mid v \in \tau(u)\}$ is a finite subset of X^*.

Definition. A family of languages L is a rational cone (resp., faithful rational cone) iff for all rational transductions τ (resp., faithful rational transductions τ) and all $L \in L$, $\tau(L) = \cup\{\tau(u) \mid u \in L\}$ belongs to L.

A rational cone is called a full trio in [22].

We introduce also the substitution operation extensively studied by Greibach.

Definition [26]. If L_1 and L_2 are two families of languages $L_1 \square L_2$ is the family of all languages obtained as images of languages of L_1 under L_2-substitution, i.e., $L_1 \square L_2 = \{\sigma(L) \mid L \in L_1$ and σ is an L_2-substitution$\}$ where an L_2-substitution σ is a morphism of X^* into the set of subsets 2^{Y^*} of Y^* satisfying for all $x \in X$, $\sigma(x) \in L_2$.

If we call Rat the family of rational languages (i.e., the smallest family of languages containing the finite languages and closed under union, product and star) the family Rat $\square$ L is the rational closure of the family L. Now we have

Proposition. A family of languages L is an AFL iff it is a rationally closed faithful cone or equivalently Rat $\square$ $L \subset L$ and for all $L \in L$ and faithful transductions τ, $\tau(L) \in L$. A family of languages is a full AFL iff it is a rationally closed cone or equivalently Rat $\square$ $L \subset L$ and for all $L \in L$ and transductions τ, $\tau(L) \in L$.

The relationship between cones and AFL's can be made more precise if one introduces the notion of generated cones and

AFL's. Since obviously the intersection of an arbitrary collection of cones (resp., AFL's) is a cone (resp., AFL) one
naturally defines for every family L the cone $T(L)$ (resp.,
the faithful cone $T_f(L)$, resp., the AFL $F_f(L)$, resp., the
full AFL $F(L)$) <u>generated</u> <u>by</u> L as the smallest cone (resp.,
faithful cone, resp., AFL, resp., full AFL) containing L. We
have the

   <u>Proposition</u>. For all families of languages L

   $F(L)$ = Rat $\square$ $T(L)$

   $F_f(L)$ = Rat $\square$ $T_f(L)$.

And we can make this relationship even more precise when
we deal with principal families thus defined:

   <u>Definition</u>. A cone (resp., faithful cone, resp., AFL,
resp., full AFL) L is said to be principal iff there exists
a language L $\in$ L such that $L = T(L)$ (resp., $L = T_f(L)$,
resp., $L = F_f(L)$, resp., $L = F(L)$).

   We get the following

   <u>Proposition</u>. For any language L

   $F(L)$ = Rat $\square$ $T(L)$ = $T((L\#)^*)$, where # is a marker,

   $F_f(L)$ = Rat $\square$ $T_f(L)$ = $T_f((L\#)^*)$.

The study of cones and AFL's which are subcones and sub-
AFL's of the family Alg of all algebraic (context-free) languages has been the most fruitful area of research concerning
this important family of languages in the past years: it led
to a number of results and also a number of yet unsolved
conjectures [6].

   However some important subfamilies of Alg are neither
cones nor AFL's. Also, if one looks at the complexity of

recognition of languages, it is very clear that both the inverse morphic image $g^{-1}(L)$ of a language and the intersection $L \cap R$ of a language with a rational set R are of the same order of recognition complexity as L. On the other hand the direct morphic image $g(L)$ is a priori exponentially more difficult to recognize than the language L. Whence recently two new notions have been introduced by several authors [18,1].

<u>Definition</u>. The family of languages L is an <u>abstract family of deterministic languages</u> iff L is closed under inverse gsm mappings, marked union, marked star and removing of end-markers.

<u>Definition</u>. The family of languages L is a <u>cylinder</u> iff L is closed under inverse morphisms and intersection with a rational set.

And a third notion will be discussed later on in this paper.

<u>Definition</u>. The family of languages L is an <u>a-cylinder</u> iff it is closed under inverse a-gsm mappings, i.e., for all $L \in L$ and a-gsm mappings $\tau : \tau^{-1}(L) \in L$.

We shall denote by $C(L)$ (resp., $G(L)$, resp., $D(L)$) the smallest cylinder (resp., a-cylinder, resp., AFDL) containing L, also called the cylinder (resp., a-cylinder, resp., AFDL) generated by L. Obvious inclusion relations hold.

<u>Proposition</u>. For all L, $C(L) \subseteq G(L) \subseteq D(L) \subseteq T_f(L)$.

Now we can raise a very general problem: let A be a set of primitive operations on languages, we call A-<u>cone</u>, and denote $A(L)$ the smallest family of languages containing L and closed under all the operations in A. And we call A-<u>basis</u> of the A-cone L every set of languages $L' \subseteq L$ such that

$A(L') = L$: in an obvious way L is said to be an A-<u>principal</u> A-cone iff there exists an $L \in L$ such that $L = A(L)$ that is an A-basis reduced to a single language. We have already introduced the following meaningful sets of operations:

T_f = {faithful rational transduction},

C = {inverse morphism, intersection with a rational set},

G = {inverse a-gsm mapping},

D = {inverse gsm mapping, marked union, marked star, removing of markers}.

As a more specific problem we can raise the question of, given two sets A and B of operations, characterizing the families which are both A-principal and B-principal. A typical positive result of this type is the proof that D-principality implies G-principality.

<u>Proposition.</u> For all languages L, $D(L) = G((L\#)^*)$, where # is a marker.

And a typical negative result pertaining to the same area is that D-principality does not imply C-principality, as is shown by the example.

<u>Proposition.</u> Let $L = \{a^n b^n \mid n \in \mathbb{N}_+\}$. Then $D(L)$ is not C-principal (though it is a C-cone, i.e., a cylinder).

Many other questions may be raised in this framework. We can say for example that the full AFL L is <u>conic</u> iff for all L', $L = F(L') \Rightarrow L = T(L')$. The full AFL which is formed by all algebraic languages, already denoted Alg, is conic, as will be proved below. We do not know, up to now, any characterization of the conic sub full AFL's of Alg.

II.   THE CONE OF ALGEBRAIC LANGUAGES

A.   Generators

When looking at the family of algebraic languages, it can
be considered as a full AFL or as an AFL; it can be considered
too as a rational cone or as a faithful rational cone. This
simple fact suggests that we may think some languages could be
able to generate the family Alg as one of these and not as
another, that is to say, for instance, that we could find some
language L such that $F(L) = Alg$ and $T(L) \subseteq Alg$ ... . It
turns out that this is impossible, as shown below, so that we
can speak of generators without other indications. (It should
be noted, however, that this is no longer true when looking at
the family Alg as a cylinder so that this convention will hold
only in this section.) Before showing how this "independence"
result is proved, we will first present some classical generators and sketch out the usual way of proving these to be
generators.

1. The first one is surely the most classical one: it is
the one-sided Dyck set over two pairs of letters. It is denoted here $D_2'^*$. When considering n pairs of letters, we
will get similarly $D_n'^*$. The classical proof that $D_2'^*$ is a
generator states in fact that $T(D_2'^*) = Alg$. It generally
goes in two steps:

a. Prove the Chomsky-Schützenberger theorem:

The language L over X is algebraic iff there exists an
integer n, a regular set R over the alphabet Z_n of n
pairs of letters and a morphism h from Z_n^* to X^* such that

$$L = h(D_n'^* \cap R).$$

In the classical proof, h is an erasing morphism. It should be noted, however, that it is possible to give a proof with the added property that h is ε-limited on R.

b. Use the usual encoding of $D_n'^*$ by $D_2'^*$ through an inverse morphism. (If (a) is proved with h ε-limited on R, you get a more precise result: $D_2'^*$ is a generator of the faithful rational cone Alg). This situation leads to the question dealing with the families $T(D_1'^*)$, $F(D_1'^*)$ and their faithful versions. These questions will not be treated here (see [10], for instance).

2. The second language to be presented here is denoted E. It is defined over $\{a, b, c, d\}$ and generated by the grammar $<S \to aSbSc + d>$. As in the case of the Dyck languages, we define the alphabet $Y_n = \{a_i, b_i, c_i, d_i \mid 1 \leq i \leq n\}$ which has $4n$ letters, and the language E_n generated by the grammar $<S \to a_iSb_iSc_i + d_i \mid 1 \leq i \leq n>$. To prove that E is a generator one can use the fact that $D_2'^*$ is one. It can be done directly, too, using two steps very similar to the above steps.

a. Prove a Chomsky-Schützenberger-like theorem:

The language L over X is algebraic iff there exists an integer n, a regular set over Y_n and a morphism h from Y_n^* to X^* such that

$$L = h(E_n \cap R).$$

Sketch of the proof: the "if" part being immediate, we will just sketch out the "only if" part of the proof. Given an algebraic language L over X, it is well known [30] that it can be generated by an algebraic grammar in double quadratic

Greibach normal form: the rules of G are of three types.

type 1: $V_1 \to xV_2V_3y$, $x, y \in X$, V_1, V_2, V_3 variables

type 2: $V_1 \to xV_2y$, $x, y \in X$, V_1, V_2 variables

type 3: $V_1 \to x$, $x \in X \cup XX$, V_1 a variable.

Numbering the rules of G, you build up a new grammar $\bar{G}$ as follows:

•if the ith rule of G is $V_1 \to xV_2V_3y$, define the ith rule of $\bar{G}$ by $V_1 \to a_iV_2b_iV_3c_i$ and set $h(a_i) = x$, $h(c_i) = y$, $h(b_i) = h(d_i) = 1$.

•if the ith rule of G is $V_1 \to xV_2y$, define the ith rule of $\bar{G}$ by $V_1 \to a_id_ib_iV_2c_i$ and set $h(a_i) = x$, $h(c_i) = y$, $h(b_i) = h(d_i) = 1$.

•if the ith rule of G is $V_1 \to x$, define the ith rule of $\bar{G}$ by $V_1 \to d_i$ and set $h(a_i) = h(b_i) = h(c_i) = 1$ and $h(d_i) = x$.

It is immediately proved that, for any variable v,

$$L(G,v) = h(L(\bar{G},v)).$$

Moreover, it is clear too that $L(\bar{G},v) \subseteq E_n$. You then define a regular set R over Y_n just by looking at the possible transitions in the words generated by $\bar{G}$: for instance a letter a_i can be followed by a_j iff

the ith rule of $\bar{G}$ is $V_1 \to a_iV_2 \cdots$

and

the jth rule of $\bar{G}$ is $V_2 \to a_j \cdots$.

Then, to each variable v is associated a regular set R_v which is the set of those words which are in R with their first letter being a_i (or d_i) if v is the left member of the ith rule of G. This construction ensures trivially that $L(\bar{G},v) \subseteq R_v$, so that $L(\bar{G},v) \subseteq E_n \cap R_v$. Exactly as in the usual Chomsky-Schützenberger theorem, you prove the inverse inclusion to hold, so that $L(\bar{G},v) = E_n \cap R_v$, getting the desired theorem. Remark that, in this proof, h is ε-limited on R, so it is ε-limited on R_v. We then go through our second step:

   b. Encode E_n by E_1 through an inverse morphism.

   Using the "classical" encodings it is clear that one can encode E_n by E_2. It is then enough to show how to encode E_2 by E_1 (which is impossible for the Dyck sets: you cannot encode $D_2'^*$ by $D_1'^*$). This can be done by using

$$h(a_1) = aa \qquad h(b_1) = bdcbadb \qquad h(c_1) = cc \qquad h(d_1) = d$$
$$h(a_2) = aadb \qquad h(b_2) = cba \qquad h(c_2) = bdcc \qquad h(d_2) = d$$

having $h(a_1 d_i b_1 d_i c_1) = h(a_2 d_i b_2 d_i c_2) = aadbdcbadbdcc \in E$ we are sure that $h(E_2) = E_1$. We just have to prove then that $h^{-1}(E_1) \subseteq E_2$ which is done by induction on the length of the words.

   Putting then together (a) and (b), we get

   E is a generator of the family Alg,

and, more precisely:

   $T_f(E) = Alg.$

   3. The last language to be presented here is δ, the language over $\{a,b\}$ generated by the grammar $<S \to aSSb + ab>$. The simplest way to prove δ to be a generator is to prove that there exists a morphism h such that $h^{-1}(\delta) = E$. Such

a morphism can be "guessed" using the derivation $S \to aSSb$ $\overset{(2)}{\to}$

$aaSSbaSSbb$ $\overset{(2)}{\to}$ $aaabSbaSabbb$ which suggests to set $h(a) =$

$aaab$, $h(b) = ba$, $h(c) = abbb$ and $h(d) = ab$. A careful

checking ensures it works, that is to say that $h^{-1}(\delta) = E$.

So that $T_f(\delta) = Alg$.

We gave this example here, because it often happens that

this way of building up a morphism satisfying $h^{-1}(L) = E$

really works. This is not really a pure miracle and is par-

tially explained by Beauquier's theorem (see below).

We now start to explain how our initial claim about gener-

ators can be proved. We will first show that whenever $F(L) =$

Alg, then $T(L) = Alg$. This result will come from a proposi-

tion and a simple fact. Given a language L over an alphabet

X, define $<L>$ as being the language over $X \cup \{a,b\}$ (where

a and b are new letters not in X):

$$<L> = \{a^n f b^n \mid n \geq 1, \quad f \in L\}.$$

Define a family of languages L to be <u>translatable</u> whenever

$L \in L$ implies $<L>$ in L [15]. Then

    <u>Proposition</u>. Any translatable full principal AFL L has

the property that

$$F(L) = L \iff T(L) = L.$$

This proposition, together with the classical fact that

the family of algebraic languages is translatable, gives rise

to the desired result.

    <u>Corollary</u>. Given an algebraic language L, $T(L) = Alg$

iff $F(L) = Alg$.

We now turn to the faithful generators problem. Once more our initial claim will come from a general proposition and a simple fact. The general proposition deals with rational transductions. Recall first a language meets the I.R.S. condition iff it contains no Infinite Regular Set [28]. We then have

Proposition [15]. Given a rational transduction τ and an algebraic language L such that τL meets the I.R.S. condition, there exists a faithful rational transduction σ such that $\sigma L = \tau L$. (We have decided to omit any detail about the empty word.)

The associated fact is then the following:

Fact: The language E is a faithful generator meeting the I.R.S. condition;

from which we derive

Corollary. Given an algebraic language L, $T(L) = \text{Alg}$ iff $T_f(L) = \text{Alg}$.

Proof. $T_f(L) = \text{Alg}$ clearly implies $T(L) = \text{Alg}$. So we are left with the other direction to prove. Given any language L such that $T(L) = \text{Alg}$, we know that there exists a rational transduction τ such that $\tau L = E$. Using the last proposition, we may assume τ to be faithful; that is, $E \in T_f(L)$ and $T_f(E) \subseteq T_f(L) \subseteq T(L) = \text{Alg}$. The above fact then ensures $T_f(L) = T(L)$.

These results are then summarized in

Fact. For any algebraic language L, the following are equivalent:

$$T_f(L) = Alg,$$
$$T(L) = Alg,$$
$$F_f(L) = Alg,$$
$$F(L) = Alg.$$

So that, from now, a language will be called a generator whenever one of these can be proved. (In particular, we shall
omit the precision that it is a T-generator.)

B.   Beauquier's Theorem

When looking carefully at the already presented generators,
some common features of them can be pointed out: all of them
are nonambiguous (and even deterministic). A more precise
study shows that

- there exists a regular set R such that $E_n \cap R = E$;
- there exists a morphism h such that $h^{-1}(\delta) = E$;
- there exists a morphism h such that $h^{-1}(D_2'^*) = E$

(given by $h(a) = xy$, $h(b) = \bar{y}x$, $h(c) = \bar{x}\bar{x}$, $h(d) = y\bar{y}$).

It could be asked then to find a generator L either ambiguous or such that any rational transduction mapping L onto E
has to use direct morphism. The first question is easy to
answer: just take any generator, say E, add to it on a disjoint alphabet any classical ambiguous language, and you get
what you want. However, clearly, everybody would say this is
an unsatisfactory answer to the question. There is some
cheating in doing so. We may so ask for a "better looking"
example. This could be, for instance, the following:

L_1 is the language over {a,b} generated by the grammar

    <S → aSbSa + a>;

L_1 has been proved [7] to be inherently ambiguous and to
be a generator.

As far as proving L_1 is a generator, the technique used once
more is the following: find a morphism h such that $h^{-1}(L_1)$
= E. in this case, such a morphism could be given by:
u = aaab, v = aba, and w = baaa with h(a) = uuav, h(b) =
wvu, h(c) = vaww and h(d) = a. It seems, with this example,
that we have a positive answer to our first question: is it
possible to be both generator and ambiguous? However, the
fact the answer could be considered as a real one is purely a
question of feeling and the remark that h(E) = L_1 ∩ h(X*) is
a nonambiguous generator included in L leaves open the following precise question:

Is it possible to find out an ambiguous generator L such
that, for any regular set K, L ∩ K is either ambiguous
or non-generator?

Beauquier's theorem will answer negatively to this question as
well as to the other one asked at the beginning of this paragraph (about using necessarily morphism to get E from a
generator). In its full detailed version, giving the more
precise information known about these questions, it can be
stated:

Beauquier's Theorem [8]. An algebraic language L over
X is a generator iff there exist six words over X,
$\#_1$, $\#_2$, α, β, γ, δ, and a regular set R over X, such
that

(i) the grammar $\langle A \to \#_1 S \#_2; \quad S \to \alpha S \beta S \gamma + \delta \rangle$ is non-ambiguous;

(ii) it generates $L \cap R$;

(iii) defining $h(a) = \alpha$, $h(b) = \beta$, $h(c) = \gamma$, $h(\#_1) = x$, $h(\#_2) = y$, $h^{-1}(L \cap R) = h^{-1}(L) = xEy$ (so that $L \cap R$ is still a generator).

From this theorem you can get two more readable corollaries:

Corollary 1. Given a generator L, there exists a regular set R such that $L \cap R$ is a nonambiguous generator.

Corollary 2. Given a generator L, there exists a morphism h such that $h^{-1}(L) = xEy$; or, equivalently, xEy is a member of the cylinder generated by any generator.

The proof of the theorem is technical and rather complicated. It is given in [8]. It does not seem to be possible with the tools we have now to make it really simple, but it surely explains the "strange" facts quoted above: roughly speaking, it says that E is encoded in any generator. This is really "roughly" speaking because when looking precisely at the proof of the theorem, you should remark it states that any word of the regular language R has a unique factorization over α, β, γ, δ, but it does not say so for any word of X^*. It is an

Open Question. The four words α, β, γ, δ of Beauquier's theorem can always be chosen such that they are a code.

Apart from its interest in its own, Beauquier's theorem can be used to prove that some languages are not generators. We will end this paragraph by giving such an example. Over the alphabet {a, b, c, d}, to each word f we associate its longest left factor e(f) which is a left factor of E. As E is the class of d in the congruence adbdc ≡ d, we can then reduce e(f) in a word h the length of which will be denoted $\|e(f)\|$. We then define

$$L_1 = \{f \in X^* \mid f = e(f)g \text{ and } \|e(f)\| \leq |g| \leq 2\|e(f)\|\}.$$

To show that L_2 is algebraic, you can easily describe a push-down automata (derived from the one recognizing E) which recognizes L_2. To show that L_2 is not a generator, you may use (i) and (ii) of Beauquier's theorem. If it were, you would have a regular set R such that

$$\#_1 \alpha^n (\alpha\delta\beta)^p \delta\gamma^p \gamma^* \#_2 \subseteq R$$

and you surely can find an integer r such that

$$\#_1 \alpha^n (\alpha\delta\beta)^p \delta\gamma^p \gamma^r \#_2 \in L_1.$$

This word being not generated by the grammar (i), you get a contradiction. (A detailed proof of this fact is given in [13].)

C. The Non-Generators

Given a substitution closed full principal AFL L, you may define the largest full sub-AFL properly contained in L: it is the family of those languages in L which do not generate L through the AFL operations. This new full AFL is substitution closed [26]. Similarly, given a principal rational cone, it contains a largest proper subcone. In the special case of Alg, this largest subcone is denoted Nge (standing for

Non-Generators' family). Clearly, because of the above-given

results concerning generators, Nge is a substitution-closed

full AFL: it is the largest full sub-AFL of Alg. One of the

major conjectures standing in this field can now be stated:

Conjecture [25]: Nge is a non-prinicipal full AFL.

This conjecture raised a lot of work which provided the

language   theory with new results; we would like to limit

this presentation to the two major ways which have been used

to attack the question.

First Approach: Describe Nge through already known

families. At its early beginning, this approach was tightly

related to a conjecture of S. Greibach [25]: within Alg, we

know two classical subfamilies, the one of linear languages

and the one of one-counter languages. Each of these is well-

known to be rational cones (see [9] for instance). Looking

then at the substitution closure of each of them, you get two

families which are non-principal full AFL's. (This comes from

general AFL-theoretic results [26].) The first one is the

family of quasi-rational (or non-expansive) languages; the

second one is the family of iterated counter languages. From

these, you may then build a larger family: the least

substitution-closed full AFL containing these two families.

Once more, this full AFL is non-principal. We call it Gre,

the full AFL of Greibach languages. As this full AFL is the

largest "really known" contained in Alg, it was conjectured

that Gre and Nge coincide. Though disproved [11], this con-

jecture was at the origin of several results and other ques-

tions. For instance, working on these questions, you may come

across a result [28] stating that any iterated counter

language meeting the I.R.S. condition is non-expansive. That is equivalent to the fact that the Greibach languages meeting the I.R.S. condition are exactly the non-expansive languages meeting this condition. It was then conjectured [28] that any expansive language meeting the I.R.S. condition was a generator. This conjecture has been disproved too: the above-given language L_2 is a counterexample to it [13]. However, some results of the same kind are known to be true: any expansive parenthesis language is a generator [16]. Or, any very simple expansive language meeting the I.R.S. condition is a generator [21].

In some sense, the oldest open question related to this approach could be considered to be the following:

Conjecture [6]. The least principal rational cone containing the family of non-expansive languages is the whole family Alg.

This conjecture could be attached to the

Second Approach: Give a direct proof that Nge is non-principal. This second approach is very different. It leads to new results on the structure of the family Alg. These may be full AFL results (such as the already mentioned syntactical lemma [26]). They may be too specific to the family Alg. We include in these all the work on iterative pairs. Given a language L, an iterative pair is a factorization $(\alpha, u, \beta, v, \gamma)$ of a word in L such that $\alpha u^n \beta v^n \gamma$ is in L for any integer n. The pairs have been classified following the properties of the set $\{(n,m) \in \mathbb{N} \times \mathbb{N} \mid \alpha u^n \beta v^m \gamma \in L\}$ [12]. In particular, the pair is strict iff this set reduced to $\{(n,n) \mid n \in \mathbb{N}\}$. The use of such a concept appears as related

to our non-generator problem when we look at the results we
have, explaining how these pairs go through the rational transductions. Typically, one of the simplest results of this sort
can be stated [12]:

Proposition (Transfer Theorem). Given two algebraic languages A and B, and a rational transduction τ such that
B = τA, if B admits a strict iterative pair, so does A.

From such a proposition, you easily get that $\{a^n b^n \mid$
$n \in \mathbb{N}\}$ will not be in the rational cone generated by
$\{a^n b^m \mid n \geq m \geq 1\}$ for instance. This result about pairs can
be extended to simultaneous pairs, when these simultaneous
pairs are independent, that is whenever their sets of exponents are independent: taking $x\bar{x}x\bar{x}$ as a word in $D_1'^*$, it
clearly has two strict pairs $(1, x, 1, \bar{x}, x\bar{x})$ and
$(x\bar{x}, x, 1, \bar{x}, 1)$. Those are not independent because $x^2\bar{x}x\bar{x}^2$
is in $D_1'^*$ and $x^2\bar{x}x\bar{x}$ is not; that is, $(2, 1, 1, 2)$ is a
possible vector of exponents so that the set of exponents does
not reduce to (n, n, m, m). A formal definition of independence can be found in [8]. A second aspect of this generalization takes into account the geometrical disposition of
the pairs: they may be nested or successive. Roughly speaking, the Transfer Theorem can be now extended to any system of
independent strict iterative pairs, so that for instance
$\{a^n b^n a^p b^p \mid n, p \geq 1\}$ is surely incomparable in terms of generated cones with $\{a^n b^p a^p b^n \mid n, p \geq 1\}$. This sort of structural result would give for instance another proof of the non-
principality of the quasi-rational languages family Qrt. The
informal conjecture on which rely a lot of conjectures about
Nge is that an algebraic languages is a generator iff it

admits any system of independent strict iterative pairs (just
as $D'_2{}^*$ or E do). Look for instance at the

Conjecture [15]. The smallest translatable principal rational cone closed under product is Alg.

It may be "explained" or "justified" by the following: in
such a cone, you surely have $\{a^n b^n \mid n \geq 1\}$. So, you have
too $\{x^n a^{n_1} b^{n_1} a^{n_2} b^{n_2} y^n \mid n, n_1, n_2 \geq 1\}$ etc. ... . Clearly,
any system of pairs should then be a system of pairs admitted
by the generator of this cone, whence the conjecture. It
should be noted that proving this conjecture would prove our
first conjecture: Nge is a translatable, product-closed full
AFL.

You should remark too that this conjecture is very similar
to our second one. This approach clearly shows that, when
meeting a non-principal cone, we may have two different situations: we have any measure on the languages of this cone
which is preserved by transduction or we have not. In the
first case, we immediately have a non-principality proof:
that is the one given by the order of quasi-rational languages,
as well as by the system of pairs such languages may have. In
the second case we are left with a conjecture: that is the
case for the Nge family itself. To illustrate this point of
view, we will briefly show two other examples, one for each
situation, which are less classical. In [14], the rational
index of language is defined: given a language L, build up
all the nondeterministic finite automata with n states; for
each of them, select the length of the shortest word of L it
recognizes (if none, set this length to 0). From this finite
set of integers, select then the maximum and set index(L,n)

to this maximum. This measure is proved [14] to be compatible with rational transductions, so that the family of languages whose index is bounded by a polynomial is a rational cone. The degree of the bounding polynomial gives us an easy way to prove this family to be a non-principal cone (after proving any such degree is accessible to ensure the family to give rise to a hierarchy of nonempty families!). This family Pol of polynomially bounded languages was hoped for a while to be the same as Nge (we know this is not true [13]), because we know any generator has a rational index growing at least like an exponential. This measure leads to questions showing that we really do not know much about the structure of the family Alg: whenever we may prove we have languages whose index is bounded by a family of functions with a growth speed between the polynomials and the exponential, we will get new non-principal subcones of Alg. We do not even know a single language having such a rational index.

A non-classical example of the second situation could be given by the following: from the Transfer Theorem, you immediately get that Nsi, the family of the algebraic languages having No Strict Iterative pair, is a rational cone. As this definition does not give rise to any "measure", we only have

Conjecture. Nsi is a non-principal rational cone.

So, our second approach can be described as an approach leading to define good structural measures on languages allowing to describe any language in Nge through such a measure. This sort of attempt is surely difficult, but it is surely too very important: it is the only one which can really give a

better understanding of the structure of Alg. There seems to
be there a lot to be done; the following conjecture indicates
that such a work could lead to some "density" result:

Conjecture. Given two algebraic languages A and B
such that $B \in T(A)$, either $T(B) = T(A)$ or there exists a
language C such that $T(B) \subsetneq T(C) \subsetneq T(A)$.

III. CYLINDERS OF ALGEBRAIC LANGUAGES

We have seen that the family Alg is a T-principal family
and that any generator of this family as a full-AFL is a generator as a rational cone. We also mentioned that some T-
generators could fail to be C-generators: as the cylinder
operations preserve the degree of ambiguity (as well as the
determinism) of languages, and as there exist algebraic languages with nonbounded degree of inherent ambiguity, any C-
generator of the family Alg would have to be of unbounded
degree of ambiguity. In particular, this simple fact excludes
the possibility for the T-generator $D_2'^*$, which is a deterministic language, to be a C-generator of the family Alg. So,
the C-domination, denoted >, defined by $L > M$ if $M \in C(L)$
allows a classification of T-generators. L and M are said
to be C-equivalent iff $L > M$ and $M > L$. Modulo this C-
equivalence, Beauquier's theorem implies that the class of the
language xEy is a smaller element among T-generators. It
can easily be shown that the Dyck sets $D_n'^*$ $(n \geq 2)$ and the
prime factors of these sets $D_n' = D_n'^* \setminus (D_n'^* - \varepsilon)^2$ are incomparable T-generator in this classification.

The question now is: does there exist a greater element
in this classification? This question is only another

formulation of the following: does there exist a C-generator
of Alg? The answer is yes as shown below, and the proof is
again an instance of the general scheme for proving either
principality or non-principality, which can be decomposed into
two steps:

- find a basis of the family;

- prove, or disprove, that one element of this basis can

  generate all others.

It happens that finding a C-basis for the family Alg can
be done in a general frame for constructing C-basis. We will
not discuss here this construction in its whole generality
(see [4]). However, as very little work is needed to show how
to get also a C-basis for deterministic realtime algebraic
languages (and for other families of algebraic languages), we
will do these various constructions at the same time.

A.   Principal Families

The construction given here is a generalization of the one
of S. Greibach for the hardest algebraic language [27], which
allows us to show at the same time that determinism can be
taken in account.

Let A be a specific realtime pushdown automaton, recognizing a language L:

$$A = \ <X, \ Q, \ Y, \ q_1, \ z_1, \ Q', \ \lambda >$$

where

X   is the input alphabet

Q   is the set of states where $Q = \{q_1, q_2, \ldots, q_p\}$

Y   is the storage alphabet $Y = \{z_1, z_2, \ldots, z_n\}$

q_1 is the initial state

z_1 is the initial store symbol

Q'   is the set of final states

λ is the transition function, i.e., an application

$\lambda : X \times Q \times Y \to 2^{Q \times Y^*}$.

A is <u>deterministic</u> if for all $(x, q, z) \in X \times Q \times Y$:
$\|\lambda(x, q, z)\| = 1$, i.e., there is only one possible transition
(λ is in fact an application $\lambda : X \times Q \times Y \to Q \times Y^*$). If
$(q_k, h) \in \lambda(x, q_i, z_j)$, this possible transition, or rule, is
usually denoted $(x, q_i, z_j) \to (q_k, h)$. This means that if x
is the input letter to be read, and q_i is the current state
of the automaton and if z_j is the top-most symbol in the
pushdown store, then the automaton moves to the new state q_k,
and the top symbol z_j is erased and replaced by the word h
at the top of the pushdown store. It is a classical construction to associate to the store alphabet Y a Dyck alphabet
$Z = Y \cup \bar{Y}$ (where $\bar{Y} = \{\bar{z}_1, \bar{z}_2, \ldots, \bar{z}_n\}$). Considering what
is going on in the store, a deletion of top-most symbol z_j
can be denoted by the letter $\bar{z}_j$, while putting the word h
on the top of the pushdown store is denoted h. So the two
changes are noted $\bar{z}_j h$.

     This leads us to define the following reduction ρ :

$\rho(\varepsilon) = \varepsilon$;

$\rho(fz_i) = \rho(f)z_i$, which corresponds to a letter z_i
     added at the top of the pushdown store;

$$\rho(f\bar{z}_i) = \begin{cases} f' & \text{if } \rho(f) = f'z_i, \text{ which corresponds to a} \\ & \text{letter } z_i \text{ erased at the top of the} \\ & \text{pushdown store,} \\ & \text{undefined if not; it is not possible to} \\ & \text{delete the letter } z_i \text{ if it is not the} \\ & \text{top-most symbol in the store: the} \\ & \text{automaton blocks.} \end{cases}$$

If f is the word obtained by concatenation of all the words denoting the changes in the store during a computation, the computation ends with an empty storage iff $z_i\rho(f) = \varepsilon$ (z_1 is the initial pushdown store). This reduction itself defines a language that we will call the characteristic language (characteristic of pushdown automata), and which is the set of words over Z such that their reduction is defined: $\hat{D} =$ $\{f \in Z* \mid \rho(f)$ is defined$\}$. Of course, this language is here the language of all left factors of words in the Dyck set, the Dyck set itself being the set of all words whose reduction is equal to the empty word ε.

But the change of configuration of the automaton is not only a change in the pushdown store, but also a change of state. If we want to encode all the changes of the automaton according to the rule $(x, q_i, z_j) \to (q_k, h)$ we can do it with the word $a^i \bar{z}_j hc^k$, where a and c are two new letters. We will call such a word an elementary factor.

In the same way we can encode all possible changes of configuration of the automaton when it reads the letter x, so that we associate to the letter x the word $\phi(x) = g_1 g_2 \cdots g_r d$ where d is a marker and every g_i is one elementary

factor encoding one possible change of configuration when
reading the letter x. Such a word $\phi(x)$ will be called a
block.

An important remark is that the number of rules, and consequently of elementary factors, is finite, and so ϕ can be
looked at as a homomorphism. If a word f is the image by
ϕ of a word $w \in X^*$, $f = \phi(w)$, then f belongs to a regular set R_A: the regular set recognized by a finite automaton
checking if f is a sequence of blocks and, A having p
states, if the number of consecutive a letters and also the
number of consecutive c letters are not more than p.

For a word f in R_A, we will call g a choice in f
if g is the concatenation of one elementary factor in each
block of f. g will be called a valid choice iff it satisfies two conditions:

•the number of a in the first elementary factor is exactly one, corresponding to the fact that g is the initial
state, and if the number of c of an elementary factor is j,
coding state q_j, then the number of a of the next elementary factor is also j;

•if we erase all a's and c's of g we get a word
$\theta(g)$ (corresponding to the succession of all changes of the
store) such that $z_1 \theta(g) \in \hat{D}$.
It is now obvious that if the word f in R_A is a succession
of blocks corresponding to the succession of letters of a word
w in X^*, then a valid choice in f corresponds exactly to
a valid computation of the automaton A when reading the word

w. We will denote $\gamma(f)$ the set of all valid choices in f,

and write $\gamma(f) = g$ rather than $(f) = \{g\}$ if g is the

unique valid choice in f.

Remark. Until now we have not said anything of the pos-

sible determinicity of the automaton. We have not described

either the recognition process.

We have associated to an automaton A a language which

is the set of all words in R_A possessing a valid choice.

This language can be defined without any reference to A but

the one induced by R_A, namely the number p of states and

the number n of pushdown store symbols. Let's call it $L_{n,p}$.

Clearly, if $Comp_A$ is the set of all words in X* for which

there is a possible computation in the automaton A, then

$Comp_A = \phi^{-1}(L_{n,p})$.

If we come now to determinism, A being deterministic

means that for every letter $x \in X$, for every state q_i and

store symbol z_j there is at most one element in $\lambda(x, q_i, z_j)$.

On our encoding this can be read: in every block, there must

be at most one elementary factor beginning with $a^i \bar{z}_j$. This

can easily be checked by a finite automaton, and so, if we call

K_A the set of all words in R_A satisfying this condition, we

get a new language $M_{n,p}$ which is the set of all words in K_A

having a valid choice. If A is deterministic we have

$Comp_A = \phi^{-1}(M_{n,p})$. Note that $M_{n,p}$ is obtained from $L_{n,p}$

only through an intersection with a regular set. L being the

language recognized by the deterministic pda A, a word f

belongs to L if at the end of the computation the state q_r

which is encoded by r consecutive letters c in the last

elementary factor belongs to Q', the set of final states.

If we note $M_{n,p}^{Q'}$ the set of words of $M_{n,p}$ satisfying this
condition on the number of c's in the last elementary factor
in the valid choice, we of course have $L = \phi^{-1}(M_{n,p}^{Q'})$. The
same thing can be done in the nondeterministic case, and if L
is recognized by a pada, we have $L = \phi^{-1}(L_{n,p}^{Q'})$.

Proposition. The family of all languages $M_{n,p}^{Q'}$ is a
C-basis of the family of languages recognized by realtime deterministic automata.

To prove the above proposition, one has only to prove that
every language $M_{n,p}^{Q'}$ is itself recognized by a realtime deterministic automaton: the final-state control of the automaton will check if the word in input belongs to K_A and will
be used to have a choice such that the number of c in the
elementary factor of the choice is equal to the number of a
in the next elementary factor of the choice (i.e., the starting state at a step of computation is the arrival state of the
preceding step), the number of a in the first elementary
factor is one (corresponding to the initial state q_1) and
the number of c in the last elementary factor of the choice
is so that it corresponds to a state in Q', the set of final
states.

The pushdown store of the automaton will be used to make
the reduction of the word obtained from the choice when deleting all a's and c's. When a block has been read, this automaton is in some state telling the number i of c's of the
last elementary factor of the choice and has a top-most symbol
z_j in its store which is the right symbol of the word obtained by reduction of the word in the beginning of the choice
to this point. These two pieces of information are enough for

the automaton to find in the next block an elementary factor
beginning with $a^i \bar{z}_j$. As the automaton is deterministic this
elementary factor is the one to be taken for the valid choice.

In the nondeterministic case, we have an analogous
proposition:

   <u>Proposition</u>. The family of all languages $L^{Q'}_{n,p}$ is a
C-basis of the family of languages recognized by pushdown
automata.

To prove this proposition again we have to prove that every
language $L^{Q'}_{n,p}$ is itself recognized by some pushdown automaton.
A possible automaton for that is basically the same as in the
deterministic case, but when it comes to an elementary factor
beginnning with $a^i \bar{z}_j$ the automaton has the possibility not
to take it in account and try to find another elementary factor in the same block having the same beginning.

   <u>Remark 1</u>. If we had chosen an empty storage recognition,
we could have done the same construction, but then the condition that $z_1 \gamma(f) = \varepsilon$ at the end of the computation of the
automaton when it recognizes f would lead to a slightly different C-basis, for example in the nondeterministic case, to
the family of all languages $L^\varepsilon_{n,p}$ where $L^\varepsilon_{n,p}$ is the set of
all words f in R_A such that $z_1 \gamma(f) \cap D'^*_n \neq \emptyset$.

One can of course combine this condition with the condition on the number of c's in the last elementary factor to
get a C-basis in the case of recognition by both final states
and empty storage process. (Note that we know that these
three kinds of recognition all lead in the nondeterministic
case to the same family recognized: the family of algebraic
languages.)

Remark 2. If we require our automata to be "simple", i.e., to have one single state, this condition can be ensured by an intersection with a regular set: the regular set checks that there is no factor aa nor cc in the words. The languages obtained from the C-basis through this intersection with a regular set are, in both deterministic and nondeterministic cases, languages of the corresponding family. (In the deterministic case, one has in fact to take a slightly more sophisticated encoding than the one described above.) Hence, we get C-basis for these families. It can be noted that in the nondeterministic case, the family is still Alg, so that the C-basis is exactly composed of the nondeterministic version of the Dyck sets used in [27].

Remark 3. If we now allow a bounded number of consecutive ε-moves, we still have a finite number of possible changes of configuration of the automata when reading one letter. All these changes may be encoded in the same way by a block having a finite length. φ is still a homomorphism and the construction can be achieved.

If we consider the family of algebraic languages, we can think of it as the family of languages recognized by realtime simple (nondeterministic) pushdown automata, with empty storage recognition. As already mentioned in Remark 2, we get this way a C-basis of Alg obtained from the C-basis obtained for general realtime pushdown machines, using an intersection with regular sets.

Proposition [27]. The family of algebraic languages is a principal cylinder.

To prove this proposition, one has to prove that all the elements of the C-basis can be obtained from one of them through cylinder operations. This C-basis is, in our notation, $\{L_{n,1} \mid n > 0\}$. The usual encoding of n letters by two letters allows us to do it, and the proposition is proved with $L_{2,1}^{\varepsilon}$ as C-generator. If we consider now the family of deterministic realtime algebraic languages, we also have a C-basis for this family also obtained from the general one by an intersection with a regular set.

The basically same encoding (though technically more complicated) leads to the analogous proposition:

Proposition [5]. The family of deterministic realtime algebraic languages is a principal cylinder.

B.   Non-C-Principal Families and Further Developments

From the general C-basis given by the above construction for realtime pushdown automata, we have deduced a C-basis for languages recognized by realtime deterministic pushdown automata. In the same way, we can deduce C-basis for other subfamilies of Alg, families recognized by realtime or, as remarked before, quasi-realtime, pushdown automata with some restrictions.

One classical restriction concerns the number of pushdown symbols: the classical family Roc1 of (restricted) one-counter languages is the family recognized by pushdown automata having only one store symbol, and we know [23] that this can be done in quasi-realtime.

On our encoding the fact only one symbol is used in the store can be read easily, and from our general C-basis which is the set of all $L_{n,p}^{Q'}$ we deduce a new family, again with an intersection with a regular set: the family of all $L_{1,p}^{Q'}$. Looking at the proof that all $L_{n,p}^{Q'}$ are recognized by push-down automata, we immediately get that all the $L_{1,p}^{Q'}$ are recognized by one-counter automata. So, the family of all $L_{1,p}^{Q'}$ is a C-basis of the family of restricted one-counter languages. This C-basis allows us to give a proof of the proposition:

Proposition [1]. The family of restricted one-counter languages is not C-principal.

Another very classical family of algebraic languages, the family Lin of linear languages, can be characterized as the family of languages recognized (in realtime) by "one-peak" pushdown automata. Again, this restriction can be worked out on our construction:

Recall that empty storage is characterized by the condition $z_1\gamma(f) \cap D_n'^* \neq \emptyset$. Having only one peak can be read on the words of $\gamma(f)$ the following way: increasing the store height is done by a factor in $\bar{Y}Y^+$ (so that the balance between letters of Y and letters of $\bar{Y}$ is positive) and the beginning of the word in $\gamma(f)$ must belong to $(\bar{Y}Y^+)^*$, and in the same way, to decrease the store height the end of the word in $\gamma(f)$ must belong to $(\bar{Y}(Y \cup \{\varepsilon\}))^*$, and so the condition is:

$$(z_1\gamma(f) \cap D_n'^*) \cap z_1(\bar{Y}Y^+)^*(\bar{Y}(Y \cup \{\varepsilon\}))^* \neq \emptyset.$$

From this we can define a new set of languages which is a C-basis for the family of linear languages, and again this C-basis allows us to give a proof of the proposition:

Proposition [7]. The family of linear languages is not C-principal.

Again, the C-basis obtained here has been obtained from the general one with an intersection with regular sets, though of a different nature from the preceding ones (instead of intersection on sets of words, this one is an intersection with sets of choices in words).

One could imagine other restrictions, which could be expressed by an intersection with regular sets, and would lead to C-basis for the families recognized in realtime (or quasi-realtime) by pda's with these restrictions. A condition which can by no means be expressed by any intersection with regular sets is the following: for every word of a language, there is only one valid computation leading to the recognition of this word. Such a language is a nonambiguous language. So there is no way to derive from our construction a C-basis for the family of nonambiguous algebraic languages, and up to now there is still no easy-to-handle C-basis for this family.

Looking at all proofs of D-principality in the literature it should be noticed that all are proofs of C-principality of the family. But we have seen that there exists a D-principal family which fails to be C-principal, namely the family $\mathcal{D}(L_0)$ where $L_0 = \{a^n b^n \mid n > 0\}$. So, the question is raised for non-C-principal families such as the family of one-counter languages or the family of linear languages whether they are G-principal or not, and more generally, which among the families of languages could be D-principal, or G-principal, without being C-principal. A partial answer is given by the following

Fact. Let L be a language over an alphabet X and a, c and d be three new symbols and call $Y = X \cup \{a, c, d\}$. Define the language V over Y:

$$V = \{\varepsilon\} \cup \{c^n a(X \cup \{a,c\})*d[(X \cup \{c\})*a]^n \mid n \geq 0\}$$

and let $A = \{a\}$ and $B = \{c^+(aX*c^+)*d\}$. We can now define a special kind of substitution S by:

$$\text{for } L \subseteq X*, \quad S(L) = \{Af_1 Vf_2 V \ldots Vf_n B \mid f_1 f_2 \ldots f_n \in L\}.$$

It can be shown that if L is a G-generator of a family L, and if $S(L)$ belongs to L, then L is C-principal with $S(L)$ as G-generator.

Moreover, it can be easily shown that if a family L is G-principal with L as G-generator, then $S(L)$ belongs to L if and only if L is closed under substitution S.

As a family is D-principal if and only if it is G-principal, we can state the proposition:

Proposition [2]. If L is an AFDL closed under the substitution S, then L is D-principal if and only if L is C-principal.

One can easily check this closure property for particular families of languages: clearly the families of algebraic languages and of deterministic realtime algebraic languages are closed under the S-substitution; obviously, $\mathcal{D}(L_0)$ is not. It is also easy to see that the families of one-counter languages and of linear languages are not closed under this substitution. This leaves open the problem whether they are G-principal or not.

Coming back to our last proposition, it could be strengthened in the following way:

Conjecture. If L is a G-principal family of algebraic languages, L is C-principal if and only if L is closed under the S-substitution.

This conjecture is in fact related to the

Conjecture. The family of unambiguous algebraic languages
is a non-principal cylinder.

Solving any of them would give valuable indications of how
to solve older conjectures, some of which are given in Chapter II. Moreover, when working on any of these, we somehow
come up to the same difficulties as the ones already mentioned
in our previous chapter. Namely, it makes clear we are lacking some reasonable measure dealing with iterative pairs (or
any other structural complexity device). Getting such a measure would surely help in several open problems on algebraic
languages.

IV. CONCLUSION

We will briefly conclude this short presentation by some
general remarks. The work on algebraic languages has three
main goals which can be described as follows:

·know as much as possible on the structure of algebraic
languages;

·know as much as possible on the structure of the family
of algebraic languages;

·relate the structure of a language and the structure of
the rational cone it generates.

A way the first goal can be attacked is illustrated by
another communcation included in this book. The present one
shows how the two last problems can be worked out: it presents some notions which are essentially looked at as tools;

it leads to a better understanding of these (transductions,
full AFL's) as well as the definition of some new notions
(iterative pairs, cylinders).

   From a language theoretician's point of view, studying these
notions is only a step towards some applications to the study
of the structure of families of languages. Reading our short
text should convince the reader that these tools are relevant
and helpful: they shed a new light on several open problems;
they may even allow a precise formulation of these, which is a
step towards their solution. Moreover, the results that can
be proved with them, and especially Beauquier's theorem, give
some evidence for the adequacy of this formalism to our
purposes.

REFERENCES

1. Autebert, J.M., Non principalité due cylindre des langages
   à compteur. Math. Syst. Theory 11, 157-167 (1977).
2. Autebert, J.M., Pushdown automata and families of languages
   generating cylinders. MFCS 77 Conference. Lecture Notes
   in Computer Science 53, 231-239 (1977).
3. Autebert, J.M., Opérations de cylindres et applications
   séquentielles gauches inverses. Acta Informatica 11,
   241-258 (1979).
4. Autebert, J.M., Familles d'automates et C-bases de familles
   de langages, to appear.
5. Autebert, J.M., The ADFL of realtime deterministic context-
   free languages is principal, submitted.
6. Autebert, J.M., Beauquier, J., Boasson, L., et Nivat, M.,
   Quelques problemes ouverts en théorie des langages algébriques. RAIRO-Informatique Théorique, 13, 363-379 (1979).
7. Beauquier, J., Un générateur inhéremment ambigu du cone
   des langages algébriques. RAIRO-Informatique Théorique 12,
   99-108 (1978).
8. Beauquier, J., Générateurs algébriques et systèmes de
   paires itérantes. Theoretical Computer Science 8, 293-323
   (1979).
9. Berstel, J., "Transductions and Context-Free Languages."
   Teubner-Verlag (1979).
10. Boasson, L., Two iteration theorems for some families of
    languages. JCSS 7, 583-596 (1973).

11. Boasson, L., The inclusion of the substitution closure of linear and one-counter languages in the largest sub-AFL of the family of CFL is proper. Information Processing Letter 2, 135-140 (1973).
12. Boasson, L., Langages algébriques, paires itérantes et transductions rationnelles. Theoretical Computer Science 2, 209-223 (1976).
13. Boasson, L., Un langage algébrique particulier. RAIRO-Informatique Théorique, to appear.
14. Boasson, L., Courcelle, B., and Nivat, M., A new complexity measure for languages. A Conference on Theoretical Computer Science, Waterloo, 130-138 (1977).
15. Boasson, L., et Nivat, M., Sur diverses familles des langages fermées par transductions rationnelles. Acta Informatica 2, 180-188 (1973).
16. Boasson, L., and Nivat, M., Parenthesis generators. 17th Annual IEEE FOCS Symposium, Houston, 253-257 (1976).
17. Boasson, L., and Nivat, M., Le cylindre des languages linéaires. Math. Syst. Theory 11, 147-155 (1977).
18. Chandler, W.J., Abstract families of deterministic languages. Proc. 1st ACM Symp. on Theory of Computing, 21-30 (1969).
19. Choffrut, C., Une caractérisation des fonctions séquentielles et des fonctions sous-séquentielles en tant que relations rationnelles. Theoretical Computer Science 5, 325-338 (1977).
20. Elgot, C.C., and Mezei, G., On relations defined by generalized finite automata. IBM J. of Res. and Dev. 9, 47-65 (1965).
21. Frougny, C., Langages très simples générateurs. RAIRO-Informatique Théorique 13, 69-86 (1979).
22. Ginsburg, S., "Algebraic and Automata Theoretic Properties of Formal Languages." North-Holland (1975).
23. Ginsburg, S., Goldstine, J., and Greibach, S., Some uniformly erasable families of languages. Theoretical Computer Science 2, 29-44 (1976).
24. Ginsburg, S., and Greibach, S., Abstract families of languages. Memoir of the Amer. Math. Soc. 87, 1-32 (1969).
25. Ginsburg, S., and Rose, G.F., A characterization of machine mappings. Canadian J. Math. 18, 381-388 (1966).
26. Greibach, S., Chains of full-AFLs. Math. Syst. Theory 4, 231-242 (1970).
27. Greibach, S., The hardest context-free language. SIAM J. Comput. 2, 304-310 (1973).
28. Greibach, S., One-counter languages and the IRS condition. JCSS 10, 237-247 (1975).
29. Greibach, S., Jump PDA's, deterministic context-free languages, principal AFDL's and polynomial time recognition. Proc. 5th ACM Symp. on Theory of Computing, 20-28 (1973).
30. Hotz, G., Normal form transformations of context-free grammars. Acta Cybernetica 4, 65-84 (1978).
31. Nivat, M., Transductions des langages de Chomsky. Annales de l'Institut Fourier 18, 339-456 (1968).
32. Schützenberger, M.P., A remark on finite transducers. Information and Control 4, 185-196 (1961).

VERY SMALL FAMILIES OF ALGEBRAIC
NONRATIONAL LANGUAGES[1]

Jean-Michel Autebert[2]
Joffroy Beauquier[3]
Luc Boasson[2]

LA 248 "Informatique Théorique et Programmation"
Université Paris VI et Paris VII
Paris, France

Michel Latteux

Université de Lille I
Villeneuve-d'Ascq, France

One of the main goals of formal language theory is to propose some notions which enable us to derive from local properties of words, global properties of languages. This point of view justifies all the studies on regularity in words of rational or algebraic languages. Unfortunately, in this area, there are more conjectures than results, and there is no known characterization of algebraic languages that are rational in terms of local properties on their words. In a way that will be apparent in the following, this problem is closely related to the study of algebraic languages that are nearly rational and to questions about very small rational cones.

This paper is divided into three parts: in the first one, about the languages that are nearly rational, deals with what

[1]Preparation of this paper was supported in part by the National Science Foundation under Grant No. MCS79-04012.
[2]Université Paris VII, Paris, France.
[3]Université de Picardie, Amiens, France.

could be a characterization of rationality of algebraic languages; the second one recalls some partial results obtained
on the problem of minimal cones; in the last one we prove,
using this general frame, a new result by building an infinite
decreasing hierarchy of principal rational cones.

In the following, we will use the definitions and notations introduced in another paper in this book [3].

I.   LANGUAGES THAT ARE NEARLY REGULAR

It is well known [17] that it is an undecidable question
whether an algebraic language is rational or not. Nevertheless, one can try to give some characterizations of those algebraic languages that are rational.

Necessary conditions are given by the iteration theorems
for rational languages. Among these, the most powerful one is
the Ogden-like version of the star theorem. To state this
theorem we introduce some definitions that will be used later:

Definition. L being a language over an alphabet X, a
word f has an iterative factor u in L if and only if
f = xuy and xu*y ⊂ L.

Definition [19]. A language L ⊆ X* is one-locally-
linear (abbreviated 1-ℓℓ) if there exists some integer N_0
such that for every word f in L, if any N_0 or more letters in f are marked, then f has an iterative factor u
in L (f = xuy) such that x, u and y contain marked
letters.

Ogden's Theorem. If L is a rational language, then L
is 1-ℓℓ.

The condition to be 1-ℓℓ is also verified by some nonrational languages:

Let $X = a,b,c,d$. Call K the rational language

$K = X*\{aa,ac,ad,bb,bd,ca,cb,cc,da,db,dd\}X*.$

The language $L = \{(ab)^n(cd)^n \mid n > 0\} \cup K$ is a nonrational algebraic language which is $1-\ell\ell$. Intuitively, L is the disjoint union of a rational language K and of a nonrational algebraic language. For a word f in this last part, every iteration of one (marked) letter will give a word in K. For a word f in K there is one "forbidden" subword such as aa, ac, ... If 5 letters are marked, among the 3 interior ones there is one which does not belong to this subword, and every iteration of this letter will give a word in K. So L is a $1-\ell\ell$ language with $N_0 = 5$.

In the same way, one can easily check that the nonrational algebraic language

$L = \{(abcd)^n(\overline{abcd})^n \mid n > 0\} \cup X*\{ad,\overline{ad},cb,\overline{cb}\}X*,$

is such that both L and $X* \setminus L$ are $1-\ell\ell$.

From these examples, it is obvious that these languages can be intersected with rational languages, such that the result is not a $1-\ell\ell$ language.

So the question is: does there exist some nonrational $1-\ell\ell$ language such that for all rational languages R, $L \cap R$ is $1-\ell\ell$? Or, more generally, does there exist any $1-\ell\ell$ language L such that the full AFL generated by L is a full AFL of $1-\ell\ell$ languages? This last question was stated by Van der Walt [19], and from his results, it reduces to the problem of the existence of a cylinder of $1-\ell\ell$ languages. It has been proved [4] that such a cylinder exists, but this was proved with non-algebraic languages, so that the following conjecture remains open:

Conjecture 1 [4]. The only cylinder of 1-$\ell\ell$ algebraic languages is Rat, the family of rational languages.

Another possible way to attack this problem is to try to find sufficient conditions for an algebraic language to be rational. Some answers have been given in particular cases such as the deterministic case [18], or the nonambiguous case [14]. A study can be done in the general case, by the means of iterative pairs.

Definition [8]. L being a language over an alphabet X, a word f in L has an iterative pair p = (x,u,y,v,z) in L if and only if uv $\neq \varepsilon$, f = xuyvz, and

$$\forall\, n \geq 1 : xu^n yv^n z \in L.$$

The study of algebraic languages leads to defining different kinds of iterative pairs [7]. For example, an iterative pair p = (x,u,y,v,z) of f in L is said to be very strict if $xu^r yv^s z \in L \Rightarrow r = s$. If one is asked to give an example of a nonrational algebraic language, one will probably produce a language with a very strict iterative pair, such as $\{a^n b^n \mid n > 0\}$. To be rational, an algebraic language must not have such features. This leads us to define a special kind of iterative pairs, whose character is the opposite of very strict.

Definition [6]. An iterative pair p = (x,u,y,v,z) of f in L is said to be very degenerate if and only if

$$\{xu^n yv^n z \mid n > 0\} \subset L \iff xu^*yv^*z \subset L.$$

In relation to this definition, we state a definition for languages:

Definition. A language satisfies the P_* condition if and only if all its iterative pairs are very degenerate.

We can then state:

Proposition 1 [6]. Every algebraic language satisfying

the P_* condition is rational.

But not all rational languages satisfy the P_* condition.

For example, the language $K = (a^2)^*(b^2)^* \cup a(a^2)^*b(b^2)^*$ is

a rational language, and $p = (\varepsilon,a,\varepsilon,b,\varepsilon)$ is an iterative

pair of the word ab in K. But a^*b^* is not included in K

and so K does not satisfy the P_* condition. Of course, K

satisfies a less restrictive condition, the condition P_2:

for every iterative pair $p = (x,u,y,v,z)$ of any word in this

language, we have $x(u^2)^*y(v^2)^*z \subset K$. More generally, one can

define the following.

Definition [6]. A language L satisfies the P_k condi-

tion if, for every iterative pair $p = (x,u,y,v,z)$ of a word

f in L,

$$x(u^k)^*y(v^k)^*z \subset L.$$

We can then state:

Conjecture 2 [6]. If L is an algebraic language and if

there exists an integer k such that L satisfies P_k, then

L is rational.

Noting that $P_1 = P_*$, Proposition 1 above states that the

conjecture is true for $k = 1$. As soon as $k \geq 2$, we have no

answer. However, it can be easily seen that there exist ra-

tional languages meeting none of the P_k conditions. Such a

language could be, for instance,

$$L = \{\varepsilon\} \cup aX^*\overline{X}^*\overline{a} \cup bX^*\overline{X}^*\overline{b}$$

where

$$X = \{a,b\} \quad \text{and} \quad \overline{X} = \{\overline{a},\overline{b}\}.$$

If we then try to get a necessary and sufficient condition for an algebraic language to be regular, we obviously have to look at conditions which are always satisfied by rational languages (which is not the case of P_k). One can easily check that the following is such a property (Q_k). There exists an integer k such that whenever $p = (x,u,y,v,z)$ is an iterative pair of a word in L, $x(u^k)^+ y(v^k)^+ z$ is included in L.

This leads us to state:

Conjecture 3 [2]. An algebraic language L is rational if and only if there exists an integer k such that L satisfies (Q_k).

This conjecture being akin to the previous one, it is then natural to study the special case $k = 1$ (which is solved for Conjecture 2), i.e., try to prove that if an algebraic language L satisfies the following conditions, then L is rational: for any integers $n, m \geq 1$, if $xu^n yv^n z$ is in L, then $xu^n yv^m z$ is also in L. It is not known whether this is true or not, so that the above conjecture still stands even with $k = 1$. It should be remarked that the problems looked at here are very closely related to other questions appearing in a quite different approach. We shall just quote the following conjecture.

Conjecture 4 [2]. If L is an algebraic language then either it is rational (its syntactic monoid is finite) or its syntactic monoid does not contain elements of infinite order.

Coming back to our Conjecture 3, it seems natural too to ask the same question, dropping the condition that the language be algebraic. It can easily be shown that this new conjecture then does not hold, considering over a three-letter alphabet the following languages:

$$C_k = \{f \mid f \text{ contains a factor } u^k \text{ (with } u \text{ non-empty)}\}.$$

It can be seen that C_k does satisfy the property (Q_{k-1}) though it is not rational (its complement is not 1-$\ell\ell$). This remark naturally raises the following question: are the C_k non-algebraic? If they were, we would have a counter-example to Conjecture 3. At this point, we have some new surprising facts: we do not know how to prove that the C_k's are not algebraic. (In fact, using combinatorial arguments on words, one can check, using the usual pumping lemmas, that none of the C_k's for $k \geq 11$ is algebraic.) For instance, when looking at C_2, the pumping lemmas appear as totally ineffi-cient. By the way, it can be remarked that this is very often the case when the language has a rather loose structure (for instance, when one asks for various exponents to be different in a bounded language).

We are then left with the following conjecture:

Conjecture 5 [2]. C_2 is not an algebraic language.

This question can even be sharpened, as any language con-taining C_2 satisfies (Q_1) and as the only algebraic lan-guages contained in the complement of C_2 are the finite lan-guages; this leads to the following:

Conjecture 6 [2]. The complement of an algebraic language is either finite or it contains infinitely many words in C_2.

We may remark that this conjecture is obviously true for deterministic algebraic languages. We may even prove Conjec-ture 3 for these particular languages.

II. MINIMAL CONES

Looking for nearly regular algebraic languages, as well as
trying to find a characterization of the algebraic languages
which are regular are two problems clearly related to questions
about "very small rational cones." More precisely, as we know
that any rational cone does contain the family Rat, we define
a minimal cone as a cone properly containing no other cone
than Rat. Such a rational cone L is surely principal: if
it were not, we could pick in it any non-regular language L
and we would have Rat $\subsetneq T(L) \subsetneq L$. Moreover, we may even prove
that, for the same reasons, L is the disjoint union of Rat
and of its generators; that is to say, any L in L is either
a generator or a regular language.

This definition of a minimal rational cone may be restricted to some subfamilies; for instance, we may look for a
minimal cone of algebraic languages. Recall the conjecture
given in another communication of this book [3].

Conjecture 7. Given two algebraic languages A and B
such that $B \in T(A)$, either $T(B) = T(A)$ or there exists a
language C such that $T(B) \subsetneq T(C) \subsetneq T(A)$.

It should be remarked that if this conjecture is true then
the following holds:

Conjecture 8 [2]. The family Alg does not contain any
minimal rational cone.

Indeed, if L were a minimal cone of algebraic languages,
we could find a language A such that $T(A) = L$ and B such
that $T(B) = $ Rat. Then because L is minimal, any language
C in L would be either rational $(T(C) = T(B))$, or generating L $(T(C) = T(A))$, disproving our first conjecture.

The aim of this section is just to recall two very particular cases for which we do have minimal cones. The first one
deals with bounded languages; the second one with commutative
languages.

A.   Bounded Languages

We will say that a language   L   is <u>strictly</u> <u>bounded</u> <u>of</u>
<u>degree</u>   k   whenever it is contained in the regular set
$a_1^*\ a_2^*\ \ldots\ a_k^*$ where the a_i's are letters. It is <u>bounded</u> <u>of</u>
<u>degree</u>   k   when the a_i's   are words. The first remark is
very easy: any bounded language is rationally equivalent to a
strictly bounded language of the same degree. So, as far as
we are interested in minimal cones with respect to bounded
languages, we may restrict our attention to strictly bounded
languages. The main result we have can then be stated as
follows:

We say that a cone L is <u>minimal</u> <u>with</u> <u>respect</u> <u>to</u> <u>bounded</u>
<u>languages</u> <u>of</u> <u>degree</u>   k   iff any bounded language of degree   k
in L is either regular or generating L.

<u>Proposition 2</u> [5]. There are exactly three rational cones
which are minimal with respect to bounded algebraic languages
of degree   2.   They are those generated by

$$s_< = \{a^m b^n \mid n \leq m\}$$
$$s_{\neq} = \{a^m b^n \mid n \neq m\}$$
$$s_> = \{a^m b^n \mid n \geq m\}.$$

This result can be made precise: any non-regular algebraic
bounded language of degree   2   generates a rational cone containing at least one of these languages. Two questions then

naturally arise: Are these cones minimal with respect to bounded languages of any degree? If not, can we find such a minimal cone?

The answer to the first question is already known to be negative. Defining over a k-letter alphabet the strictly bounded languages of degree k,

$$S_{\neq}^{(k)} = \{a_1^{n_1} a_2^{n_2} \ldots a_k^{n_k} \mid \exists j, \ 0 < j < k, \ n_j \neq n_{j+1}\}$$

(so that $S_{\neq} = S_{\neq}^{(2)}$), we have

Fact [5]. For any integer $k \geq 2$, $T(S_{\neq}^{(k)}) \supsetneq T(S_{\neq}^{(k+1)})$; or, equivalently, the $S_{\neq}^{(k)}$ give rise to an infinite decreasing chain of rational cones.

From this fact, we derive easily that none of the $T(S_{\neq}^{(k)})$ is a minimal cone with respect to bounded languages. Turning then to the non-minimality of $S_{<}$ and $S_{>}$, the same sort of arguments can be performed by using some $S_{<}^{(k)}$ and $S_{>}^{(k)}$ languages. However, we are left with

Conjecture 9. For any $k \geq 3$, $T(S_{\neq}^{(k)})$ is a minimal cone with respect to bounded algebraic languages of degree k.

About this conjecture, the following can be recalled [11]: any bounded language of degree $(k-1)$ in $T(S_{\neq}^{(k)})$ is regular.

If we turn now to our second question, we do not know anything:

Conjecture 10. There does not exist any minimal cone with respect to bounded algebraic languages.

We will end this section with two remarks:

From Proposition 2, we can easily derive that there cannot exist any minimal cone generated by a deterministic language because we know [18] such a non-regular language always generates a cone containing a bounded algebraic language of degree 2.

Proving our last conjecture would not imply that there does not exist any minimal cone at all; this comes from the fact that there do exist algebraic languages generating a cone which contains no non-regular bounded language. (We will have such an example in Section III).

B. Commutative Languages

For a word w, we denote $c(w)$ the set of words obtained from w by permuting the letters of w (i.e., its commutative image). Let L be a language over the alphabet $\{a_1, a_2, \ldots, a_k\}$, we say that L is <u>commutative</u> <u>of</u> <u>degree</u> k iff $L = c(L) = \underset{w \in L}{\cup} c(w)$. Commutative languages and strictly bounded languages are closely related (see [12], for instance). In particular, in both families, the languages are characterized by their Parikh range. Moreover, for each language

$$L' \subseteq a_1^* a_2^* \ldots a_k^*, \quad L' = c(L') \cap a_1^* a_2^* \ldots a_k^*.$$

Another link between commutative and bounded languages is indicated by an old conjecture which should permit us to characterize algebraic commutative languages.

<u>Conjecture 11</u> [9]: A commutative language L over $\{a_1, a_2, \ldots, a_k\}$ is algebraic iff for each permutation M over $\{1, 2, \ldots, k\}$,

$$L \cap a_{M(1)}^* a_{M(2)}^* \cdots a_{M(k)}^*$$

is algebraic.

Notice that this conjecture does hold for commutative languages of degree 3 (k = 3) [15]. The connection between commutative and bounded languages is even more tight when looking at rational transductions: if L is a commutative language and L' a strictly bounded language in $T(L)$, then $c(L')$ is in $T(L)$ [12].

Now consider the commutative languages of degree 2. A commutative language included in $\{a,b\}*$ is algebraic if and only if $L \cap a*b*$ is algebraic. Let $\overline{D}_1^* = c(S_{\neq})$. Clearly, $T(c(S_<)) = T(c(S_>)) \subsetneq T(\overline{D}_1^*)$. Then by using the above result and proposition, one can prove:

Proposition 3 [12]. Let L be an algebraic commutative language of degree 2. If L is non-regular, then $T(\overline{D}_1^*) \subseteq T(L)$.

So, $T(\overline{D}_1^*)$ is a minimal cone with respect to commutative languages of degree 2. In fact, contrary to the case of bounded languages, this property can be extended to commutative languages of arbitrary degree:

Proposition 4 [12]. $T(\overline{D}_1^*)$ is a minimal cone with respect to commutative languages.

It seems that the above two propositions can be improved. Let $c(Rat) = \{c(R) \mid R \text{ is regular}\}$. One can state the following conjecture:

Conjecture 12 [12]. If L is a non-regular language in $c(Rat)$, then $T(\overline{D}_1^*) \subseteq T(L)$.

III. THE DECREASING HIERARCHY

Until recently, all the known algebraic languages generated cones containing a nonrational bounded language. So,
one could think that any possible minimal algebraic language
had to be bounded. Goldstine was the first to intensively
study the first question, and he showed that there does exist
an algebraic language the generated cone of which does not
contain any nonrational bounded language. This precise language is at the starting point of our infinite decreasing
hierarchy of rational cones. It is defined by

$$G = \{a^{i_1}ba^{i_2}b \ldots a^{i_p}b \mid p \geq 1, \exists j \text{ such that } i_j \neq j\}.$$

Proposition 5 [10]. Any bounded language in $T(G)$ is
rational.

The language G can be easily defined by its complement
in $(a^*b)^+$, $G' = \{aba^2ba^3b \ldots a^pb \mid p \geq 1\}$ which is (nearly)
the set of the left factors of an infinite word. The above
proposition can then be explained by the following general
result:

Proposition 6 [13]. Let $L \subseteq X^*$ be the set of left factors of an infinite word and $\bar{L} = X^* \setminus L$. Then each bounded
language in $T(\bar{L})$ is regular.

In connection with Section II, let us notice, also, that
it can be easily checked that for each $k \geq 2$, $T(G) \subseteq T(S_{\neq}^k)$.

Another interesting particularity of the language G is
that, since its definition in 1972 until now, no non-regular
language L such that $T(L) \subsetneq T(G)$ was known. A recent result shows that such a language L cannot be found in the
cylinder generated by G.

Proposition 7 [1]. Let L be a non-regular language be-
longing to the cylinder generated by G. Then $T(L) = T(G)$.

Our aim, in this section, is not only to prove the conjecture [1] which says that $T(G)$ is not a minimal cone, but
also to find an infinite decreasing hierarchy of rational
cones within $T(G)$. Thus, we will construct an infinite sequence of languages $G_2, G_3, \ldots, G_n, \ldots$ such that $T(G) =$
$T(G_2) \supsetneq T(G_3) \supsetneq \ldots$. These languages can be easily defined
as complements of DOL-languages.

For each n in $\mathbb{N}$, Let $X_n = \{b_0, b_1, \ldots, b_n\}$ and let
$h_{(n)}$ be the homomorphism defined on X_n^* by

$$\forall i \in \{0, \ldots, n\}, \quad h_{(n)}(b_i) = b_i b_{i-1} \ldots b_0.$$

For each n in $\mathbb{N}$, let $\bar{G}_n$ be the language generated by
the DOL-system $\langle X_n, h_{(n)}, b_n \ldots b_0 \rangle$ that is the language
$\{h_{(n)}^i(b_n) \mid i \geq 1\}$ and let $G_n = X_n^* \setminus \bar{G}_n$.

First, we will prove that, for each $n \geq 2$, $T(G_{n+1}) \subseteq$
$T(G_n)$. For each i and n in $\mathbb{N}$ we note $w_i^{(n)}$ the word
$h_{(n)}^i(b_n)$. Then, we can state:

Lemma. For each $i, n \in \mathbb{N}$,

$$w_i^{(n+1)} = b_{n+1} w_1^{(n)} \ldots w_i^{(n)}.$$

Proof. It will be shown by induction on i.

In the case $i = 0$, we have $w_0 = h_{(n+1)}^0(b_{n+1}) = b_{n+1}$.

Now let us consider the word $w_{i+1}^{(n+1)} = h_{(n+1)}^{i+1}(b_{n+1}) =$
$h_{(n+1)}(w_i^{(n+1)})$. From the induction hypothesis, $w^{(n+1)}$ is
equal to $b_{n+1} w_1^{(n)} \ldots w_i^{(n)}$ and belongs to $b_{n+1} X_n^*$. Thus,
$w_{i+1}^{(n+1)} = h_{n+1}(b_{n+1}) h_{(n+1)}(w_1^{(n)}) \ldots h_{(n+1)}(w_i^{(n)})$. For each

$j \in \{1,\ldots,i\}$, $w_j^{(n)} \in X_n^*$ which implies $h_{(n+1)}(w_j^{(n)}) = h_{(n)}(w_j^{(n)}) = w_{j+1}^{(n)} \in X_n^*$. Moreover, $h_{(n+1)}(b_{n+1})$ is equal to $b_{n+1} \cdots b_0 = b_{n+1} w_1^{(n)}$. Hence the result. $\square$

We shall use the following languages defined for each integer $n \geq 2$:

$$R_{n+1} = X_{n+1}^* \setminus b_{n+1} b_n X_n^*,$$

$$A_{n+1} = X_{n+1}^* (b_n X_{n-1}^* \cap G_n)(\{\varepsilon\} \cup b_n X_{n+1}^*),$$

$$B_{n+1} = s_{(n)}(b_n b_{n-1} X_{n-1}^* \cap G_n), \quad \text{where } s_{(n)} \text{ is the}$$

rational substitution defined on X_n by $s_{(n)}(b_n)$
$= \{b_{n+1}\}$, $s_{(n)}(b_{n-1}) = b_n X_{n-1}^* b_{n-1}$ and $\forall x \in X_{n-2}$,
$s_{(n)}(x) = \{x\}$.

Then we can state:

<u>Lemma.</u> For each integer $n \geq 2$, G_{n+1} is equal to $R_{n+1} \cup A_{n+1} \cup B_{n+1}$ and belongs to $T(G_n)$.

<u>Proof.</u> Let us show, first, the inclusion of $R_{n+1} \cup A_{n+1} \cup B_{n+1}$ in G_{n+1}. By the previous lemma, $\overline{G}_{n+1} \subseteq b_{n+1} b_n X_n^*$, which implies

$$R_{n+1} = X_{n+1}^* \setminus b_{n+1} b_n X_n^* \subseteq X_{n+1}^* \setminus \overline{G}_{n+1} = G_{n+1}.$$

In order to prove that A_{n+1} is included in G_{n+1}, let us consider $w \in b_n X_{n-1}^* \cap RF(\overline{G}_{n+1})$ (where $RF(\overline{G}_{n+1})$ denotes the set of right factors of the words of $\overline{G}_{n+1}$). Then, there exists a positive integer i such that $w_i^{(n+1)} = w'w$ and, from the previous lemma,

$$w'w = w_i^{(n+1)} = b_{n+1} w_1^{(n)} \ldots w_i^{(n)} \quad \text{with } w_i^{(n)} \in b_n X_{n-1}^*.$$

Then, w is equal to $w_i^{(n)}$ and belongs to $\overline{G}_n$. We deduce from this that $u \in b_n X_{n-1}^* \cap G_n$ implies $u \notin RF(\overline{G}_{n+1})$, thus that $X_{n+1}^*(b_n X_{n-1} \cap G_n) \subseteq G_{n+1}$. In the same way it follows from the lemma that $wb_n \in b_n X_{n-1}^* b_n \cap F(\overline{G}_{n+1})$ (where $F(\overline{G}_{n+1})$ denotes the set of factors of words of $\overline{G}_{n+1}$) implies $w \in \overline{G}_n$. Hence, $u \in b_n X_{n-1}^* \cap G_n$ implies $ub_n \notin F(\overline{G}_{n+1})$, and so $X_{n+1}^*(b_n X_{n-1}^* \cap G_n) b_n X_{n+1}^* \subseteq G_{n+1}$ and $A_{n+1} \subseteq G_{n+1}$.

Let us show now $B_{n+1} \subseteq G_{n+1}$. Let w be a word, $w \in b_n b_{n-1} X_{n-1}^* \cap G_n$. Then, w has a factorization $w = b_n b_{n-1} u_1 b_{n-1} u_2 \cdots b_{n-1} u_k$ with $k \geq 1$ and $\forall i \in \{1, \dots, k\}$, $u_i \in X_{n-2}^*$. Each word y in $s_{(n)}(w)$ has a factorization $y = b_{n+1} b_n v_1 b_{n-1} u_1 b_n v_2 b_{n-1} u_2 \cdots b_n v_k b_{n-1} u_k$, with, $\forall i \in \{1, \dots, k\}$, $v_i \in X_{n-1}^*$. Let us suppose that y belongs to $\overline{G}_{n+1}$. Then, there exists a positive integer t such that $y = w_t^{(n+1)}$ and, from the previous lemma,

$$y = b_{n+1} w_1^{(n)} \cdots w_t^{(n)} \text{ with, } \forall i \in \{1, \dots, t\},$$
$$w_i^{(n)} \in b_n X_{n-1}^*.$$

Hence, $t = k$ and $\forall i \in \{1, \dots, k\}$, $b_n v_i b_{n-1} u_i = w_i^{(n)} \in \overline{G}_n$ with $u_i \in X_{n-2}^*$. Always using the previous lemma, this implies that $b_{n-1} u_i = w_i^{(n-1)}$. Then, $w = b_n w_1^{(n-1)} \cdots w_k^{(n-1)} = w_k^{(n)} \in \overline{G}_n$, hence a contradiction, and $y \in G_n$, which implies $B_{n+1} \subseteq G_{n+1}$.

For proving the other inclusion, it suffices to prove that $G_{n+1} \cap b_{n+1} b_n X_n^*$ is included in $A_{n+1} \cup B_{n+1}$. Let us consider a word w in $G_{n+1} \cap b_{n+1} b_n X_n^*$. Then, w has factorization $w = b_{n+1} b_n u_1 \cdots b_n u_k$ with $k \geq 1$ and $\forall j \in \{1, \dots, k\}$, $u_j \in X_{n-1}^*$. There, two cases are to be examined:

(1) There exists $i \in \{1, \ldots, k\}$ such that $b_n u_i \in G_n$.

Then, $w \in X_{n+1}^* (b_n X_{n-1}^* \cap G_n)(\{\varepsilon\} \cup b_n X_{n+1}^*) \subseteq A_{n+1}$.

(2) For each $j \in \{1, \ldots, k\}$, $b_n u_j \in \overline{G}_n$.

Let us suppose that, $\forall j \in \{1, \ldots, k\}$, $b_n u_j = w_j^{(n)}$. Then,

$w = b_{n+1} b_n u_1 \cdots b_n u_k = b_{n+1} w_1^{(n)} \cdots w_k^{(n)} = w_k^{(n+1)}$ with

$k \geq 1$, hence $w \in \overline{G}_{n+1}$ and we obtain a contradiction. Thus,

there exists $i \in \{1, \ldots, k\}$ and $t \geq 1$ such that $b_n u_i = $

$w_t^{(n)} \neq w_i^{(n)}$. For each $j \in \{1, \ldots, k\}$, $b_n u_j \in \overline{G}_n$, hence

$u_j \in b_{n-1} X_{n-1}^*$ and $u_j = u_j' b_{n-1} u_j''$ with $u_j'' \in X_{n-2}^*$. From the

equality $b_n u_i = w_t^{(n)}$, we can deduce $b_{n-1} u_i'' = w_t^{(n-1)} \neq$

$w_i^{(n-1)}$. Clearly the word $w' = b_n b_{n-1} u_1'' \cdots b_{n-1} u_k''$ belongs

to $b_n b_{n-1} X_{n-1}^* \cap G_n$. For each $j \in \{1, \ldots, k\}$, $b_n u_j' b_{n-1} \in$

$b_n X_{n-1}^* b_{n-1} = s_{(n)}(b_{n-1})$, $u_j'' \in s_{(n)}(u_j'')$ and $b_{n+1} \in s_{(n)}(b_n)$.

Then $w = b_{n+1} b_n u_1' b_{n-1} u_1'' \cdots b_n u_k' b_{n-1} u_k''$ belongs to

$s_{(n)}(b_n b_{n-1} u_1'' \cdots b_{n-1} u_k'') = s_{(n)}(w') \subseteq s_{(n)}(b_n b_{n-1} X_{n-1}^* \cap G_n) =$

B_{n+1}. So the second inclusion is proved and we have: $G_{n+1} =$

$R_{n+1} \cup A_{n+1} \cup B_{n+1}$. Now, it suffices to remark that the lan-

guage R_{n+1} is rational and that, clearly, A_{n+1} and B_{n+1}

belong to $T(G_n)$. Thus $G_{n+1} = R_{n+1} \cup A_{n+1} \cup B_{n+1}$ belongs to

$T(G_n)$, which ends the proof. □

Now, in order to prove that $T(G_{n+1})$ is strictly included

in $T(G_n)$, it suffices to show that, for $n \geq 2$, the lan-

guage G_n does not belong to $T(G_{n+1})$. That will be done

using a result on rational transductions and complements. For

languages $L \subseteq X^*$ and $L' \subseteq X'^*$, let us denote $\overline{L} = X^* \setminus L$

and $\overline{L}' = X'^* \setminus L$. Then, we have

Proposition 8 [11]. Let L' be a nonrational language in

$T(L)$. Then there exists in $T(\overline{L}')$ a nonrational language L''

included in $\overline{L}$.

In the case where $\overline{L}$ is the set of left factors of an infinite word, L'' being infinite, $\overline{L}$ is exactly the set of the left factors of L' as well. This implies that $\overline{L}$ is a language in $T(\overline{L}')$. The same argument allows us to state:

Corollary. Let I be the set of left factors of an infinite word, and let $L \subseteq I$ be a language in $T(I)$. If L' is a non-rational language in $T(\overline{L})$, then L belongs to $T(\overline{L}')$.

Let us consider the language $\overline{G}_n = \{w_i^{(n)} \mid i \geq 1\}$ for some $n \geq 2$. From the first lemma, $w_i^{(n)} = b_n w_1^{(n-1)} \ldots w_i^{(n-1)}$. Thus, for $i < j$, $w_i^{(n)}$ is a left factor of $w_j^{(n)}$, which implies that $I_n = LF(\overline{G}_n)$ is the set of left factors of an infinite word. Moreover, $\overline{G}_n$ is equal to $(I_n \setminus b_{n-1}) \cap b_n b_{n-1} X_{n-1}^*$ and $\overline{G}_n$ belongs to $T(I_n)$. Then, by using the previous corollary to prove that G_n does not belong to $T(G_{n+1})$, we just have to show that $\overline{G}_{n+1}$ does not belong to $T(\overline{G}_n)$.

It is easy to verify that the DOL-system $\langle X_n, h_{(n)}, b_n \ldots b_0 \rangle$, which generates $\overline{G}_n$, is an ETOL-system of rank n (see [16]). So, each language L in $T(\overline{G}_n)$ is an ETOL-language of rank n and, from [16], there exists a strictly growing polynomial P of degree not larger than n such that $\{P(j) \mid j \geq 0\}$ is included in the set $\{|w| \mid w \in L\}$. By using the equality $w_i^{(n+1)} = b_{n+1} w_1^{(n)} \ldots w_i^{(n)}$, one can easily show, by induction, that there exists a polynomial Q of degree $n + 1$ such that $\{|w| \mid w \in \overline{G}_{n+1}\}$ is equal to $\{Q(j) \mid j \geq 0\}$. Clearly, we can deduce that $\overline{G}_{n+1}$ is not an ETOL-language of rank n and does not belong to $T(\overline{G}_n)$. Then, we can state

<u>Proposition 9</u>. The languages G_n do generate an infinite decreasing chain of rational cones:

$$T(G) = T(G_2) \supset T(G_3) \supset \ldots \supset T(G_n) \supset T(G_{n+1}) \ldots .$$

From this proposition, one can immediately think to ask

<u>Question</u>. Does there exist a nonrational language L belonging to all the $T(G_k)$?

It should be noted that any answer to this question would not contradict Conjecture 8.

REFERENCES

1. Autebert, J.M, Beauquier, J., and Boasson, L., Contribution à l'étude des cônes minimaux. Note au CRAS Paris 287, Série A, 353-355 (1978).
2. Autebert, J.M., Beauquier, J., Boasson, L., and Nivat, M., Quelques problèmes ouverts en théorie des languages algébriques. RAIRO Informatique Théorique 13, 363-379 (1979).
3. Autebert, J.M., and Boasson, L., Generators of cones and cylinders (this volume).
4. Autebert, J.M., Boasson, L., and Cousineau, G., A note on 1-locally linear languages. Info. and Control 37, 1-4 (1978).
5. Berstel, J., and Boasson, L., Une suite décroissante de cônes rationnels. In "Automata, Languages and Programming" (J. Loeckx, ed.), Lecture Notes in Computer Science 14, 383-397 (1974).
6. Boasson, L., Un critère de rationnalité des languages algébriques. In "Automata, Languages and Programming (M. Nivat, ed.), North Holland, 359-365 (1973).
7. Boasson, L., Paires itérantes et languages algébriques. Thèse de Doctorat d'Etat, Université Paris VII (1974).
8. Boasson, L., Langages algébriques, paires itérantes et transductions rationnelles. Theoret. Comp. Sci. 2, 209-223 (1976).
9. Fliess, M., Personal communication.
10. Goldstine, J., Substitution and bounded languages. J. Comp. Syst. Sci. 6, 9-29 (1972).
11. Latteux, M., Sur deux langages linéaires. 4th GI Conference, Aachen, Lecture Notes in Computer Science 67, 185-192 (1979).
12. Latteux, M., Cônes rationnels commutatifs. J. Comp. Syst. Sci. 18, 307-333 (1979).
13. Latteux, M., Transduction rationnelle, substitution et complémentaire. Information and Control (to appear).
14. Nivat, M., Une propriété des langages compilables. Note au CRAS Paris 267, Série A, 244-246 (1968).
15. Perrot, J.-F., Sur la fermeture commutative des C-langages. Note au CRAS Paris 265, Série A, 597 (1967).

Jean-Michel Autebert *et al.*

16. Rozenberg, G., and Vermeir, D., Extending the notion of
    finite index.   6th ICALP, Lecture Notes in Computer Sci-
    ence 71, 479-488 (1979).
17. Salomaa, A., "Formal Languages." Academic Press, New York
    (1973).
18. Stearns, R.E., A regularity test for pushdown machines.
    Info. and Control 11, 323-340 (1967).
19. Van der Walt, A.P.J., Locally linear families of languages.
    Info. and Control 32, 27-32 (1976).

FORMAL LANGUAGES AND THEIR RELATION TO AUTOMATA:
WHAT HOPCROFT & ULLMAN DIDN'T TELL US

Jonathan Goldstine[1]

Department of Computer Science
The Pennsylvania State University
University Park, Pennsylvania

I. INTRODUCTION

In 1969, Hopcroft and Ullman wrote Formal Languages and
their Relation to Automata (12), which has become perhaps the
standard text on the subject. As the title promises, the
relationship between automata and languages is stressed. But
that relationship is a weak one and proceeds in only one
direction. Automata are used as acceptors to define languages; hence, languages can be considered the external
behavior of their acceptors. Period. That ends the relationship. There is no meaningful discussion of the effect
that operations on acceptors will have on their external
behavior, nor of automata used for other purposes than as
acceptors. And most significantly, there is no application
of results from language theory to the study of automata.
These remarks are not meant as a criticism of the authors of
that textbook, but rather of the state of development of the
field at the time the textbook was written. Shortly there-
after, Ginsburg and Greibach did develop a theory that shed
some light on the effect that operations on acceptors have on

[1]Preparation of this paper was supported in part by the
National Science Foundation under Grants No. MCS76-10076A01
and MCS79-04012.

109

their external behavior. (The first paper is by Ginsburg and

Greibach (8); the most complete treatment is by Ginsburg (7).)

But this theory of AFLs (AFL = Abstract Family of Languages)

was not completely successful because the role of automata in

the theory was so unwieldy that the theory was of little

practical use to those who use automata. Thus, Eilenberg

says, "I have serious doubts whether this notion [of automata

in AFL theory] will survive the test of time and taste." (5)

And to this day, little if any significant work has been done

on the applications of language theory to automaton theory[2].

It is my intention here to argue that these lacks are

deficiencies in the theory of automata, that these deficien-

cies are reparable, and that they should be repaired. Some

would denigrate this topic by suggesting that it deals merely

with the choice of notation to be used in describing automata,

but such a criticism would be misleading on two counts.

First, the subject concerns the broader issue of choosing the

right concepts and tools for developing automaton theory.

Second, there is nothing trivial about matters of notation,

and I do not apologize for stressing the importance of good

notation. It is indeed true that Gauss once said (as quoted

recently by deMillo, Lipton, and Perlis (4)) that one of his

colleagues "...needs notions, not notations." But Gauss

also said (as quoted by Bell in (2)), "To what heights would

science now be raised if Archimedes had made that discovery

---

[2]As Eilenberg points out, the phrase "automata theory" is
no more grammatical than the phrase "groups theory" would be
(5).

[of decimal notation]!" Let me begin, then, by considering notation. The following example is taken from Goldstine (9). The empty string is denoted by 1.

Consider the prototypical one-way nondeterministic automaton, the pushdown automaton, as classically defined (6,12).

Definition: A pushdown automaton is a 7-tuple $A = (K, \Sigma, \Gamma, \delta, q_0, Z_0, F)$, where K, Σ, Γ are finite, $q_0 \in K$, $Z_0 \in \Gamma$, $F \subseteq K$, and $\delta: K \times (\Sigma \cup \{1\}) \times \Gamma \to \{S \subseteq K \times \Gamma^* | S \text{ finite}\}$. Define a binary relation $\vdash$ on $K \times \Sigma^* \times \Gamma^*$ by

$$(p, xu, vy) \vdash (q, u, vz) \quad \text{if} \quad (q, z) \in \delta(p, x, y),$$

and let $\vdash^*$ be its transitive reflexive closure. Then the language defined by A is

$$L(A) = \{u \in \Sigma^* | (q_0, u, Z_0) \vdash^* (q, 1, v)$$

$$\text{for some } (q, v) \in F \times \Gamma^*\}.$$

The fact that A is taken to be a 7-tuple, that δ is an object of an awkward type (a function from $K \times (\Sigma \cup \{1\}) \times \Gamma$ to the set of finite subsets of $K \times \Gamma^*$) which cannot even be used directly to describe $L(A)$, and that A is arbitrarily constrained to pop exactly one stack symbol per move, all suggest that this formalism is very poor. To test this suggestion, choose a very simple context-free language L and write down a pushdown automaton for it. Let $L = \{a^n b^n | n \geq 0\}$. Then $L = L(A)$ for the following pushdown automaton A.

$$A = (\{q_0, q_1, q_2\}, \{a, b\}, \{Z_0, Z\}, \delta, q_0, Z_0, \{q_2\}),$$

$$\delta(q_0, 1, Z_0) = \{(q_2, 1)\} \tag{1.1}$$

$$\delta(q_0, a, Z_0) = \{(q_0, Z_0 Z), (q_1, Z_0 Z)\} \tag{1.2}$$

$$\delta(q_0, a, Z) = \{(q_0, ZZ), (q_1, ZZ)\} \tag{1.3}$$

$$\delta(q_1, b, Z) = \{(q_1, 1)\} \tag{1.4}$$

$$\delta(q_1, 1, Z_0) = \{(q_2, 1)\} \tag{1.5}$$

In all other cases, $\delta(q,x,X) = \emptyset$ (1.6)

Certainly, A is more complicated than a context-free grammar or set of equations for L, e.g., L = aLb + 1. Examples
like this lend credence to the belief that, while the behavior of automata may often be more intuitive than that of
grammars, automata are so much more complicated that they
would be used in formal proofs only with great awkwardness
and when a proof by means of grammars is for some reason not
feasible. In his book on context-free languages, Ginsburg
summarizes this widespread feeling very well (6, p. 71):

> The reader has probably observed already that pda
> are complicated objects to treat formally....
> This should not be surprising, since the movement
> of a pda depends on three variables, [state, input,
> and top of stack]. In view of the length of the
> proofs involved, it is customary to avoid using a
> pda in a mathematical proof whenever possible.
> In practice, we employ a pda informally to convince
> ourselves that a specific set is a language and
> then construct appropriate grammars (which experi-
> ence indicates are easier to handle than pda) to
> present a formal proof.

Before accepting this view, consider the alternative that
these automata are awkward to write down or manipulate
largely because the formalism is bad. Surely, if the preceding notation were regarded as a language for describing or
programming pushdown automata, it would be a programming
language so poor that it would never be tolerated by a
language designer or user. Equations (1.1) through (1.5) are
in effect instructions in a programming language in which
every instruction is labelled (by a state, which may be
shared with other instructions) and has a goto field. Not
only is the syntax of this language extremely awkward, but
it does not support well-structured, "goto-less" programming.

To design an alternate notation, observe first that replacing "$(q,z) \in \delta(p,x,y)$" by the 5-tuple "(p,x,y,z,q)" and
permitting x, y, z to be arbitrary strings improves the
syntax and power of the language.   (What one has now is
similar to a "generalized pda"; see Ginsburg (6, p. 62).)
Second, note that the 5-tuple "(p,x,y,z,q)" represents the
move "go from state p to q while reading x , popping y
and pushing z (on the stack)", and this can be replaced by
a 4-tuple "$(p,x,y^{-1}z,q)$".   Here, "$y^{-1}z$" means "pop y and
push z".   Third, note that the states in the 4-tuple are
merely a mechanism for specifying a regular set of sequences
of moves, in precisely the same way that a finite-state
automaton specifies a regular set.   But there are many ways
besides a finite-state automaton to define a regular set,
and there is no reason to confine oneself to a single method.
In particular, converting a finite-state automaton to an
equivalent regular expression is similar to converting an
unstructured program to a well-structured program.   Using
regular expressions to describe regular sets leads to the
following description of a pushdown automaton B   for
$L = \{a^n b^n \mid n \geq 0\}$.   (Compare this with Conway's treatment of
transducers (3, Chap. 7).)

$$B = \langle a,Z \rangle \ast \ \langle b,Z^{-1} \rangle \ast \ \langle 1,Z_0^{-1} \rangle$$

The pushdown automaton B is about as simple as a grammar
for L, but it cannot be written in the usual 7-tuple notation because that notation does not have instructions corresponding to "push Z" (since every move must begin with a
pop) and does not permit spontaneous transitions between
states (to get from the "read a" state to the "read b" state

you must pass through a transition that pops and pushes the stack). Thus, two additional conclusions may be drawn. First, if arbitrary restrictions are placed on the form a pushdown instruction can take, then a pushdown automaton for even a very simple language may become quite complicated. Therefore, such restrictions should be avoided. Second, a finite-state automaton is not always the best way to describe a regular set. In fact, there is no single method of representing regular sets that is always the most convenient to use. Therefore, pushdown automata should be defined to be regular sets (of strings of moves), and not be tied by definition to any one method of describing such sets. In this way, one can retain the freedom to describe a pushdown automaton by a finite-state automaton (obtaining more or less the usual notation), or by a regular expression, or a graph, or a transition matrix, or any other method of description that may be convenient for a particular purpose.

This last point cannot be stressed too strongly. Surely, computer scientists have long understood the distinction between word and object, between pointer and "pointee" (cf. ALGOL 68). To say that an automaton is a regular expression would be as wrong as to say that it is a 7-tuple. Both statements confuse an object with its name. The object is the regular set of strings representing the computations of the automaton. (Not all of these computations succeed: some fail by doing something illegal to the stack.) It is true that this set of computations can be described or named by specifying a finite-state automaton (and that this can be done by writing down a 7-tuple if one is masochistically inclined), or alternatively by specifying a regular expression; but the automaton _is_ neither of these. This distinction is similar to the one that is now maintained in mathematics between a vector and the n-tuple of its coordinates in one particular basis; the advantage of defining vectors in abstraction from any particular coordinate system has long been recognized. (The advantage is even clearer with tensors, which were once unhappily defined as arrays of indices that transform in certain ways as the coordinate axes are changed.) In the present case, there are several advantages to maintaining the distinction between an automaton and its various names. For one thing, no one naming scheme is best. A regular expression is frequently better than a finite-state description, for it corresponds closely to the well-structured presentations used in Dijkstra D-charts and it is frequently as perspicacious as the finite-state description is ill structured. On the other hand, certain common regular sets are difficult to describe by regular expressions but easy to describe by finite-state automata: the set of all paths through a finite maze is the canonical example. Yet even if one naming scheme were always the best, it would still be inadvisable to identify automata with their names in that scheme. The reason is that formal language theory has developed many powerful and elegant results about regular sets, but not primarily about names for regular sets. If automata are not confused with their names, then all of these results can be brought to bear on their study.

Section II defines automata to be regular sets. Such a definition may be considered, if you will, a coordinate-free

definition. Section III studies a particular problem in
automaton theory in order to illustrate some of the manipu-
lations of automata that such a theory needs to support.
This problem is the speed-up problem for pushdown automata:
to show that nondeterministic pushdown automata can be sped
up to run in real time. This is usually proved by establishing the equivalent result that context-free grammars can
be converted to Greibach normal form. But the ability to
support an automaton-based proof of the speed-up result is
a stringent test for any theory of pushdown automata.
Section IV discusses a coordinate-free approach to deterministic automata lacking input tapes, specifically, to Turing
machines. Section V contains some concluding remarks.

II.   COORDINATE-FREE AUTOMATA

This section discusses nondeterministic automata with
one-way input tapes. Section IV illustrates the application
of a coordinate-free approach to automata that are deterministic or lack an input tape.

As explained in the introduction, an automaton should be
defined to be a regular set of computations, existing independently of any particular method of describing that regular
set. Although it is not necessary in an unsophisticated
treatment of this idea, it is convenient to consider a
homomorphism from such an automaton to a (nonfree) monoid in
order to achieve the maximum flexibility inherent in this
approach. The image of the automaton will then be a rational
set in a monoid. (In general, the rational sets in a monoid
are just the homomorphic images of the regular languages in a
free monoid.)

Let Σ be a countably infinite alphabet from which all names of symbols used in any formal language will be drawn. A <u>monoid</u> is a set M with an associative binary operation and a two-sided identity 1. If S is a subset of Σ, let S^* denote the free monoid generated by S. Thus, S^* consists of all finite strings of symbols from S. If S is not a subset of Σ but is a countable subset of a monoid M, let $S \to \Sigma : s \mapsto \langle s \rangle$ be an embedding of S into Σ, and let S^* denote the submonoid of M generated by S. Note that $\langle S \rangle^*$ is a free monoid in Σ^*, whereas S^* is a (not necessarily free) submonoid of M. For example, if $S = \{a, b, ab\} \subseteq \Sigma^* = M$ then S^* has its usual meaning as the Kleene closure of the language S, which equals $\{a, b\}^*$, whereas $\langle S \rangle^*$ consists of strings such as $\langle a \rangle \langle ab \rangle \langle b \rangle$ and is isomorphic to $\{a, b, c\}^*$. (This use of angle brackets is similar to their use in Backus Naur form to construct a single atomic element, e.g. $\langle \text{digit} \rangle$, from a compound string of symbols.) Since the mapping $S \to \langle S \rangle$ is a bijection, there is an inverse mapping $\langle S \rangle \to S : s \mapsto \hat{s}$, which defines a homomorphism

$$\langle S \rangle^* \to S^* : w = \langle s_1 \rangle \ldots \langle s_n \rangle \mapsto \hat{w} = s_1 \ldots s_n.$$

If M is any monoid, then the collection of <u>rational</u> subsets of M, denoted $\text{RAT}(M)$, is the smallest collection $\mathcal{C}$ of subsets of M containing all finite subsets and satisfying the condition that, if A and B are in $\mathcal{C}$, then $A \cup B$, $A \cdot B = \{a \cdot b \mid a \in A, \, b \in B\}$, and A^* are in $\mathcal{C}$.

If $\Sigma_1, \Sigma_2 \subseteq \Sigma$ then $\Sigma_1^* \times \Sigma_2^*$ is a product monoid, where $(u, v) \cdot (x, y) = (ux, vy)$. If $T \subseteq \langle \Sigma_1^* \times \Sigma_2^* \rangle^*$ then $\hat{T} \subseteq \Sigma_1^* \times \Sigma_2^*$. Any $z \in T$ has the form

$$z = <u_1,v_1><u_2,v_2>\ldots<u_n,v_n>, \quad n \geq 0, \quad u_i \in \Sigma_1^*, \quad v_i \in \Sigma_2^*,$$

and $\hat{z} = (u_1 u_2 \ldots u_n, v_1 v_2 \ldots v_n)$. When T is a rational sub-

set of $<\Sigma_1^* \times \Sigma_2^*>^*$, $T \in \text{RAT}(<\Sigma_1^* \times \Sigma_2^*>^*)$, then T is called

a (rational) <u>transducer</u> and $\hat{T}$, which will then be in

$\text{RAT}(\Sigma_1^* \times \Sigma_2^*)$, is called a (rational) <u>transduction</u>. In

general, any set $S \subseteq U \times V$ is considered to be a binary

relation mapping the set U into the set V, and one writes

$S:u \mapsto v$ if $(u,v) \in S$; $S:U_0 \mapsto V_0$ if $S:u \mapsto v$ for some

$u \in U_0 \subseteq U$, $v \in V_0 \subseteq V$; and (if δ is a set of such S),

$\delta:U_0 \mapsto V_0$ if $S:U_0 \mapsto V_0$ for some $S \in \delta$. Furthermore,

$S(u) = \{v | S:u \mapsto v\}$, $S(U_0) = \bigcup\{S(u) | u \in U_0\}$, $S^{-1} = \{(v,u) |$

$(u,v) \in S\}$. Thus, $\hat{T}$ is a mapping from Σ_1^* to Σ_2^* and

$\hat{T}^{-1}$ is a mapping from Σ_2^* to Σ_1^*. Note that if $T \subseteq <\Sigma^* \times$

$\Sigma^*>^*$ is rational then $T \subseteq <\Sigma_1^* \times \Sigma_2^*>^*$ for some finite

$\Sigma_1, \Sigma_2 \subseteq \Sigma$.

For any set U, let $\text{Rel}(U) = \{S | S \subseteq U \times U\}$ be the set of

binary relations on U. This is a monoid under the composi-

tion of relations $S \cdot T = \{(x,z) | \exists y, (x,y) \in S, (y,z) \in T\}$.

For $S \subseteq \Sigma^*$ and $w \in \Sigma^*$, let $w \backslash S = \{z \in \Sigma^* | wz \in S\}$,

$S/w = \{z \in \Sigma^* | zw \in S\}$, and $\text{PREFIX}(S) = \{w \in \Sigma^* | w \backslash S \neq \emptyset\}$. Call

S <u>nonsingular</u> if $1 \notin S$. Let $\text{Alph}(S)$ be the set of symbols

occurring in the strings of S.

Let Γ and I be countably infinite alphabets from

which all names of storage symbols and storage manipulation

instructions for automata will be chosen. The set of formal

languages is defined to be

$$\text{LANG} = \{L \subseteq \Sigma^* | \text{Alph}(L) \text{ finite}\},$$

but it is also convenient to treat $L \subseteq I^*$ as a language if

only finitely many different symbols occur in its strings;

hence it is tacitly assumed that I is embedded in Σ.
Storage contents will be described by strings in Γ^*, so
storage manipulation instructions act as binary relations on
Γ^*. Thus, a function ACTION is assumed to be given that maps
the name of an instruction to the instruction named; that is,
ACTION maps I into $\text{Rel}(\Gamma^*)$, the monoid of binary relations
on Γ^* under composition, and hence it extends uniquely to a
homomorphism

ACTION: $I^* \to \text{Rel}(\Gamma^*)$.

Thus, $\text{ACTION}(v_1 \ldots v_n)$ is the action of the instructions
$v_1, \ldots, v_n \in I$ acting in sequence from left to right on Γ^*.
(In some contexts, it is desirable to generalize to the case
where $\text{Rel}(\Gamma^*)$ is replaced by $\text{Rel}(C)$, C an abstract
set of storage configurations. For example, one might want
to let $C = \Gamma^* \times \Gamma^*$ for automata with two auxiliary data
stores; or $C = \Gamma \times \Gamma^*$ in a proof of the very useful fact
that automata of any type may be permitted to have a global
variable, i.e. an auxiliary finite register, since this can
always be simulated in the finite-state control.)

A <u>data storage mechanism</u> is specified by giving a subset
$M \subseteq I^*$ to be used as an instruction set for the corresponding
automata, together with two subsets of Γ^* called IN and
OUT to be used as the sets of initial and terminal storage
configurations for those automata. More generally, M may
be a subset of 2^{I^*}, in which case a whole set of instructions
may be used by each move of an automaton.

Let $\Sigma^1 = \Sigma \cup \{1\}$. If M is a data storage mechanism
then $\text{RAT}(\langle \Sigma^1 \times M \rangle^*)$ and $\text{RAT}(\langle \Sigma \times M \rangle^*)$ are the sets of
M-<u>automata</u> and <u>realtime</u> M-automata. (It is sometimes

convenient to replace Σ^1 by Σ^*, but that will not be done here.)   If   A   is an M-automaton, $M \subseteq I^*$,   then each move of A, i.e. each symbol in a computation string $\alpha \in A$, has the form $<u,v>$, where $u \in \Sigma^1$ is the input consumed by the move and $v \in M \subseteq I^*$ is the name of the transformation to be performed on the storage.   Hence the language defined by   A is

$$L(A) = \{u_1 \ldots u_n \mid \exists <u_1,v_1> \ldots <u_n,v_n> \in A,$$
$$\text{ACTION}(v_1 \ldots v_n) : \text{IN} \mapsto \text{OUT}\}$$

$$= \{u \in \Sigma^* \mid \exists \, \alpha \in A, \, \hat{\alpha} = (u,v), \, \text{ACTION}(v) : \text{IN} \mapsto \text{OUT}\}$$

$$= \{u \in \Sigma^* \mid \exists (u,v) \in \hat{A}, \, \text{ACTION}(v) : \text{IN} \mapsto \text{OUT}\}$$

$$= \hat{A}^{-1}(K_M), \, K_M = \{v \in M^* \mid \text{ACTION}(v) : \text{IN} \mapsto \text{OUT}\}.$$

Here, K_M is called the characteristic set of   M, but it is not generally a language because its alphabet is not generally a finite subset of   I, except in the case where   M   is a finite subset of I^*.   If $M \subseteq 2^{I^*}$, then each move of   A has the form $<u,V>$, $V \subseteq I^*$, where   u   is the input consumed by the move and   V   is the set of names of storage transformations any one of which (nondeterministically) can act to transform the storage.   Thus,

$$L(A) = \{u_1 \ldots u_n \mid \exists <u_1,V_1> \ldots <u_n,V_n> \in A, \, \exists \, v_i \in V_i,$$
$$\text{ACTION}(v_1 \ldots v_n) : \text{IN} \mapsto \text{OUT}\}.$$

In general,   A   is nonsingular if $1 \notin L(A)$, and   A   and   B are equivalent if $L(A) = L(B)$.

For each $a \in \Gamma$, let   a   and a^{-1} be distinct symbols in I, and define their actions to be the pushdown operations "push(a)" and "pop(a)" as follows:

$ACTION(a):w \mapsto wa, \ w \in \Gamma*$

$ACTION(a^{-1}):wa \mapsto w, \ w \in \Gamma*$

Let $\Gamma^{-1} = \{a^{-1}|a \in \Gamma\}$. Then $M = \Gamma^{-1}\Gamma*$ is the pushdown storage mechanism. It is customary to let $IN = \{Z_0\}$ and $OUT = \Gamma*$. If $M_2 = \{a,a^{-1},b,b^{-1}\}$ and $IN = OUT = \{1\}$, then the binary pushdown mechanism is obtained; its characteristic set is K_2, the Dyck language on two generators. Since every context-free language can be defined by an M_2-automaton, every context-free language has the form

$$\hat{A}^{-1}(K_2) = \{u|(u,v) \in \hat{A}, v \in K_2\} = h_1(A \cap h_2^{-1}(K_2)),$$

where $\langle\Sigma* \times I*\rangle* \to \Sigma* \times I* : w \mapsto \hat{w} = (h_1(w),h_2(w))$ defines h_1 and h_2. Since A is regular and h_1 and h_2 are homomorphisms, this result is the Chomsky-Schutzenberger Theorem. It is usually proved, with some difficulty, by manipulating grammars. It is easier to obtain the result by first showing that every pushdown automaton is equivalent to a binary pushdown automaton and then applying the preceding formula. Incidentally, the derivation of the corresponding formula relating M_2 and K_2 in AFL theory is hideously complicated: see Section 5.3 of Ginsburg (7).

Finally, if α is the initial part of a computation in A, i.e. $\alpha \in PREFIX(A)$, it is convenient to have a notation for the set of storage configurations that α produces. Thus, for $\alpha \in \langle\Sigma* \times I*\rangle*$ and $S \subseteq \langle\Sigma* \times I*\rangle*$, let $\hat{\alpha} = (u,v)$, $v \in I*$, let $f = ACTION(v)$ and define

$$STORE(\alpha) = \bigcup\{f(z)|z \in IN\}$$

and

$$STORE(S) = \bigcup\{STORE(\alpha)|\alpha \in S\}.$$

Let Σ_A denote the input alphabet of A, i.e. the minimum alphabet such that $A \subseteq <(\Sigma_A \cup \{1\}) \times M>^*$, and let Γ_A denote the tape alphabet of A, i.e. the minimal alphabet such that STORE(PREFIX(A)) $\subseteq \Gamma_A^*$. (If A is rational, Σ_A will be finite but Γ_A need not be.)

III. PUSHDOWN AUTOMATA

In this section, it is proved that every nonsingular pushdown automaton is equivalent to a realtime pushdown automaton. Corollaries are the Greibach and Chomsky normal form theorems for context-free grammars and the existence of a hardest context-free language. The purpose of this exercise is to determine what features must be available in a theory of automata in order to support a purely automaton-theoretic proof of this result. While grammars can be used in place of pushdown automata, this alternative is not available for most other kinds of automata. Thus, it is important that any theory of automata be powerful enough to handle problems such as this one. The proof is achieved by a series of transformations on automata.

Unless otherwise specified, IN = $\{Z_0\}$ and OUT = $\{1\}$. Let

$$M_1 = \{c^{-1}v \mid c \in \Gamma, v \in \Gamma^*\},$$

$$M_2 = \{c^{-1}R \mid c \in \Gamma, R \in \text{RAT}((\Gamma \cup \Gamma^{-1})^*)\}.$$

<u>3.1 Lemma</u>. Each nonsingular M_1-automaton A is equivalent to a realtime M_2-automaton B.

<u>Proof</u>. The moves of A may be grouped together into regular segments, each segment reading exactly one input symbol. Then B can simulate each segment in a single move. More formally,

since A is regular there is a finite labelled directed

graph G, with a set of IN nodes and a set of OUT nodes, that

defines A in the sense that A is the set of all labels

of paths from IN to OUT. For each pair of nodes i and j,

let A_{ij} be the set of labels of paths from i to j. Now

form a new graph G' by deleting the edges of G and adding,

for each pair of nodes (i,j) and each $a \in \Sigma$, an edge from i

to j labelled by $<a, \hat{A}_{ij}(a)>$. Then G' defines the

required B. □

Let $M_3 = \{R^{-1}S | R, S \in RAT(\Gamma*), 1 \nmid R\}$, where $R^{-1} =$

$\{a_n^{-1} \ldots a_1^{-1} | a_1 \ldots a_n \in R, a_i \in \Gamma\}$.

3.2 Lemma. Each realtime M_2-automaton A is equivalent to a

realtime M_3-automaton B.

Proof. Consider each $<a, c^{-1}R>$ in Alph(A). Let R' be

the set of strings obtainable from those in $c^{-1}R$ by

repeatedly performing zero or more cancellations of the form

$bb^{-1} \to 1, b \in \Gamma$. Then $R' = \sigma^{-1}(c^{-1}R)$, where σ is the sub-

stitution $\sigma(z) = KzK, z \in \Gamma \cup \Gamma^{-1}$, K the set of all strings

that can be cancelled to 1. Hence, R' is regular. (If σ

is an arbitrary substitution then $w \backslash \sigma^{-1}(L) = \{z | wz \in \sigma^{-1}(L)\}$

$= \{z | \sigma(w) \cdot \sigma(z) \cap L \neq \emptyset\} = \{z | \sigma(z) \cap (\sigma(w) \backslash L) \neq \emptyset\}$

$= \sigma^{-1}(\sigma(w) \backslash L)$. Thus, σ^{-1} preserves the property of having

finitely many left quotients $y \backslash L$ and hence preserves

regularity.) Since $ACTION(bb^{-1}) = ACTION(1)$ and

$ACTION(bd^{-1}) = \emptyset$ for $b \neq d$,

$ACTION(R' \cap (\Gamma^{-1})*\Gamma*) = ACTION(R)$.

This is so because if a string in R is cancelled as far

as possible then it has the same action as before; and either

it contains bd^{-1}, $b \neq d$, and can be discarded, or it lies in

$(\Gamma^{-1})*\Gamma*$. Since $R' \cap (\Gamma^{-1})*\Gamma*$ is regular and is a subset of $(\Gamma^{-1})*\Gamma*$, it has the form

$$R_1^{-1}S_1 \cup \ldots \cup R_n^{-1}S_n, \quad R_i, S_i \subseteq \Gamma*,$$

where each R_i and S_i is regular. Let τ be the finite substitution

$$\tau: <a, c^{-1}R> \mapsto \{<a, R_i^{-1}S_i>|1 \leq i \leq n\}.$$

Then $B = \tau(A)$ is as required. $\square$

Let $M_4 = \{v^{-1}S|1 \leq |v| \leq 2, S \in RAT(\Gamma*), |v| = 2 \Rightarrow 1 \notin S\}$.

3.3 Lemma. Each realtime M_3-automaton A is equivalent to a realtime M_4-automaton B.

Proof. Let $R = \{R|\exists<a, R^{-1}S> \in Alph(A)\}$. Since R is a finite collection of regular sets, there is a congruence $\equiv$ of finite index under which each $R \in R$ is closed, i.e. $\equiv$ is an equivalence relation on Σ_0^* where $\Sigma_0 = \cup \{Alph(R)|R \in R\}$, $x \equiv x'$ and $y \equiv y'$ implies $xy \equiv x'y'$, $x \equiv y \in R \in R$ implies $x \in R$, and if $E(x)$ is the equivalence class of x then $\mathcal{E} = \{E(x)|x \in \Sigma_0^*\}$ is finite. By adding $\{Z_0\}$ and $\{1\}$ to R if necessary, it may be assured that $E(Z_0) = \{Z_0\}$ and $E(1) = \{1\}$.

The idea is to store tokens on the stack to represent elements in each equivalence class so that long elements can be popped by popping a single token. For $x \in \Sigma_0^+$, let $[E(x)]$ be a unique name for $E(x)$ in Γ, where $[E(Z_0)] = Z_0$. For convenience, define $[E(1)] = 1$. Let $\Sigma_1 = \{[E(x)]|x \in \Sigma_0^+\}$ and let π be the substitution from Σ_1^* to $2^{\Sigma_0^*}$ that replaces the token $[E]$ by the set E. Define $E(x) \otimes E(y) = E(xy)$, a well-defined operation, let σ be the finite substitution

$$\sigma:<a, R^{-1}S> \mapsto \{<a,([F][E])^{-1}[F \otimes G]([G]\backslash\pi^{-1}(S))> | E,F,G \in \mathcal{C},$$
$$E \subseteq R\},$$

and let $B = \sigma(A)$. Intuitively, what happens is this: when A changes its stack from $bc...fe$ to $bc...fgh...k$ where $b,...,k$ are strings with $e \in R$ and $gh...k \in S$, then B changes its stack from

$$[E(b)][E(c)]...[E(f)][E(e)] \quad \text{to}$$
$$[E(b)][E(c)]...[E(fg)][E(h)]...[E(k)].$$

Thus, B always maintains on its stack all possible factorizations of A's stack. Note that f may be 1 in which case $[E(f)]$ vanishes and B simply replaces $[E(e)]$ with $[E(g)]...[E(k)]$.

To continue with the formal proof, note that $E \subseteq R$ implies $1 \notin E$, so $[E] \neq 1$; and if $[F] \neq 1$ then $[F \otimes G] \neq 1$. Hence, the moves of B have the right form. It remains to show that B is equivalent to A. First note that, for any sets X and Y,

$$\pi^{-1}(X)/Y = \{z | \pi(zy) \cap X \neq \emptyset \text{ for some } y \in Y\} \tag{3.4}$$
$$= \{z | (\pi(z) \cdot \pi(Y)) \cap X \neq \emptyset\}$$
$$= \{z | \pi(z) \cap (X/\pi(Y)) \neq \emptyset\}$$
$$= \pi^{-1}(X/\pi(Y)).$$

Second, note that

$$\pi^{-1}(XS) = \bigcup\{(\pi^{-1}(X)/[F]) \cdot [F \otimes G] \cdot ([G]\backslash\pi^{-1}(S)) | F, G \in \mathcal{C}\}. \tag{3.5}$$

For suppose first that $[E_1]...[E_p]$ is in $\pi^{-1}(XS)$, $[E_i] \neq 1$. Then $e_1...e_p \in XS$ for some $e_1 \in E_1,...,e_p \in E_p$. So $(e_1...e_{k-1}f, ge_{k+1}...e_p) \in X \times S$ for some k and some $fg = e_k$. Let $F = E(f)$ and $G = E(g)$. Then

$[E_1]\ldots[E_{k-1}] \in \pi^{-1}(X)/[F]$, since $e_1\ldots e_{k-1}f \in X$;

$[E_k] = [F \otimes G]$, since $e_k = fg$;

$[E_{k+1}]\ldots[E_p] \in [G]\backslash\pi^{-1}(S)$, since $ge_{k+1}\ldots e_p \in S$.

Hence,

$$[E_1]\ldots[E_p] \in (\pi^{-1}(X)/[F]) \cdot [F \otimes G] \cdot ([G]\backslash\pi^{-1}(S)).$$

And suppose next that

$$[E_1]\ldots[E_{k-1}] \in \pi^{-1}(X)/[F], \text{ and}$$

$$[E_{k+1}]\ldots[E_p] \in [G]\backslash\pi^{-1}(S),$$

where each $[E_i] \neq 1$. Then

$$e_1\ldots e_{k-1}f \in X \text{ for some } e_1 \in E_1,\ldots,f \in F;$$

$$ge_{k+1}\ldots e_p \in S \text{ for some } g \in G,\ldots,e_p \in E_p.$$

Then

$$[E_1]\ldots[E_{k-1}][F \otimes G][E_{k+1}]\ldots[E_p] \in \pi^{-1}(XS),$$

since $e_1\ldots e_{k-1}fge_{k+1}\ldots e_p$ is in XS. This proves (3.5).

But (3.5) implies that, for any $\alpha \in \text{PREFIX}(A)$,

$$\text{STORE}(\sigma(\alpha)) = \pi^{-1}(\text{STORE}(\alpha)). \tag{3.6}$$

For if $\alpha = 1$ then $\text{STORE}(\sigma(\alpha)) = \{Z_0\} = \{[E(Z_0)]\} = \pi^{-1}(\{Z_0\}) = \pi^{-1}(\text{STORE}(\alpha))$. And if $\alpha = \alpha_0 \cdot <a, R^{-1}S>$ and $\text{STORE}(\sigma(\alpha_0)) = \pi^{-1}(\text{STORE}(\alpha_0))$ then

$\text{STORE}(\sigma(\alpha))$

$\quad = \text{STORE}(\sigma(\alpha_0) \cdot \sigma(<a, R^{-1}S>))$

$\quad = \bigcup\{(\text{STORE}(\sigma(\alpha_0))/[F][E]) \cdot [F \otimes G] \cdot ([G]\backslash\pi^{-1}(S))$
$\qquad\qquad |E,F,G \in \mathcal{E}, E \subseteq R\}$

$$= \bigcup \{ (\pi^{-1}(\mathrm{STORE}(\alpha_0))/[F][E]) \cdot [F \otimes G] \cdot ([G] \backslash \pi^{-1}(S)) $$
$$| E, F, G \in \mathcal{E}, \ E \subseteq R \}$$

$$= \bigcup \{ (\pi^{-1}(\mathrm{STORE}(\alpha_0)/E)/[F]) \cdot [F \otimes G] \cdot ([G] \backslash \pi^{-1}(S)) $$
$$| E, F, G \in \mathcal{E}, \ E \subseteq R \}, \ \text{by (3.4)}$$

$$= \bigcup \{ \pi^{-1}((\mathrm{STORE}(\alpha_0)/E) \cdot S) | E \in \mathcal{E}, \ E \subseteq R \}, \ \text{by (3.5)}$$

$$= \pi^{-1}((\mathrm{STORE}(\alpha_0)/R) \cdot S), \ \text{since} \ R = \bigcup \{ E \in \mathcal{E} | E \subseteq R \}$$

$$= \pi^{-1}(\mathrm{STORE}(\alpha)).$$

Hence, $1 \in \mathrm{STORE}(\sigma(\alpha))$ iff $1 \in \pi^{-1}(\mathrm{STORE}(\alpha))$ iff $\pi(1) \cap \mathrm{STORE}(\alpha) \neq \emptyset$ iff $1 \in \mathrm{STORE}(\alpha)$. So $\alpha \in A$ has $1 \in \mathrm{STORE}(\alpha)$ (and hence the input to α is in $L(A)$) iff some $\beta \in \sigma(\alpha) \subseteq \sigma(A) = B$ has $1 \in \mathrm{STORE}(\beta)$ (and hence the input to β is in $L(B)$). Since σ preserves inputs, $L(A) = L(B)$. □

Let $M_5 = \{ c^{-1}S | c \in \Gamma, \ S \in \mathrm{RAT}(\Gamma^*) \}$.

3.7 Lemma. Each realtime M_4-automaton A is equivalent to a realtime M_5-automaton B.

Proof. It obviously suffices to construct a suitable B that initially has a new symbol $\#$ rather than Z_0 on its stack. Furthermore, B can be permitted to have an extra pushdown stack P whose capacity is limited to one symbol, and extra instructions $\hat{c}$ (push c on P if P empty) and $\hat{c}^{-1}$ (pop c off P), for this may be implemented in the finite-state control. One may further require that the initial and terminal contents of P be Z_0 and $\#$, respectively. Let σ be the finite substitution

$$\sigma : <a, \ b^{-1}c^{-1}R> \ \mapsto \ \{ <a, \ \hat{b}^{-1}c^{-1}(R/d)\hat{d}> \ | \ d \in \Gamma_A \}$$

$$<a, \ b^{-1}R> \ \mapsto \ \{ <a, \ \hat{b}^{-1}c^{-1}((c \cdot R)/d)\hat{d}> \ | \ c, \ d \in \Gamma_A \cup \{\#\} \},$$

and let $B = \sigma(A)$. Recall that $b^{-1}c^{-1}R \in M_4$ implies R is nonsingular. It is easy to see that B is equivalent to A, with B storing A's stack contents $c_1 \ldots c_n$, $n \geq 0$, in the form $c_0 c_1 \ldots c_{n-1}$, with $c_0 = \#$ and c_n in P. $\square$

Let $M_6 = \{c^{-1}w \mid c \in \Gamma, w \in \Gamma^*, 0 \leq |w| \leq 2\}$.

<u>3.8 Lemma</u>. Each realtime M_5-automaton A is equivalent to a realtime M_6-automaton B.

<u>Proof</u>. Let $\delta = \{S \mid \exists \langle a, c^{-1}S \rangle \in \mathrm{Alph}(A)\}$ and let

$$R = \{\{Z_0\}, \; S/w \mid S \in \delta, \; w \in \Gamma^*, \; S/w \neq \{1\}\}.$$

Then R is finite since a regular set S has only finitely many right quotients S/w.

The idea is to represent a regular set R on the stack by a single token $[R]$ and to implement $\mathrm{ACTION}(c^{-1}S)$ by sending $[R]$ to $[R/c][S]$. However, some care must be taken to pop $[R/c]$ at the appropriate time. For each $R \in R$, let $[R]$ be a new symbol in Γ, with $[\{Z_0\}] = Z_0$. Let σ be the finite substitution

$$\sigma : \langle a, c^{-1}S \rangle \mapsto \{\langle a, [R]^{-1}[R/c][S] \rangle \mid R, R/c, S \in R\} \quad (3.9)$$

$$\cup \; \{\langle a, [R]^{-1}[R/c] \rangle \mid R, R/c \in R, 1 \in S\}$$

$$\cup \; \{\langle a, [R]^{-1}[S] \rangle \mid R, S \in R, 1 \in R/c\}$$

$$\cup \; \{\langle a, [R]^{-1} \rangle \mid R \in R, 1 \in R/c, 1 \in S\},$$

and let $B = \sigma(A)$. If L is a language, let $L' = L - \{1\}$. Then

$$((L \cdot R')/c) \cdot S = L \cdot (R/c) \cdot S \quad (3.10)$$

$$= \{w \in L \cdot (R/c)' \cdot S' \mid R/c \neq \{1\}, S \neq \{1\}\}$$

$$\cup \; \{w \in L \cdot (R/c)' \mid R/c \neq \{1\}, 1 \in S\}$$

$$\cup \; \{w \in L \cdot S' \mid 1 \in R/c, S \neq \{1\}\}$$

$$\cup \ \{w \in L \mid 1 \in R/c, \ 1 \in S\}.$$

It follows from (3.10) that σ was defined in just such a way that, for every $\alpha \in \text{PREFIX}(A)$,

$$\text{STORE}(\alpha) = \cup\{R_1'\ldots R_n' \mid [R_1]\ldots[R_n] \in \text{STORE}(\sigma(\alpha)), \ n \geq 0\}$$

$$(3.11)$$

For if $\alpha = 1$ then $z \in \text{STORE}(\sigma(\alpha))$ iff $z = [\{Z_0\}]$, and $\{Z_0\}' = \{Z_0\} = \text{STORE}(\alpha)$ as required. And if $\alpha = \alpha_0 \cdot \ <a, \ c^{-1}S>$ and (3.11) is true of α_0 then

$\text{STORE}(\alpha)$

$$= \text{STORE}(\alpha_0 \cdot <a, \ c^{-1}S>)$$

$$= (\text{STORE}(\alpha_0)/c) \cdot S$$

$$= (\cup\{R_1'\ldots R_n' \mid [R_1]\ldots[R_n] \in \text{STORE}(\sigma(\alpha_0))\}/c) \cdot S$$

$$= \cup\{((R_1'\ldots R_n')/c) \cdot S \mid [R_1]\ldots[R_n] \in \text{STORE}(\sigma(\alpha_0))\}$$

$$= \cup\{S_1'\ldots S_m' \mid [S_1]\ldots[S_m] \in \text{STORE}(\sigma(\alpha_0) \cdot \sigma(<a,c^{-1}S>))\},$$

$$\text{by (3.9) and (3.10)}$$

$$= \cup\{S_1'\ldots S_m' \mid [S_1]\ldots[S_m] \in \text{STORE}(\sigma(\alpha))\},$$

as required.

It follows that 1 is in $\text{STORE}(\alpha)$, $\alpha \in A$, iff 1 is in $\text{STORE}(\sigma(\alpha))$. Hence, A and B are equivalent. □

3.12 Theorem. Each nonsingular pushdown automaton is equivalent to a realtime pushdown automaton with instructions of the form $c^{-1}w$, $c \in \Gamma$, $w \in \Gamma^*$, $0 \leq |w| \leq 2$.

Proof. An ordinary pushdown automaton A is the same as an M_1-automaton except that OUT is Γ^* instead of $\{1\}$, so

$$B = A \cdot \{<1,c^{-1}> \mid c \in \Gamma_A\}^*$$

is an equivalent M_1-automaton. Hence, the theorem follows from the preceding lemmas. □

3.13 Corollary. (Greibach-Chomsky normal form). Each non-singular context-free language can be generated by productions of the form $A \to a$, $A \to aB$, $A \to aBC$ (where A, B, C range over nonterminals and a ranges over terminal symbols).

Proof. The usual construction for converting a pushdown automaton to a context-free grammar converts a move of the form $\langle a, c^{-1}c_1 \ldots c_n \rangle$ to productions of the form $A \to aB_1 \ldots B_n$. □

The following continuation of this development is worth mentioning briefly. Let $M_7 = (\Gamma \cup \Gamma^{-1})^*$. Then an M_7-automaton B can simulate an ordinary pushdown automaton A without using its finite-state control by storing the state of A on top of its stack. That is, assume without loss of generality that the moves of A never contain Z_0 (the instruction that pushes Z_0 on the stack). For each edge labelled $\langle u, c^{-1}c_1 \ldots c_n \rangle$, $n \geq 0$, from node p to node q in a graph for A, let Alph(B) contain the following moves:

$\langle u, Z_0^{-1}c_1 \ldots c_n q \rangle$, if $c = Z_0$, $p \in$ IN

$\langle u, p^{-1}c^{-1}c_1 \ldots c_n q \rangle$

$\langle u, p^{-1}c^{-1} \rangle$, if $n = 0$, $q \in$ OUT

$\langle u, Z_0^{-1} \rangle$, if $c = Z_0$, $p \in$ IN, $n = 0$, $q \in$ OUT

Then if B is taken to be stateless in the sense that $B = \text{Alph}(B)^*$, then B will be equivalent to A and will be realtime assuming A was. By coding $\Gamma - \{Z_0\}$ into a two-symbol alphabet $\Gamma_2 \subseteq \Gamma - \{Z_0\}$, B may be converted to an equivalent stateless realtime automaton C lying in a class with characteristic set $Z_0^{-1}K_2$, where $K_2 \subseteq (\Gamma_2 \cup \Gamma_2^{-1})^*$ is the Dyck language on two generators. But C is equivalent to

$$D = \{<a, <V>> \,|\, V = \{v\,|\,<a,v> \in Alph(C)\}, \, a \in \Sigma_C\}^*,$$

where $ACTION(<V>) = \bigcup \{ACTION(v)\,|\,v \in V\}$. Since $\hat{D}$ is merely a homomorphism, any nonsingular context-free language L has the form $L = \hat{D}^{-1}(K) = h^{-1}(K)$, h a homomorphism,

$$K = \{<V_1>\ldots<V_n> \,|\, \exists v_i \in V_i, \, v_1 \ldots v_n \in Z_0^{-1}K_2\}.$$

Here, K is not a language since its alphabet is not finite. But it can be coded into a language by using ordered sets $V = (v_1, \ldots, v_n)$ instead of $V = \{v_1, \ldots, v_n\}$ and coding $<V>$ by

$$f: <(v_1, \ldots, v_n)> \mapsto v_1 c \ldots v_n c\#,$$

where c and # are separator symbols. This is indeed a code (in fact, a prefix code), so the homomorphism determined by f is injective. Hence, $K = f^{-1}(f(K))$, and so every nonsingular context-free language is the inverse homomorphic image of the language f(K). Therefore, f(K) is the hardest context-free language since every nonsingular context-free language can be homomorphically reduced to it. This result, with Z_0^{-1} replaced by \$, is due to Greibach (11). The alternate derivation of Greibach's result given here illustrates the value of allowing instructions to have a nondeterministic effect on the storage. (Note that

$$ACTION(v_1 c \ldots v_n c\#) = ACTION(<\{v_1, \ldots, v_n\}>)$$

$$= ACTION(v_1) \cup \ldots \cup ACTION(v_n)$$

is nondeterministic; that is, it is a binary relation on Γ^* but not a partial function.)

IV. TURING MACHINES

This section contains a very brief illustration of how to
develop a coordinate-free theory of deterministic automata
that do not have separate input tapes. The automata considered are Turing machines. The problem studied is that of
showing that nondeterministic Turing machines are no more
powerful than deterministic ones (when resource consumption
and conciseness are ignored). Among the noteworthy features
of the development are these. Treating Turing machines as
regular sets gives rise in a natural way to the use of
macros in programming them. And it is easy to use the approach of top-down development by stepwise refinement with
explicit specifications of the actions of each module, an
approach that is recommended by many software engineers for
dealing with complex problems.

Let $\not b$ be a special "blank" symbol in Γ, let $\#$ be
another symbol in Γ, and assume $\Sigma \subseteq \Gamma - \{\not b, \#\}$. Let
$\bar{\Gamma} = \{\bar a \mid a \in \Gamma\}$ be disjoint from Γ. The Turing machine
instructions are

$$M = \{LEFT, RIGHT, READ(a), WRITE(a) \mid a \in \Gamma\},$$

where M is assumed to be embedded in I. The actions are
the following, where $a, c \in \Gamma$ and $\alpha, \beta \in \Gamma^*$.

$$\begin{array}{lll}
\text{ACTION(LEFT):} & \alpha a \bar c \beta & \vdash \alpha \bar a c \beta \\[4pt]
 & \bar a \beta & \vdash \not b a \beta \\[4pt]
\text{ACTION(RIGHT):} & \alpha \bar a c \beta & \vdash \alpha a \bar c \beta \\[4pt]
 & \alpha \bar a & \vdash \alpha a \bar{\not b} \\[4pt]
\text{ACTION(READ(a)):} & \alpha \bar a \beta & \vdash \alpha \bar a \beta \\[4pt]
\text{ACTION(WRITE(a)):} & \alpha \bar c \beta & \vdash \alpha \bar a \beta
\end{array}$$

A Turing machine is a set $T \in RAT(M*)$. Define

$$T(\alpha\bar{a}\beta) = \{\gamma \mid ACTION(T): \alpha\bar{a}\beta \vdash \gamma\}.$$

The language defined by T is

$$L(T) = \{w \in \Sigma* \mid T(\bar{\emptyset}w) \neq \emptyset\}.$$

Finally, T is <u>deterministic</u> if, for any $m, m' \in M$ and any quotient $Q = w\backslash PREFIX(T\$)$, if $m, m' \in Q$ then $(m,m') \in \{(READ(a), READ(c)) \mid a, c \in \Gamma\}$ or $m = m'$.

The definition of determinism is coordinate-free in the sense that it does not involve choosing a graph (and hence an explicit finite-state control) for the regular set T, but it does require some explanation. The symbol $\$$ is an end-marker which could be read as "halt". Take the graph of a deterministic finite-state automaton for the regular set $T\$$ and discard any nodes that are not on some IN-OUT path. Suppose m and m' label two different edges leaving the same node p. Then $m \neq m'$ since the graph is deterministic. Let w label any path from IN to p. Then wm and wm' are in $PREFIX(T\$)$, so if T is deterministic, $m = READ(a)$ and $m' = READ(c)$, where $a \neq c$ since $m \neq m'$. These two moves can compatibly branch from the same node p in a deterministic Turing machine because the contents of the square being read will determine which edge to take. (Note that no other types of move pairs are compatible in this sense.)

The following theorems are of central importance. The proofs are simple applications of the definitions, and are omitted.

<u>4.1 Theorem</u>. If T_1 and T_2 are deterministic Turing machines then so is $T_1 \cdot T_2$.

4.2 Theorem. If T is a deterministic Turing machine and $R \subseteq \Gamma$ is finite then

$$\mathrm{UNTIL}(R{:}T) = (\{\mathrm{READ}(a) \mid a \notin R\} \cdot T)^* \cdot \{\mathrm{READ}(a) \mid a \in R\}$$

and

$$\mathrm{IF}(R{:}T) = (\{\mathrm{READ}(a) \mid a \in R\} \cdot T) \cup \{\mathrm{READ}(a) \mid a \notin R\}$$

are deterministic Turing machines.

Theorem 4.3 can be generalized to the case where R is any regular set of tape configurations by suitably defining $\mathrm{UNTIL}(R{:}T)$ and $\mathrm{IF}(R{:}T)$ with the aid of a flag, which could be implemented by storing the flag either in the finite-state control or on the tape. The details are omitted, but it is assumed this has been done.

Let T be a nondeterministic Turing machine and $m_1, \ldots, m_n$ a listing of its alphabet, i.e. of the moves it can make. The states that T could be in following $\alpha \in \mathrm{PREFIX}(T)$ can be represented by the quotient $\alpha \backslash T$ (so the final states are the singular quotients) and an instantaneous description of T can be represented by a string of the form

$$w = a_1 \ldots a_{k-1}{}^{<Q, a_k>}a_{k+1} \ldots a_m$$

representing the state $Q = \alpha \backslash T$, the tape contents $a_1 \ldots a_k \ldots a_m$, and the head positioned on a_k. The action of m_i on w to yield $m_i(w)$ may be defined in the obvious way, with Q going to $m_i \backslash Q$, and with $m_i(w) = w$ if the move m_i is not applicable to w.

To simulate T with a deterministic Turing machine T_0 that computes the instantaneous descriptions of T, one may proceed in a top-down way as follows. Let

$$T_0 = \mathrm{START} \cdot \mathrm{UNTIL}(\mathrm{DONE}{:}\mathrm{MOVE})$$

where START and MOVE are to be designed in such a way that

$$\text{ACTION(START)} : \bar{\not{b}}w \mapsto \not{b}<T,\not{b}>w,$$

and

$$\text{ACTION(MOVE)} : \bar{\not{b}}w \# w_1 \# \ldots \# w_k \mapsto$$

$$\bar{\not{b}}w_1 \# \ldots \# w_k \# m_1(w) \# \ldots \# m_n(w)$$

are true and where DONE is the regular set of all strings
containing a symbol $<Q,a>$, Q singular. (Recall that the
assertion $R:x \mapsto y$ merely means that the relation R can
map x to y, i.e. that (x,y) is in R. It does not assert
what other pairs are in R. In the present case, it does not
matter what ACTION(START) does on strings not of the form
$\bar{\not{b}}w$. However, since T_0 is deterministic, ACTION(START)
will be a partial function.) Then let

$$\text{START} = \text{WRITE}(<T,\not{b}>) \cdot \text{LEFT},$$

which clearly has the right action. Let

$$\text{MOVE} = \text{MOVE}(m_1) \cdot \text{MOVE}(m_2) \ldots \text{MOVE}(m_n) \cdot \text{REMOVE},$$

where

$$\text{ACTION(MOVE}(m_i)) : \bar{\not{b}}w \# w_1 \# \ldots \# w_k \mapsto \bar{\not{b}}w \# w_1 \# \ldots \# w_k \# m_i(w)$$

and

$$\text{ACTION(REMOVE)} : \bar{\not{b}}w \# w_1 \# \ldots \# w_k \mapsto \bar{\not{b}}w_1 \# \ldots \# w_k.$$

And so forth. Along the way, the following tools will prove
useful, among others, and could be defined when first needed
or at the outset.

$$\text{LEFT}(S) = \text{LEFT} \cdot \text{UNTIL}(S:\text{LEFT}), \ S \subseteq \Gamma_T$$

$$\text{RIGHT}(S) = \text{RIGHT} \cdot \text{UNTIL}(S:\text{RIGHT}), \ S \subseteq \Gamma_T$$

$$\text{MARK} = \{\text{READ}(a) \cdot \text{WRITE}(a') \,|\, a \in \Gamma_T\}$$

$$\text{UNMARK} = \{\text{READ}(a') \cdot \text{WRITE}(a) \,|\, a \in \Gamma_T\}$$

PUSH(a) = MARK $\bullet$ RIGHT($\{\not{b}\}$) $\cdot$ WRITE(a) $\bullet$ LEFT(Γ_T') $\cdot$ UNMARK.

Here, Γ_T is the tape alphabet of T and $\Gamma_T' = \{a' | a \in \Gamma_T\}$ is a disjoint alphabet of new symbols.

V. CONCLUSIONS

It is not the purpose of this paper to present a finished theory of automata, but rather to propose that such a theory be developed. It should be flexible enough to permit the easy manipulation of automata, as well as the application of results from formal language theory to automata. For example, the regular sets are closed under regular substitution, and indeed it frequently proves convenient to obtain new automata from old ones by substitution. Another example occurs in Goldstine (10), where two transducers are shuffled together to construct a new one, a procedure which is valid because the family of regular sets is closed under the shuffle operation. In addition, a satisfactory theory of automata should provide great flexibility in moving from one set of instructions to another, and should even allow an automaton to use instructions that have a nondeterministic effect on storage, either because an entire set of instructions is used in a move or because the individual instructions are nondeterministic. (For an example of the latter, see the derivation of Greibach's hardest language in Section III.) Furthermore, any theory of automata should support the construction of highly complex automata, such as universal Turing machines and the machines needed for simulations in the study of computational complexity. These constructions should employ methods intrinsic to the theory and applicable to all automata, and not merely employ an ad hoc programming language approach as is sometimes done in the development of Turing machines. The theory should facilitate the application of good software engineering practices, as discussed in Section IV. It should also facilitate the measurement of resource consumption, a topic not discussed here. In addition, it is important in the case of automata with one-way input tapes to have a simple relationship between an automaton A and the language it defines; in Sections II and III this relationship is expressed by the formula $L = \hat{A}^{-1}(K)$ (and when A reduces to a homomorphism, this becomes $L = h^{-1}(K)$ as with Greibach's hardest language K). This relationship, incidentally, ought to be taken as the starting point for a reworked development of AFL theory, and such a development can yield a theory which merges smoothly into automaton theory instead of existing on a higher plane of abstraction (see Goldstine (10)). A further development of the calculus of regular events would also be desirable: most of the details in proving the realtime speed-up result in Section III involved just such calculations and if a suitable calculus were available, such a derivation might become trivial.

Would there be any practical significance to such a theory? I think there would. A cleaner theory would be easier to use and might find a larger number of practical applications than at present. Such a theory might shed light on the formal specification of data structures. Also, a suitable algebra for manipulating and combining automata might serve as a paradigm for programming language designers.

(For example, in his 1977 Turing Award lecture, John Backus strongly argued the need for an algebra of programs (1).) It is ironic that automaton theorists, who deal with objects far simpler than programming languages, have made little effort to construct such an algebra if only to see how successfully the central problem of software engineering, the problem of managing complexity, could be handled in a relatively simple arena. Whether or not there is an algebra for combining automata, whenever a specific automaton is programmed (i.e. defined), it ought to be programmed in a well-structured way. To put this in pedagogical terms, whenever a student encounters any part of automaton theory, it would be beneficial for him to see structured design techniques in their purest form. In fact, such techniques ought to be applied in automaton theory with even greater clarity than is feasible in other areas, because automata are vastly simplified models of real world objects and because theoreticians should be more concerned with elegance and polish than practitioners can afford to be. Yet at present, a student learns good design in his other courses; in his course in automaton theory, he is likely to see design techniques that would be red penciled in a freshman programming course, and while he may learn something about automata in such a course, he is likely to learn nothing about the systematic management of complexity, even though this would be of great educational value. Finally, the simplifications that can arise from cleaning up any theory can sometimes be large enough to greatly enhance its utility. I believe that this is true, for example, in AFL theory. (This is discussed

at greater length in Goldstine (10).) This suggests that
serious research should be done on developing cleaner treat-
ments of other areas of theoretical computer science. (The
theory of parsing immediately leaps to mind.)

Anyone who works on improving existing theories may have
to work outside of current fashion. Much of the research
community thinks that if it's not new, it's not good. Worse,
if it's not difficult, it's not good. Make something too
easy and you decrease its perceived worth. This view is
unfortunate. For example, I can justify the critique of
automaton theory outlined earlier by appealing (with hind-
sight) to broad philosophical or psychological maxims or
lessons from software engineering, but that is not the
origin of this critique. What actually happened was this:
unwilling to memorize the definition of an automaton used
in AFL theory, I started to simplify the definition by
throwing away everything that wasn't needed; this gradually
forced on me the realization that the definition of an
automaton in classical formal language theory as well as in
AFL theory is thoroughly indefensible. What seems curious
about all of this is that some of the most technically
skilled and creative theoreticians have worked with or
criticized the definition of an automaton in AFL theory; yet
none changed the definition, although it is a trivial
technical task to perform the necessary simplifications.
Why? Apparently, no one thought it worthwhile to tinker with
an established definition when there were new research vistas
to explore. Polishing and improving old results is simply
not considered real research. And that's a shame. Taking

a new look at old work ought to be just as valid a research
activity as solving old problems or posing new ones. But
for anyone willing to resist the fashionable trends, one way
to find worthwhile areas of research may be to reopen areas
that the trendsetters have declared closed.

REFERENCES

1. J. Backus, Can programming be liberated from the
    von Neumann style? A functional style and its algebra
    of programs, Comm. ACM 21 (1978), 613-641.
2. E. T. Bell, The prince of mathematicians, in The World
    of Mathematics (J. R. Newman, ed.), pp. 295-339, Simon
    and Schuster, New York, 1956.
3. J. H. Conway, Regular Algebra and Finite Machines,
    Chapman and Hall, London, 1971.
4. R. A. deMillo, R. J. Lipton, and A. J. Perlis, letter to
    ACM Forum, Comm. ACM 22 (1979), 629-630.
5. S. Eilenberg, review of Ginsburg's book (7), SIGACT
    News 8 (October-December, 1976), 11-12.
6. S. Ginsburg, The Mathematical Theory of Context-Free
    Languages, McGraw-Hill, New York, 1966.
7. S. Ginsburg, Algebraic and Automata-Theoretic Properties
    of Formal Languages, North-Holland, Amsterdam, 1975.
8. S. Ginsburg and S. A. Greibach, Abstract families of
    languages, in "Studies in Abstract Families of Lan-
    guages," Memoirs of the Am. Math. Soc., No. 87 (1969),
    1-32.
9. J. Goldstine, Automata with data storage, Proc. Conf. on
    Theoretical Computer Science, Univ. of Waterloo, Ontario,
    Canada (August, 1977), 239-246.
10. J. Goldstine, A rational theory of AFLs, Sixth Colloqui-
    um on Automata, Languages and Programming (Graz, Austria,
    July, 1979), Lecture Notes in Computer Science, No. 71,
    pp. 271-281, Springer-Verlag, Berlin, 1979.
11. S. A. Greibach, The hardest context-free language, SIAM
    J. Comput. 2 (1973), 304-310.
12. J. Hopcroft and J. Ullman, Formal Languages and their
    Relation to Automata, Addison-Wesley, Reading, Mass.,
    1969.

MORPHISMS ON FREE MONOIDS
AND LANGUAGE THEORY[1]

Arto Salomaa

Mathematics Department
University of Turku
Turku, Finland

Mathematically perhaps the simplest and most natural operation considered in language theory is a morphism between two free monoids. However, many of the very basic problems concerning such morphisms are difficult and challenging. Indeed, throughout the history of formal language theory many of the outstanding open problems as well as many of the mainstream topics have been reducible to or at least closely linked with questions about morphisms between two free monoids (or from a free monoid into itself).

The purpose of this paper is to discuss problems of this nature in formal language theory. We do not try to be exhaustive in any sense. However, our presentation includes the oldest work in formal language theory, as well as very recent topics. In fact, two of the presently very active areas of research, equality sets and grammar forms, fit very well into the framework of studies dealing with morphisms.

In the first section we study a problem of Thue that is very conveniently presentable in terms of DOL systems.

---

[1]Preparation of this paper was supported in part by the National Science Foundation under Grant No. MCS79-04012.

Related questions and open problems are discussed in the second section. The last two sections are devoted to equality
sets and forms, respectively.

I.   THUE AND LINDENMAYER

The oldest papers in formal language theory, as we see the
field today, are the papers of Thue at the beginning of this
century, such as (21) and (22). The papers are very well
written and contain a tremendous amount of material. Some of
the results, such as the existence of square-free ω-words,
have been rediscovered many times in the literature in various
disguises. The original arguments of Thue are, in general,
much more convincing than the later ones.

The heading of this section is justified by the observation that DOL systems constitute a convenient framework, both
as regards definitions and proofs, for certain properties of
ω-words. Because of this reason we want to present the arguments of this section in a rather detailed fashion. This section deals with the original problems of Thue. Modifications
and some recent results along the same lines are discussed in
Section II.

We now begin the formal details.

Triples $G = (\Sigma, h, w)$, where Σ is an alphabet,
$h : \Sigma^* \rightarrow \Sigma^*$ is a morphism and w is a word over Σ, are
referred to as <u>DOL</u> <u>systems</u>. A DOL system G defines the
following sequence $E(G)$ of words over Σ:

$$w = h^0(w), \quad h(w) = h^1(w), \quad h(h(w)) = h^2, \quad h^3(w), \quad \dots \; .$$

It also defines the following language:

$$L(G) = \{h^i(w) \mid i \geq 0\}.$$

Thus, a DOL system constitutes a very simple finitary device for language definition. Languages defined by a DOL system are referred to as DOL languages.

An infinite sequence of elements of an alphabet Σ is called an ω-word. Thus, an ω-word can be identified with a mapping of the set of nonnegative integers into Σ. A very convenient way of defining some special ω-words is provided by DOL systems as follows. Consider a DOL system $G = (\Sigma, h, w)$ such that

$$h(w) = wx, \quad \text{where} \quad x \in \Sigma^+,$$

that is, w is a proper prefix of $h(w)$, and furthermore, h is nonerasing: $h(a) \neq \lambda$ for every a in Σ. Then

$$h^2(w) = wxh(x), \quad h^3(w) = wxh(x)h^2(x)$$

and, in general,

$$h^{i+1}(w) = h^i(w)h^i(x) \quad \text{for all} \quad i \geq 0.$$

This equation shows that, for any i, $h^i(w)$ is a proper prefix of $h^{i+1}(w)$. (Observe that $h^i(x) \neq \lambda$ because h is nonerasing.) Consequently, an ω-word α can be defined as the "limit" of the sequence $h^i(w)$, $i = 0, 1, 2, \ldots$. More explicitly, α is the ω-word whose prefix of length $|h^i(w)|$ equals $h^i(w)$, for all i. The ω-word α obtained in this fashion is said to be generated by the DOL system G.

Thue's problem deals with repetitions occurring in words and ω-words. A word or an ω-word over an alphabet Σ is termed square-free (resp., cube-free) if it contains no subword of the form x^2 (resp., x^3), where x is a nonempty word. A word or an ω-word is termed strongly cube-free if it contains no subword of the form x^2a, where x is a nonempty word and a is the first letter of x. Clearly, every square-free word or ω-word is also strongly cube-free, and every strongly cube-free word or ω-word is also cube-free.

Thue's problem consists of constructing square-free words, as long as possible, over a given alphabet Σ, and preferably square-free ω-words. Whenever this is not possible, strongly cube-free words or ω-words should be constructed, again as long as possible. Applications of Thue's problem arise in a variety of quite different situations, ranging from unending chess to group theory, and also in various constructions in formal language theory.

As an initial observation, it should be noted that Thue's problem becomes easier (in a sense made precise below) if the cardinality of the alphabet Σ increases. Intuitively, this provides more "leeway." In particular, if Σ consists of only one letter then no word of length ≥ 3 is cube-free. If Σ consists of two letters, then very short words only can be square-free, as seen in the following lemma.

Lemma 1.1. No word of length ≥ 4 over an alphabet Σ with cardinality 2 is square-free. Consequently, no ω-word over Σ is square-free.

Let α be a word (resp., an ω-word) over an alphabet Σ. A word α' of the same length as α (resp., an ω-word α')

is called an <u>interpretation</u> of α if the following condition is satisfied: whenever the ith symbol (counted from the beginning) differs from the jth symbol in α, then also the ith symbol differs from the jth symbol in α'. Thus, both $a_1a_2a_3b_1a_4b_2$ and $a_1a_2a_1a_3a_1a_3$ are interpretations of the word a^3bab, whereas $a_1a_2a_3a_4a_5a_1$ is not an interpretation of a^3bab. Apart from a possible renaming of the letters, every interpretation of a word or ω-word α is obtained by providing, for each letter a in α, every occurrence of a with some lower index, where only finitely many indices may be used. Interpretations defined as above are exactly the ones used in the theory of grammar forms, cf. Section 4.

Lemma 1.2. If α (a word or an ω-word) is square-free, strongly cube-free or cube-free, then so is every interpretation α' of α.

Lemma 1.2 shows that if α is a square-free (resp., strongly cube-free, cube-free) ω-word strictly over an alphabet Σ (meaning that all letters of Σ actually occur in α) and Σ_1 is an alphabet of cardinality greater than that of Σ, then a square-free (resp., strongly cube-free, cube-free) ω-word strictly over Σ_1 can be constructed from α.

Returning to Thue's problem, we see that it is obvious that if we are able to construct a square-free (resp., strongly cube-free) ω-word over an alphabet Σ, then we can also construct arbitrarily long square-free (resp., strongly cube-free) words over Σ. (The converse implication is not so obvious; however, it turns out to be true as we shall see below.) Consequently, in view of Lemma 1.1, the best results we can hope for are the solutions to the following two problems.

(i) Construct a strongly cube-free ω-word over an alphabet with cardinality 2 (<u>strong</u> <u>cube-freeness</u> <u>problem</u>).

(ii) Construct a square-free ω-word over an alphabet with cardinality 3 (<u>square-freeness</u> <u>problem</u>).

(i) Solution to the strong cube-freeness problem. Consider a DOL system $G = (\{a,b\}, h, a)$, where the morphism h is defined by

$h(a) = ab$, $h(b) = ba$.

Then the first few words in the sequence $E(G)$ are

a, ab, abba, abbabaab, abbabaabbaababba, ...

In general, for any $i \geq 1$, the $(i+1)$st word w_{i+1} in the sequence $E(G)$ satisfies

$$w_{i+1} = w_i w_i',$$

where we denote by x' the word obtained from the word x by interchanging a and b.

Denote now by α the ω-word generated by G. We claim that α is strongly cube-free. In the proof we use the following two easily obtainable lemmas.

<u>Lemma 1.3.</u> Neither a^3 nor b^3 occurs as a subword in α. Neither $ababa$ nor $babab$ occurs as a subword in α. Consequently, every subword x of α such that $|x| = 5$ contains either a^2 or b^2 as a subword.

<u>Lemma 1.4.</u> Assume that a^2 or b^2 occurs as a subword of α, starting with the jth letter of α. Then j is even.

<u>Theorem 1.5</u>. The ω-word α is strongly cube-free.

<u>Proof</u>. Arguing indirectly, we assume that xxc, where c
is the first letter of x, is a subword of α and, furthermore, no word yyd, where d is the first letter of y and
$|y| < |x|$, is a subword of α. (In other words, xxc provides the shortest possible counterexample to Theorem 1.5.)
If $|x|$ equals 1 or 2, one of the words a^3, b^3, ababa,
babab occurs as a subword of α. Since this is impossible by
Lemma 1.3, we conclude that

$$|x| = t \geq 3.$$

Assume that the occurrence of xxc we are considering
starts with the jth letter of α. Hence, denoting the ith
letter of α by c_i,

$$c_j \ldots c_{j+2t} = xxc.$$

By Lemma 1.3, either a^2 or b^2 occurs as a subword in
xx. This implies that either a^2 or b^2 occurs twice as a
subword in xxc. Indeed, a^2 or b^2 must occur as a subword
either in x or else in xc. In both cases, it occurs twice
as a subword in xxc.

We can now conclude by Lemma 1.4 that $|x| = t$ is even.
For if t is odd then at least one of the occurrences of a^2
or b^2 in xxc must start with the kth letter of α, for
some odd k. But this is impossible by Lemma 1.4.

Consequently, t = 2u for some natural number u. We
assume first that j is even and, hence, $j \geq 2$. We now
choose a large enough i (such that $|w_i| \geq j + 2t$) and make
use of the relation $w_i = h(w_{i-1})$. We conclude that

$$c_{j-1}c_j = ab \quad \text{or} \quad c_{j-1}c_j = ba.$$

That implies that also

$$c_{j-1+t}c_{j+t} = ab \quad \text{or} \quad c_{j-1+t}c_{j+t} = ba$$

because $j + t$ is even. But $c_j = c_{j+t}$ which now gives the
result $c_{j-1} = c_{j-1+t}$. Consequently,

$$c_n = c_{n+t} \quad \text{for every} \quad n \quad \text{with} \quad j - 1 \le n \le j + t.$$

For $0 \le n \le t$, the word $c_{j-1+2n}c_{n+2n}$ equals either $h(a)$
or $h(b)$. This follows because of the relation $w_i = h(w_{i-1})$
and because $j - 1$ is odd. We now infer that w_{i-1} contains
a subword yyd, where d is the first letter of y and
$|y| = \frac{t}{2} = u$. Hence, also α contains yyd as a subword.
But this contradicts the choice of x.

The case of j being odd is handled in the same way, considering the letter c_{j+2t+1} instead of c_{j-1}. $\square$

(ii) Solution to the square-freeness problem. We now turn
to the discussion of the problem of constructing a square-free
ω-word over an alphabet with cardinality 3. In fact, we are
able to reduce the entire matter to the already established
Theorem 1.5. This becomes possible by applying a technique
very common and useful in formal language theory. The technique consists of grouping several letters into one. By this
technique, we obtain first the following lemma.

Lemma 1.6. There exists a square-free ω-word β over an
alphabet with four letters.

Proof. Consider the ω-word α of Theorem 1.5. We define
a new alphabet Σ_1 by

$$\Sigma_1 = \{[aa], [ab], [ba], [bb]\}.$$

We now define an ω-word

$$\beta = d_1 \, d_2 \, d_3 \, \ldots$$

over the alphabet Σ_1 by the condition

$$d_j = [c_j c_{j+1}] \quad \text{for every} \quad j \geq 1,$$

where c_j is the jth letter of α. Lemma 1.6 is now an immediate consequence of Theorem 1.5. $\square$

We now strengthen Lemma 1.6 to the result we are looking for. For this purpose it will be convenient to abbreviate the letters of Σ_1 as follows:

$$[aa] = 1, \quad [ab] = 2, \quad [ba] = 3, \quad [bb] = 4.$$

In this notation, the beginning of β is

$$\beta = 24323124312324323123243123432312\ldots \; .$$

The following lemma is easy to establish.

Lemma 1.7. Every occurrence of the letter 1 in β is preceded by an occurrence of 3 and followed by an occurrence of 2. Every occurrence of the letter 4 in β is preceded by an occurrence of 2 and followed by an occurrence of 3.

We are now ready for the main result.

Theorem 1.8. There exists a square-free ω-word γ over an alphabet with three letters.

Proof. Consider the alphabet $\Sigma_2 = \{1, 2, 3\}$. The ω-word γ is obtained from β by replacing 4 with 1. Thus, the beginning of γ is

$\gamma = 213231213123213231232132132312...$.

We will show that γ is square-free.

Assume the contrary: xx occurs as a subword in γ, where x is a nonempty word. This implies that β contains a subword $y_1 y_2$ such that

$$|y_1| = |y_2| = |x| = t$$

and, furthermore, y_1 and y_2 become identical when every occurrence of the letter 4 is replaced by the letter 1.

We observe first that $t \geq 2$ because, by Lemma 1.7, none of the words 11, 14, 41, 44 occurs as a subword in β.

Let

$$y_1 = d_{j+1} \cdots d_{j+t}, \quad y_2 = d_{j+t+1} \cdots d_{j+2t}.$$

Thus, for every n satisfying $1 \leq n \leq t$, $d_{j+n} = d_{j+n+t}$ with the possible exception of the case where one of the numbers d_{j+n} and d_{j+n+t} equals 1 and the other equals 4. We shall prove that this exceptional case is, in fact, impossible.

Consider first a fixed value of n satisfying $1 \leq n < t$. By Lemma 1.7, if d_{j+n} equals 1 (resp., 4) then d_{j+n+1} equals 2 (resp., 3). Hence, also $d_{j+n+1+t}$ equals 2 (resp., 3), by our assumption concerning y_1 and y_2. Thus, another application of Lemma 1.7 gives us the result

$$d_{j+n} = d_{j+n+t} \quad \text{whenever} \quad 1 \leq n < t.$$

Consider, secondly, the letters d_{j+t} and d_{j+2t}. Instead of successors, we use now predecessors in our argument based on Lemma 1.7. If d_{j+t} equals 1 (resp., 4), then

d_{j+t-1} equals 3 (resp., 2). Consequently, also d_{j+2t-1} equals 3 (resp., 2). Hence, $d_{j+t} = d_{j+2t}$, which combined with our previous result shows that $(d_{j+1} \cdots d_{j+t})^2$ occurs as a subword in β, contradicting Lemma 1.6. Our assumption about xx occurring as a subword in γ is wrong, whence Theorem 1.8 follows. $\square$

II. PROBLEMS ABOUT INFINITE WORDS

By definition, a word or an ω-word w is square-free if it does not contain a subword of the form xx, where x is nonempty. It is still conceivable that w could contain two "overlapping" occurrences of x, i.e., a subword $xy = zx$, where

$$1 \leq |y| = |z| < |x|.$$

However, the following lemma shows that this is not possible.

Lemma 2.1. Assume that a word or an ω-word w contains a subword xy such that $xy = zx$ and $1 \leq |y| = |z| < |x|$. Then w is not square-free.

Proof. It is easily seen that the equation $xy = zx$, where y and z are nonempty, implies the existence of words u, v and an integer k such that

$$z = uv, \quad y = vu, \quad x = (uv)^k u.$$

From this the lemma immediately follows. $\square$

Thue considered also a notion stronger than square-freeness. He called an ω-word over Σ with cardinality n "irreducible" if, whenever it contains a subword xyx where x is nonempty, then $|y| \geq n - 2$. Thus, for $n = 3$, this

notion coincides with the notion of square-freeness. Given
any alphabet Σ , an irreducible ω -word over Σ can be constructed. (Observe that for n $\leq$ 2 every ω -word is trivially
irreducible.)

The condition of two occurrences of x lying apart can be
further strengthened by requiring that the length of the word
y separating the occurrences is bounded from below by $|x|$.
Along these lines, the following result can be obtained.

Theorem 2.2. If Σ is of cardinality $\geq$ 3, there is an
ω -word w over Σ such that, whenever xyx with $x \neq \lambda$ is
a subword of w, then $|y| \geq \frac{1}{3}|x|$.

The proof of Theorem 2.2 is given in [11]. A w as required is generated by the DOL system $(\{a, b, c\}, h, a)$,
where

    h(a) = abc acb cab c bac bca cba,

    h(b) = bca bac abc a cba cab acb,

    h(c) = cab cba bca b acb abc bac.

It is also discussed in [11] why $|h(a)|$ cannot be smaller
and shown that the constant $\frac{1}{3}$ is the best possible in the
following sense. Assume that the cardinality of Σ equals
3. Then every word over Σ with length $\geq$ 39 contains a
subword xyx with the properties $x \neq \lambda$ and $|y| \leq \frac{1}{3}|x|$.

Not much is known about the ω -words generated by DOL systems. We now discuss some problems in this area. Many of
them are at least closely linked with some currently very
active research topics.

Observe first that the ω -word α of Theorem 1.5 is also
generated by the DOL system

$G_1 = (\{a,b\}, h, abba)$, where $h(a) = ab$, $h(b) = ba$,

as well as by the DOL system

$G_2 = (\{a,b\}, h_1, a)$, where $h_1(a) = abba$, $h_1(b) = baab$.

This is a special case of the following more general result, the proof of which is immediate by the definitions.

Lemma 2.3. Assume that δ is the ω-word generated by the DOL system (Σ, h, w) and that $i \geq 1$ and $j \geq 0$ are integers. Then δ is generated also by the DOL system $(\Sigma, h^i, h^j(w))$.

It may also happen that the original DOL system does not generate an ω-word (because w is not a prefix of $h(w)$) but there still exist numbers i and j such that the DOL system $(\Sigma, h^i, h^j(w))$ generates an ω-word.

It is difficult to decide whether or not an ω-word defined by some other effective method can also be defined by a DOL system. This can be stated as a precise decision problem for each class of effective methods defining ω-words.

For instance, the ω-word β of Lemma 1.6 was not originally defined by a DOL system. However, β is generated by the DOL system $(\{1, 2, 3, 4\}, h, 2)$, where

$h(1) = 2\ 4\ 3\ 1, \quad h(2) = 2\ 4\ 3\ 2,$
$h(3) = 3\ 1\ 2\ 3, \quad h(4) = 3\ 1\ 2\ 4.$

On the other hand, Berstel [2] has shown that a certain square-free ω-word, due originally to Arson, is not generated by any DOL system.

No general method is known for deciding whether or not the ω-word generated by a DOL system G is square-free. In [1], such a method is given for the case where the alphabet of G consists of three letters.

We say that a morphism h preserves square-freeness if h(x) is square-free whenever x is square-free. Clearly, the ω-word δ generated by the DOL system (Σ, h, w), where w is square-free and h preserves square-freeness, is itself square-free (providing, of course, that the conditions for generating an ω-word are satisfied). For instance, Thue shows in [22] that the morphism h_1 defined by

$h_1(a)$ = abcab, $h_1(b)$ = acabcb, $h_1(c)$ = acbcacb

is square-free. Thus, the DOL system ({a, b, c}, h_1, a) generates a square-free ω-word.

However, a DOL system (Σ, h, w) may generate a square-free ω-word although h does not preserve square-freeness. An example is provided by the DOL system ({a, b, c}, h_2, a), where h_2 is defined by

$h_2(a)$ = abc, $h_2(b)$ = ac, $h_2(c)$ = b.

It can be shown that the generated ω-word is square-free. However, h_2 does not preserve square-freeness because

$h_2(aba)$ = abcacabc.

Perhaps the most celebrated decision problem dealing with morphisms is the DOL (sequence) equivalence problem: to construct an algorithm for deciding whether or not two DOL systems generate the same sequence. The problem was first solved in [6]; [12] gives an essentially simpler solution.   The

reader is referred to [18] for further details, and to [18]

and [20] for related topics.

As regards ω-words, the analogous problem is still open.

Consider two DOL systems

$$G_i = (\Sigma, h_i, w_i), \quad i = 1, 2,$$

with the same alphabet Σ,   and satisfying the condition for

generating ω-words: w_i is a proper prefix of $h_i(w_i)$.   We

then state the following.

Conjecture.   It is decidable whether or not the systems

G_i generate the same ω-word.

There is no direct interrelation between the sequence

equivalence and ω-word equivalence of two DOL systems: the

systems can generate the same ω-word without being sequence

equivalent.   Clearly, if the systems are sequence equivalent

and generate ω-words then they generate the same ω-words.

A DOL system $G = (\Sigma, h, w)$ may also generate several

ω-words in the sense that different ω-words may be generated

by the systems

$$(\Sigma, h^i, h^j(w))$$

obtained by "decomposing" the original system.   The collection

of all such ω-words is referred to as the ω-language generated

by the DOL system G.   Clearly, an ω-language generated by a

DOL system is always finite, i.e., consists of only finitely

many ω-words.

Consider now the following "ω-language equivalence" prob-

lem for DOL systems: given two arbitrary DOL systems G_1 and

G_2, decide whether or not G_1 and G_2 generate the same
ω-language. By the sophisticated technique of [15], we may
first decide whether or not the ω-language of G_i is empty.
In case it is not empty, we obtain also a bound for the powers
of the morphism giving rise to possibly different ω-words.
The identity of such words can be tested pairwise, provided
the above conjecture is true. Hence, we have established the
following result.

Lemma 2.4. Assuming the conjecture above is true then the
ω-language equivalence problem is decidable for DOL systems.

III.   EQUALITY SETS

Consider two homomorphisms h_1 and h_2 mapping Σ^* into
Σ_1^*, where Σ_1 is a possibly different alphabet. The equality set for the pair (h_1, h_2) is defined by

$$E(h_1, h_2) = \{w \in \Sigma^* \mid h_1(w) = h_2(w)\}.$$

Equality sets have been the object of an intensive study
during the past two years. This study was initiated by considerations connected with the DOL sequence equivalence problem: two DOL systems

$$G_i = (\Sigma, h_i, w), \quad i = 1, 2,$$

are sequence equivalent if and only if

$$L(G_1) \subseteq E(h_1, h_2).$$

The purpose of this section is to give a brief overview
on equality sets.

By standard coding techniques it is immediately seen that
we may always assume that Σ_1 consists of two letters only,
i.e., every equality set is obtained using such a range alphabet. A further reduction to a one-letter alphabet is not
possible: it is shown in [19] that equality sets, where the
range alphabet consists of one letter only, are context-free,
which is not true of equality sets in general.

On the other hand, coding techniques are not applicable
for the reduction of the domain alphabet Σ. For instance,
[7] and [10] investigate the case where Σ consists of two
letters. The techniques and results cannot be extended to the
general case.

What kind of languages are equality sets? This is quite
a widely investigated topic. The following result gives an
indication of the "expressive power" of equality sets. For a
proof, as well as for other similar results, the reader is referred to [19], [13] or [8].

Theorem 3.1. For every recursively enumerable language L,
one can effectively construct an equality set E, a regular
language R and a homomorphism h such that $L = h(E \cap R)$.

This result can be further strengthened, [5], to a purely
homomorphic characterization as follows. Observe first that
every equality set is a star event, i.e., of the form L^* for
some language L. We say that a language is a minimal equality set if it equals the minimal star root of an equality set.

Theorem 3.2. For every recursively enumerable language L,
one can effectively construct a minimal equality set E_{min}
and a homomorphism h such that $L = h(E_{min})$.

We give now some examples of equality sets of different complexities. Consider first two homomorphisms h_1 and h_2 defined by

$$h_1(a) = h_2(b) = a, \quad h_2(a) = h_1(b) = aa.$$

It is immediately verified that $E(h_1, h_2)$ consists of all words w such that the number of occurrences of a in w equals that of b in w. Thus, we have here a simple example of a context-free nonregular equality set.

The following example due to [14] is very interesting in many respects.

Let

$$g, h : \{a, b, c, d, e, f\}^* \rightarrow \{1, 2, 3, 4, 5\}^*$$

be homomorphisms defined by the table

	a	b	c	d	e	f
g	1234	2323	4	24	32	5
h	1	23	4	42	3232	4325

Then it is easy to verify that

$$E(g, h) = (\{abcb^2 \ldots cb^{2^n} de^{2^n} c \ldots e^2 cef \mid n \geq 0\} \cup c)^*.$$

In fact, if words c^i are disregarded, then every word in the equality set must begin with an occurrence of a. After that the continuation is determined by the requirement that h must "catch up the faster running" g. The only nondeterministic choice is that concerning the middle position. It is interesting to observe that the idea behind the proofs of

Theorems 3.1 and 3.2 is the same: there one considers two homomorphisms, one of which runs faster on a derivation sequence.

The above example is interesting also because of the following reason. In the applications of equality sets to decidability questions it is very desirable that the equality sets considered belong to a family of languages with strong decidability properties, such as the family of regular languages. In some cases this is indeed true, as we shall now see.

We say that a homomorphism $h : \Sigma^* \to \Sigma_1^*$ has <u>bounded delay</u> from left to right if there exists a natural number k such that, for all u and v in Σ^* and all a and b in Σ, whenever $h(au)$ is a prefix of $h(bv)$ and $|u| \geq k - 1$, then a = b. The notion of bounded delay from right to left is defined analogously. (Clearly, every bounded delay homomorphism is a code.)

<u>Theorem 3.3</u>. If h_1 and h_2 are homomorphisms with bounded delay in the same direction then $E(h_1, h_2)$ is regular. If h_1 has bounded delay in both directions and h_2 is arbitrary then $E(h_1, h_2)$ is regular.

Theorem 3.3 is established in [14], following the ideas of [12], where it was shown that the equality set between two elementary homomorphisms is always regular. (Indeed, this result was an important step in the proof of the decidability of the DOL sequence equivalence problem.)

Returning to the above example with the morphisms g and h, we see now that Theorem 3.3 cannot be strengthened to concern the case where h_1 and h_2 have bounded delay in different directions. This follows because g has bounded delay

from left to right with k = 1 (i.e., g is a prefix code),
and h has bounded delay from right to left also with k = 1.

We would like to emphasize that it is not known whether
the equality sets of Theorem 3.3 are effectively regular. If
this were the case, then the Post correspondence problem (PCP)
would be decidable for the corresponding class of homomorphisms. (Observe that solving PCP amounts to deciding the emptiness of an equality set.) In particular, this would imply the
decidability of PCP's with only two words in the lists. But
even the latter problem is still open, although [7] contains
some partial results. In fact, the decidability of PCP has
not been established so far for any class of homomorphisms.
[14] contains the result that the emptiness of $E(h_1, h_2)$ is
decidable if one of h_1 and h_2, say h_1, is periodic, i.e.,
$h_1(\Sigma) \subseteq w^*$ for some word w.

We conclude this section with a brief mention of some other
results. [3] gives characterizations of complexity classes in
terms of equality sets. In [4] the notion of an equality set
is extended to concern the equality of n homomorphisms.
According to [9] it is decidable whether a given context-free
language is contained in a given equality set. It is shown in
[10] that every language L over {a, b} possesses a finite
subset (test set) L_0 with the following property. L is
contained in an equality set E if and only if L_0 is contained in E.

IV. FORMS

Grammar and L forms have constituted during the past few years one of the most vividly investigated research areas in language theory. For an overview the reader is referred to [23]. The purpose of this section is only to point out some interesting recent results and open problems that fit nicely into the framework of morphisms. The attention is restricted to grammar forms only. We give first the basic definitions.

A finite substitution μ defined on an alphabet V is said to be a <u>dfl-substitution</u> (a disjoint finite letter substitution) if, for any a in V, μ(a) is a finite set of letters and, moreover, a ≠ b implies μ(a) ∩ μ(b) = φ.

A (<u>context-free</u>) <u>grammar</u> <u>form</u> is a context-free grammar G = (V, Σ, P, S). (Here V is the total alphabet, Σ the terminal alphabet, P the production set, and S the initial letter.) Given a dfl-substitution μ defined on V, we say that a context-free grammar G' = (V', Σ', P', S') is an <u>interpretation</u> of G modulo μ, in symbols G' ◁ G(μ), if the following conditions (i) - (iv) obtain:

(i) μ(A) ⊆ V' - Σ' for all A in V - Σ;

(ii) μ(a) ⊆ Σ' for all a in Σ;

(iii) P' ⊆ μ(P), where μ(P) = {B → y : B is in μ(A),
                y is in μ(x), for some A → x in P};

(iv) S' is in μ(S).

The <u>language</u> <u>family</u> generated by the grammar form G is defined by

$L(G) = \{L(G') : G' \lhd G(\mu) \quad \text{for some} \quad \mu\}.$

Language families generated by grammar forms are referred to as <u>grammatical</u>.

Observe that if $G' \lhd G$ then every word of $L(G')$ is an interpretation (in the sense defined in Section I) of a word in $L(G)$. Observe also that μ^{-1} is always a length preserving homomorphism.

Consider the following examples. Each grammar form is given by listing the productions.

F_1 : $S \to ab$, $S \to ba$;

F_2 : $S \to aa$;

F_3 : $S \to aS$, $S \to a$;

F_4 : $S \to aSa$, $S \to a$, $S \to a^2$;

F_5 : $S \to aS$, $S \to Sa$, $S \to a$;

F_6 : $S \to A$, $S \to B$, $A \to A^2$, $A \to a^2$, $B \to aB$, $B \to Ba$, $B \to a$;

F_7 : $S \to SS$, $S \to a$.

Here F_1 and F_2 are finite forms: their language is finite and, consequently, every language in their language family is finite. The family of F_3 equals the family $L(REG)$ of regular languages. (Indeed, we get only regular languages not containing λ. However, we make the customary convention that languages and language families are considered modulo λ.) Similarly, F_5 and F_7 generate the families $L(LIN)$ and $L(CF)$ of linear and context-free languages, respectively. It can also be shown that, for every $i \leq 6$, $L(F_i)$ is strictly contained in $L(F_{i+1})$. The reason why F_6 does not generate

$L(CF)$ is that expansions are possible in the generation of even-length words only--words of odd length are generated in a linear fashion. Similarly, the reason why F_4 does not generate the whole $L(LIN)$ is in the restricted capability for "pumping": for instance, the language

$$\{a^{2n}b^n \mid n \geq 1\}$$

is not in the family of F_4.

The above examples indicate some of the phenomena typical for the language families of grammar forms. With the exception of the form F_1, all of the forms are unary, i.e., have only one terminal letter. Forms with several terminal letters are, in general, more difficult to handle. In such cases it is often useful to consider a-restrictions F_a of a given form F. Such an a-restriction (where a is a terminal letter) is obtained from F by removing all productions containing terminals $b \neq a$.

We say that a grammatical family L is unary-complete if, whenever a grammar form F satisfies $L(F) = L$, then F also possesses an a-restriction F_a satisfying $L(F_a) = L$.

Theorem 4.1. The families of regular and linear languages are unary-complete.

Theorem 4.2. There is an algorithm for deciding whether or not a given grammar form F satisfies (i) $L(F) = L(REG)$, (ii) $L(F) = L(LIN)$.

Theorems 4.1 and 4.2 are from [16]. In fact, a stronger version of Theorem 4.2 is given in [16]: not only an algorithm but a rather easily verifiable characterization for the satisfaction of (i) and (ii). Observe that each form F such that $L(F) = L(LIN)$ can be viewed as a "normal form" for linear grammars. Thus, a characterization of (ii) gives a characterization of all possible normal forms.

Theorems 4.1 and 4.2 can be extended to concern the family $L(CF)$ as well, provided the following conjecture is true.

Conjecture. Assume that (i, j, k) is a triple of non-negative integers. Then every context-free language L is generated by a grammar whose productions are of the two types (i) $A \to w$ and (ii) $A \to w_i Bw_j Cw_k$, where A, B, C are non-terminals and w's are terminals such that $|w_i| = i$, $|w_j| = j$, $|w_k| = k$. Moreover, $|w|$ in type (i) productions assumes values from the length set of L only.

If the last sentence ("Moreover...") is removed from the above conjecture, then the resulting statement is known to be true.

Perhaps the most interesting phenomena about grammatical families deal with density. In fact, no other collections of language families obtained by generative devices are known to possess such a density property. We conclude the paper with a few remarks about this topic.

Assume that L and L' are grammatical families such that $L \subsetneq L'$. The pair (L, L') is said to be dense if, whenever L_1 and L_2 are grammatical families satisfying

$$L \subseteq L_1 \subsetneq L_2 \subseteq L',$$

then there is a grammatical family L_3 such that

$$L_1 \subsetneq L_3 \subsetneq L_2.$$

Theorem 4.3. The pair $(L(REG), L(CF))$ is dense.

Theorem 4.3 is established in [17], where also other dense pairs are given and the question of the "maximality of such pairs (for instance, whether $(L_1, L(CF))$ is dense for some $L_1 \subsetneq L(REG)$ is investigated.

As regards finite forms, very interesting problems remain open. Moreover, these problems can be considered as basic problems about morphisms.

For instance, it is not known whether there are dense pairs whose components are generated by finite forms. (It is easy to see that if F is a finite and G an infinite form then the pair $(L(F), L(G))$ is not dense.) As regards the examples listed above,

$$(L(F_1), L(F_2))$$

is a reasonable candidate for such a dense pair. We can at least show that if L_3 is a grammatical family satisfying

$$L(F_1) \subsetneq L_3 \subsetneq L(F_2),$$

then there are grammatical families L_4 and L_5 such that

$$L(F_1) \subsetneq L_4 \subsetneq L_3 \subsetneq L_5 \subsetneq L(F_2).$$

REFERENCES

1. Berstel, J., Sur les mots sans carré définis par un morphisme. Springer Lecture Notes in Computer Science 71, 16-25 (1979).
2. Berstel, J., Most sans carré et morphismes itérés. Univ. Paris 7, Institut de Programmation, Tech. Rep. 78-42 (1978).
3. Book, R.V., and Brandenburg, F.-J., Representing complexity classes by equality sets. Springer Lecture Notes in Computer Science 71, 49-57 (1979).
4. Brandenburg, F.-J., Multiple equality sets and Post machines. Submitted for publication.
5. Culik, II, K., A purely homomorphic characterization of recursively enumerable sets. JACM 26, 345-350 (1979).
6. Culik, II, K, and Fris, I., The decidability of the equivalence problem for DOL-systems. Information and Control 35, 20-39 (1977).

7. Culik, II, K., and Karhumäki, J., On the equality sets for homomorphisms on free monoids with two generators. RAIRO, to appear.

8. Culik, II, K., and Maurer, H., On simple representations of language families. RAIRO, to appear.

9. Culik, II, K., and Salomaa, A., On the decidability of homomorphism equivalence for languages. JCSS 17, 163-175 (1978).

10. Culik, II, K., and Salomaa, A., Test sets and checking words for homomorphism equivalence. Univ. Waterloo, Computer Science Res. Rep. CS-79-04 (1979).

11. Dejean, F., Sur un théorème de Thue. J. Combinatorial Theory 13, Ser. A, 90-99 (1972).

12. Ehrenfeucht, A., and Rozenberg, G., Elementary homomorphisms and a solution of the DOL sequence equivalence problem. Theoretical Computer Science 7, 169-183 (1978).

13. Engelfriet, J., and Rozenberg, G., Equality languages and fixed point languages. Information and Control, to appear.

14. Karhumäki, J., and Simon, I., A note on elementary homomorphisms and the regularity of equality sets. EATCS Bulletin, to appear.

15. Linna, M., The decidability of the DOL prefix problem. International Journal of Computer Mathematics 6, 127-142 (1977).

16. Maurer, H., Salomaa, A., and Wood, D., Context-free grammar forms with strict interpretations. JCSS, to appear.

17. Maurer, H., Salomaa, A., and Wood, D., Dense hierarchies of grammatical families. JACM, to appear.

18. Rozenberg, G., and Salomaa, A., "The Mathematical Theory of L Systems." Academic Press (1980).

19. Salomaa, A., Equality sets for homomorphisms of free monoids. Acta Cybernetica 4, 127-139 (1978).

20. Salomaa, A., and Soittola, M., "Automata-Theoretic Aspects of Formal Power Series." Springer-Verlag (1978).

21. Thue, A., Über unendliche Zeichenreihen. Norsk. Vid. Selsk. Skr. I, Mat.-Nat. Kl. Nr. 7, 1-22 (1906).

22. Thue, A., Über die gegenseitige Lage gleicher Teile gewisser Zeichenreihen. Norsk. Vid. Selsk. Skr. I, Mat.-Nat. Kl. Nr. 1, 1-67 (1912).

23. Wood, D., "Grammar and L Forms." Springer-Verlag, in preparation.

HOMOMORPHISMS: DECIDABILITY, EQUALITY
AND TEST SETS[1]

Karel Culik II

Department of Computer Science
University of Waterloo
Waterloo, Ontario, Canada

I.   INTRODUCTION

We survey a number of recent results and open problems on homomorphisms on free monoids. Except for the last section, dealing with representation of language families, most of the results are decidability results. They were motivated or directly constitute problems in L-systems theory. However all of them are basic problems about free monoids and as such are not only of purely mathematical interest but also, since they are all simply formulated decidability problems, are of fundamental interest for theoretical computer science.

Whenever possible we give an algebraic formulation of each problem so that reading, not only the whole paper, but even a particular problem or theorem does not require any specialized knowledge. Open problems are specifically of interest.

[1]Research supported in part by the Natural Sciences and Engineering Research Council of Canada under Grant No. A-7403. Preparation of this paper was supported in part by the National Science Foundation under Grant No. MCS79-04012.

which makes us stress some topics. The only new results in
this paper are some relations among the open problems (conjectures) mostly very easily shown.

In Section II we deal with iterations of one or more homomorphisms (DOL, HDOL, DTOL systems) and some generalizations
thereof. The next section is about "homomorphism equivalence
on languages," i.e., the problem whether two given homomorphisms agree "string by string" on a given language, and its
applications to transducers.

In Section IV we consider elementary homomorphisms and
questions about equality sets, in particular over a binary
alphabet. In the next section we consider "homomorphism compatibility on languages," i.e., the problem whether there exists a string in given languages on which two given
homomorphisms agree, in particular various restricted forms
of the Post Correspondence Problem.

In Section VI we discuss the Ehrenfeucht conjecture: Each
language possesses a finite subset such that any two homomorphisms which agree (string by string) on the subset agree also
on the whole language. Some partial solutions are discussed.
Finally in the last section we list some new representation
theorems for language families based on equality sets and related phenomena.

Preliminaries

We consider homomorphisms $\Sigma^* \to \Delta^*$, where Σ^*, Δ^* are free
monoids generated by finite alphabets Σ, Δ. The monoid unit
(empty word) is denoted by ε, the length of a word w in Σ^* by
$|w|$. We also use $|n|$ to denote the absolute value of number n.
The cardinality of set S is denoted by card S.

An alphabet Σ, homomorphism $h : \Sigma^* \to \Sigma^*$ and an (initial) word w in Σ^* form a DOL system $G = (\Sigma,h,w)$. The sequence generated by G, denoted $E(G)$, is defined by $E(G) = w$, $h(w)$, $h^2(w)$, $\ldots,$; the language generated by G, denoted $L(G)$, is defined by $L(G) = \{h^n(w) \mid n \geq 0\}$.

A DOL system G and another homomorphism g form an HDOL system $K = \langle G,g \rangle$. It generates the sequence

$$E(K) = g(w), \ g(h(w)), \ g(h^2(w)), \ \ldots$$

and the language

$$L(K) = g(L(G)) = \{g(h^n(w)) \mid n \geq 0\}.$$

A DTOL system G is a tuple $(\Sigma, h_1, \ldots, h_n, w)$ where $h_i : \Sigma^* \to \Sigma^*$ for $i = 1, \ldots, n$. It generates a set of sequences

$$\{w, h_{i_1}(w), h_{i_1}(h_{i_2}(w)), \ldots \mid \text{each } i_j \in \{1, \ldots, n\}\}$$

and the language

$$L(G) = \{h_{i_1}(h_{i_2}(\ldots h_{i_k}(w)\ldots)) \mid i_1, \ldots, i_k \in \{1,\ldots,n\}\}$$

For homomorphisms g, $h : \Sigma^* \to \Delta^*$ the equality set for the pair (g,h) is denoted by $E(g,h)$ and defined by $E(g,h) = \{x \in \Sigma^* \mid g(x) = h(x)\}$.

A deterministic generalized sequential mapping (dgsm mapping) is a mapping defined by deterministic generalized sequential machine with accepting states (dgsm) as in [32].

For other standard definitions and notations we refer the reader to [40], [41], or [47].

II.   ITERATED HOMOMORPHISMS

We will discuss a number of decision problems about iterative homomorphisms. The following problem and techniques
used in its proof stimulated most of the research reported in
this paper.

Theorem 2.1 [15].   (DOL sequence equivalence problem)
Given two homomorphisms g, h : $\Sigma^* \rightarrow \Sigma^*$ and w in Σ^*, it is decidable whether $g^n(w) = h^n(w)$ for all $n \geq 0$.

The strategy of the solution of this problem is to show
that any two (normal) equivalent systems must behave in certain "similar" ways and then to show the decidability for
similar systems only. Here a pair of DOL systems is similar
if the pair (g,h) has "bounded balance" on the language
$\{g^n(w) \mid n \geq 0\}$.

The <u>balance</u> of a string w in Σ^* with respect to a pair of
homomorphisms g, h on Σ^* is defined as

$$B(w) = |g(w)| - |h(w)|.$$

The pair (g,h) is said to have <u>bounded balance</u> on language L
if there is a C > 0 so that $|B(w)| \leq C$ for each prefix of
every word in L.

A property of a pair of DOL systems $G_1 = (\Sigma,g,w)$ and
$G_2 = (\Sigma,h,w)$ equivalent to "bounded balance" is introduced in
[15]. The pair (G_1,G_2) is said to have a <u>true</u> <u>envelope</u> R if
$L(G_1) \cup L(G_2) \subseteq R \subseteq E(g,h)$. Obviously, if a pair (G_1,G_2) has
a true envelope, then G_1 and G_2 are sequence equivalent. It
is shown in [15] that a pair of equivalent DOL systems
(G_1,G_2) has a regular true envelope iff the pair of homomorphisms (g,h) has bounded balance on $L(G_1)$, and consequently

that each pair of equivalent normal DOL systems has a regular true envelope. The latter result is extended in [25] to all pairs of equivalent DOL systems.

The "bounded balance technique" is also useful when testing homomorphism equivalence discussed in Section III   (see [20]). The same holds also for another technique introduced in [8], the "shifting argument." Roughly speaking, it is used to show that if homomorphisms g, h agree on two words of the form xwy and uwv, i.e., with a common subword w, where w is "sufficiently long" and $|B(x) - B(u)|$ "sufficiently small," then either $B(x) = B(u)$ or $g(w)$ and $h(w)$ are periodic.

The bounded balance technique is not helpful in proving the following generalization of the DOL sequence equivalence problem.

Conjecture 2.2.   (HDOL equivalence problem)   Given four homomorphisms $g_1 : \Sigma_1^* \to \Sigma_1^*$, $g_2 : \Sigma_1^* \to \Sigma_2^*$, $h_1 : \Delta_1^* \to \Delta_1^*$, $h_2 : \Delta_1^* \to \Delta_2^*$ and strings $u \in \Sigma_1^*$, $v \in \Delta_1^*$, it is decidable whether $g_2(g_1^n(u)) = h_2(h_1^n(v))$.

We show later a problem equivalent to the HDOL equivalence problem (Theorem 3.3). There are two other interesting extensions of DOL equivalence which have been shown decidable by reducing them to DOL equivalence (Theorems 2.3 and 2.6). The proof of the following theorem also uses results about monoids generated by integer matrices obtained by [34] and by [37].

Theorem 2.3 [10].   (Ultimate sequence equivalence)   Given two homomorphisms g, h : $\Sigma^* \to \Sigma^*$ and u, v in Σ^* it is decidable whether there exists $n \geq 0$ such that $g^k(u) = h^k(v)$ for all $k \geq n$.

It is natural to ask whether sequence equivalence remains decidable for more complicated mappings than homomorphisms, in particular for mappings defined symbol by symbol but in a context dependent manner. This is also strongly biologically motivated since such mappings abstract developmental systems of higher level where individual cells interact, i.e., their behavior is context dependent. The simplest case is dependence on one symbol at the left, the so-called D1L system. The sequence equivalence has been shown undecidable even for propagating (nonerasing) version of these systems.

Theorem 2.4 [52]. The PD1L sequence equivalence problem is undecidable.

In the view of the last theorem it is rather surprising that the equivalence problem becomes decidable when the rewriting of a letter might depend on one neighbor from each side but only when the letter is being rewritten by at least two new letters. That is any letter-to-letter rewriting must be context free (no erasing is allowed). A deterministic system based on this type of rewriting is introduced in [16] and called an e-GD2L system. Two main results of [16] are that e-GD2L systems have essentially context-free behavior and that the sequence equivalence for them is decidable. The former result could be compared to "Baker's Theorem" [29, Theorem 10.2.1] giving a condition under which context-sensitive grammar generates a context-free language.

Theorem 2.5. If the sequence s_0, s_1, ... is generated by an e-GD2L system, then there exist a nonerasing homomorphism h and a letter-to-letter homomorphism (coding) g so that $s_n = g(h^n(s_0))$ for all $n \geq 0$.

Theorem 2.6 [16].   The sequence equivalence problem for e-GD2L systems is decidable.

We are not directing our attention here to the languages generated by various parallel rewriting systems, but for completeness of the decidability results we mention the following two theorems.   The DOL language equivalence had already been reduced to DOL sequence equivalence in [38] before the latter was shown to be decidable.   Recently even the inclusion problem has been shown decidable.

Theorem 2.7 [45].   The inclusion problem for DOL languages is decidable.

In the nondeterministic case we have the following result which follows from the undecidability of the equality problem for sentential forms of context-free languages.

Theorem 2.8 [3].   The equivalence problem for OL (even POL) languages is undecidable.

Another biologically important generalization of DOL systems is obtained when several starting strings and several homomorphisms (tables) are considered.   Given two such systems with matching starting strings and matching pairs of homomorphisms we can ask whether all "matching" sequences are identical.

Consider

$$(h_1, \ldots, h_n), (h_1', \ldots, h_n') \tag{2.1}$$

where h_i, h_i' are homomorphisms $\Sigma^* \to \Sigma^*$, for $i = 1, \ldots, n$.

Conjecture 2.9.   (DTOL sequence equivalence)   Given strings $w, w' \in \Sigma^*$ and homomorphisms (2.1) it is decidable whether

$$h_{i_1}(h_{i_2}(\ldots h_{i_k}(w)\ldots)) = h'_{i_1}(h'_{i_2}(\ldots h'_{i_k}(w')\ldots))$$

for all $i_1 i_2 \ldots i_k$ in $\{1, \ldots, n\}^*$.

Lemma 2.10 [20]. Conjecture 2.9 holds if it holds for $n = 2$ (two tables).

Later we show another conjecture equivalent to Conjecture 2.9 (Theorem 3.4).

Note that the DTOL language equivalence problem has been shown undecidable in [39] and recently [46] it has been shown that it becomes decidable if only one system is a DTOL system and the other is DOL. This is a strengthening of the decidability of DOL language equivalence.

All the decidable problems mentioned in this section, as well as some other problems in L-systems (see, e.g., [22]) have been shown decidable by reducing them to the DOL sequence equivalence problem (Theorem 2.1). Another problem shown decidable in the same way has been the equivalence problem for simple single loops programs with respect to symbolic evaluation [33].

III.   HOMOMORPHISM EQUIVALENCE
ON A LANGUAGE

The problems discussed in this section originated in a simple observation in the proof of decidability of DOL equivalence problem [8,15]. The first step in the proof was that given homomorphisms g, h : $\Sigma^* \to \Sigma^*$ and w in Σ^* the following two conditions are clearly equivalent.

(i) $g^n(w) = h^n(w)$ for all $n \geq 0$;

(ii) $g(u) = h(u)$ for all u in L, $L = \{g^n(w) : n \geq 0\}$.

So, the testing of iterative equivalence of two homomorphisms g, h can be reduced to the testing of string-by-string equivalence of g and h on a certain language, namely the language generated by g from the "starting string" w. It is natural and also very useful (cf. Theorems 3.10 and 3.11) to attempt such testing also for other types of languages.

The problem to test whether two homomorphisms agree (string by string) on a given language from family L is called the homomorphic equivalence problem for L [20]. Its decidability for regular sets was already implicitly contained in [15]. The following is the main result from [20].

Theorem 3.1 [20]. (Homomorphism equivalence for CFL) Given a context-free language $L \subseteq \Sigma^*$ and homomorphisms h, g : $\Sigma^* \to \Delta^*$, it is decidable whether h(x) = g(x) for each x $\in$ L.

The decidability of homomorphic equivalence is open for all families of languages between DOL and indexed. In particular we have the following:

Conjecture 3.2. (Homomorphism equivalence for DOL languages) Given w in Σ^* and homomorphism h : $\Sigma^* \to \Sigma^*$ and f, g : $\Sigma^* \to \Delta^*$ it is decidable whether

$$f(h^n(w)) = g(h^n(w)) \qquad\qquad (3.1)$$

for all n $\geq$ 0.

The following is mentioned in [20].

Theorem 3.3. Conjecture 2.2 is equivalent to Conjecture 3.2, i.e., the HDOL equivalence problem is decidable iff the homomorphism equivalence problem for DOL languages is decidable.

Proof. (1) To test (3.1) means to compare two HDOL sequences based on the same DOL system. (2) Given $u \in \Sigma^*$, $v \in \Delta^*$ and homomorphisms $g_1 : \Sigma^* \to \Sigma^*$, $g_2 : \Sigma^* \to \Gamma^*$, $h_1 : \Delta^* \to \Delta^*$, $h_2 : \Delta^* \to \Gamma^*$. Assume without loss of generality that $\Sigma \cap \Delta = \emptyset$ and define homomorphisms f, f_1 and f_2 : $(\Sigma \cup \Delta)^* \to (\Sigma \cup \Delta)^*$ by $f(a) = g_1(a)$ for $a \in \Sigma$, $f(b) = h_1(b)$ for $b \in \Delta$, $f_1(a) = g_2(a)$, $f_2(a) = \varepsilon$ for $a \in \Sigma$, $f_1(b) = \varepsilon$, $f_2(b) = h_2(b)$ for $b \in \Delta$. Then, clearly, $f_1(f^n(uv)) = f_2(f^n(uv))$ for all n iff $g_2(g_1^n(u)) = h_2(h_1^n(v))$ for all n. $\square$

Using similar techniques as in the proof of Theorem 3.2 we also get the following reduction result.

Theorem 3.4. The following three problems are equivalent (and thus all conjectured to be decidable by Conjecture 2.9):

(a) DTOL sequence equivalence problem;

(b) HDTOL sequence equivalence problem;

(c) homomorphism equivalence problem for DTOL languages.

Proof. We show the reduction (c) to (a); the others are easier.

Let $\bar{\Sigma} = \{\bar{a} \mid a \in \Sigma\}$ and for w in Σ let $\bar{w}$ denote the word obtained from w by "barring" each symbol. Given DTOL system $G = (\Sigma, h_1, h_2, w)$ and homomorphisms g_1, g_2, we construct DTOL systems $G_i = (\Sigma \cup \bar{\Sigma}, h_1', h_2', f_i, w)$ for $i = 1$, 2, where $h_j'(a) = h_j(a)$, $h_j(\bar{a}) = \varepsilon$ for all $a \in \Sigma$ and $j = 1$, 2; $f_i(a) = \overline{g_i(a)}$, $f_i(\bar{a}) = \varepsilon$ for all a in Σ and $i = 1$, 2. $\square$

Since $h_j'(f_i(j) = \varepsilon$ for all i, $j = 1$, 2 and $u \in \Sigma^*$, it is easy to verify that G_1 and G_2 are sequence equivalent iff homomorphisms g_1 and g_2 are equivalent on $L(G)$.

In [20] it has been conjectured that even a much stronger result than Conjecture 3.2 holds. However, in the view of Theorem 3.3 we cannot expect it to be easy to prove the following.

Conjecture 3.5. The homomorphism equivalence problem for indexed languages is decidable.

For the special case of elementary homomorphisms (see Section IV) decidability has been shown using Theorem 4.4.

Theorem 3.6 [49]. It is decidable whether two given elementary homomorphisms are equivalent on a given indexed language.

The following is a partial solution of Conjecture 3.5, which is incomparable with Theorem 3.1. It is based on the fact that every homomorphism on a binary alphabet is either elementary or periodic with the same period for each letter (see Section IV), and on Theorem 3.6.

Theorem 3.7 [19]. The homomorphism equivalence problem for ETOL languages over a binary alphabet is decidable.

Finally, we have an easy undecidability result:

Theorem 3.8 [20]. The homomorphism equivalence problem for (deterministic) context-sensitive languages is undecidable.

We conclude this section with applications of Theorem 3.1 to problems about finite and pushdown transducers [12]. All these quite powerful results follow easily from Theorem 3.1. Note, for example, that the equivalence problem for deterministic generalized sequential machines is a very special case of Theorem 3.11.

We call a transducer defining a regular (rational) translation a finite transducer (a-transducer in [28]). In [1] it

has been shown that regular (rational) and pushdown translations can be homomorphically characterized, i.e., each regular
or pushdown translation t can be expressed as

$$t = \{(g(w), h(w)) : w \in L\}$$

where g, h are homomorphisms and L is regular or context free,
respectively. Therefore, we immediately obtain by Theorem 3.1:

Theorem 3.9 [12]. Given a finite transducer or a pushdown
transducer it is decidable whether it defines an identity relation restricted to its domain.

From Theorem 3.9 we easily obtain the following:

Theorem 3.10 [12]. Given a finite transducer M and a
context-free grammar G, it is decidable whether t_M (the relation defined by M) is functional on L(G).

The inverse relation of the restriction of t_M to L(G) is
not necessarily equal to the restriction of t_M^{-1} to $t_M(L(G))$.
Hence it does not follow as a corollary of Theorem 3.10, as
claimed in [12], that it is decidable whether t_M is one-to-one
on L(G). Actually this problem has been shown to be undecidable in [30]. However, we can test whether t_M is one-to-one
(on its domain).

Among the other consequences of Theorem 3.1 shown in [12]
is the decidability of the equivalence problem for functional
finite transducers, or the even stronger result which follows,
where an unambiguous pushdown transducer is a pdt based on an
unambiguous pushdown automaton [32].

Theorem 3.11 [12]. (Equivalence between a functional
finite transducer and an unambiguous pushdown transducer)
Given an unambiguous pushdown transducer P and a functional
finite transducer it is decidable whether $t_P = t_M$.

IV.   ELEMENTARY HOMOMORPHISMS
AND EQUALITY SETS

Here we consider a very useful special type of homomorphism first introduced in [23], equality sets for them and
equality sets over a binary alphabet.

A homomorphism h : $\Sigma^* \to \Delta^*$ is <u>elementary</u> if there is no
decomposition of h into homomorphisms f and g, that is, $h = gf$:

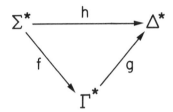

such that card Γ < card Σ. Similarly, a finite language L is
<u>elementary</u> if there is no language K such that card K < card L
and $L \subseteq K^*$. Let $L_h = \{h(a) : a \in \Sigma\}$. Clearly, a homomorphism
h : $\Sigma^* \to \Delta^*$ is elementary iff card L_h = card   and L_h is
elementary.

Properties of elementary homomorphisms and languages were
studied in [23,24,35,41]. We mention a few of them.

<u>Theorem 4.1</u> [23].   Each elementary homomorphism is
injective.

<u>Theorem 4.2</u> [41].   Let $L = \{u_1, \ldots, u_n\}$ be an elementary
language over the alphabet Σ.   If $u_i xz = u_j y$ for some $i \neq j$,
x, $y \in L^*$ and $z \in \Sigma^*$, then $|u_i x| \leq |u_1 u_2 \ldots u_n| - n$.

<u>Corollary 4.3</u> [41].   Every elementary language is a code
with bounded delay (both from left to right and from right to
left).

The following is an important result. In particular it has made it possible to simplify the proof of the decidability of DOL sequence equivalence.

Theorem 4.4 [24]. If homomorphisms g and h are elementary, then the equality set E(g,h) is regular.

This result has been strengthened in [26] for the weaker assumption that at least one of g and h is elementary and then for even weaker assumptions in [35]. No effective proof even for the weakest result is known so we have the following open problem and its even harder versions.

Open Problem 4.5. Given elementary homomorphisms g, h : $\Sigma^* \to \Delta^*$, can the regular set E(g,h) (represented, e.g., by a regular expression) be found effectively?

This problem is presently open even for the case of binary alphabets [17]. A positive answer in this special case already implies the validity of Conjecture 5.2, the decidability of PCP restricted to lists of length two.

The fact that every homomorphism on a binary alphabet is either elementary or periodic severely restricts the form of equality sets for homomorphisms over a binary alphabet (on free monoids with two generators). Each equality set is either regular or of the form $\{w \in \{a,b\}^* \mid \#a(w)/\#b(w) = k\}$ for some rational $k \neq 0$, where $\#a(w)$ is the number of occurrences of letter a in w. In [17] an attempt has been made to fully classify such equality sets. In particular for some words all possible homomorphisms agreeing on them are shown. On the other hand a number of sets or words (singleton sets) are shown to be "periodicity forcing," meaning that only periodic homomorphisms could agree on them. These results support the following.

Conjecture 4.6. Every regular equality set for homomorphisms over a binary alphabet is of the form F* where F is of
cardinality at most two.

This conjecture would imply a simple proof of Theorem 6.2
and also sharpen this theorem, namely it would imply that for
L ⊆ {a,b}* there always exists (noneffectively) a test set
(see Section VI) of cardinality at most three. Some other implications of Conjecture 4.6 are discussed in [17].

Note that there is no loss of generality in assuming that
the range of considered homomorphisms is over a binary alphabet, since a larger alphabet can always be encoded into a
binary one, preserving the equality set. This is, of course,
not the case for the domain. Hence, we have a rather unusual
situation that many problems considered here are much easier
for a binary alphabet than in the general case. One such example is the DOL equivalence problem.

V.   HOMOMORPHISM COMPATIBILITY

In Section III we were interested in testing whether two
given homomorphisms agree "string by string" on a given language. In [20] four kinds of "homomorphism agreements" were
considered, namely, compatibility, strong compatibility, ultimate equivalence and equivalence. The last one was considered
in Section III; here we will consider the first one; the other
two are omitted since the results for them are similar to the
two cases considered.

Homomorphisms g and h are compatible on a language L if
g(w) = h(w) for some w in L, that is, if L ∩ E(g,h) ≠ ∅.

To decide whether homomorphisms g and h are compatible on Σ^+, i.e., whether $E(g,h) - \{\varepsilon\} \neq \emptyset$, is nothing else but the Post Correspondence Problem (PCP). An instance of PCP(g,h) is given by two nonerasing homomorphisms g, h : $\{1, \ldots, n\}^* \to \Sigma^*$, traditionally called <u>lists</u> of length n.

The problem of homomorphism compatibility for a family of languages L can be stated as: given L in L and homomorphisms g and h, to decide whether there is w in L such that g(w) = h(w). Hence, this problem is undecidable for any family containing Σ^+ for arbitrarily large alphabet Σ. Actually, it is known that there is a certain fixed size for Σ, which is sufficient to make the PCP undecidable. However the minimal size is not known. We have the following open problem and conjecture.

<u>Open Problem 5.1</u>. What is the minimal integer n such that PCP with only lists of length n is undecidable?

The results in [17] support the following generally accepted but not yet proven

<u>Conjecture 5.2</u>. The PCP with the restriction to lists of length two, i.e., homomorphic compatibility on Σ^+ for a binary Σ, is decidable.

More difficult to prove would be the following:

<u>Conjecture 5.3</u>. The PCP restricted to instances PCP(g,h) with elementary homomorphisms (lists) g and h is decidable.

Open also is the modification of Conjecture 5.3 obtained by assuming that the homomorphisms are injective rather than elementary.

<u>Theorem 5.4</u>. The positive solution of Problem 4.5 implies the validity of Conjectures 5.2 and 5.3.

Proof. If g and h are elementary, then we can effectively find a regular set E(g,h) and test whether E(g,h) $\neq$ {ε}. This validates Conjecture 5.3, in the case of Conjecture 5.2. There remains the easy case when at least one of g, h is periodic (see [17]).

Obviously, #Σ*, for every alphabet Σ and # $\notin$ Σ, is a DTOL language. Hence, the homomorphism compatibility problem is clearly undecidable for the family of DTOL languages. However, we have the following:

Open Problem 5.5. (Homomorphism compatibility on DOL languages) Given w in Σ*, and homomorphisms h : Σ* $\rightarrow$ Σ*, g, f : Σ* $\rightarrow$ Δ*, is it decidable whether there is an n $\geq$ 0 such that g(h^n(w)) = f(h^n(w))?

Related are the following two problems:

Open Problem 5.6. (Intersecting DOL sequences) Given u, v in Σ* and homomorphisms g, h : Σ* $\rightarrow$ Σ*, is it decidable whether g^n(u) = h^n(v) for some n $\geq$ 0?

Open Problem 5.7. (Intersecting HDOL sequences) Given u in Σ*, v in Δ* and homomorphisms

g_1 : Σ* $\rightarrow$ Σ*,

g_2 : Σ* $\rightarrow$ Γ*,

h_1 : Δ* $\rightarrow$ Δ*,

h_2 : Δ* $\rightarrow$ Γ*,

is it decidable whether g_2(g_1^n(u)) = h_2(h_1^n(v)) for some n?

Theorem 5.8. Problems 5.5 and 5.7 are equivalent; the decidability of Problem 5.5 implies the decidability of Problem 5.6.

Proof. Similar to the proof of Theorem 3.3.

If we modify Problem 5.6 so that only the length of generated strings is compared we obtain the following problem which is shown in [51] to be equivalent to the well known open problem of finding zeros of Z-rational functions.

Open Problem 5.9. (Intersecting DOL growth sequences) Given u in Σ^*, v in Δ^* and h : $\Delta^* \to \Delta^*$, decide whether $|g^n(u)| = |h^n(v)|$ for some n.

There are a large number of results (and open problems) concerning growth (length) and Parikh vector sequences generated by one or more iterative homomorphisms. Mathematically, they belong to the theory of noncommutative formal power series, and we refer the interested reader to [51]. We have included Problem 5.9 here because of its strong implications to our other open problems shown in the following theorem. The first part was shown in the terminology of Z-rational functions in [42]; the second follows by Theorem 3.3.

Theorem 5.10. The decidability of Problem 5.9 implies

(i) the decidability of the HDOL sequence equivalence problem (Conjecture 2.2);

(ii) the decidability of the homomorphism equivalence problem for DOL languages.

Clearly, the decidability of Problem 5.7 (or 5.5) implies the decidability of Problem 5.9 and therefore, by Theorem 5.10, also the decidability of (i) and (ii) above.

In [17] a problem which can be considered dual to the Post Correspondence Problem is shown to be decidable by reducing it to Makanin's result concerning solvability of equations in free monoids [36].

Theorem 5.11. Given a string w in Σ^*, it is decidable whether there exist two distinct homomorphisms g, h : $\Sigma^* \to \Delta^*$ for some Δ, such that at least one of them is aperiodic and g(w) = h(w).

Note that the problem is trivial if g and h are not required to be distinct or aperiodic.

VI.   TEST SETS AND CHECKING WORDS

The very interesting "Ehrenfeuch conjecture" (Conjecture 6.1) is at least several years older than the notion of homomorphism equivalence to which it is closely related.

We say that a finite subset F of a language L is a test set for L if, for any pair of homomorphisms (g,h), g(x) = h(x) for all x in L if and only if g(x) = h(x) for all x in F, i.e., g and h are equivalent on L iff g and h are equivalent on F.

Conjecture 6.1. For every language there exists a test set.

It immediately follows by Theorem 3.8 that given a context-sensitive grammar G a test set for L(G) cannot be effectively constructed, since the effective existence of a test set for a family L obviously implies the decidability of homomorphism equivalence for L.

The discussion in Section IV indicates that proving the validity of the Ehrenfeucht conjecture is considerably easier for languages over a binary alphabet. This has actually been done recently in [21].

Theorem 6.2 [21]. For each language $L \subseteq \Sigma^*$, where Σ is a binary alphabet, there exists a test set F, i.e., a finite set F, such that for each pair of homomorphisms g, h, g(x) = h(x) for all x in F.

It easily follows from the discussion in [15] or [20] that for each regular set there effectively exists a test set. Recently this result has been extended to context-free languages.

Theorem 6.3 [2]. For each context-free language there effectively exists a test set.

As mentioned above, this result immediately implies the decidability of homomorphism equivalence on the CFL (Theorem 3.1).

Actually, a somewhat stronger form of Theorem 6.3 is shown in [2], namely that given a CFG, $G = (N,T,P,S)$ with $n = $ card N and m the maximal length of the right side of the production in P,

$$F = \{w \in L : |w| \leq m^{3n+1}\}$$

is a test set for $L(G)$.

This result is then used to obtain also finite "test sets" for CFL with respect to gsm mappings realized by gsm with a uniformly bounded number of states. Despite our reasons for expecting it to be hard to prove Conjecture 3.2 (equivalent to Conjecture 2.2) we venture to make an even stronger one:

Conjecture 6.4. For every indexed language (given by an indexed grammar) there effectively exists a test set.

According to [21] a word in Σ^* is a __checking__ __word__ for a language $L \subseteq \Sigma^*$ if, for any pair of homomorphisms (g,h), $g(x) = h(x)$ for all x in L if and only if $g(w) = h(w)$. Observe that it is not required that w be in L, hence $\{w\}$ might not be a test set for L.

A language L is __rich__ if two homomorphisms g and h are equivalent on L only in case $g = h$. Somewhat surprisingly it is easier to show the following result than Theorem 6.2.

Theorem 6.5 [21]. Every language over a binary alphabet is either rich or possesses a checking word.

VII.   REPRESENTATION OF LANGUAGE FAMILIES

Equality sets have already been discussed in the previous sections mainly in relation to decidability problems about homomorphisms. They were explicitly introduced in [24] under a different name and their basic properties were studied in [49]. A generalization of equality sets to more than two homomorphisms is considered by [6].

It turned out that equality sets and similarly fixed-point languages [26] provide simple representations of the recursively enumerable languages [11,27,49] which can also be extended to various time and complexity classes [4,5,13,14]. The first results say that the closure of equality sets under dgsm mappings is the family of recursively enumerable languages.

Theorem 7.1 [27,49]. For every recursively enumerable (r.e.) set L, there exists a pair of homomorphisms (h_1, h_2) and a dgsm mapping g such that $L = g(E(h_1, h_2))$.

This result has been strengthened in [11] by replacing dgsm's by erasings and equality sets by minimal equality sets.

A homomorphism $h : \Sigma^* \to \Delta^*$ is called erasing if, for each $a \in \Sigma$ either $h(a) = a$ or $h(a) = \varepsilon$. For homomorphisms $g, h : \Sigma^* \to \Delta^*$, the minimal equality set is the set $e(g,h) = \{w \in \Sigma^+ \mid g(w) = h(w)$ and if $w = uv$ for $u, v \in \Sigma^+$, then $g(u) \neq h(u)\}$, that is, using the notation of [32],

$$e(g,h) = \min(E(g,h)) - \{\varepsilon\}.$$

Theorem 7.2 [11]. For every r.e. language L, there exist
homomorphisms h_1, h_2 and an erasing h_0 so that L =
$h_0(e(h_1,h_2))$.

Also we have a representation based on fixed points of
dgsm mappings. Let g : $\Sigma^* \to \Sigma^*$ be a function. The fixed-
point language $F_p(g)$ of the function g is defined to be
$F_p(g) = \{w \in \Sigma^* \mid g(w) = w\}$.

Theorem 7.3 [27]. For every r.e. language L, there exists
a dgsm mapping g and an erasing h such that L = $h(F_p(g))$.

By imposing simple restrictions on the mappings used in
Theorems 7.1, 7.2 and 7.3, we obtain a simple "machine independent" characterization of many time and space complexity
classes of languages. Similar results have been shown independently in [4,5] and in [13,14]. We give here a few of
these results.

We say that C is a class of complexity functions if C is a
class of functions closed under addition of and multiplication
by a constant. A language L is of time (space) complexity C
if L is accepted by a nondeterministic multitape on-line
Turing machine M which operates within time bound (space
bound) f, for some f in C we write L $\in$ NTIME(C)
(L $\in$ NSPACE(C)).

We generalize the notion of k-limited erasing [32] as
follows: For a function f on the integers we say that an
erasing h is f-bounded on a language L if for each w in L,
w = xyz and h(y) = ε implies $|y| \le f(|w|)$, that is, at most
$f(|w|)$ consecutive symbols of w may be erased. We say that h
is C-bounded, for a class C of complexity functions, if h is
f-bounded for some f from C.

We get the following "machine independent" characterization of the time complexity classes of languages.

Theorem 7.4 [5,14]. Let C be a class of complexity functions closed under squaring. Then the following three conditions are equivalent.

(i) $L \in$ NTIME (C).

(ii) $L = h_0(e(h_1,h_2))$ where h_1, h_2 are homomorphisms and
h_0 is C-bounded erasing on $e(h_1,h_2)$.

(iii) $L = h(F_p(g))$ where g is a dgsm mapping and h is
erasing on $F_p(g)$.

Corollary. A language L is in NP iff there exist homomorphisms h_0, h_1, h_2 such that $h_0(e(h_1,h_2)) = L$ and h_0 is
polynomial-bounded erasing on $e(h_1,h_2)$.

Corollary. A language L is primitive recursive (recursive)
iff there exist homomorphisms h_0, h_1, h_2 such that
$h_0(e(h_1,h_2)) = L$ and h_0 is primitive recursive- (recursive-)
bounded erasing on $e(h_1,h_2)$.

In order to get a characterization of space complexity
classes we need to generalize the notion of bounded balance
on a language considered in Section III.

Consider two fixed homomorphisms g, h : $\Sigma^* \to \Delta^*$. Recall
that for each w in Σ^*, the balance of w is defined as $B(w) =$
$|g(w)| - |h(w)|$. Now, for a monotone function f on the integers, an erasing π and $L \subseteq \Sigma^*$, we say that the pair (g,h) has
f-bounded balance on language L, with respect to erasing π, if
for each x in L and each prefix w of x we have $|B(w)| \leq$
$f(|h(x)|)$. For a complexity class C, we say that (g,h) has
C-bounded balance on L, with respect to π, if the same holds
true for some $f \in C$.

Theorem 7.5 [14]. Let C be any class of complexity functions. Then $L \in \text{NSPACE}(C)$ iff $L = h_0(e(h_1,h_2))$ where h_0 is
erasing and the pair (h_1,h_2) has C-bounded balance on $e(h_1,h_2)$
with respect to h_0.

Corollary. A language L is context sensitive iff there
exist an erasing h_0 and homomorphisms h_1, h_2 such that $L = h_0(e(h_1,h_2))$ and the pair (h_1,h_2) has linear-bounded balance
on $e(h_1,h_2)$.

The class NP also has an alternative characterization:

Theorem 7.6 [5]. The class NP is the smallest class containing all equality sets $E(h_1,h_2)$ (of nonerasing homomorphisms) with square-root-bounded balance (i.e., with the pair
(h_1,h_2) having square-root-bounded balance on $E(h_1,h_2)$ with
respect to the identity) and closed under intersection with
regular sets and polynomial-bounded erasings.

We also have an alternative necessary condition for PSPACE:

Theorem 7.7 [5]. For every language L in PSPACE there is
a pair of nonerasing homomorphisms (h_1,h_2) with log n-bounded
balance, a regular set R, and an erasing h such that $L = h(E(h_1,h_2) \cap R)$ and for some constants $c > 1$, $k > 0$, h is
c^{n^k}-bounded on $E(h_1,h_2) \cap R$.

The study of equality sets has contributed representation
theorems of the following form:

Let L be a family of languages over an alphabet Σ. Then
there exist a language L_Σ and an erasing π_Σ such that $L \in L$
iff $L = \pi_\Sigma(L_\Sigma \cap R_L)$ for some regular set R_L.

Letting L be the family of context-free languages we have
the well known Chomsky-Schützenberger theorem with L_Σ being

the Dyck language over Σ; for the families of EOL and ETOL

languages such representation has been established in [7].

Now, given Σ let $\bar{\Sigma}$ denote the alphabet disjoint from Σ

consisting of "barred" symbols, $\bar{\Sigma} = \{\bar{a} \mid a \in \Sigma\}$, and for any

word x in Σ^*, let $\bar{x}$ denote the word obtained from x by barring

each symbol. To get a representation as above for the r.e.

sets, the twin shuffle over Σ has been defined in [27] as

$$L(\Sigma) = \{x \in (\Sigma \cup \bar{\Sigma})^* \mid \overline{\pi_\Sigma(x)} = \pi_{\bar{\Sigma}}(x)\}$$

where π_Σ, $\pi_{\bar{\Sigma}}$ are erasing on $(\Sigma \cup \bar{\Sigma})$, which only preserve the

symbols from Σ, $\bar{\Sigma}$ respectively.

Clearly, the twin shuffle $L(\Sigma)$ is an equality set of two

homomorphisms. They cannot be nonerasing as shown in [5].

Theorem 7.8 [27]. Let L be an r.e. language over Σ.

There exists a regular set $R_L \subseteq (\Sigma \cup \bar{\Sigma} \cup \{0,0,1,1\}^*)$ such that

$L = \pi_\Sigma(L(\Sigma \cup \{0,1\}) \cap R_L)$, where π_Σ is erasing and only pre-

serves the symbols from Σ.

This theorem has essentially been shown in [27] using

Theorem 7.3. It also follows by Theorem 7.2 (see [13,18]).

It is actually not difficult to show that every principal

cone has a representation as above. A family of languages L

is a principal cone if there is an L in L such that L is the

closure of {L} under the operations of homomorphism, inverse

homomorphism and intersection with a regular set, or equiva-

lently, L is the closure of {L} under finite transducers (ra-

tional realtions) (see [28]).

Theorem 7.9 [13,18]. Let Σ be an alphabet and L a princi-

pal cone. There exists a language L_Σ in L such that for each

L in L, $L \subseteq \Sigma^*$, there exists a regular set R_L such that $L = \pi_\Sigma(L_\Sigma \cap R_L)$ where π_Σ is erasing and only preserves the symbols in Σ.

The reader is referred to [4,5,13,14,18,27] for a number of additional representation results.

REFERENCES

1. Aho, A.V., and Ullman, J.D., "The Theory of Parsing, Translation, and Compiling." Prentice-Hall (1972).
2. Albert, J., and Culik II, K., Test sets for homomorphism equivalence on context-free languages. Research Report CS-79-39, University of Waterloo (1979).
3. Blattner, M., The unsolvability of the equality problem for sentential forms of context-free languages. J. Comp. System Sci. 7, 463-468 (1973).
4. Book, R., and Brandenburg, F.-J., Representing complexity classes by equality sets. Proceedings of the Sixth ICALP, Graz, Lecture Notes in Computer Science 71, Springer Verlag, 49-57 (1979).
5. Book, R., and Brandenburg, F.-J., Equality sets and complexity classes. SIAM J. Computing 9(1980), to appear.
6. Brandenburg, F.-J., Multiple equality sets and Post machines. Technical Report, Dept. of Mathematics, University of California, Santa Barbara (1979).
7. Culik II, K., On some families of languages related to development systems. Internat. J. Computer Math., Sec. A, 4, 31-42 (1974).
8. Culik II, K., On the decidability of the sequence equivalence problem for DOL-systems. Theoret. Comp. Sci. 3, 75-84 (1977).
9. Culik II, K., The decidability of v-local catenativity and of other problems of DOL systems. Inf. Proc. Letters 7 (1), 33-35 (1978).
10. Culik II, K., The ultimate equivalence problem for DOL systems. Acta Informatica 10, 69-84 (1978).
11. Culik II, K., A purely homomorphic characterization of recursively enumerable sets. JACM 6, 345-350 (1979).
12. Culik II, K., Some decidability results about regular and push down translations. Info. Proc. Letters 8, 5-8 (1979).
13. Culik II, K., On homomorphic characterization of families of languages. Proceedings of the Sixth ICALP, Graz, Lecture Notes in Computer Science 71, Springer Verlag, 161-170 (1979).
14. Culik II, K., and Diamond, N.D., A homomorphic characterization of time and space complexity classes of languages. Internat. J. Computer Math., to appear.
15. Culik II, K., and Fris, J., The decidability of the equivalence problem for DOL-systems. Inf. and Control 35, 20-39 (1977).

16. Culik II, K., and Karhumaki, J., Interactive L-systems with almost interactionless behaviour. Inf. and Control 43, 83-100 (1979).
17. Culik II, K., and Karhumaki, J., On the equality sets for homomorphisms on free monoids with two generators. RAIRO, to appear. Also Research Report CS-79-17, University of Waterloo (1979).
18. Culik II, K., and Maurer, H.A., On simple representations of language families. RAIRO, to appear. Also Research Report CS-78-41, University of Waterloo (1978).
19. Culik II, K., and Richier, J.L., Homomorphism equivalence on ETOL languages. Internat. J. Computer Math., Sec. A, 7, 43-51 (1979).
20. Culik II, K., and Salomaa, A., On the decidability of homomorphism equivalence for languages. J. Comp. System Sci. 17, 163-175 (1978).
21. Culik II, K., and Salomaa, A., Test sets and checking words for homomorphism equivalence. Research Report CS-79-04, University of Waterloo (1979).
22. Culik II, K., and Wood, D., Double deterministic tabled OL systems. Internat. J. Comp. and Inf. Science 8, 335-347 (1979).
23. Ehrenfeucht, A., and Rozenberg, G., Simplifications of homomorphisms. Inf. and Control 38, 298-308 (1978).
24. Ehrenfeucht, A., and Rozenberg, G., Elementary homomorphisms and a solution to the DOL sequence equivalence problem. Theoret. Comp. Sci. 7, 169-183 (1978).
25. Ehrenfeucht, A., and Rozenberg, G., Every two equivalent DOL systems have a regular true envelope. Theoret. Comp. Sci., to appear.
26. Engelfriet, J., and Rozenberg, G., Equality languages and fixed point languages. Inf. and Control 43, 20-49 (1979).
27. Engelfriet, J., and Rozenberg, G., Fixed point languages, equality languages and representation of recursively enumerable languages. JACM, to appear.
28. Ginsburg, S., "Algebraic and Automata-Theoretic Properties of Formal Languages." North Holland/American Elsevier (1975).
29. Harrison, M.A., "Introduction to Formal Language Theory." Addison-Wesley (1978).
30. Head, T., Unique decipherability relative to a language. Unpublished manuscript (1979).
31. Herman, G.T., and Rozenberg, G., "Developmental Systems and Languages." North-Holland, New York (1975).
32. Hopcroft, J.E., and Ullman, J.D., "Formal Languages and Their Relation to Automata." Addison-Wesley (1969).
33. Howden, W.E., Lindenmayer grammars and symbolic testing. Inf. Proc. Letters 7, 36-45 (1978).
34. Jacob, G., Un algorithme calculant le cardinal, fini ou infini, des demi groups de matrices. Theoret. Comp. Sci. 5, 183-204 (1977).
35. Karhumaki, J., and Simon, I., A note on elementary homomorphisms and the regularity of equality sets. Bulletin EATCS 9, 16-24 (Oct. 1979).
36. Makanin, G.S., The problem of solvability of equations in a free semigroup (in Russian). Matematiceskij Sbornik 103 (145), 148-236 (1977).

37. Mandel, A., and Simon, I., On finite semigroups of matrices. Theoret. Comp. Sci. 5, 101-111 (1977).
38. Nielsen, M., On the decidability of some equivalence problems for DOL-systems. Info. and Control 25, 166-193 (1974).
39. Rozenberg, G., The equivalence problem for deterministic TOL systems is indecidable. Inf. Proc. Letters 1, 201-204; errata, 252 (1972).
40. Rozenberg, G., and Salomaa, A., The mathematical theory of L systems. In "Advances in Information Systems Science" (J. Tou, ed.), vol. 6, chap. 4, New York, Plenum Press (1976).
41. Rozenberg, G., and Salomaa, A., "The Mathematical Theory of L Systems." Academic Press (1980).
42. Ruohonen, K., Zeros of Z-rational functions and DOL-equivalence. Theoret. Comp. Sci. 3, 283-292 (1976).
43. Ruohonen, K., On the decidability of the OL-DOL equivalence problem. Info. and Control 40, 301-318 (1979).
44. Ruohonen, K., The decidability of the FOL-DOL equivalence problem. Inf. Proc. Letters 8, 257-260 (1979).
45. Ruohonen, K., The inclusion problem for DOL languages, Info. and Control, to appear.
46. Ruohonen, K., The decidability of the DOL-DTOL equivalence problem. Unpublished manuscript (1979).
47. Salomaa, A., "Formal Languages." New York, Academic Press (1973).
48. Salomaa, A., DOL equivalence: the problem of iterated and morphisms. Bulletin EATCS 4, 5-12 (1978).
49. Salomaa, A., Equality sets for homomorphisms of free monoids. Acta Cybernetica 4, 127-139 (1978).
50. Salomaa, A., DOL language equivalence. Bulletin EATCS 8, 4-12 (July 1979).
51. Salomaa, A., and Soittola, M., "Automata-Theoretic Aspects of Formal Power Series." Springer-Verlag (1978).
52. Vitanyi, P.M.B., Growth of strings in context dependent Lindenmayer systems. In "L Systems" (G. Rozenberg and A. Salomaa, eds.), Lecture Notes in Computer Science 15, 104-123, Springer-Verlag (1974).

A SURVEY OF RESULTS AND OPEN PROBLEMS
IN THE MATHEMATICAL THEORY OF L SYSTEMS[1]

Grzegorz Rozenberg

Institute of Applied Mathematics and Computer Science
University of Leiden
Leiden, The Netherlands

INTRODUCTION

L systems were originated by Aristid Lindenmayer in connection with biological considerations in 1968 (see [71]).
Independently of its biological interest, the theory of L
systems had a great impact on formal language theory. Two
main novel features brought about by the theory of L systems
from its very beginning are (i) parallelism in the rewriting
process and (ii) the notion of a grammar conceived as a description of a dynamic process (taking place in time), rather
than of a static one. The latter feature initiated an intensive study of sequences (in contrast to sets) of words, as
well as of grammars without nonterminal symbols. L systems
have not only enriched the theory of formal languages but have
also been able to put the latter theory in a totally new perspective. It is our firm opinion that nowadays a course in
formal language theory which does not present L systems misses
some of the very essential points in the area. Indeed, a

---

[1]Preparation of this paper was supported in part by the
National Science Foundation under Grant No. MCS79-04012.

a course in formal language theory can be based on the mathematical framework of L systems because the traditional areas
of the theory, such as context-free languages, have their natural counterparts within this framework. On the other hand,
there is no way of presenting iterated morphisms or parallel
rewriting in a natural way within the framework of sequential
rewriting.

This paper is concerned with the mathematical theory of L
systems (the reader interested in the biological aspects of L
systems is referred to [48,71,73,84,124]) which constitutes today an extensive body of knowledge within formal language theory. The literature concerning L systems consists of several
books [56,75,103,104] and more than 600 publications. Therefore it is virtually impossible to write a survey of this area
which gives a full account of its development. In preparing
this paper we were faced with many (often drastic) decisions
of what should and what should not be included in this survey.

One of the outstanding features of the theory of L systems
is that its core (the theory of ETOL systems) fits into a very
systematic and basic mathematical framework formed by single
or several iterated homomorphisms or finite substitutions on a
free monoid. The basic part of our paper (its first four sections) consists of an outline of this systematic framework.
The choice of particular topics discussed is clearly influenced
by the research preferences of the author of this survey; it
is also considerably influenced by the fact that two other
papers in this volume [7,116] deal in one way or the other
with the theory of L systems. We have tried to stress two
points: (1) the theory of word sequences as a very novel topic
in formal language theory, and (2) the results on the

combinatorial structure of languages--a topic which in our
opinion is a central topic of formal language theory. Throughout the paper we illustrate our points by giving both classical
(older) and recent results. In Section V we discuss a number
of results pointing out the relationship of the theory of L
systems to several other topics of formal language theory. We
conclude the paper by a short discussion (Section VI).

   The basic part of the paper follows an outline of the theory of L systems as presented in the recent monograph [104].
However, this paper contains quite a number of old and recent
results and topics not discussed in [104]. We assume the
reader to be familiar with the basics of formal language theory, e.g., in the scope of [111]. We are often somewhat informal in describing various results; however, the interested
reader will find formal details in the references cited. We
use the standard formal language theoretic notation and terminology and perhaps only the following notational matters
require an additional explanation.

   (1) N, N_+, Z, R_+ denote the set of non-negative integers,
       integers and positive reals, respectively.

   (2) For a finite set V, $^{\#}V$ denotes its cardinality. We
       often identify a singleton {x} with its element x.

   (3) We consider finite alphabets only. For an alphabet Σ
       and i $\in N$, Σ^i denotes the set of all words over Σ
       of length i.

   (4) Λ denotes the empty word and $|x|$ denotes the length
       of a word x. For an alphabet Σ and a word x, $\#_\Sigma x$
       denotes the number of occurrences of elements from Σ
       in x; <u>alph</u> x denotes the set of letters occurring

in x. For a language K, <u>length</u> K denotes the
length set of K, i.e., <u>length</u> K = {$|x|$: x $\in$ K}.

(5) A homomorphism h : $\Sigma^* \rightarrow \Delta^*$ is called a <u>coding</u> if
$|h(a)|$ = 1 for each a $\in$ Σ; it is called a <u>weak</u>
<u>identity</u> if for each a $\in$ Σ either h(a) = a or
h(a) = Λ. In particular, <u>pres</u>$_{\Sigma,\Theta}$ denotes the weak
identity on Σ^* such that <u>pres</u>$_{\Sigma,\Theta}$ a = a if and only
if a $\in$ Θ; we write <u>pres</u>$_\Theta$ whenever Σ is understood.

(6) Given a class X of rewriting systems, L(X) denotes
the class of languages generated by elements of X.
In particular we use L(CF) to denote the class of
context-free languages and L(CS) to denote the class
of context-sensitive languages; L(RE) denotes the
class of recursively enumerable languages.

I. SINGLE HOMOMORPHISMS ITERATED

The basic construct of L systems theory is the DOL system
which is formally defined as follows.

<u>Definition</u> [71]. A DOL <u>system</u> is a construct G = (Σ,h,ω)
where Σ is an alphabet, h : $\Sigma^* \rightarrow \Sigma^*$ is a homomorphism and
$\omega \in \Sigma^*$ (ω is referred to as the <u>axiom</u> of G). The <u>sequence</u>
of G, denoted E(G), is defined by E(G) = ω_0, ω_1, $\ldots$
where $\omega_0 = \omega$ and $\omega_{i+1} = h(\omega_i)$ for i $\geq$ 0. The <u>language</u> of
G, denoted L(G), is defined by L(G) = {$h^n(\omega)$: n $\geq$ 0}.
The <u>length sequence</u> of G, denoted LS(G), is defined by
LS(G) = $|\omega_0|$, $|\omega_1|$, $\ldots$. The <u>growth function</u> of G, denoted
f_G, is the function from N into N defined by $f_G(n) =$
$|h^n(\omega_0)|$, n $\geq$ 0. E(G) is referred to as a DOL <u>sequence</u>,
L(G) as a DOL <u>language</u>, LS(G) as a DOL <u>length sequence</u> and
f_G as a DOL <u>growth function</u>. $\square$

A DOL system represents thus a very basic mathematical structure--the iteration of a single homomorphism on a free monoid. Although mathematically most simple, DOL systems give a clear insight into the essential ideas and techniques behind L systems and parallel rewriting in general. At the same time the theory of DOL systems contributes to our understanding of the very basic mathematical notion of an endomorphism defined on a free monoid.

The theory of DOL systems brought to formal language theory a totally new topic: the theory of sequences of words (rather than their sets--languages). We shall survey now several research areas concerning DOL sequences.

The theory of locally catenative DOL systems (originated in [102]) is one of the more fascinating areas of the DOL systems theory.

On the one hand, it is a typical example of the more general research area: global versus local behavior of rewriting systems. Roughly speaking, a global property of an L system is a property which can be expressed independently of the system itself (for example, a property expressed in terms of its language or its sequence) and a local property of an L system is a property of its underlying mapping (for example, a property of the "graph of productions" of a given system).

On the other hand, locally catenative DOL systems form perhaps the most natural generalization to words of linear homogeneous recurrence relations.

Formally they are defined as follows.

Definition [102]. A locally catenative formula (LCF in short) is an ordered k-tuple $(i_1, \ldots, i_k)$ of positive integers, where $k \geq 1$ (we refer to k as the width of v and to $\max\{i_1,\ldots,i_k\}$ as the depth of v). An infinite sequence

of words ω_0, ω_1, ... satisfies an LCF $(i_1,\ldots,i_k)$ with a

cut $p \geq \max\{i_1,\ldots,i_k\}$ if, for all $n \geq p$, $\omega_n =$

$\omega_{n-i_1} \cdots \omega_{n-i_k}$. A sequence of words satisfying some LCF v

with some cut is called (v-) locally catenative. A DOL sys-

tem G is locally catenative if E(G) is locally catenative;

moreover, G is locally catenative of depth (width) d if G

is v-locally catenative for some LCF v with depth (width)

of v equal to d. □

Hence locally catenativeness is a typical example of a

global property of a rewriting system. Thus a natural research

direction concerning locally catenative DOL systems is to look

for "structural" (hence local) properties of the homomorphism

of a DOL system responsible for its locally catenative (hence

global) behavior. To this aim, given a DOL system G =

(Σ,h,ω), one defines its graph $G(G)$ to be the directed

graph the nodes of which are elements of Σ and for which a

directed edge leads from node a to node b if and only if

$b \in$ alph h(a). (If for no $a \in \Sigma$, $h(a) = \Lambda$, then we say that

G is a propagating DOL system abbreviated as a PDOL system.)

Theorem I.1 [102]. Let $G = (\Sigma,h,\omega)$ be a PDOL system.

If there exists a letter $b \in \Sigma$ such that $b \in L(G)$ and each

cycle in $G(G)$ goes through b then G is locally

catenative. □

One can also define a "structural" property of E(G)

yielding the locally catenative behavior of a DOL system G.

If G is a DOL system and $E(G) = \omega_0$, ω_1, ... then we say

that E(G) is covered if there exist $k \geq 0$, $j \geq k+2$ and

a sequence s of occurrences of ω_k in (some of the) strings

ω_{k+1}, ..., ω_{j-1} such that ω_j is the catenation of the sequence of its subwords derived from the respective elements of
s (a more formal definition is given in [102,103]).

Theorem I.2 [102]. A DOL system G is locally catenative
if and only if E(G) is covered. □

However, the above results about the structure of locally
catenative DOL systems are not strong enough to provide a solution of the following.

Open Problem. Is it decidable whether or not an arbitrary
DOL system is locally catenative? □

The above open problem constitutes today perhaps the most
important open problem concerning DOL systems. The most advanced result towards the solution of this problem is the following one.

Theorem I.3 [24,110]. (1) It is decidable whether or not
an arbitrary DOL system is locally catenative of depth d,
where d is an arbitrary positive integer. (2) It is decidable whether or not an arbitrary DOL system is locally catenative of width d, where d is an arbitrary positive
integer. □

Obviously the above theorem yields a positive solution of
the decidability of the locally catenative problem for DOL
systems providing that one proves the following.

Conjecture. A DOL system over an alphabet Σ with $^{\#}\Sigma = n$
is locally catenative if and only if it is locally catenative
of depth d with d $\leq$ n!. □

One of the more intriguing mathematical problems concerning
DOL systems is the DOL sequence equivalence problem: "Is it

decidable whether or not $E(G_1) = E(G_2)$ for two arbitrary DOL systems G_1 and G_2?" This problem was open for a long time; its first solution appears in [9].

Theorem I.4 [9]. The DOL sequence equivalence problem is decidable. □

The solution in [9] uses quite complicated structural analysis. Another solution is presented in [25]--it uses some algebraic constructs and is simpler than the solution from [9].

We would like to stress here that although two different positive solutions of the DOL equivalence problem are available by now, the matter is not closed yet by far. This point is best illustrated by the following. One would like a positive solution to the DOL equivalence problem to provide an algorithm which, given two DOL systems G_1 and G_2, will give a bound $e(G_1,G_2)$ such that $E(G_1) = E(G_2)$ if and only if the $e(G_1,G_2)$ first elements of $E(G_1)$ and $E(G_2)$ are pairwise identical. It is not clear whether or not the solution from [9] yields such a bound, whereas the solution from [25] yields a bound $e(G_1,G_2)$ (see [29]) which tremendously exceeds $2n$, where n is the size of the alphabet involved. At the same time the common conjecture is (see [114]):

Conjecture. Let G_1 and G_2 be DOL systems over an alphabet Σ with $^\#\Sigma = n$. $E(G_1) = E(G_2)$ if and only if the first $2n$ elements of G_1 are identical to the first $2n$ elements of G_2. □

Various efforts to prove Theorem I.4 created quite a number of notions and results that are of interest in themselves and which in fact opened quite new research areas within formal language theory. Thus, for example, the solution in [9] gave rise to a very useful "bounded balance technique" and the solution in [25] gives (under a different name) an explicit formulation (and first results) concerning the notion of equality languages (a very vivid topic by now) as well as it introduces the topic of elementary homomorphisms and elementary languages. We now will discuss briefly elementary homomorphisms, while in Section V we will come back to the topic of equality languages.

Definition [24]. A homomorphism $h : \Sigma^* \to \Delta^*$ is simplifiable if there is an alphabet Θ with $^\#\Theta < {}^\#\Sigma$ and homomorphisms $f : \Sigma^* \to \Theta^*$ and $g : \Theta^* \to \Delta^*$ such that $h = gf$. Otherwise h is called elementary. A finite language K is elementary if there is no language K_1 such that $^\#K_1 < {}^\#K$ and $K \subseteq K_1^*$. □

Clearly elementary homomorphisms and elementary languages are very closely connected: if a homomorphism h defined on Σ is elementary then so is the language $\{h(a) : a \in \Sigma\}$; conversely, if the language $\{h(a) : a \in \Sigma\}$ is elementary and consists of $^\#\Sigma$ words then h is elementary.

The following are examples of basic results on the structure of elementary languages and homomorphisms.

Theorem I.5 [43]. If a homomorphism $h : \Sigma^* \to \Delta^*$ is elementary, then there is an injective mapping $g : \Sigma \to \Delta$ with the following property. For each letter a of Σ there are words x_a and y_a in Δ^* such that $h(a) = x_a g(a) y_a$. □

Theorem I.6 [25]. Let $K = \{u_1, \ldots, u_k\}$ be an elementary language over the alphabet Σ. Assume that $u_i xy = u_j y$ for some $i \neq j$, $y \in \Sigma^*$ and $x, y \in K^*$. Then $|u_i x| \leq |u_1 \ldots u_k| - k$. □

The above result yields the following corollary which constitutes an interesting link between the theory of DOL systems
and coding theory.

Theorem I.7 [83]. Every elementary language is both a
code with a bounded delay from left to right and a code with a
bounded delay from right to left. □

We need some additional notions to state our next result.
A bounded delay homomorphism from left to right (resp., from
right to left) with the delay equal 1 is called a prefix
(resp., a suffix). A biprefix is a homomorphism which is both
a prefix and a suffix. A homomorphism $h : \Sigma^* \to \Sigma^*$ is atomic
if there exist b and $\bar{b}$ in Σ such that either $h(b) = b\bar{b}$
and $h(x) = x$ for $x \neq b$, or $h(b) = \bar{b}b$ and $h(x) = x$ for
$x \neq b$. If h is a composition of atomic homomorphisms then
we call h quasiatomic.

Theorem I.8 [65]. A homomorphism $h : \Sigma^* \to \Delta^*$ is elementary if and only if there exist a quasiatomic homomorphism
$g : \Sigma^* \to \Sigma^*$ and an elementary biprefix $f : \Sigma^* \to \Delta^*$ such that
$h = fg$. □

We move now to the theory of growth functions of DOL systems (initiated in [94,123]). This theory forms a mathematically very natural and application-wise well motivated topic
of investigation. It is perhaps mathematically the best understood area of L systems theory. Its basic mathematical framework is that of formal power series in noncommuting variables.
One may safely say that the theory of formal power series and
the theory of DOL growth functions have mutually contributed
to each other's development--which is best illustrated in [117].

The relationship between DOL length sequences and Z-rational sequences of numbers is by now sufficiently understood. Here are two typical results.

Theorem I.9 [120]. Assume that an N-rational sequence of numbers has a matrix representation $u(n) = \pi M^n \eta$, $n = 0, 1, 2,$ ... with either only positive entries in π or only positive entries in η. Then $u(n)$ is a DOL length sequence. $\square$

Theorem I.10 [117]. Every Z-rational seqeunce can be expressed as the difference of two DOL length sequences. $\square$

Generating functions form a very useful tool in investigating DOL growth functions. The following result is typical in characterizing generating functions of DOL growth functions.

Theorem I.11 [117]. A rational function $F(x)$ with integral coefficients and written in lowest terms is the generating function of a DOL growth function not identical to the zero function if and only if either $F(x) = a_0 + a_1 x + \ldots + a_n x^n$ where $a_0, \ldots, a_n$ are positive integers, or else $F(x)$ satisfies each of the following conditions:

(i) The constant term of its denominator equals 1;

(ii) The coefficients of the Taylor expansion $F(x) = \sum_{n=0}^{\infty} a_n x^n$ are positive integers and, moreover, the ratio a_{n+1}/a_n is bounded by a constant;

(iii) Every pole x_0 of $F(x)$ of the minimal absolute value is of the form $x_0 = r\varepsilon$ where $r = |x_0|$ and ε is a root of unity. $\square$

We close this section by giving two major open problems concerning DOL growth functions.

Open Problem. Is it decidable whether or not the growth function f_G of an arbitrary DOL system G is monotonic, i.e., it satisfies $f_G(n) \leq f_G(n + 1)$ for all $n \in N$? □

Open Problem. Is it decidable whether or not the growth function f_G of an arbitrary DOL system G possesses a "constant level," i.e., it satisfies $f_G(n) = f_G(n + 1)$ for some $n \in N$? □

II. SINGLE FINITE SUBSTITUTIONS ITERATED

A natural way to generalize DOL systems is to consider the iteration of a finite substitution rather than the iteration of a homomorphism. From the mathematical point of view such a generalization is very natural: rather than to allow only singletons we allow now finite sets to be images of letters from the alphabet considered. From the formal language theory point of view this corresponds to transition from deterministic to nondeterministic rewriting: in each rewriting step for each letter we have now a finite number of possible rewritings rather than one only.

Definition [72]. An OL system is a construct $G = (\Sigma, h, \omega)$ where Σ is an alphabet, h is a finite substitution on Σ (into the set of subsets of Σ^*) and $\omega \in \Sigma^*$. The language of G is defined by $L(G) = \bigcup_{n \geq 0} h^n(\omega)$. $L(G)$ is referred to as an OL language. □

In contradistinction to DOL systems, the theory of OL systems concentrates on OL languages, that is, languages generated by OL systems. This is quite natural because a finite substitution is a nondeterministic mapping and so there is no single sequence that is naturally associated with an OL system.

However, we want to stress the following point: each OL sys-

tem G defines in an obvious way a set of (derivation) se-

quences E(G). Those objects--the OL sequence languages--

certainly deserve more attention than they have received until

now. Thus we get the following.

Open Problem Area. Investigate the theory of OL sequence

languages. □

In particular, the following problem seems to be a natural

counterpart of the above-mentioned DOL sequence equivalence

problem.

Open Problem. Is it decidable whether or not $E(G_1)$ =

$E(G_2)$ for arbitrary OL systems G_1 and G_2? □

We conjecture that the answer to the above problem is

positive.

The structure of OL languages is at present not too well

understood. A rather well understood subclass is OL languages

over a one-letter alphabet (see [55]). One of the very few

results on the combinatorial structure of OL languages is the

following one [28]. Let Σ be an alphabet, $\alpha \in \Sigma^+$, and t

be a positive integer, $t \geq 2$. A t-disjoint decomposition of

α is a vector $(\alpha_1, \ldots, \alpha_t)$ such that $\alpha_1 \cdots \alpha_t = \alpha$,

$\alpha_1, \ldots, \alpha_t \in \Sigma^+$ and alph $\alpha_i \cap$ alph $\alpha_{i+1} = \emptyset$ for

$1 \leq i \leq t-1$. A language $K \subseteq \Sigma^*$ is t-balanced if there exist

positive rational numbers $c_1, \ldots, c_t$ with $\sum_{i=1}^{t} c_i = 1$ and

a positive integer d such that for every α in K there

exists a t-disjoint decomposition $(\alpha_1, \ldots, \alpha_t)$ of α such

that $c_i |\alpha| - d \leq |\alpha_i| \leq c_i |\alpha| + d$ for $1 \leq i \leq t$. We say

that K is t-counting if $K = \{a_1^n a_2^n \ldots a_t^n : n \geq 1\}$ where

$a_i \in \Sigma$ for $1 \leq i \leq t$ and $a_j \neq a_{j+1}$ for $1 \leq j \leq t-1$. A language generated by a propagating OL system which has a finite number of starting words (axioms), rather than one only, is referred to as a FPOL language.

Theorem II.1 [28]. Let $t \geq 3$, M be a t-counting language, L be a t-balanced FPOL language and $K = M \cap L$. There exists a constant c such that $\#\{x \in K : |x| \leq n\} \leq$ c log n for every positive integer n. □

Corollary II.2 [28]. Let K be an FPOL language such that $\{a^n b^n c^n : n \geq 1\} \subseteq K$. For no finite language M, $K \setminus M$ is 3-balanced. □

An interesting and mathematically very elegant way of providing conditions under which a language is or is not an OL language is to investigate length sets of OL languages. A typical example of such a research is the following result.

Theorem II.3 [63]. Assume that $X = \{x_i : i = 1, 2, ...\}$ where $x_i < x_{i+1}$ for $i \geq 1$, is a set of natural numbers satisfying the following conditions:

(i) $\lim_{i \to \infty} (x_{i+1} - x_i) = \infty$,

(ii) for each $n \in N$, $\lim_{i \to \infty} \frac{i^n}{x_i} = 0$, and

(iii) for each $m > 1$, $\lim_{i \to \infty} \frac{x_i}{m^i} = 0$.

Then X is not an OL length set. □

OL languages represent an exhaustive approach to language definition: given a rewriting system (here an OL system) one defines its language to be the set of all strings that can be derived in the system. Various mathematical and application-oriented motivations lead to the consideration of various other "language squeezing" mechanisms. We will consider now two of them:

(1) the mechanism of nonterminals--a very traditional mechanism of language definition within formal language theory, and

(2) the mechanism of coding, the consideration of which in the theory of L systems is due to a biological motivation (see, e.g., [19]).

Definition [54]. An EOL system is a construct $G = (\Sigma, h, \omega, \Delta)$ where $U(G) = (\Sigma, h, \omega)$ is an OL system and $\Delta \subseteq \Sigma$ (Δ is referred to as a terminal alphabet and $\Sigma \setminus \Delta$ is referred to as a nonterminal alphabet). The language of G is defined by $L(G) = L(U(G)) \cap \Delta^*$ and referred to as an EOL language. □

Definition [19]. A COL system is a construct $G = (\Sigma, h, \omega, g)$ where $U(G) = (\Sigma, h, \omega)$ is an OL system and g is a coding on Σ^*. The language of G is defined by $L(G) = g(L(U(G)))$ and is referred to as a COL language. □

The following result is quite instructive for understanding the language defining power of both of the above mechanisms.

Theorem II.4 [19]. $L(\text{EOL}) = L(\text{COL})$. □

Various ramifications of the above result are considered in [11,31].

Theorem II.4 forms also an additional motivation to study $L(\text{EOL})$--the class of languages quite central within the theory of L systems. Quite a number of results concerning the combinatorial structure of EOL languages are available by now. Here are some examples.

Let K be a language over Σ and let Θ be a nonempty subset of Σ. Let $N(K, \Theta) = \{n : \#_\Theta x = n \text{ for some } x \in K\}$. We say that Θ is numerically dispersed in K if $N(K, \Theta)$ is infinite and, for every natural number k, there exists a natural number n_k such that, for all u_1, $u_2 \in N(K,\Theta)$, $u_1 > u_2 > n_k$ implies $u_1 - u_2 > k$. We say that Θ is <u>clus-tered</u> in K if $N(K,\Theta)$ is infinite and there exist natural numbers k_1, k_2 both larger than 1 such that if a word $x \in K$ satisfies $\#_\Theta x \geq k_1$ then x contains at least two occurrences of letters from Θ which lie at a distance smaller than k_2 from each other.

<u>Theorem II.5</u> [21]. Let K be an EOL language over Σ and let Θ be a nonempty subset of Σ. If Θ is numerically dispersed in K then Θ is clustered in K. □

<u>Corollary II.6</u> [54]. $L_0 = \{x \in \{a,b\}^* : \#_a x = 2^n$ and $n \geq 0\}$ is not an EOL language. □

Let K be a language over an alphabet Σ and let Θ be a nonempty subset of Σ. We say that K is Θ-<u>determined</u> if for every positive integer k there exists a positive integer n_k such that for every x, y in K, if $|x|$, $|y| > n_k$, $x = x_1 u x_2$, $y = x_1 v x_2$ and $|u|$, $|v| < k$ then $\underline{pres}_\Theta u = \underline{pres}_\Theta v$.

<u>Theorem II.7</u> [21]. Let K be a Θ-determined EOL language. There exist positive integer constants c and d such that, for every $x \in K$, if $\#_\Theta x > c$ then $|x| < d^{\#_\Theta x}$. □

<u>Corollary II.8</u> [21]. $L_1 = \{a^k b^\ell a^k : \ell \geq k \geq 1\}$ is not an EOL language. □

<u>Theorem II.9</u> [21]. Let K be an EOL language over an alphabet Σ. If K is Σ-determined then there exist a finite number of DOL languages K_1, ..., K_n and a homomorphism h such that $K = h\left(\bigcup_{i=1}^{n} K_i\right)$. □

A classical aspect of the combinatorial structure of a class of languages (defined by a class of rewriting systems) is that of ambiguity. The ambiguity of an EOL system is defined in the same way as for context-free grammars (see, e.g., [111]), i.e., through the number of different derivation trees. Also the notion of the ambiguity of an EOL language follows then in the same way as in the case of a context-free language.

A quite counterintuitive result concerning the ambiguity of EOL languages (actually disproving a conjecture from [89]) is the following one.

Theorem II.10 [27]. There exist EOL languages of finite degree of ambiguity. □

An interesting study of different aspects of ambiguity of OL languages is presented in [96].

We conclude this section by giving typical examples of results concerning decision problems for EOL systems.

Theorem II.11 [100,113]. It is undecidable whether or not an arbitrary EOL language is an OL language. □

Theorem II.12 [113]. It is undecidable whether or not an arbitrary EOL language is regular. The validity of the inclusion $K \subseteq R$ is decidable, given an EOL language K and a regular language R. □

Open Problem. Is it decidable whether or not an arbitrary OL language is regular? Is it decidable whether or not an arbitrary regular language is an OL language? □

III. SEVERAL HOMOMORPHISMS ITERATED

The language of a DOL system is obtained by applying to a fixed word an arbitrary homomorphism from the semigroup generated by a single homomorphism. Semigroups generated by a finite number of homomorphisms form a natural next step.

Definition [98]. A DTOL system is a construct $G = (\Sigma, H, \omega)$ where Σ is an alphabet, $\omega \in \Sigma^*$ and H is a finite set of homomorphisms from Σ^* into Σ^* (referred to as tables of G). The language of G is defined by $L(G) = \{x \in \Sigma^* : x = h_n \ldots h_1(\omega)$ for some $n \geq 0$ and $h_1, \ldots, h_n \in H\}$ and referred to as a DTOL language. □

A useful way of looking at the combinatorial structure of a DTOL language is to investigate the structure of its set of subwords. The basic result in this direction is the following one. (For a language K and a positive integer ℓ, $\text{sub}_\ell K$ denotes the set of all subwords of length ℓ occurring in words of K.)

Theorem III.1 [18]. Let Σ be a finite alphabet such that $^\#\Sigma = n \geq 2$. If K is a DTOL language over Σ then $\lim_{\ell \to \infty} \dfrac{^\#\text{sub}_\ell K}{n^\ell} = 0$. □

Corollary III.2 [18]. Let F be a finite language over Σ. Then $\Sigma^* \setminus F$ is not a DTOL language. □

Theorem III.1 points very clearly to the source of the "poor" language generating power of DTOL systems. It turns out that the "subword point of view" is very convenient in the investigation of the influence of various structural restrictions (on DTOL systems) on the language generating power of resulting systems (for proofs see, e.g., [76,103]).

Theorem III.3. (1) For every DOL language K there exists a constant c such that, for every $\ell > 0$, $^{\#}\underline{sub}_\ell K \leq c\ell^2$. (2) For every positive integer c there exists a DOL language K such that $^{\#}\underline{sub}_\ell K \geq c\ell^2$ for infinitely many positive integers ℓ. □

The above result together with Theorem II.9 yields then an interesting result on the combinatorial structure of EOL languages.

Theorem III.4 [21]. Let K be an EOL language over an alphabet Σ. If K is Σ-determined then there exists a constant c such that, for each natural number ℓ,
$^{\#}\underline{sub}_\ell K \leq c\ell^3$. □

Corollary III.5 [21]. $L_3 = \{\omega\$\omega\$\omega : \omega \in \{a,b\}*\}$ is not an EOL language. □

If we restrict ourselves to languages generated by DOL systems in which every letter is rewritten as a word of length at least two (called growing DOL systems) then the resulting languages are "poorer" as far as their subwords are concerned.

Theorem III.6. (1) For every growing DOL language K there exists a positive integer constant c such that, for every $\ell > 0$, $^{\#}\underline{sub}_\ell K \leq c\ell \log \ell$. (2) For every positive integer c there exists a growing DOL language K such that $^{\#}\underline{sub}_\ell K \geq c\ell \log \ell$ for infinitely many positive integers ℓ. □

The theory of DTOL systems offers quite a number of interesting results concerning growth functions and length sets. We will discuss now some of them.

Definition. Given an alphabet $\Sigma = \{a_1,...,a_k\}$, a function $f : \Sigma^* \to Z$ is termed Z-rational (resp., N-rational) if there is a row vector π, a column vector η and square matrices $M_1, \ldots, M_k$, all of the same dimension m and with integral (resp., nonnegative integral) entries, such that for any word $x = a_{i_1} \ldots a_{i_t}$, $f(x) = \pi M_{i_1} \ldots M_{i_t} \eta$ (where for $x = \Lambda$ we set $f(\Lambda) = \pi\eta$). An N-rational function is called a DTOL <u>function</u> if all entries in η equal 1; moreover if for all words x, y with a common Parikh vector $f(x) = f(y)$, then we say that f is a <u>commutative</u> DTOL <u>function</u>. $\square$

The following two results describe the interconnection between commutative DTOL functions and DOL growth functions.

<u>Theorem III.7</u> [64]. For any DOL growth functions f_{ij}, $1 \leq i \leq k$, $1 \leq j \leq u$, one may construct a DTOL system G defining the commutative function $f : \{a_1, \ldots, a_k\}^* \to N$ such that $f(x) = \sum_{j=1}^{u} f_{1j}(\#_{a_1} x) \ldots f_{kj}(\#_{a_k} x)$. $\square$

The converse of the above theorem is not true: there are commutative DTOL functions not expressible in the above form. However, the following result holds.

<u>Theorem III.8</u> [64]. Any commutative DTOL function $f : \{a_1, \ldots, a_k\}^* \to N$ is of the form $f(x) = \sum_{j=1}^{u} f_{1j}(\#_{a_1} x) \ldots f_{kj}(\#_{a_k} x)$ where all of the functions f_{ij} are N-rational and, furthermore, the functions f_{kj} are DOL growth functions. $\square$

An interesting aspect of the length set of a language is its length density: given a language K its <u>length</u> <u>density</u> is defined by $\underline{lgd}\ K = \lim_{\ell \to \infty} \dfrac{\#\{|x| : x \in K \text{ and } |x| \leq \ell\}}{\ell}$ provided the limit exists. For DOL languages the situation concerning length density is rather simple.

Theorem III.9 [103]. Every DOL language has a rational length density which can be computed effectively. Every rational number between 0 and 1 equals the length density of some DOL language. □

In view of the above, the following result sheds an additional light on the language generating power of DTOL systems.

Theorem III.10 [64]. There are DTOL languages with a transcendental length density, as well as DTOL languages with no length density at all. □

Enriching DTOL systems with the mechanism of nonterminal symbols yields EDTOL systems.

Definition [99]. An EDTOL system is a construct G = $(\Sigma, H, \omega, \Delta)$ where $U(G) = (\Sigma, H, \omega)$ is a DTOL system and $\Delta \subseteq \Sigma$. The language of G is defined by $L(G) = L(U(G)) \cap \Delta^*$ and it is referred to as an EDTOL language. □

The following is a major result on the combinatorial structure of EDTOL languages. It is an analogue of the celebrated pumping lemma for context-free languages. A function $f : R_+ \rightarrow R_+$ is called slow if for every $\alpha \in R_+$ there exists $n_\alpha \in R_+$ such that for every $x \in R_+$, if $x > n_\alpha$ then $f(x) < x^\alpha$. Let Σ be a finite alphabet and let f be a function, $f : R_+ \rightarrow R_+$. A word x over Σ is called f-random if every two disjoint subwords of x longer than $f(|x|)$ are different.

Theorem III.11 [20]. Let K be an EDTOL language over an alphabet Σ with $^\#\Sigma = t$ and let f be a slow function. There exists a positive integer constant p such that for every f-random word x in K longer than p there exist words $x_0, \ldots, x_{2t}, y_1, \ldots, y_{2t}$ with $y_1 \ldots y_{2t} \neq \Lambda$ and $x_0 \ldots x_{2t} = x$ such that $x_0 y_1^n x_1 y_2^n x_2 \ldots y_{2t}^n x_{2t}$ is in K for every positive integer n. □

One easily notices that Σ^* is an EDTOL language for every alphabet Σ. Hence the "subword complexity" consider- ations analogous to those for DTOL languages do not go through. However, based on the above theorem one can prove a result somewhat analogous to Theorem III.1 but concerning the number of words of the given length (rather than the number of sub- words of the given length).

Theorem III.12 [20]. Let K be an EDTOL language over an alphabet Σ where $^\#\Sigma = n \geq 2$. If length K does not contain an infinite arithmetic progression, then

$$\lim_{\ell \to \infty} \frac{^\#\{x \in K : |x| = \ell\}}{n^\ell} = 0. \quad \square$$

Corollary III.13 [20]. Let Σ be a finite alphabet with $^\#\Sigma \geq 2$. Let k be a positive integer larger than 1. Then neither $\{x \in \Sigma^* : |x| = k^n \text{ for some } n \geq 0\}$ nor $\{x \in \Sigma^* : |x| = n^k \text{ for some } n \geq 0\}$ are EDTOL languages. □

IV. SEVERAL FINITE SUBSTITUTIONS ITERATED

In the same way as DOL systems are generalized to yield DTOL systems, OL systems are generalized to yield TOL systems.

Definition [98]. A TOL system is a construct $G = (\Sigma, H, \omega)$ where Σ is an alphabet, $\omega \in \Sigma^*$ and H is a finite set of finite substitutions from Σ^* into subsets of Σ^* (referred to as tables of G). The language of G is defined by $L(G) = \{x \in \Sigma^* : x \in h_n \ldots h_1(\omega) \text{ for some } n \geq 0, h_1, \ldots, h_n \in H\}$ and referred to as a TOL language. □

Very little is known about the combinatorial structure of TOL languages; perhaps the best understood case is that of TOL languages over a one-letter alphabet [68].

A natural area of investigation concerns properties of TOL transformations: here one considers a TOL scheme (that is, a TOL system without the axiom) $G = (\Sigma, H)$ and investigates it as a function from the set of subsets of Σ^* into itself. The basic situation under examination consists of being given two of the following three sets: a set K_1 of (start) words over Σ, a set K_2 of (target) words of Σ and a (control) set C of finite sequences of applications of elements from H. The problem is to ascertain information about the remaining set. (Note that we can consider a sequence of elements from H either as a word over H^*, called a control word, or a mapping from subsets of Σ^* into subsets of Σ^*. We shall do both in the sequel but this should not lead to confusion.) The following are examples of known results concerning this problem.

Theorem IV.1 [50]. If K_2 is a regular language, and K_1 an arbitrary language, then the set C of control words leading from K_1 to K_2 is regular. $\square$

Theorem IV.2 [50]. If K_2 is a regular language and C is an arbitrary set of control words, then the set of all words mapped into K_2 by C is regular. $\square$

Theorem IV.3 [50]. There is no TOL scheme $G = (\Sigma, H)$ such that H^* is the set of all finite nonempty subsitutions on Σ^*. $\square$

Again, TOL systems can be augmented with the mechanism of nonterminals yielding ETOL systems.

Definition [99]. An ETOL system is a construct $G =$ $(\Sigma, H, \omega, \Delta)$ where $U(G) = (\Sigma, H, \omega)$ is a TOL system and $\Delta \subseteq \Sigma$. The language of G is defined by $L(G) = L(U(G)) \cap \Delta^*$ and referred to as an ETOL language. □

A number of results are available describing the combinatorial structure of ETOL languages (which form a larger class than $L(\text{EDTOL})$). We discuss some of them now.

Theorem IV.4 [30]. Let K be an ETOL language over an alphabet Δ. Then for every $\Delta_1 \subseteq \Delta$, $\Delta_1 \neq \emptyset$, there exists a positive integer k such that for every x in K either (i) $\#_{\Delta_1} x \leq 1$, or (ii) x contains a subword w such that $|w| \leq k$ and $\#_{\Delta_1} x \geq 2$, or (iii) there exists an infinite subset M of K such that for every y in M, $\#_{\Delta_1} y = \#_{\Delta_1} x$. □

Corollary IV.5 [30]. $L_4 = \{(ab^n)^m : m \geq n \geq 1\}$ is not an ETOL language. □

Theorem IV.6 [30]. Let K be an ETOL language over an alphabet Δ and let Δ_1, Δ_2 be a partition of Δ. If there exists a function ϕ from nonnegative integers into nonnegative integers such that, for every x in K, $\#_{\Delta_2} x < \phi(\#_{\Delta_1} x)$, then Δ_1 is clustered in K. □

Corollary IV.7 [30]. $L_5 = \{x \in \{a,b\}^* : \#_b x = 2^{\#_a x}\}$ is not an ETOL language. □

The following result is a typical "bridging" result. It allows one to construct examples of non-ETOL languages providing that one has examples of languages that are not EDTOL.

Theorem IV.8 [35]. Let Σ_1, Σ_2 be two disjoint alphabets and let $K_1 \subseteq \Sigma_1^*$, $K_2 \subseteq \Sigma_2^*$. Let f be a surjective function from K_1 into K_2 and let $K = \{xf(x) : x \in K_1\}$. If K is an ETOL language then K_2 is an ETOL language. □

The above theorem and Corollary III.13 yield then the following result.

Corollary IV.9 [35]. Let f be the coding $f : \{a,b\}^* \to \{c,d\}^*$ defined by $f(a) = c$ and $f(b) = d$, and let $L_6 = \{x \in \{a,b\}^* : |x| = 2^n$ for some $n \geq 0\}$. Then $L_7 = \{xf(x) : x \in L_5\}$ is not an ETOL language. $\square$

A classical way to investigate the effect of structural restrictions on rewriting systems on their language generating power is to consider "rewriting systems of finite index." To determine "the index of a rewriting" in context-free grammars one counts the number of nonterminals in "intermediate" sentential forms. Since in an ETOL system both terminal and nonterminal symbols can be rewritten, one has to count active symbols rather than nonterminal symbols. A letter a in an ETOL system $G = (\Sigma, H, \omega, \Delta)$ is called active (in G) if $x \in h(a)$ for some $x \neq a$ and $h \in H$. Then $A(G) = \{a \in \Sigma : a$ is active in $G\}$. The notion of a derivation and its trace has the usual meaning also within the theory of ETOL systems.

Definition [104]. (1) Let G be an ETOL system. For a positive integer k, we say that G is of index k if for every word x in $L(G)$ there exists a derivation of x in G with the trace $x_1, \ldots, x_n$ such that, for $1 \leq j \leq n$, $\#_{A(G)} x_j \leq k$. We say that G is of finite index if G is of index k for some $k \geq 1$. (2) Let K be an ETOL language. For a positive integer k we say that K is of index k if there exists an ETOL system G of index k such that $L(G) = K$. We say that K is of finite index if K is of index k for some $k \geq 1$. $\square$

Among ETOL systems of finite index one can naturally distinguish these in which every successful derivation satisfies
a finite index restriction.

Definition [104]. (1) Let G be an ETOL system. For a
positive integer k, we say that G is of uncontrolled index
k, if for every word x in L(G), whenever x_1, ..., x_n is
the trace of a derivation of x in G, then $\#_{A(G)} x_j \leq k$
for $1 \leq j \leq n$. We say that G is of uncontrolled finite
index if G is of uncontrolled index k for some $k \geq 1$.
(2) Let K be an ETOL language. For a positive integer k
we say that K is of uncontrolled index k if there exists
an ETOL system G of uncontrolled index k such that L(G) =
K. We say that K is of uncontrolled finite index if K is
of uncontrolled index k for some $k \geq 1$. □

We will use $L(\text{ETOL})_{FIN}$ and $L(\text{ETOL})_{FINU}$ to denote the
class of languages generated by ETOL systems of finite index
and the class of languages generated by ETOL systems of uncontrolled finite index respectively. If we want to fix a
particular index k then we use $L(\text{ETOL})_{FIN(k)}$ and
$L(\text{ETOL})_{FINU(k)}$ respectively.

The following result is the basic technical tool in investigating ETOL languages of finite index.

Theorem IV.10 [105]. There exists an algorithm which,
given an arbitrary ETOL system G of index k, produces an
equivalent EPDTOL system H which is of uncontrolled index
k. □

Increasing the index of ETOL systems leads to the following infinite hierarchy.

Theorem IV.11 [105]. For every positive integer i,

$L(\text{ETOL})_{\text{FIN}(i)} \subsetneq L(\text{ETOL})_{\text{FIN}(i+1)}.$ □

It turns out that $L(\text{ETOL})_{\text{FIN}}$ has a nice algebraic structure.

Theorem IV.12 [105]. (1) For every $k \geq 1$, $L(\text{ETOL})_{\text{FIN}(k)}$ is a full semiAFL (which is full principal); (2) $L(\text{ETOL})_{\text{FIN}}$ is a substitution-closed full AFL (which is not full principal). □

Languages in $L(\text{ETOL})_{\text{FIN}}$ admit the following intercalation property.

Theorem IV.13 [105]. Let K be an ETOL language of index k. There exist positive integers n, m such that for every word x in K longer than n, $x = x_0\alpha_1 x_1 \cdots \alpha_{2k}x_{2k}$, with $\alpha_1\ldots\alpha_{2k} \neq \Lambda$, $|\alpha_i| \leq m$ for $1 \leq i \leq k$ and $x_0\alpha_1^t x_1\alpha_2^t \cdots \alpha_{2k}^t x_{2k} \in K$ for every $t \geq 0$. □

It is possible to get one "universal" system representing all ETOL languages of index k over Σ (for given k and Σ). Given an ETOL system $G = (\Sigma, h, \omega, \Delta)$ and a (control) language $C \subseteq H^*$, we define $L_C(G)$ to be the set of all those words in $L(G)$ that can be derived in G using a sequence of tables from C.

Theorem IV.14 [105]. Let Σ be a finite alphabet. For every positive integer k there exists an EPDTOL system G_k of uncontrolled index k such that $\{L_C(G_k) : C$ is a regular set} is identical with the family of ETOL languages of index k over Σ. □

The subject of ETOL systems of finite index is also treated in detail in [70] and a very comprehensive study of this topic is presented in [125]. Using a machine-model

approach, $L(\text{ETOL})_{\text{FIN}}$ is studied in [95] and quite extensively in [51], where also the above three results occur. The
notion of an ETOL system of finite index admits interesting
generalizations to an ETOL system of finite rank and to an
ETOL system of finite tree rank (see, e.g., [108]). The
theory of those systems gives a real insight into the structure of (the derivations in) ETOL systems and at the same time
it accentuates some of the basic differences between parallel
and sequential rewriting systems.

ETOL systems constitute today a central model of parallel
rewriting. Hence a way to understand the nature of parallel
rewriting is to look for those features of ETOL systems that
are responsible for their language generating power. An example of a research in this direction is presented now.

Intuitively it is clear that the considerable language
generating power of ETOL systems comes from the fact that in
rewriting a string x an ETOL system G can "force" different sorts of letters to behave synchronously. For example, if
occurrences of a letter b in x are rewritten by elements
of a set B then at the same time occurrences of a letter c
must be rewritten by elements of a set C, occurrences of a
letter d must be rewritten by elements of a set D, etc.
Hence, intuitively, it seems conceivable that if more letters
can be forced to behave synchronously then the language generating power increases. Let us investigate first the simplest case: 1-<u>restricted</u> ETOL <u>systems</u>; an ETOL system G =
 $(\Sigma, H, \omega, \Delta)$ is called 1-<u>restricted</u>, abbreviated
ETOL$_{[1]}$<u>system</u>, if for every $h \in H$ there exists $b \in \Sigma$ such
that h(c) = {c} for each $c \in \Sigma \setminus b$. To state a result on

the combinatorial structure of languages in $L(\text{ETOL}_{[1]})$, we need the following two notions. Let K be an infinite language over Σ. For $b \in \Sigma$ we say that K is <u>logarithmically</u> <u>b-clustered</u> if there exists a positive integer q such that for every word x in K, if $b \in \underline{\text{alph}}\ x$, then $x = x_0 b x_1 \ldots b x_n$, $n \geq 1$, $x_0, \ldots, x_n \in \Sigma^*$, $b \notin \underline{\text{alph}}\ x_0 \cdots x_n$ and $|x_j| \leq q \log n$ for $0 \leq j \leq n$. We say that K is <u>logarithmically</u> <u>clustered</u> if there exists a letter $b \in \Sigma$ such that K is logarithmically b-clustered. We say that K is <u>pump-generated</u> if there exist positive integers r, q and words $x_0, \ldots, x_r$, u, w, $z \in \Sigma^*$ with $uz \neq \Lambda$ and $|uz| < q$ such that $K = \bigcup\limits_{i>0} x_0 u^i w z^i x_1 \ldots u^i w z^i x$.

<u>Theorem IV.15</u> [66]. If K is an infinite $\text{ETOL}_{[1]}$ language then either K contains an infinite logarithmically clustered language or K contains a pump-generated language. □

<u>Corollary IV.16</u> [66]. $\{a^n b^n c^n : n \geq 0\} \notin L(\text{ETOL}_{[1]})$. □

The notion of a 1-restricted ETOL system is generalized in an obvious way to a k-<u>restricted</u> ETOL <u>system</u>--that is, an ETOL system G in each table of which at most k different symbols can be rewritten by a mapping different from the identity mapping; we say that G is an $\text{ETOL}_{[k]}$ <u>system</u>. Clearly, Corollary IV.16 yields easily the following result.

<u>Theorem IV.17</u> [66]. $L(\text{ETOL}_{[1]}) \subsetneq L(\text{ETOL}_{[2]})$. □

It is quite surprising that the above result does not generalize as to yield an infinite hierarchy within $L(\text{ETOL})$. We have the following result.

<u>Theorem IV.18</u> [66]. For every $k \geq 8$, $L(\text{ETOL}_{[k]}) = L(\text{ETOL}_{[k+1]})$. □

In order to give a more precise answer to the quite natural question "How parallel must parallel rewriting be?" one needs a solution of the following.

Open Problem. What is the minimal positive integer ℓ such that $L(\text{ETOL}_{[k]}) = L(\text{ETOL}_{[k+1]})$ for every $k \geq \ell$? □

It is instructive to notice that k-restricted ETOL systems form a very natural extension of Indian parallel grammars introduced in [119].

We end this section by giving the following open problem, the solution of which could provide an additional link between L systems and the rest of the formal language theory.

Open Problem. Does there exist an ETOL language which is the hardest (in the sense of [51]) for $L(\text{ETOL})$? □

Partial results concerning the above problem can be found in [10,32].

V. THE RELATIONSHIP TO OTHER CLASSES OF LANGUAGES

In this section we discuss the relationship of $L(\text{ETOL})$ and its subclasses to various classes of languages considered in formal language theory. $L(\text{ETOL})$ and $L(\text{EOL})$ fit into the classical Chomsky framework as follows.

Theorem V.1 [54,99]. $L(\text{CF}) \subsetneq L(\text{EOL}) \subsetneq L(\text{ETOL}) \subsetneq L(\text{CS})$. □

It turns out that ETOL systems and EOL systems have an interesting connection to the classical tag systems with deletion number $n = 1$ (called context-free tag systems and referred to as 1-TAG systems). The existence of a natural relationship between 1-TAG systems and EOL systems is pointed out in [78] and this relationship is investigated in [17,67].

Theorem V.2 [17,67]. L(EOL) $\subsetneq$ L(1-TAG) $\subsetneq$ L(ETOL). $\square$

Moreover, [17] provides a characterization of L(1-TAG) in terms L(EOL).

A natural way of investigating the relationship between sequential and parallel rewriting systems is by investigating that between context-free grammars and EOL systems. The usefulness of the class of EOL systems is indicated (among others) by the fact that it admits several characterizations of the class of context-free languages. For example, we have the following result.

Theorem V.3 [72,101]. A language is context-free if and only if it is generated by an EOL system $G = (\Sigma,h,\omega,\Delta)$ such that $a \in h(a)$ for every $a \in \Sigma$. $\square$

An interesting and well motivated mechanism of language definition using OL systems is that of adult languages introduced in [57]. For an OL system $G = (\Sigma,h,\omega)$ we define its adult language by $L_A(G) = \{x \in L(G) : y \in h(x)$ implies $y = x$ for all $y \in \Sigma^*\}$--it is referred to as an AOL language. It turns out that one can characterize L(CF) as follows.

Theorem V.4 [57]. L(AOL) = L(CF). $\square$

Results obtained for the time complexity of EOL parsing are similar to the results known for context-free grammars.

Theorem V.5 [93]. L(EOL) $\subseteq$ DTIME(n^4). $\square$

It was established in [122] that EOL languages are in DTAPE($\log^2 n$) (the same tape bound has been obtained also for context-free languages). A very close connection between L(EOL) and L(CF) is pointed out by the following result.

Theorem V.6 [122]. For any real number $k \geq 1$,

$L(\text{EOL}) \subseteq \text{DTAPE}(\log^k n)$ if and only if $L(\text{CF}) \subseteq \text{DTAPE}(\log^k n)$

and

$L(\text{EOL}) \subseteq \text{NTAPE}(\log^k n)$ if and only if $L(\text{CF}) \subseteq \text{NTAPE}(\log^k n)$.

$\square$

Hence, as far as (time or tape) complexity of parsing is concerned, there is little difference between $L(\text{EOL})$ and $L(\text{CF})$. However, $L(\text{EOL})$ is a "much" bigger class of languages than $L(\text{CF})$. The attractiveness of $L(\text{EOL})$ is even more obvious when one considers the traditional (and very important) issue of ambiguity. It was observed in [89] that there exist CF inherently ambiguous languages which are EOL unambiguous--hence one can "repair" the ambiguity by (re)defining a context-free language by an EOL system. Moreover, the situation is even more favorable to EOL systems as pointed out by the following result.

Theorem V.7 [26]. For every context-free language K, the degree of EOL ambiguity of K cannot exceed the degree of CF ambiguity of K. $\square$

The comparison of $L(\text{CF})$ and $L(\text{EDTOL})$ is very important for the understanding of the role of "generative determinism" in the theory of parallel rewriting. Here are two typical results in this direction.

Theorem V.8 [23,69]. There exist context-free languages that are not EDTOL languages. In particular, no generator of $L(\text{CF})$ is an EDTOL language. $\square$

Theorem V.9 [3]. If $L_1, \ldots, L_n$ are context-free languages, one of which is bounded, then $L_1 \cap \ldots \cap L_n$ is an EDTOL language. $\square$

To get a more complete picture of the relationship between L(CF) and L(EDTOL) one would have to prove or disprove the following.

Conjecture. L(EDTOL) $\cap$ L(CF) equals the class of context-free languages of finite index. $\square$

The area of finite index restrictions on rewriting systems provides numerous bridges between the class of ETOL systems and various other classes of language-defining mechanisms. Here are some results in this direction.

Theorem V.10 [106,107]. Under the finite index restrictions the following classes of language-generating systems produce exactly L(ETOL)$_{FIN}$:

(1) the class of scattered grammars,

(2) the class of context-free programmed grammars,

(3) the class of matrix grammars,

(4) the class of ordered grammars,

(5) the class of state grammars,

(6) the class of random context grammars. $\square$

Theorem V.11 [95]. The class of output languages of two-way dgsm's coincides with L(ETOL)$_{FIN}$. $\square$

Theorem V.12 [46]. Under the finite index restriction macro grammars generate the class of EDTOL languages. $\square$

As a matter of fact there exists a quite strong relationship between macro grammars and ETOL systems as illustrated further by the following results (see also [45,47] for a comprehensive treatment of this topic).

Theorem V.13 [16]. The class of extended linear basic macro languages coincides with the class of ETOL languages. $\square$

Theorem V.14 [1,16]. The class of linear basic macro languages coincides with the class of EDTOL languages. □

The connection between indexed grammars and ETOL languages
was pointed out first in [6] (in particular it is shown there
that L(ETOL) is included in the class of indexed languages).
An interesting result in this direction was recently obtained
in [42]. An indexed ETOL system is an (obvious) combination
of an indexed grammar and a slightly generalized ETOL system.

Theorem V.15 [42]. The class of Szilard languages of
indexed ETOL systems equals the class of languages defined by
one-way alternating pushdown automata. □

The underlying mappings of the ETOL framework outlined in
the first four sections of this paper are homomorphisms and
finite substitutions. Clearly a systematic study of various
properties of ETOL systems requires a systematic study of
homomorphisms. There are several examples of such studies
initiated within the framework of L systems which either led
to new research areas within formal language theory or shed
new light on the existing topics. We consider some of these
now.

The area of equality languages was initiated in connection
with efforts to solve the DOL sequence equivalence problem.
The equality language of homomorphisms h, g on an alphabet
Σ is defined by $Eq(g,h) = \{x \in \Sigma^* : g(x) = h(x)\}$. Equality
languages of homomorphisms were explicitly introduced (under
a different name) in [25]; they provide an interesting representation of recursively enumerable languages, as, e.g., the
following two results.

Theorem V.16 [25,115]. For every recursively enumerable language K there exist homomorphisms h, g, a weak identity f and a regular set R such that K = f(Eq(h,g) ∩ R). □

For homomorphisms h, g : $\Sigma^* \to \Delta^*$ the minimal equality set is the set eq(h,g) = $\{x \in \Sigma^+ : h(x) = g(x)$ and if x = yz for y, z $\in \Sigma^+$ then $h(y) \neq g(y)\}$.

Theorem V.17 [8]. For every recursively enumerable language K there exist homomorphisms h, g and a weak identity f such that K = f(eq(h,g)). □

There exists a single (and "simple") equality language encoding all recursively enumerable languages as follows. For an alphabet Σ let $\bar{\Sigma} = \{\bar{a} : a \in \Sigma\}$ and then for each x $\in \Sigma^*$ let $\bar{x}$ denote the word obtained from x by barring each symbol in it. Then the complete twin shuffle over Σ is defined by $L_\Sigma = \{x \in (\Sigma \cup \bar{\Sigma})^* : \overline{\text{pres}_\Sigma x} = \underline{\text{pres}_{\bar{\Sigma}} x}\}$. Obviously L is an equality language.

Theorem V.18 [44]. For every recursively enumerable language K there exists a dgsm mapping f such that K = $f(L_{\{0,1\}})$. □

Another basic notion concerning homomorphisms is that of a fixed point. The fixed point of a mapping h on Σ^* is the language defined by Fp(h) = $\{x \in \Sigma^* : h(x) = x\}$. It turns out that from the point of view of fixed-point languages, homomorphisms are "weak" mappings.

Theorem V.19 [57]. For every homomorphism h there exists a finite language K such that Fp(h) = K*. □

Hence it is natural to consider fixed-point languages of mappings more general than homomorphisms. For dgsm mappings we get the following result.

Theorem V.20 [44]. For every recursively enumerable language K there exist a dgsm mapping h and a weak identity
f such that K = f(Fp(h)). □

Comparing Theorems V.19 and V.20 we see that dgsm's form
a "too powerful" generalization of homomorphisms. This leads
one to consider a new subclass of dgsm mappings: symmetric
dgsm mappings. Informally speaking, a symmetric dgsm mapping
(see [43]) is a dgsm mapping which can be also defined by a
reversed dgsm, that is, a dgsm which reads its input (and
writes its output) from right to left (rather than from left
to right). Then we have the following result.

Theorem V.21 [43]. The class of fixed-point languages of
symmetric dgsm mappings equals the class of regular languages.
□

Investigating symmetric dgsm mappings turns out to be useful for the investigation of elementary homomorphisms which
are very important in the theory of DOL systems. For example,
as a corollary of the above result, we get the following
theorem.

Theorem V.22 [43]. Eq(h,g) is regular if g is a homomorphism and h is the composition of elementary
homomorphisms. □

To put the above result in the proper persective we mention that the composition of elementary homomorphisms does not
have to be an elementary homomorphism. The theory of symmetric dgsm mappings is at its very beginnings. Quite a number
of basic questions concerning those mappings are still open.
An example of such a basic open problem is the following one.

Open Problem. Is it decidable whether or not an arbitrary dgsm mapping is symmetric? □

We have seen above examples of expressive power of homomorphisms. The area of basic properties of homomorphisms, including the representation of recursively enumerable languages using homomorphisms, is by now a subject of a very active research surveyed extensively in [7]. We close this section by giving a very instructive result concerning the expressive power of homomorphisms (see [33,34]). For homomorphisms h and g we denote by max(h,g) the maximal solution of the equation h(X) = g(X), where X is a variable of language type.

Theorem V.22 [33]. A language K is the complement of a recursively enumerable language if and only if there exist Λ-free homomorphisms h, g, f and a regular language R such that K = f(max(h,g) ∩ R). □

Moreover, it is shown in [33] that if one considers arbitrary homomorphisms h, g then the class of languages of the form f(max(h,g) ∩ R), with f and R as above, strictly contains both the class of all recursively enumerable languages and the class of complements of recursively enumerable languages!

VI. DISCUSSION

In this paper we have tried to survey some aspects of the theory of L systems. Since the theory of L systems forms today a very rich body of knowledge, the restriction on the size of this paper made it unavoidable to skip a number of very important problem areas and to be rather sketchy with the topics covered. In particular, we had no opportunity to cover the following areas of research.

(1) The theory of L forms constitutes today one of the most vigorous areas within the theory of L systems. It was initiated in [85], and [86-89] are some of the papers representative for this area; [127] is a monograph covering in detail the theory of grammar and L forms. We have decided not to cover it in our paper because the paper of A. Salomaa in the same volume [116] treats it very thoroughly.

(2) The theory of iteration grammars generalizes the theory of ETOL systems by allowing to iterate mappings more general than finite substitutions only. It was initiated in [77] while [2,41,79,112] are some of the papers representative for the area.

(3) Complexity of recognizing and parsing of ETOL languages constitutes a very natural topic. The most basic results are presented in [53,61,78,82,93,122].

(4) The theory of machine models for ETOL languages constitutes an important link with automata theory. Two most important models are considered in [81,109]; another representative paper is [47]. A more general model is considered in [118]. This area is closely related to (3).

(5) Stochastic ETOL systems constitute an extension of ETOL systems that is quite natural from both mathematical and biological points of view. The area was initiated in [37,59] and is further considered in [38,60].

(6) Context-dependent L systems constitute an extension of ETOL systems (referred to as context independent L systems)

following a classical line within formal language theory: the rewriting of a letter in a context-dependent L system may depend on the neighboring letters. It was already considered in [71] and the first paper devoted to mathematical properties of those systems is [15]. The most comprehensive treatment of context-dependent L systems is in [126] while [4,12] are very interesting recent results on this subject.

(7) The theory of multidimensional L systems considers L systems generating sets of graphs or sets of maps (rather than sets of strings). In our opinion this theory forms perhaps the most natural and the most needed extension of the "usual" theory of L systems. The theory of multidimensional L systems originates from [90]. The mathematical theory of L systems generating graph languages is for the first time considered in [13] and then further explored in [14]; [36,91] are examples of different approaches to this problem. The theory of L systems generating map languages is for the first time considered in [5] and a different approach is presented in [74].

The topics mentioned above and the material presented in this paper indicate only some of the research areas incorporated in the framework of L systems. The author of this paper is strongly convinced that today the theory of L systems occupies a very central position within formal language theory. It offers to a formal language theorist a possibility of pursuing almost any of the traditional research interests, it offers new perspectives on the traditional topics and it offers totally new problem areas. At the same time the theory of L systems offers very interesting links with other areas of science: links with some traditional mathematical topics are illustrated, e.g., in [117], links with developmental biology are discussed, e.g., in [48,73,84,124], links with systems theory are discussed in [62] and links with the modelling of social systems are discussed in [92].

Several links between the theory of L systems and various areas of computer science outside of formal language theory were established already. A connection to operating systems is pointed out in [40], a connection to program validation is discussed in [39,58], a connection to systematic programming is discussed in [97] and a link with parallel processing is discussed in [49]. We would like to close this paper by calling for more research in this direction. We are convinced that both the theory of L systems and computer science can profit when closer relationships are established.

ACKNOWLEDGMENTS

The author is indebted to J. Engelfriet, A. Lindenmayer and R. Verraedt for useful comments on the first version of this paper.

REFERENCES

1. Arnold, A., and Dauchet, M., Translations de forets re-connaissables monadiques; forets coregulieres. RAIRO 10, 5-28 (1976).
2. Asveld, P.R.J., Iterated context-independent rewriting. Ph.D. thesis, Technical University of Twente (1978).
3. Blattner, M., and Cremers, A., Observations about bounded languages and developmental systems. Math. Syst. Theory 10, 253-258 (1978).
4. Brandenburg, F.J., On the coherence complexity of EIL systems and languages. Unpublished manuscript.
5. Carlyle, J.W., Greibach, S.A., and Paz, A., A two-dimensional generating system modelling growth by binary cell division. Proc. 15th Ann. Symp. Switch. and Aut. Theory, New Orleans, 1-12 (1974).
6. Culik, K., II, On some families of languages related to developmental systems. Int. J. Comp. Math. 4, 31-42 (1974).

7. Culik, K., II, Homomorphisms: decidability, equality and test sets. This volume.
8. Culik, K., II, A purely homomorphic characterization of recursively enumerable sets. JACM 6, 345-350 (1979).
9. Culik, K., II, and Fris, I., The decidability of the equivalence problem for DOL systems. Info. and Control 35, 20-39 (1977).
10. Culik, K., II, and Maurer, H.A., On simple representations of language families. RAIRO, to appear.
11. Culik, K., II, and Opatrny, Literal homomorphisms of OL languages. Int. J. Comp. Math. 4, 247-267 (1974).
12. Culik, K., II, and Karhumaki, J., Interactive L systems with almost interactionaless behaviour. Info. and Control, to appear.
13. Culik, K., II, and Lindenmayer, A., Parallel graph generating and graph recurrence systems for multicellular development. Int. J. Gen. Systems 3, 53-66 (1976).
14. Culik, K., II, and Wood, D., A mathematical investigation of parallel graph OL systems. McMaster University, Dept. of Appl. Math., Tech. Rep. 78-CS-17 (1978).
15. van Dalen, D., A note on some systems of Lindenmayer. Math. Syst. Theory 5, 128-140 (1971).
16. Downey, P.J., Formal languages and recursion schemes. Ph.D. thesis, Harvard University (1974).
17. Ehrenfeucht, A., Engelfriet, J., and Rozenberg, G., Context free normal systems and ETOL systems. Unpublished manuscript.
18. Ehrenfeucht, A., and Rozenberg, G., A limit theorem for sets of subwords in deterministic TOL systems. Info. Proc. Letter 2, 70-73 (1973).
19. Ehrenfeucht, A., and Rozenberg, G., The equality of EOL languages and codings of OL languages. Int. J. Comp. Math. 4, 95-104 (1974).
20. Ehrenfeucht, A., and Rozenberg, G., A pumping theorem for deterministic ETOL languages. RAIRO 9, 13-23 (1975).
21. Ehrenfeucht, A., and Rozenberg, G., The number of occurrences of letters versus their distribution in some EOL languages. Info. and Control 26, 256-271 (1975).
22. Ehrenfeucht, A., and Rozenberg, G., On Θ-determined EOL languages. In [75].
23. Ehrenfeucht, A., and Rozenberg, G., On some context-free languages that are not deterministic ETOL languages. RAIRO 11, 273-291 (1977).
24. Ehrenfeucht, A., and Rozenberg, G., Simplifications of homomorphisms. Info. and Control 38, 298-309 (1978).
25. Ehrenfeucht, A., and Rozenberg, G., Elementary homomorphisms and a solution of the DOL sequence equivalence problem. TCS 7, 169-183 (1978).
26. Ehrenfeucht, A., and Rozenberg, G., On ambiguity in EOL systems. TCS, to appear.
27. Ehrenfeucht, A., and Rozenberg, G., On EOL languages of finite degree of ambiguity. Unpublished manuscript.
28. Ehrenfeucht, A., and Rozenberg, G., FPOL systems generating counting languages. RAIRO, to appear.
29. Ehrenfeucht, A., and Rozenberg, G., On a bound for the DOL sequence equivalence problem. TCS, to appear.
30. Ehrenfeucht, A., and Rozenberg, G., A result on the structure of ETOL languages. Found. of Cont. Eng., to appear.

31. Ehrenfeucht, A., and Rozenberg, G., EOL languages are not codings of FPOL languages. TCS 6, 327-341 (1978).

32. Ehrenfeucht, A., and Rozenberg, G., On inverse homomorphic images of deterministic ETOL languages. In [75].

33. Ehrenfeucht, A., Rozenberg, G., and Ruohonen, K., A morphic characterization of complements of recursively enumerable languages. Unpublished manuscript.

34. Ehrenfeucht, A., Rozenberg, G., and Ruohonen, K., Structurally restricted maximal solutions of language equations involving morphisms. Unpublished manuscript.

35. Ehrenfeucht, A., Rozenberg, G., and Skyum, S., A relationship between ETOL languages and EDTOL languages. TCS 1, 325-330 (1976).

36. Ehrig, H., and Kreowski, H.J., Parallel graph grammars. In [75].

37. Eichhorst, P., Stochastic Lindenmayer systems. University of California at San Diego, Dept. of Appl. Phys. & Info. Sci., Tech. Rep. (1975).

38. Eichhorst, P., and Savitch, W.J., Growth functions of stochastic Lindenmayer systems. Unpublished manuscript.

39. Eichhorst, P., and Vermeir, D., Symbolic correctness of single loop programs. Unpublished manuscript.

40. Ellis, C.A., Consistency and correctness of duplicate database systems. Proc. 6th ACM Symp. Oper. Syst. Princ., 67-84 (1977).

41. Engelfriet, J., Iterating iterated substitution. TCS 5, 85-100 (1977).

42. Engelfriet, J., Some open questions and recent results on tree transducers and tree languages. This volume.

43. Engelfriet, J., and Rozenberg, G., Equality languages and fixed point languages. Info. and Control, to appear.

44. Engelfriet, J., and Rozenberg, G., Equality languages, fixed point languages and representations of recursively enumerable languages. JACM, to appear.

45. Engelfriet, J., Rozenberg, G., and Slutzki, G., Tree transducers, L systems and two-way machines. Proc. 10th Ann. Symp. Theory of Comp., San Diego (1978).

46. Engelfriet, J., and Slutzki, G., Bounded nesting in macro grammars. Info. and Control 42, 157-193 (1979).

47. Engelfriet, J., Schmidt, E.M., and van Leeuwen, J., Stack machines and classes of nonnested macro languages. JACM, to appear.

48. Frijters, D., Principles of simulation of influorescence development: Mechanisms of developmental integration of Aster novae-angliae L. and Hieracium murorum L. Annals of Botany 42, 549-575 (1978).

49. Gati, G., On schemata and L systems for parallel algorithms. RAIRO 13, 155-184 (1979).

50. Ginsburg, S., and Rozenberg, G., TOL schemes and control sets. Info. and Control 27, 109-125 (1974).

51. Greibach, S.A., The hardest context free language. SIAM J. of Comp. 2, 304-310 (1973).

52. Greibach, S.A., One-way finite visit automata. TCS 6, 175-221 (1978).

53. Harju, T., A polynomial recognition algorithm for the EDTOL languages. EIK 13, 167-177 (1977).

54. Herman, G.T., Closure properties of some families of languages associated with biological systems. Info. and Control 24, 101-121 (1974).
55. Herman, G.T., Lee, K.P., van Leeuwen, J., and Rozenberg, G., Characterization of unary developmental languages. Discr. Math., 235-247 (1973).
56. Herman, G.T., and Rozenberg, G., "Developmental Systems and Languages." North-Holland, Amsterdam (1975).
57. Herman, G.T., and Walker, A., Context free languages in biological systems. Int. J. Comp. Math. 4, 369-391 (1975).
58. Howden, W.E., Lindenmayer grammars and symbolic testing. Info. Proc. Letter 7, 38-39 (1978).
59. Jürgensen, H., Probabilistic L systems. In [75].
60. Jürgensen, H., Matthews, D., and Wood, D., Markov deterministic tabled OL systems. Unpublished manuscript.
61. Jones, N., and Skyum, S., Complexity of some problems concerning L systems. Lect. Notes in Comp. Sci. 52, 301-308 (1977).
62. Kalman, R.E., and Lindenmayer, A., DOL-realization of the growth of multi-cellular organisms. Proc. 4th Int. Symp. Math. Theory of Networks and Systems (1979).
63. Karhumaki, J., On length sets of informationless L systems. In [75].
64. Karhumaki, J., On commutative DTOL systems. TCS, to appear.
65. Karhumaki, J., and Simon, I., A note on elementary homomorphisms and the regularity of equality sets. Bulletin of the EATCS 9, 16-24 (1979).
66. Kleijn, H.C.M., and Rozenberg, G., A study in parallel rewriting systems. Info. and Control, to appear.
67. Kudlek, M., Context free normal systems. Lect. Notes in Comp. Sci. 74, 346-353 (1979).
68. Latteux, M., Sur les TOL-systèmes unaires. RAIRO 9, 51-62 (1975).
69. Latteux, M., Générateurs algebraiques et languages EDTOL. Lille, Lab. Calcul, Tech. Rep. No. 109 (1978).
70. Latteux, M., Substitutions dans les EDTOL systèmes ultra-linéaires. Info. and Control 42, 194-260 (1979).
71. Lindenmayer, A., Mathematical models for cellular interactions in development, Parts I & II. J. Theoret. Biol. 18, 280-315 (1968).
72. Lindenmayer, A., Developmental systems without cellular interactions, their languages and grammars. J. Theoret. Biol. 30, 455-484 (1971).
73. Lindenmayer, A., Developmental systems and languages in their biological context. In [56].
74. Lindenmayer, A., and Rozenberg, G., Parallel generation of maps: developmental systems for cell layers. Lect. Notes in Comp. Sci. 73, 301-316 (1979).
75. Lindenmayer, A., and Rozenberg, G. (eds.), "Automata, Languages, Development." North-Holland, Amsterdam (1976).
76. Lee, K.P., Subwords of developmental languages. Ph.D. dissertation, SUNY at Buffalo (1975).
77. van Leeuwen, J., F-iteration grammars. University of California at Berkeley, Dept. of Comp. Sci., Tech. Rep. (1973).

78. van Leeuwen, J., A forgotten connection between tag sys-
     tems and parallel rewriting. SIGACT News 6, 19-20 (1975).
79. van Leeuwen, J., A study of complexity in hyper algebraic
     families. In [75].
80. van Leeuwen, J., The tape complexity of context independ-
     ent developmental languages. JCSS 11, 203-211 (1975).
81. van Leeuwen, J., Variations of a new machine model. Proc.
     17th Ann. Symp. Found. Comp. Sci., Houston, Tx., 228-235
     (1976).
82. van Leeuwen, J., The membership question for ETOL lan-
     guages is polynomial complete. Info. Proc. Letter 3,
     138-143 (1975).
83. Linna, M., The decidability of the DOL prefix problem.
     Int. J. Comp. Math. 6, 127-142 (1977).
84. Lück, H.B., Elementary behavioural rules as a foundation
     for morphogenesis. J. Theoret. Biol. 54, 23-34 (1975).
85. Maurer, H., Salomaa, A., and Wood, D., EOL forms. Acta
     Informatica 8, 75-96 (1977).
86. Maurer, H., Salomaa, A., and Wood, D., On good EOL forms.
     SIAM J. Comput. 7, 158-166 (1978).
87. Maurer, H., Salomaa, A., and Wood, D., Uniform interpre-
     tations of L forms. Info. and Control 36, 157-173 (1978).
88. Maurer, H., Salomaa, A., and Wood, D., On generators and
     generative capacity of EOL forms. Acta Informatica, to
     appear.
89. Maurer, H., Salomaa, A., and Wood, D., Synchronized EOL
     forms. McMaster University, Tech. Rep. No. 79-CS-2
     (1979).
90. Mayoh, B.H., Multidimensional Lindenmayer systems. In
     [104].
91. Nagl, M., On a generalization of Lindenmayer systems to
     labelled graphs. In [75].
92. Nurmi, H., Some lessons from the study of biolgoical sys-
     tems for the modelling of social systems. Prog. Cyber.
     Syst. Res. 1, 237-246 (1975).
93. Opatrny, J., and Culik, K., II, Time complexity of recog-
     nition and parsing of EOL languages. In [75].
94. Paz, A., and Salomaa, A., Integral sequential word func-
     tions and growth equivalence of Lindenmayer systems.
     Info. and Control 23, 313-343 (1973).
95. Rajlich, V., Absolutely parallel grammars and two-way
     finite state transducers. JCSS 13, 339-354 (1976).
96. Reedy, A., and Savitch, W., Ambiguity in the develop-
     mental systems of Lindenmayer. JCSS 11, 262-283 (1975).
97. Roman, G.C., R-systems and their relationship to system-
     atic programming. Ph.D. dissertation, Moore School of
     Electrical Engineering, University of Pennsylvania (1976).
98. Rozenberg, G., TOL systems and languages. Info. and
     Control 23, 357-381 (1973).
99. Rozenberg, G., Extension of tabled OL systems and lan-
     guages. Int. J. Comp. Info. Sci. 2, 311-334 (1973).
100. Rozenberg, G., Theory of L systems from the point of view
     of formal language theory. In [104].
101. Rozenberg, G., and Doucet, P., On OL languages. Info.
     and Control 19, 302-318 (1971).
102. Rozenberg, G., and Lindenmayer, A., Developmental systems
     with locally catenative formulas. Acta Informatica 2,
     214-248 (1973).

103. Rozenberg, G., and Salomaa, A., "The Mathematical Theory of L Systems." Academic Press, to appear.

104. Rozenberg, G., and Salomaa, A. (eds.), "L Systems." Lect. Notes in Comp. Sci. 15 (1974).

105. Rozenberg, G., and Vermeir, D., On ETOL systems of finite index. Info. and Control 38, 103-133 (1978).

106. Rozenberg, G., and Vermeir, D., On the effect of the finite index restriction on several families of grammars. Info. and Control 39, 284-302 (1978).

107. Rozenberg, G., and Vermeir, D., On the effect of the finite index restriction on several families of grammars, Part 2. Found. of Contr. Eng. 3, 125-142 (1978).

108. Rozenberg, G., and Vermeir, D., Extending the notion of finite index. Lect. Notes in Comp. Sci. 71, 479-488 (1979).

109. Rozenberg, G., and Vermeir, D., On acceptors of iteration languages. Int. J. Comp. Math. 7, 3-19 (1979).

110. Ruohonen, K., Remarks on locally catenative developmental sequences. EIK 14, 171-180 (1978).

111. Salomaa, A., "Formal Languages." Academic Press (1973).

112. Salomaa, A., Iteration grammars and Lindenmayer AFL's. Lect. Notes in Comp. Sci. 14, 250-253 (1974).

113. Salomaa, A., Comparative decision problems between sequential and parallel rewriting. Proc. Symp. Uniformly Structured Automata Logic, Tokyo, 62-66 (1975).

114. Salomaa, A., DOL equivalence: the problem of iterated morphisms. Bulletin of the EATCS 4, 5-12 (1978).

115. Salomaa, A., Equality sets for homomorphisms of free monoids. Acta Cybernetica 4, 127-139 (1978).

116. Salomaa, A., Morphisms on free monoids and language theory. This volume.

117. Salomaa, A., and Soittola, M., "Automata-Theoretic Aspects of Formal Power Series." Springer-Verlag, New York (1978).

118. Savitch, W., Some characterizations of Lindenmayer systems in Chomsky type grammars and stack machines. Info. and Control 27, 37-60 (1975).

119. Siromoney, R., and Krithivasan, K., Parallel context free languages. Info. and Control 24, 155-162 (1974).

120. Soittola, M., Remarks on DOL growth sequences. RAIRO 10, 23-34 (1976).

121. Soittola, M., Positive rational sequences. TCS 2, 317-322 (1976).

122. Sudborough, H., The time and tape complexity of developmental languages. Lect. Notes in Comp. Sci. 52, 509-523 (1977).

123. Szilard, A.L., Growth functions of Lindenmayer systems. University of West Ontario, Computer Science Dept., Tech. Rep. No. 4 (1971).

124. Veen, A.H., and Lindenmayer, A., Diffusion mechanism for phyllotaxis. Plant Physiol. 60, 127-139 (1977).

125. Vermeir, D., On structural restrictions of ETOL systems. Ph.D. thesis, U.I.A., University of Antwerp (1978).

126. Vitanyi, P., Lindenmayer systems: structure, languages and growth functions. Ph.D. thesis, Mathematisch Centrum, Amsterdam (1978).

127. Wood, D., "Grammar and L Forms." Springer-Verlag, to appear.

SOME OPEN QUESTIONS AND RECENT RESULTS
ON TREE TRANSDUCERS AND TREE LANGUAGES[1]

Joost Engelfriet

Department of Applied Mathematics
Twente University of Technology
Enschede, The Netherlands

I.   INTRODUCTION

From a general point of view the theory of tree automata
and tree grammars investigates

(a) computation on structured objects, and

(b) structure of computation.

In both cases structure is represented by a tree (for the
first case, think of the evaluation of an expression, and for
the second, of the calling hierarchy of a set of procedures;
as another example, think of a derivation tree of a context-
free grammar as representing both the structure of the derivation and the structure of the derived string). To carry out
such an investigation, tree language theory uses the methods
and results of formal language theory, often supported by algebraic methods. Since its beginnings in about 1965 tree language theory has steadily grown and proved its usefulness in
areas such as program scheme theory, theory of syntax-directed
translation and formal language theory itself. In this paper

[1]Preparation of this paper was supported in part by the
National Science Foundation under Grant No. MCS79-04012.

we discuss a number of recent results and point at some possible directions of research, based on a completely personal selection by the author; thus the paper is not the result of taking an inventory but rather of picking flowers among the trees.

Let us first have a closer look at the position of tree language theory with respect to theoretical computer science and formal language theory. An important task of theoretical computer science is to formalize and investigate the control structures and data structures used by the programmer to describe his algorithms (in some programming language). Insight into the formal power of such programming constructs, and their trade-offs, hopefully leads to a better understanding of the nature of computation, and may help the programmer to make up his mind. In order to investigate the formal power of some specific feature (or combination of features) it is essential to restrict or even eliminate the influence of the other features present. One way of doing this is to put restrictions on the available time or space, as in complexity theory. Another way is to define a programming language with this feature only, to abstract from (some or all of) the properties of the basic objects and from the meaning of the basic operations on them, and to execute programs formally (i.e., symbolically) on meaningingless objects. Thus, in formal language theory one considers algorithms which manipulate formal (i.e., meaningless) strings, whereas in program scheme theory the basic operations are given names and programs manipulate formal expressions representing structured objects (see (a) above). The advantage of strings is that they are concrete mathematical objects which are easy to handle; the advantage of expressions is that they are easy to interpret as meaningful objects and hence are closer to actual programs. Tree language theory has the advantage of both approaches: labeled trees are concrete mathematical objects (close to strings) and correspond in an obvious way to expressions.

Consider a concrete algorithm A taking elements from data type D_Σ as input and producing elements of data type D_Δ, where Σ and Δ are finite sets of operations (see Figure 1). Abstracting from the meaning of the operations, A turns into a symbolic algorithm A_s which is a tree transducer transforming elements of T_Σ (the set of labeled trees over ranked alphabet Σ) into elements of T_Δ. The concrete algorithm can be recovered from this tree transduction by interpreting the trees again as elements of the data types ($t \in T_\Sigma$ is interpreted as $d_\Sigma(t) \in D_\Sigma$, and similarly for Δ); in other words, A is the composition of d_Σ^{-1} ("parsing" of the input), A_s (tree transduction) and d_Δ (interpretation of the output). For a given class of algorithms, this

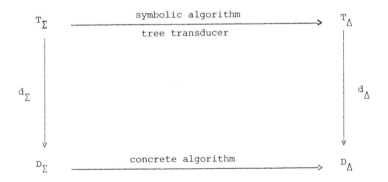

Fig. 1.   Picture of the formal approach.

possibility to view them as interpretation of symbolic algorithms (on trees) may be called a Mezei-and-Wright-like result
for the class [68].

Since every symbolic algorithm (or, program scheme) is
also a concrete algorithm (viz., a tree transducer), the abstraction process of Figure 1 may be repeated. In this sense
tree language theory is a closed theory: a symbolic tree
transducer is again a tree transducer, working on "second-
level" trees which are expressions to be evaluated as "first-
level" trees. Note that, by Figure 1, this leads to
decomposition results for (tree) transductions, a well-known
phenomenon in language theory. In some cases the whole computation of the concrete algorithm (on some input) can be represented by one symbolic tree (see (b) above); in such a case
$T_\Sigma = T_\Delta$ and the symbolic algorithm just checks whether the
input tree is a correct computation tree; the concrete algorithm may then be called a bimorphism (it is determined by a
tree language in T_Σ and two morphisms d_Σ and d_Δ; see,
e.g., [5,6,32]). Bimorphisms turn up in particular when the
concrete algorithm is some sort of recursive program: the dynamic calling structure of a set of recursive procedures is
adequately represented by a tree labeled by the names of the
procedures; this explains the close relationship between tree
grammars/transducers and recursive program (scheme)s. If the
choices made by the algorithm (as a result of tests or nondeterminism) are also executed symbolically, then even nonrecursive programs give rise to one, usually infinite, computation
tree (viz., the unraveled flowchart); see, e.g., [49].

Having argued the relevance of tree language theory in
general to the theory of computation, we now consider its
close relationship to formal language theory, cf. [80].
Firstly, turning a string into vertical position, it becomes
a monadic tree (i.e., every node has at most one son). Thus
a device from formal language theory (such as an automaton or
a grammar) may be generalized to trees in an almost automatic
way, replacing concatenation of strings by concatenation of
trees, i.e., substitution of expressions. In this way formal
language theory is "the monadic case" of tree language theory;
note the relationship between formal languages and monadic
program schemes, cf. [33,50]. Similarly, a path through a
tree can be represented by a string. As a consequence the behavior of a generalized device on the paths of a tree is usually that of the original device on strings. Secondly, the
yield of a tree is a string. Very often a simple tree automaton is turned into a complicated string automaton by considering the yields of the recognized trees, and thus offers a
tree-oriented explanation of the string automaton (and similarly for transducers and grammars). Finally, since every
tree is a string (viz., an expression), tree language theory
is part of formal language theory. These relationships explain why the two theories can exchange definitions, results
and ideas (as far as they are alive). As an example, the
finite-state transducer (gsm) can be generalized to the finite-
state top-down tree transducer which, taking yields, corresponds to the syntax-directed translation scheme (of which it
is, on the other hand, a special case when trees are viewed as
expressions); the same holds for the context-free grammar, the

context-free tree grammar and the macro grammar, respectively.
It seems like good luck that these straightforward generalizations to trees of the basic devices of finite-state transducer
and context-free grammar are also interesting from the "symbolic algorithm" point of view: syntax-directed translation
and recursive programs with parameters, respectively, cf.
[39,49,69,80]. This may, however, be due to the essentially
recursive nature of both devices. Indeed, the notion of recursion might be used as a unifying concept for a large part
of formal (tree) language theory.

In the rest of the paper we wish to illustrate the above
ideas by some not too obvious examples, related to top-down
tree transducers and context-free tree grammars. In Section
II we recall the definitions of these two devices and discuss
a few recent results in these areas. In Section III we show
how attribute grammars can be investigated formally as tree
transducers, and in Section IV we consider some relationships
between alternating automata and tree automata. Finally, in
Section V we show how the equivalence problem for deterministic tree transducers can be solved by generalizing string
theory.

II. TREE TRANSDUCERS AND TREE GRAMMARS

We need the following basic terminology. For a ranked
alphabet Σ, Σ_k is the set of symbols of rank k; Σ is
monadic if $\Sigma = \Sigma_0 \cup \Sigma_1$. The set of all labeled trees over Σ
is denoted T_Σ; $\sigma(t_1,\ldots,t_k)$ denotes a tree with root labeled $\sigma \in \Sigma_k$ and direct subtrees t_1, ..., t_k. The yield
(also denoted y) of a tree is the string of its leaf labels

($\in \Sigma_0^*$). A tree is monadic if it is in T_Σ for some monadic Σ. RECOG denotes the class of recognizable tree languages [80]. For a set S of symbols, $T_\Sigma[S]$ denotes $T_{\Sigma \cup S}$ where the elements of S have rank 0 (i.e., occur only at leaves). Let $X = \{x_1, x_2, \ldots\}$ and $X_n = \{x_1, \ldots, x_n\}$. For $t \in T_\Sigma[X_n]$ and $t_1, \ldots, t_n \in T_\Sigma[X]$, $t[t_1, \ldots, t_n]$ denotes the result of substituting t_i for x_i in t (this operation is also called tree concatenation). Viewing tree concatenation as a symbolic operation gives rise to ("second-level") trees representing trees by the YIELD operation defined as follows (cf. [39,64]). Let f be a mapping from Σ_0 to $T_\Delta[X]$. Then f is extended to a partial mapping $\text{YIELD}_f : T_\Sigma \to T_\Delta[X]$ by (i) for $\sigma \in \Sigma_0$, $\text{YIELD}_f(\sigma) = f(\sigma)$ and (ii) for $\sigma \in \Sigma_{k+1}$,
$\text{YIELD}_f(\sigma(t_0, t_1, \ldots, t_k)) = \text{YIELD}_f(t_0)[\text{YIELD}_f(t_1), \ldots, \text{YIELD}_f(t_k)]$
which is defined only if $\text{YIELD}_f(t_0) \in T_\Delta[X_k]$. We shall use YIELD to stand for any YIELD_f. Note that in case $f(\sigma) = \sigma(x_1)$ and $k = 1$, $\text{YIELD}_f(t)$ is the yield of t (as monadic tree); thus yield is the monadic case of YIELD.

A. Top-Down Tree Transducers

A top-down tree-to-string transducer (yT transducer) is a construct $M = (Q, \Sigma, \Delta, q_0, R)$ consisting of a finite set of states, ranked input and output alphabet, initial state, and a finite set of rules of the form $q(\sigma(x_1, \ldots, x_m)) \to$
$w_1 q_1(x_{i_1}) w_2 q_2(x_{i_2}) \cdots w_n q_n(x_{i_n}) w_{n+1}$ (with m, n $\geq$ 0; $q, q_1, \ldots, q_n \in Q$; $\sigma \in \Sigma_m$; $w_j \in \Delta^*$ and $1 \leq i_j \leq m$) which turn into rewriting rules by replacing each x_i by a tree $t_i \in T_\Sigma$. M realizes the translation $\{(t,w) \in T_\Sigma \times \Delta^* \mid q_0(t) \overset{*}{\Rightarrow} w\}$. M is a top-down tree transducer (T transducer)

if Δ is ranked and each right-hand side of a rule is in
$T_\Delta[Q(X_m)]$. M is deterministic (yDT or DT transducer) if
different rules have different left-hand sides. M is monadic
if Σ is monadic. For formal definitions see, e.g., [10,38,
76]. The yT transducer may be viewed as a string concept
(as far as its output is concerned) obtained from the T
transducer by the yield operation; the yDT transducer is a
notational variant of the generalized syntax-directed translation scheme of [1], except that the latter is restricted to
derivation trees of context-free grammars. Note that the T
transducer may be viewed as a symbolic algorithm assigning
(symbolic) meaning to trees.

As a typical, though somewhat artificial, example of how
the formal power of programming features can be studied, consider the composition of T transducers. In the meta language for defining T transducers there is no explicit facility to obtain composition of the translations they define
(i.e., to feed the output of one as input to another). It
turns out (see [34], based on [11,38,71,73]) that when added
to the meta language, the composition faculty gives rise to a
proper hierarchy of classes of tree translations (w.r.t. the
number of transducers composed). This is a consequence of the
simultaneous presence of two other facilities: copying (of
input subtrees) and nondeterminism. In case one of these latter facilities is dropped, the so restricted class of T
transducers is closed under composition (i.e., the explicit
addition of composition to the meta language does not give extra power). As is well known (see, e.g., [35,38]) there is a
close relationship between T transducers, L systems and

2-way (tree-walking) automata; in particular, between monadic
T transducers, ETOL systems and 2-way gsm. Composition of
these devices gives rise to proper hierarchies for the same
reason (see also [51]).

Top-down tree transducers have recently been generalized to
more powerful transducers in [5,6,59,57,62]. Other recent results can be found in [9,41,44,84].

B. Context-Free Tree Grammars and Macro Grammars

A context-free tree grammar (macro grammar) is a construct
$G = (N,\Sigma,S,R)$ consisting of ranked alphabets of nonterminals
and terminals, initial nonterminal of rank 0, and a finite
set of rules of the form $A(x_1,\ldots,x_n) \to t$ with $A \in N_n$ and
$t \in T_{N\cup\Sigma}[X_n]$, which turn into rewriting rules by replacing
x_i by a tree t_i in $T_{N\cup\Sigma}$ or in T_Σ, giving rise to unre-
stricted (OI) or inside-out (IO) derivations, respectively.
G generates the context-free tree language $\{t \in T_\Sigma \mid S \overset{*}{\underset{m}{\Rightarrow}} t\}$
and the macro (string) language $\{\text{yield}(t) \in \Sigma_0^* \mid S \overset{*}{\underset{m}{\Rightarrow}} t\}$,
where m is either OI or IO. The corresponding classes of
tree languages are denoted by OIT and IOT. For more precise definitions see, e.g., [39,45,76].

Context-free tree grammars can be viewed as symbolic nondeterministic recursive procedures with parameters [39,45,69].
As an example of the repetition of Figure 1, it can be shown
that IOT = YIELD(RECOG) (see [39,64]); this means that when
tree concatenation (i.e., substitution of expressions, i.e.,
passing of parameters) is viewed symbolically, then the IO
context-free tree grammar turns into a regular tree grammar
(in Figure 1, T_Σ and D_Σ are trivial and $d_\Delta = \text{YIELD}$). For

OIT a similar result holds, involving infinite trees rather than tree languages (because choice has to be symbolic). For a diagram of the situation for IOT see Figure 2, where "gen" abbreviates "generalization." As suggested by Figure 2, the generalization process can be repeated indefinitely, leading to a hierarchy of higher-level tree grammars (see [39,64,65, 82]) which, via a λ-calculus oriented formalism, can be shown to correspond to recursive procedures with typed procedure parameters, cf. [24,28]. Let IOT(n) and OIT(n) denote the classes of tree languages generated by level n tree grammars, corresponding to level n recursive procedures (which have procedure parameters of level n-1). Then IOT(n) = $YIELD^n$(RECOG), and similarly for OIT(n). It was proved recently by Damm [24,25] that IOT(n) and OIT(n) (and also their yields) form infinite hierarchies, thus showing that the use of procedures of higher and higher type increases the power of program (scheme)s. The hierarchy proof is based on the notion of regular index introduced in [15]. Apart from IOT(n) it is still open whether these hierarchies are proper at each level; it can be shown that level 2n is more powerful than level n [26]. We note that, using an untyped λ-calculus formalism, it was shown in [27] that untyped procedures are more powerful than typed ones (of any level).

We also wish to mention here that the DPDA equivalence problem and the equivalence problem for simple deterministic (OI) context-free tree grammars are reducible to each other [20]; the reductions are obtained by representing a tree by the (string) language of all its paths.

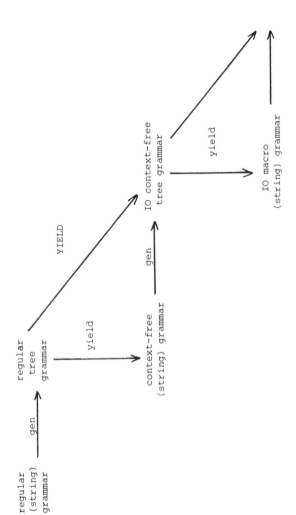

Fig. 2. Generalization and yield.

Other recent results on macro (tree) grammars or their
generalizations can be found in, e.g., [4,7,8,31,40,42,70,78].
Recent results on trees in general can be found in the proceedings of the Lille conferences (see, e.g., [43]).

III. ATTRIBUTE GRAMMARS AS TREE TRANSDUCERS

Attribute grammars [59] provide an attractive formalism
to assign meaning to the strings of a context-free language.
They are used, e.g., as a meta language for writing compilers
[74] or to process natural languages, cf. [83]. In an attribute grammar (AG) each nonterminal of the underlying
context-free grammar has a number of associated inherited
(i-) and synthesized (s-) attributes of which the values
(in a derivation tree) are computed by the use of semantic
rules. The formal power of attribute grammars can be studied
by abstracting from the meaning of the operations used in the
semantic rules; in this way the AG assigns a formal expression to each derivation tree (viz., the formal value of a
designated s-attribute of its root), and it has become a tree
transducer (see Figure 1, where d_Σ = yield), cf. [19,72].
Note that attribute grammars are sometimes also implemented in
this way: the output tree (or dag) is produced in the form
of intermediate code which is then interpreted. Only a few
papers have dealt with the formal power of attribute grammars
[30,54,61,72]; this lack of interest may be due to the complexity of the model or to its close relationship to formalisms (like van Wijngaarden grammars) which are as powerful as
the Turing machine. Restricted cases of the AG have received more attention: firstly, AGs with s-attributes only

correspond closely to (generalized) syntax-directed translation schemes, i.e., DT transducers; secondly, the i-
attributes of a nonterminal of an AG are similar to the arguments of a nonterminal of a macro (or context-free tree)
grammar. We want to indicate in this section some more relationships between AGs, top-down tree transducers and macro
(tree) grammars. Combining our knowledge concerning the latter two models may well lead to a better insight into the properties of the attribute grammar formalism.

Let us first see how one of the usual binary number examples of an AG looks as tree transducer.

Example 1. The attributes are v = value (synthesized)
and sc = scale (inherited); the operations (on integers) are
0, 1 (both constants) and exp (= 2 to the power), +. The
productions and semantic rules are as follows.

$$S \rightarrow N \qquad v(S) = v(N), \quad sc(N) = 0$$

$$N_0 \rightarrow N_1 0 \qquad v(N_0) = v(N_1), \quad sc(N_1) = +(sc(N_0),1)$$

$$N_0 \rightarrow N_1 1 \qquad v(N_0) = +(v(N_1),\exp(sc(N_0))),$$

$$sc(N_1) = +(sc(N_0),1)$$

$$N \rightarrow 1 \qquad v(N) = \exp(sc(N)).$$

This AG translates the derivation tree of 101 into the
tree of Figure 3. Note that this AG is not formally equivalent (i.e., as a program scheme) to the one which uses no
scale attribute and has, e.g., the rules $N_0 \rightarrow N_1 1 : v(N_0) = +(*(2,v(N_1)),1)$. $\square$

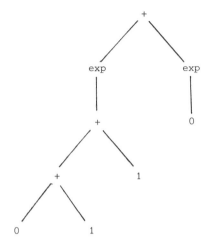

Fig. 3. Formal value.

A.   Output Tree Languages
of Attribute Grammars

The intuitive relationship between macro grammars and attribute grammars has been expressed in the following formal
result by Duske, et al. We need some terminology. An AG is
L is its attributes can be evaluated in one depth-first left-
to-right pass over the derivation tree [16]; an AG is 1S
if it has just one s-attribute (but arbitrarily many i-
attributes). If F is a class of translations then OUT(F)
denotes the class of ranges of elements of F.

Theorem 1 (Duske, et al. [30]). OUT(L-1S-AG) = IOT, i.e.,
IOT is the class of output tree languages of the tree transductions realized by L attribute grammars that are 1S.
(Actually, in [30] this result was shown for strings rather
than trees.)

Roughly speaking, the result can be explained by saying
that if A labels the root of a derivation tree of the AG
and its i-attributes have values $t_1, \ldots, t_n$, then the

value of its only s-attribute is the tree generated by

$A(t_1,\ldots,t_n)$ in the IO context-free tree grammar. In [36]

it is shown that also OUT(1S-AG) = IOT, i.e., the L re-

striction is not necessary; moreover OUT(L-AG) = DT(IOT),

which clearly shows that AGs can be studied by combining

top-down tree transducers and macro grammars! It is open whe-

ther OUT(AG) can also be characterized in terms of known

concepts. We finally note that OUT(OnlyS-AG) = DT(RECOG),

where OnlyS-AG denotes the class of AG without

i-attributes.

B. Path Languages of Attribute Grammars

Using the "path-approach" it can now be shown that arbi-

trary AGs are more powerful than L-AGs and these more pow-

erful than OnlyS-AGs, as already shown in [61] in a different

formalism. Since on paths a DT transducer behaves like a

gsm, a regular tree grammar like a regular grammar and a

context-free tree grammar like a context-free grammar, it fol-

lows from the equalities OUT(L-AG) = DT(IOT) and

OUT(OnlyS-AG) = DT(RECOG) of Section A that the path languages

of OUT(OnlyS-AG) are regular and those of OUT(L-AG) context-

free. It is easy to see that the path language of the L-AG

of Example 1 is not regular, whereas a non-context-free path

language is given in the next example.

Example 2. The underlying context-free grammar has rules

$S \rightarrow A$, $A \rightarrow A$, $A \rightarrow e$; S has attribute s, and A has at-

tributes i_1, i_2, s_1, s_2. The semantic rules are indicated by the dependency graphs in Figure 4, where arcs are labeled by the (monadic) operations applied in the rules. Since the output tree is always monadic, the path language is equal to the output language, viz. $\{ ¢a^n \#b^n rc^n \&d^n \$ \mid n \geq 0 \}$, where $¢$ is the leaf and $\$$ the root of the output tree ($¢$ is a constant). $\square$

We now take a closer look at output path languages of arbitrary AGs. It turns out [37] that they are related to "finite copying" yT transducers (denoted yT_{fc}), meaning that there is a bound on the number of copies the yT transducer can make of each input subtree, cf. [34,38]. As can be seen from the above example, output paths are closely related to paths in dependency graphs of derivation trees (indeed, in general, one may say that the formal computing power of an AG is determined by the dependency graphs of its derivation trees, cf. [54]). Thus, for a (noncircular) AG G, let $\pi(G)$ denote its dependency-path language, i.e., the set of all paths through dependency graphs of derivation trees (obtained by labeling the arcs in dependency graphs of productions, as in Example 2).

Theorem 2. For every AG G, $\pi(G) \in yT_{fc}(RECOG)$, i.e., its dependency-path language is a finite copying tree transformation language (and the same holds for its output path language).

Proof (sketch). The tree-to-string transducer has states $\langle i,s \rangle$ for every i- and s-attribute of the AG, and $\langle i,s \rangle(t) \overset{*}{\Rightarrow} w$ if and only if w is a path through the dependency graph of t, starting at i and ending at s of the root of t. It is not difficult to write down the

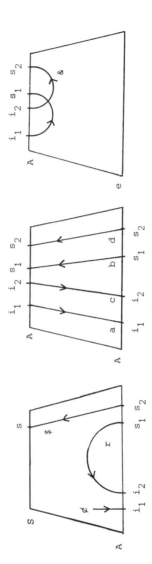

Fig. 4.   Dependency graphs.

(nondeterministic) recursive rules for generating the
dependency-paths. The tree-to-string transducer will be finite copying because a dependency-path can visit a node at
most n times, where n is the number of its attributes. □

The above construction (which is close to the one in [54]
to decide circularity) can be used to obtain results on multi-
pass and multi-visit AGs. An AG is k-pass if its attributes can be evaluated by k consecutive depth-first left-to-
right passes through the derivation tree, and it is multi-pass
if such a k exists. It can be shown that an AG is multi-
pass iff there is a bound on the number of "bad" arcs in
dependency-paths, i.e., arcs which go from a son to some left-
brother, or to himself. It was recently observed by Alblas
[3] that Bochmann's algorithm [16] does not decide the multi-
pass property but a restricted version of it (where it is
known in advance which attributes are evaluated in which pass).
Using Theorem 2 (or obvious variants of it) and the connection
between multi-pass and the dependency-paths, the following can
be shown.

• The multi-pass property can be decided in exponential
time. In fact, using a variant of the method of [54], it can
be shown that the multi-pass property is complete in exponential time.

• For each fixed k, the k-pass property can be decided
in polynomial time.

Finally we mention a result on visits by Riis and Skyum
[75]. An AG is k-visit if its attributes can be evaluated
by a walk through the derivation tree in such a way that each
subtree is visited at most k times (it can be shown that
every AG is k-visit for some k).

•[75] Attribute grammars form a proper hierarchy with respect to the k-visit property.

It is open whether the k-visit property is decidable (for
k ≥ 2; for k = 1 decidability was shown in [36]).

C.   Macro Tree Transducers

We propose [37] a new type of tree transducer which is a
combination of the top-down tree transducer and the context-
free tree grammar and is more powerful than both. It will be
called the macro tree transducer, and is meant to model both
attribute grammars and certain aspects of the meta language of
denotational semantics. Since AGs are difficult to handle
formally, it is our hope that this model can be used instead.
From the program schematic point of view, the macro tree
transducer is again a system of recursive procedures with parameters, such that exactly one parameter plays the role of
input tree. From the point of view of formal language theory
it is obtained by generalizing the "string concept" of a yT
transducer to trees.

Formally, a macro tree transducer (MTT) has ranked alphabets Q, Σ and Δ of states, input symbols and output
symbols, respectively, an initial state q_0, and a finite set
of rules; each state has a rank ≥ 1; a rule looks as follows:

$$q(y_1,\ldots,y_n, \sigma(x_1,\ldots,x_m)) \rightarrow t \qquad\qquad (*)$$

where $q \in Q_{n+1}$, $\sigma \in \Sigma_m$ and t is an expression such as
$\ldots q'(\ldots,x_i)\ldots q''(\ldots,x_j)\ldots y_k\ldots$, i.e., t is built up
from y's, elements of Δ and "calls" of q's (with expressions at the parameter positions except the last). Formally
$t \in RHS$, where RHS is a set of trees defined as follows:

(i) $\{y_1,\ldots,y_n\} \cup \Delta_0 \subseteq$ RHS,

(ii) if $t_1,\ldots,t_k \in$ RHS   and $f \in \Delta_k$,   then $f(t_1,\ldots,t_k)$
$\in$ RHS,

(iii) if $t_1,\ldots,t_k \in$ RHS, $q' \in Q_{k+1}$ and $x_i \in x_m$,   then
$q'(t_1,\ldots,t_k, x_i) \in$ RHS.

Rule (*) turns into a rewriting rule by replacing all x's
and y's by trees (of the appropriate type). M realizes the
translation $\{(t_1,t_2) \in T_\Sigma \times T_\Delta \mid q_0(t_1) \overset{*}{=}> t_2\}$. An MTT is
deterministic (DMTT) if different rules have different left-
hand sides. Note that for nondeterministic MTT (and even
for partial DMTT) we have to decide whether to expand calls
outside-in or inside-out. Here we choose IO.

   From the point of view of attribute grammars, rule (*) can
be explained as follows: σ is a production A →
$w_1B_1w_2B_2 \cdots w_mB_mw_{m+1}$ of the underlying context-free grammar,
x_i stands for B_i, state q represents an s-attribute of
A, the parameters $y_1,\ldots,y_n$ represent those i-attributes
of A the s-attribute depends on, and (*) expresses the semantic rule defining s-attribute q of A in terms of all
other attributes (where nesting of "q-calls" corresponds to
the definition of i-attributes in terms of s-attributes).

   Example 3. The AG of Example 1 can be expressed as
DMTT as follows. $\Sigma = \{<S \to N>, <N \to N0>, <N \to N1>, <N \to 1>\}$,
$\Delta = \{0,1,\exp,+\}$, $Q = \{q_0,q\}$. Attribute v is represented by
states q and q_0, and attribute sc by parameter y of
q. The rules of the DMTT are the following.

$$q_0(<S{\to}N>(x)) \to q(0,x)$$

$$q(y, <N{\to}N0>(x)) \to q(+(y,1), x)$$

$$q(y, <N{\to}N1>(x)) \to +(q(+(y,1), x), \exp(y))$$

$$q(y, <N{\to}1>) \to \exp(y). \quad \square$$

From the point of view of denotational semantics, rule (*) expresses the q-meaning of the syntactic construct σ in the environment $(y_1,\ldots,y_n)$ in terms of the meanings of the constituents of σ (in possibly different environments). Relationships between AGs and the meta language of denotational semantics have been pointed out in [19,47,67]. The model of an MTT is one way of obtaining formal results on this relationship. In [47] the MTT is suggested in an informal way.

Actually, not every AG can be transformed directly into a DMTT, because in a DMTT one has to know exactly on which i-attributes an s-attribute depends (for each production). This condition is (sufficiently) satisfied for absolutely non-circular AGs [58]. Since the required information ("i/o graphs") can be computed by a finite tree automaton, every AG translation is the composition of a finite-state tree relabeling and a DMTT (and thus OUT(AG) $\subseteq$ DMTT(RECOG)). On the other hand, DMTTs are more powerful than AGs as can be seen from the following example (using paths). Let M be a DMTT with $\Sigma = \{\rho,\sigma,\tau\}$, $\Delta = \{e,a\}$, $Q = \{q_0,q\}$ and rules

$$q_0(\tau(x)) \to q(e,x)$$

$$q(y,\sigma(x)) \to q(q(y,x),x)$$

$$q(y,\rho) \to a(y).$$

Then a monadic tree $\tau\sigma^n\rho$ is translated by M into a monadic tree $a^{2^n}e$; e.g., $q_0(\tau\sigma\rho) \Longrightarrow q(e,\sigma\rho) \Longrightarrow q(q(e,\rho),\rho) \Longrightarrow q(a(e),\rho) \Longrightarrow a(a(e))$. By Theorem 2 and the fact that languages in yT_{fc}(RECOG) have the Parikh-property [38], it follows that no AG can do this translation (in fact, any straightforward trial to construct an AG from M results in a circular AG; note that some people do use circular AGs). This shows that, in some sense, the meta language of denotational semantics is more powerful than that of attribute grammars. The basic difference between an AG and a DMTT is that, although in an AG an s-attribute of a node can be viewed as a function of its i-attributes, that function can only be evaluated for <u>one</u> set of arguments.

Since the MTT is the "appropriate" generalization to trees of the yT transducer, the following "symbolic" result can be obtained, analogous to the one for IOT as discussed in Section II.B (see Figure 5 and compare it with Figure 2).

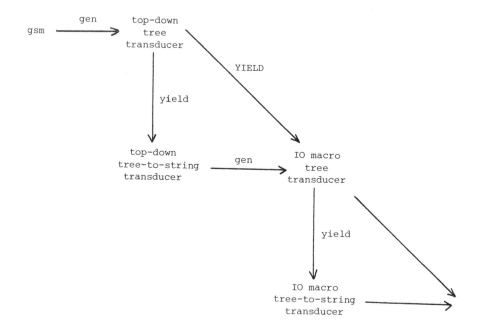

Fig. 5. Generalization and yield for transducers.

Theorem 3. $MTT = T \circ YIELD$ and $DMTT = DT \circ YIELD$ (where $R_1 \circ R_2$ means feeding the output of R_1 as input to R_2).

For the same reason, the MTT behaves on paths like a yT transducer and it can be shown that $\pi(MTT(RECOG)) = yT(RECOG)$, where π produces the output path language, cf. Theorem 2. More precisely (for one direction of this equality), $yT \subseteq MTT$ and $yDT \subseteq DMTT$ modulo a 90° turn of the output. As a very easy example we show that the yield operation can be realized by a DMTT.

Consider the easy case that $\Sigma = \Sigma_0 \cup \Sigma_2$, and let $\Delta_1 = \Delta_0 = \Sigma_0$ and $Q = \{q_0, q\}$. The DMTT has the following rules (for every $a \in \Sigma_0$ and $\sigma \in \Sigma_2$):

$$q_0(\sigma(x_1, x_2)) \rightarrow q(q_0(x_2), x_1), \quad q_0(a) \rightarrow a,$$
$$q(y, \sigma(x_1, x_2)) \rightarrow q(q(y, x_2), x_1), \quad q(y, a) \rightarrow a(y).$$

An example of a derivation is $q_0(\sigma(\sigma(a, b), c)) \Longrightarrow$ $q(q_0(c), \sigma(a, b)) \Longrightarrow q(c, \sigma(a, b)) \Longrightarrow q(q(c, b), a) \Longrightarrow q(b(c), a)$ $\Longrightarrow a(b(c))$.

It follows from Theorem 3 that $AG \subseteq DT \circ YIELD$ modulo a relabeling, and hence $OUT(AG) \subseteq YIELD(DT(RECOG))$. It is not clear how the DT transducer can be restricted so as to obtain exactly $OUT(AG)$; recall however that $OUT(1S\text{-}AG) = IOT = YIELD(RECOG)$. One way of viewing the inclusion $AG \subseteq DT \circ YIELD$ is to say that every AG can be turned into an OnlyS-AG (viz., a DT transduction) if the new s-attributes are taken to be trees (which show how the old s-attributes of the root of a subtree can be computed from its i-attributes) and tree concatenation is taken as basic operation. This way of bottom-up evaluation of an AG (with dags rather than trees) has actually been implemented in Aarhus [55,63]. In short, Theorem 3 expresses formally one of the basic ideas of denotational semantics, viz., how to "get rid of" the environment by the introduction of functions (cf. [47,49]).

To determine the formal power of the MTT the same questions can be asked as for the T transducer and the macro grammar. We list a few of these.

•On what kind of sequential (tree-walking) machine can the MTT translations be implemented? What is the relationship between such a machine and the known evaluation methods of AGs? Is there any sense in studying nondeterministic AGs?

•Figure 2 can be iterated toward the right lower corner so as to obtain the IOT(n)-hierarchy $YIELD^n(RECOG)$. Is it meaningful to do the same for Figure 5 and consider the hierarchy $DT \circ YIELD^n$? Can the methods of Damm [25] be used to prove it proper? How is this hierarchy (or its OI version) related to a more detailed model of denotational semantics in which higher-type functions may be used to describe the meaning of a derivation tree of a context-free grammar?

•What about composition of AGs and macro tree transducers: does one get a proper hierarchy, and if so, how is it related to the tree transducer hierarchy and the IOT(n)-hierarchy? Note that, by Theorem 3 and the remarks following it, the (union of all classes of the) MTT hierarchy contains both the tree transducer hierarchy, the IOT(n)-hierarchy and the hierarchy obtained by iterating controlled ETOL systems (i.e., the $(yT)^n$ hierarchy). One may well ask how large this hierarchy is and how complex its elements get.

IV. COMPUTATION TREES OF ALTERNATING AUTOMATA

An automaton is alternating [18] if its nonfinal states and hence its nonfinal configurations are divided into universal and existential ones. A computation of the automaton on some input x can most clearly be modeled by a tree as follows [60]: the nodes of the computation tree are labeled by configurations, the root by the initial configuration for input x and the leaves by accepting configurations; if a node is labeled by a universal (existential) configuration, then it has all possible (exactly one) successor configurations as sons. The input x is accepted iff there exists at least one such computation tree. Thus, in terms of Figure 1, this is the case of a bimorphism: the whole computation can be modeled as a tree. We want to show in this section how this leads to a natural relationship between alternating automata and tree automata. It is not clear yet whether tree automata can be helpful in the study of alternation.

A. Complexity Classes

It is shown in [46] that the NSPACE(n) Turing machine is equivalent to a bug automaton working on rectangles, which in its turn is equivalent to the 2-way 2-tape finite automaton. Both automata act like "checking automata" in the sense that they are able to check a computation sequence of the NSPACE(n) Turing machine. Here we want to show that a completely similar relationship holds between the ASPACE(n) Turing machine (where A stands for alternating), a special kind of tree bug automaton and a 2-way checking tree automaton.

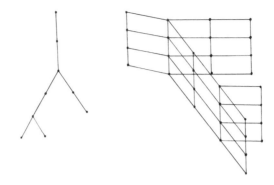

Fig. 6. A tree and a layered cake (with 4 layers).

Let us start with the tree bug automaton (TBA). The input to a TBA is a graph consisting of an arbitrary tree
which is turned into a layered piece of cake by putting the
tree on top of itself some number of times, as indicated in
Figure 6; the nodes of the graph are then labeled with symbols
from some finite alphabet. At each moment of time the (finite-
state) tree bug is at some node of the graph, initially at the
root of the bottom layer. Depending on state and node symbol
it may move either (down or up) to a different layer, or to
the father or one of the sons in the same layer. The bug accepts by moving off the graph in an accepting state; a string
x is accepted by the TBA iff there is an accepted layered
tree such that x is the string of labels formed by the roots
of all layers.

Theorem 4. ASPACE(n) = TBA.

Proof (sketch).

⊆: If M is an ASPACE(n) Turing machine with input x,
each computation tree of M on x can be turned into a layered tree by putting each configuration vertically on top of
the node it labels (note that if M is an ordinary NSPACE(n)

machine then its computation tree is monadic and hence the layered tree is a rectangle). It should be clear that a tree bug can check whether a given layered tree corresponds in this way to a computation tree (walking through the tree in a depth-first fashion, each time comparing two vertical configurations symbol by symbol).

⊇: For a given walk of the tree bug on the graph one can associate a "visit set" with each node, containing all information about the visits of the bug to that node. Starting with a given "root-string," the alternating Turing machine can guess a tree in a top-down fashion node by node (making a universal move at each splitting of the tree) and keep the visiting sets corresponding to all nodes of one vertical pile in linear space. See [46] for details in the monadic case. □

We now consider another tree-walking automaton: the 2-way checking tree automaton (2CTA), (cf. [2,35,38]). It has a 2-way reading head on the input string, and a reading head pointing to a node in a labeled tree (the "checking tree") which can go to the father or one of the sons in one move: see Figure 7. An input string is accepted if there is at

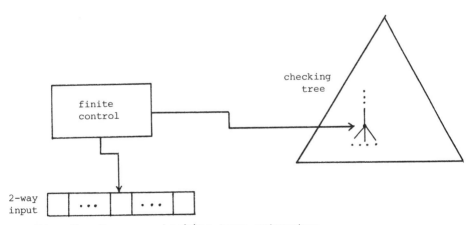

Fig. 7. Two-way checking tree automaton.

least one checking tree such that the 2CTA has an accepting computation on this string and tree. For the next result, cf. [35].

Theorem 5. ASPACE(n) = 2CTA.

Proof (sketch).

⊆: A computation tree of an ASPACE(n) Turing machine on input x can be turned into a checking tree by putting each configuration as a monadic tree between the node it labels and the father, as suggested in Figure 8. With x on its input the 2CTA can easily check that a given checking tree corresponds in this way to a computation tree of M, using x as a yardstick to measure the distance n when comparing configurations.

⊇: For each 2CTA and equivalent TBA can be constructed which works on the 3-dimensional "product" of the input string x and the checking tree t: position i on x and node n in t together correspond to node n in layer i of the product tree (cf. [46]). □

This theorem can easily be extended: the NSPACE(S(n)) auxiliary CTA is equivalent to the ASPACE($c^{S(n)}$) Turing machine, just as the NSPACE(S(n)) auxiliary checking stack

Fig. 8.   Configuration tree.

automaton is equivalent to the NSPACE($c^{S(n)}$) Turing machine
(see [53]). Auxiliary checking stack automata can be used to
give an alternative proof of properness of the 2-way gsm
hierarchy by translating it into a hierarchy of space complexity classes [35]; it is an interesting question whether this
could also be done for the tree transducer hierarchy (note
that the T transducer is closely related to the CTA (see
[2,38]).

Another question is what happens to Theorem 5 and its generalization when restrictions are put on the size or the
height of the trees (cf. [77,81]).

B.   Alternating Automata Theory

We now want to show that the computation of an alternating
automaton (of any storage type) is strongly related to the
top-down tree transducer. Intuitively the parallelism of the
alternating automaton due to universality corresponds to the
parallelism of the top-down tree transducer (due to recursion).
Viewing an alternating automaton as a concrete algorithm
(Figure 1 with D = {true, false}) the symbolic algorithm
will be a T transducer transforming the input string
(viewed as monadic tree) into an "instruction tree" which has
to be interpreted in the storage (by d_Δ). In other words,
for alternating AFA theory the monadic top-down tree transducer (i.e., the ETOL system) plays the same role as the
a-transducer for ordinary AFA theory [48]!

Consider as an example the 1-way alternating pushdown
automaton (1APDA) (see [18,60]), known to be equivalent to
ASPACE(n) = DTIME(c^n). Let M be a 1APDA with a finite set
of rules of the form

$$(q,\sigma) \rightarrow (q_1,\alpha_1) \quad \text{AND} \quad (q_2,\alpha_2) \quad \text{AND} \quad \ldots \quad \text{AND} \quad (q_n,\alpha_n) \quad (*)$$

where the q's are states, σ is an input symbol (or empty) and each "instruction" α_i is a pair (A,γ_i) meaning that top-symbol A should be replaced by string γ_i on the pushdown. Application of rule (*) leads to a node with n sons in the computation tree of M (this is an inessential generalization of alternation: universality and existentiality are modeled in the rules instead of being a property of states). Rule (*) could also be written in the form

$$q(\sigma x, Ay) \rightarrow q_1(x,\gamma_1 y) \quad \text{AND} \quad \ldots \quad \text{AND} \quad q_n(x,\gamma_n y)$$

showing that M is essentially a (monadic) T transducer of which the states have an extra argument of type pushdown. Note the similarity to indexed grammars which are context-free grammars with the nonterminals having an argument of type pushdown; thus the 1APDA could be called an indexed ETOL system.

We now show how we can separate the finite-state control (i.e., the T transducer) of M from the processing of its storage. The T transducer N corresponding to M will produce a tree whose nodes are labeled with instruction sequences like $<\alpha_1, \alpha_2, \ldots, \alpha_n>$, i.e., an instruction tree. Rule (*) is turned into the rule $q(\sigma(x)) \rightarrow$ $<\alpha_1, \ldots, \alpha_n>(q_1(x), \ldots, q_n(x))$ for N. Note that σ may be empty in which case we write $q(x)$ instead of $q(\sigma(x))$; thus N is a (generalized) T transducer with λ-moves. Let L_0 be the tree language of all instruction trees which are "accepting," i.e., the execution of all instructions along any path of the tree (where α_i should be executed when the

i^{th} son of the node labeled $<\alpha_1, \ldots, \alpha_n>$ is taken) leads

from an empty pushdown store to an empty pushdown store.

Then the language accepted by M is clearly equal to

$N^{-1}(L_0)$: the Mezei-and-Wright-like result for this case.

Now consider the top-down tree pushdown automaton (T-PDA)

introduced by Mayer [66] which works exactly as a top-down

finite tree automaton, except that during processing of the

tree each active state has an associated pushdown store. Thus

its rules are of the form $(p,\tau) \rightarrow ((p_1,\beta_1), \ldots, (p_n,\beta_n))$:

in state p with pushdown γ at a node labeled τ (of rank

n) the T-PDA splits into n copies; the ith copy goes to

the ith son in state p_i with the result of executing in-

struction β_i on γ (where β_i is again a pair (A,γ_i)).

It should be clear that L_0 can be accepted by a T-PDA

(with one state and $\tau = <\beta_1, \ldots, \beta_n>$ in the above rule).

It is not difficult to show that, vice versa, if L is ac-

cepted by a T-PDA and N is a monadic T transducer (with

λ-moves), then $N^{-1}(L)$ can be accepted by a 1APDA.

Generalizing this example to an arbitrary storage-type X

we obtain the following AAFA theorem. Let $T_{\lambda m}$ be the

class of monadic T transducers with λ-moves. Let $\mathscr{L}_1^A(X)$

be the class of languages accepted by 1-way alternating

X-automata and let $\mathscr{L}^N(T-X)$ denote the class of tree lan-

guages accepted by nondeterministic top-down tree X-automata.

Theorem 6. $\mathscr{L}_1^A(X) = T_{\lambda m}^{-1}(\mathscr{L}^N(T-X))$.

We note that $\mathscr{L}^N(T-PDA) = OIT$ and hence $1APDA =$

$T_{\lambda m}^{-1}(OIT)$. As another example, taking the trivial X, the

alternating finite automaton [18] accepts $T_m^{-1}(RECOG)$ which

is the class of regular languages because T^{-1} preserves re-
cognizability (this corresponds to Szilard languages of ETOL
systems).

Should AFA theory be developed for alternating automata?
It is, e.g., doubtful whether the $\mathscr{L}_1^A(X)$ can be characterized by closure properties (à la AFL) because T is not
closed under composition (the property of a-transducers on
which such a characterization is based in ordinary AFA
theory). Since DT is closed under composition (modulo re-
labelings), there may be some chance for alternating automata
which correspond to monadic DT transducers, i.e., deterministic automata with universality only.

We finally note that a similar relationship can be found
between 2-way alternating automata and (nondeterministic) attribute grammars (with monadic input tree). A rule like (*)
in which the direction of the input head is added to the right-
hand side, would correspond to a semantic rule of the AG defining attribute q in terms of attributes $q_1, \ldots, q_n$.

V.   THE EQUIVALENCE PROBLEM
FOR DETERMINISTIC TREE TRANSDUCERS

In this section we want to illustrate the relationship
between tree language theory and string language theory by
considering the specific example of the equivalence problem
for deterministic transducers. For strings it is well known
that the equivalence problem is undecidable for nondeterministic gsm's [52] and decidable for deterministic ones; see,
e.g., [12,14,22,56]--there seems to be no original reference.
For trees, the equivalence problem for deterministic tree
transducers has recently been investigated [17,44,84]. We

will first show decidability of this problem for deterministic

bottom-up tree transducers [84] and then, using a different

technique, for deterministic top-down tree transducers [44].

Finally we will point out the relationship between the equi-

valence problem for DT transducers and some equivalence

problems concerning L systems and attribute grammars.

A. Bottom-Up Tree Transducers

For the case of strings, equivalence of two deterministic

finite-state transducers M_1 and M_2 can, e.g., be decided

as follows. Consider a long string w_0, computations of M_1

and M_2 on w_0, and three different points in w_0 where the

pairs of states of M_1 and M_2 are the same: $w_0 = x_0 u_0 v_0 y_0$

and $(\delta^1(q_0^1, x_0),\ \delta^2(q_0^2, x_0)) = (\delta^1(q_0^1, x_0 u_0),\ \delta^2(q_0^2, x_0 u_0)) =$

$(\delta^1(q_0^1,\ x_0 u_0 v_0),\ \delta^2(q_0^2,\ x_0 u_0 v_0))$ where δ^i, q_0^i are the

transition function and initial state of M_i, respectively.

Let x_i be the output string produced by M_i when processing

x_0, and similarly for u_i, v_i and y_i. Clearly

$M_i(x_0 u_0 v_0 y_0) = x_i u_i v_i y_i$, $M_i(x_0 u_0 y_0) = x_i u_i y_i$, $M_i(x_0 v_0 y_0) =$

$x_i v_i y_i$ and $M_i(x_0 y_0) = x_i y_i$. Now equivalence of M_1 and M_2

on the shorter strings $x_0 y_0$, $x_0 u_0 y_0$ and $x_0 v_0 y_0$ implies

their equivalence on $x_0 u_0 v_0 y_0$ (and hence, to decide equi-

valence of M_1 and M_2, it suffices to check all strings of

length at most $3 N_1 N_2$ where N_i is the number of states of

M_i). This is due to the following property S1 of strings.

Let $x = (x_1, x_2)$ be a pair of strings over some alphabet

Σ, and similarly for u, v, y and z. Define concatenation on $\Sigma^* \times \Sigma^*$ coordinate-wise and let E be the diagonal of $\Sigma^* \times \Sigma^*$, i.e., $E = \{(x_0, x_0) \mid x_0 \in \Sigma^*\}$. Note that $\Sigma^* \times \Sigma^*$ is a monoid, with unity (λ, λ).

Property S1. Let x, u, v, y $\in \Sigma^* \times \Sigma^*$. If xy, xuy, xvy $\in$ E, then xuvy $\in$ E.

In fact this property can be obtained from the following more basic one, using monoid laws only (take $x' = x$, $y' = y$, $u' = xu$ and $v' = vy$).

Property S2. Let x, u, v, y $\in \Sigma^* \times \Sigma^*$. If xy, xv, uy $\in$ E, then uv $\in$ E.

(Proof: $x_1 y_1 = x_2 y_2$ implies the existence of $t \in \Sigma^*$ such that $x_2 = x_1 t$ and $y_1 = t y_2$, or vice versa. Hence $x_1 v_1 = x_2 v_2$ implies that $x_1 v_1 = x_1 t v_2$ and so $v_1 = t v_2$, $u_1 y_1 = u_2 y_2$ implies $u_1 t y_2 = u_2 y_2$ and so $u_1 t = u_2$. Finally $u_1 v_1 = u_1 t v_2 = u_2 v_2$.)

Let us now consider trees. The following notation is appropriate. For a ranked alphabet Σ, $T_\Sigma[*]$ denotes $T_\Sigma[\{*\}]$, i.e., the set of all trees over Σ in which certain leaves are "unlabeled" (labeled by *). For $x_0, y_0 \in T_\Sigma[*]$, $x_0 y_0$ denotes $x_0[y_0]$, i.e., the result of substituting y_0 for all occurrences of * in x_0. In this way $T_\Sigma[*]$ is a monoid, with unity *.

The string-approach can now be generalized to trees, due to the following property of a deterministic bottom-up tree transducer M_1 (for a definition of bottom-up tree transducers see, e.g., [9]). Suppose $t_0 = x_0 y_0$, where x_0 contains exactly one occurrence of * and let M_1 process t_0; see Figure 9. If y_1 is the output produced during processing of y_0 and x_1 that of x_0 then $M_1(x_0 y_0) = x_1 y_1$ (note

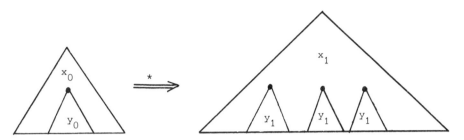

Fig. 9.   Bottom-up tree transduction.

that x_1 contains in general several occurrences of *, due to
the copying ability of M_1). Thus, given two deterministic
bottom-up tree transducers M_1 and M_2 one could consider a
large input tree with a long path, take three points on this
path with identical state-pairs, and apply property S1. Unfortunately properties S1 and S2 do not hold for trees!
to see that S1 fails, let σ have rank 2 and take $x_1 = x_2$
= *, $y_1 = y_2 \neq$ *, $u_1 = \sigma(*,y_1)$ and $u_2 = v_1 = \sigma(*,*)$. Why
do these properties fail? The proof of property S2 is based
on the left-and-right-cancellation laws for strings (these are
also special cases of S2: take $y = u = (\lambda,\lambda)$ and $x = v =$
(λ,λ), respectively). The corresponding "top-cancellation
law" for trees is valid (assuming that the top part contains
at least one *), but the "bottom-cancellation law" fails:
take $x_1 = \sigma(*,*)$ and $x_2 = \sigma(t,*)$ with $t \neq$ *, then $x_1t =$
x_2t but $x_1 \neq x_2$. This example shows the basic trouble: t
is already present at some occurrences of *; if we could
change t slightly and still have $x_1t = x_2t$, then x_1 and
x_2 had to be equal. This gives the following revised law.

Law of bottom cancellation (for trees in $T_\Sigma[*]$): if
$x_1t = x_2t$, $x_1t' = x_2t'$ and $t \neq t'$, then $x_1 = x_2$.

From this law the following analogue of property S2 can be proved.

Property T2.   Let   u, v, x, y, z $\in T_\Sigma[*] \times T_\Sigma[*]$.   Assume that x_1 or x_2 contains at least one occurrence of   *,   and assume that $y_1 \neq z_1$ and $y_2 \neq z_2$.   If   xy, xz, xv, uy, uz $\in$ E,   then   uv $\in$ E.

Note that the bottom-cancellation law is a special case of this property (take   x = v = (*,*)).   Finally, using property T2 we can obtain the following analogue of property S1.

Property T1.   Let   x, u, v, w, y $\in T_\Sigma[*] \times T_\Sigma[*]$.   If xy, xuy, xvy, xwy, xuvy, xuwy, xvwy $\in$ E,   then   xuvwy $\in$ E.

(Proof: take   x' = x,   y' = y,   z' = wy,   v' = vwy, u' = xu   and apply   T2; consider separately the cases that the assumptions of   T2   are not fulfilled.)

Note that property T1 could be weakened to the following more pleasing property: let   U   be a subset of $T_\Sigma[*] \times T_\Sigma[*]$; if   xy $\in$ E,   xUy $\subseteq$ E   and   xUUy $\subseteq$ E,   then   xU*y $\subseteq$ E.

Property T1 shows that the equivalence problem for bottom-up tree transducers M_1 and M_2 can be solved by considering four points on a long path rather than three (and thus it suffices to check trees of height at most $4N_1N_2$ where N_i is the number of states of M_i).

Theorem 7 (Zachar [84]).   The equivalence problem for deterministic bottom-up tree transducers is decidable.

The same proof shows decidability for linear (noncopying) DT transducers, and even for "unique-state" DT transducers (i.e., if $q(\sigma(x_1, \ldots, x_n)) \to t$ is a rule, and $q_1(x_i)$ and $q_2(x_i)$ occur in   t,   then $q_1 = q_2$).   Also, exactly the same technique can be used to show the decidability of the functionality problem (i.e., does a given nondeterministic finite-state transducer realize a partial function?), see [12,14,79]. A relation R is injective iff R^{-1} is functional. Since for strings nondeterministic finite-state transducers are closed under inverse, this implies the decidability of injectivity for these transducers. For trees the situation is less satisfactory: nondeterministic tree transducers are not closed under inverse (see [5,6]). In [43] several results on injectivity are obtained; it is, e.g., decidable for linear bottom-up transducers and undecidable in the general case. It would be interesting to see whether these results could be obtained by considering the equivalence problem for (generalized) tree transducers which are closed under inverse, cf. [5,6].

B.   Top-Down Tree Transducers

Recently, Esik has shown the decidability of equivalence of arbitrary DT transducers [44]. The basic idea of the proof is that equivalent transducers have "bounded balance" (see [22] where the string case is discussed), i.e., after processing a prefix of the input the difference in size of their translations is bounded. Consider as an example Figure 10. Suppose

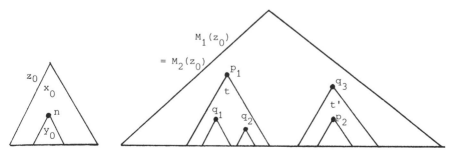

Fig. 10.   Two equivalent top-down tree transducers.

M_1 and M_2 are equivalent DT transducers. Consider the processing of an input tree $z_0 = x_0 y_0$ by M_1 and M_2. When M_1 arrives at node n, it has produced the part of the output tree outside the trees rooted at the nodes p_1 and p_2; similarly M_2 has produced the part outside the q_1, q_2, q_3 trees (where the p's and q's indicate the states of the transducers). We now claim that the size of the trees t and t' is small, i.e., their number of nodes is bounded (note that t and t' indicate how much the translation of M_2 is ahead of that of M_1, and vice versa, respectively; in general there are of course many of such trees). To see this, let y_0' be the smallest input tree which is translatable when starting in p_1, p_2, q_1, q_2 and q_3, and let k be the maximum size of the corresponding output trees. Then the sizes of t and t' are bounded by k, because otherwise $M_1(x_0 y_0') \neq M_2(x_0 y_0')$. Now let K be the maximum of all such k's. Then K bounds the size of all possible t and t'. Now the usual buffer technique can be used to define a top-down tree automaton A which at each node n keeps all "balance trees" like t and t' (together with the states) in its finite control and simulates the moves of all copies of M_1 and M_2 simultaneously, checking whether their outputs are still consistent, and rejecting when either the outputs are different or their difference in size becomes too big. M_1 and M_2 are equivalent iff A accepts all input trees (which is decidable).

   Theorem 8 (Esik [44]). The equivalence problem for deterministic top-down tree transducers is decidable.

   Again the same proof can be given to show that functionality of T transducers is decidable.

It follows from the proofs of Theorems 7 and 8 that in each case only a finite number of trees (up to some height H) has to be checked for equivalence of M_1 and M_2. In the top-down case H depends both on the number of states and on the size of the rules of M_1 and M_2. However, in the bottom-up case H only depends on the number of states of M_1 and M_2. From this the following can be concluded [44]: for each recognizable tree language R there exists (effectively) a finite subset R_0 such that, for every two tree homomorphisms h_1 and h_2, $h_1|R = h_2|R$ if and only if $h_1|R_0 = h_2|R_0$ (where | denotes restriction to a set), i.e., in the terminology of [23], every recognizable tree language has a finite test set. It is open whether in the top-down case an H can be found which depends on the number of states only.

For monadic DT transducers a relationship with automata on strings exists by the "path-approach." For a monadic DT transducer M, let π(M) be the string translation $\{(v,w) \mid$ w is a path through $M(\bar{v})\}$, where $\bar{v}$ is the monadic tree corresponding to the string v. Then two such transducers, M_1 and M_2, are equivalent iff $\pi(M_1) = \pi(M_2)$. It is easy to see that the translations π(M), for monadic DT transducers M, correspond precisely to the translations realizable by nondeterministic gsm's with the prefix property, i.e., at each moment the pieces of output produced by possible moves are not prefixes of each other. Thus equivalence of such ngsm's is decidable, cf. a remark in [52]. Such translations are also recognizable by 1-way 2-tape finite automata (cf. [17]) for which the equivalence problem is decidable [13]. Vice versa, every relation recognizable by a 1-way 2-tape

automaton can be realized (in the π sense) by a monadic DT
transducer which has infinite, but regular, trees as right-
hand sides. It might be nice to show decidability of equivalence of such infinite DT transducers in general.

C. Other Equivalence Problems

A relationship with other equivalence problems turns up
when considering that for deterministic top-down tree-to-
string transducers, i.e., yDT transducers. Very little is
known concerning decidability of this problem. Let us consider in particular monadic yDT transducers. Due to the relationship of such transducers to EDTOL systems, their
equivalence problems would be called the EDTOL sequence
equivalence problem in L system theory. It is equivalent to
the problem of homomorphism equivalence on EDTOL languages,
cf. [22]. Its decidability would imply that of the HDOL
sequence equivalence problem and the DTOL sequence equivalence problem, both open problems (thus the decidability of
the DOL sequence equivalence problem [21] seems to be the
only known subcase). Due to the relationship between ETOL
systems and 2-way automata it would also imply decidability of
the equivalence problem for 2-way deterministic finite-state
transducers (2DGSM) which is also open (in fact, this problem is equivalent to that for finite copying monadic yDT
transducers, or, EDTOL systems of finite index).

Note that Theorem 8 can be interpreted saying that for all
above-mentioned problems the structural equivalence problem is
decidable, i.e., equivalence of systems which produce parenthesized strings (expressions).

We finally mention the equivalence problems for deterministic macro tree transducers (DMTT, Section III.C) and for attribute grammars (as tree transducers, Section III). If equivalence is decidable for DMTT, then also for yDT transducers (see the remarks following Theorem 3) and for AG transductions. Decidability for AG would imply decidability for yDT_{fc} (cf. Theorem 2) and hence for 2DGSM. This shows that the problem of deciding equivalence of attribute grammars and macro tree transducers is probably very hard to solve (let alone the one for the corresponding tree-to-string transducers!).

VI.   CONCLUSION

We hope to have shown, by way of examples, that tree language theory can help to get more insight into the (formal) structure of computation. Although perhaps not many "realistic" results can be obtained in tree language and formal language theory, these theories are strong enough to offer a unifying framework for more advanced theories of computation. For this reason formal (tree) language theory itself needs continuous strengthening and unification.

ACKNOWLEDGMENTS

I wish to thank Gilberto Filè and Werner Damm for stimulating conversations.

REFERENCES

1. Aho, A.V., and Ullman, J.D., "The Theory of Parsing, Translation and Compiling." Prentice-Hall, Englewood Cliffs, N.J. (1972) (two volumes).
2. Aho, A.V., and Ullman, J.D., Translations on a context-free grammar. Inf. and Control 19, 439-475 (1971).
3. Alblas, H., The limitations of attribute evaluation in passes. Memorandum, Twente University of Technology (1979).

4. Arnold, A., Systèmes d'équations dans le magmoide: Ensembles rationnels et algébriques d'arbres. Thèse, Université de Lille (1977).
5. Arnold, A., and Dauchet, M., Bi-transductions de forêts. Proc. 3rd International Colloquium on Automata, Languages and Programming, Edinburgh, 74-86 (1976).
6. Arnold, A., and Dauchet, M., Sur l'inversion des morphismes d'arbres. Proc. 5th International Colloqium on Automata, Languages and Programming, Udine, Lecture Notes in Computer Science 62 (G. Ausiello and C. Böhm, eds.), 26-35 (1978).
7. Arnold, A., and Dauchet, M., Forêts algébriques et homomorphismes inverses. Inf. and Control 37, 182-196 (1978).
8. Asveld, P.R.J., and Engelfriet, J., Extended linear macro grammars, iteration grammars, and register programs. Acta Informatica 11, 259-285 (1979).
9. Baker, B.S., Composition of top-down and bottom-up tree transductions. Inf. and Control 41, 186-213 (1979).
10. Baker, B.S., Generalized syntax directed translation, tree transducers, and linear space. SIAM J. Comp. 7, 376-391 (1978).
11. Baker, B.S., Tree transducers and tree languages. Inf. and Control 37, 241-266 (1978).
12. Berstel, J., Tranductions and context-free languages. Teubner Studienbücher Informatik, Stuttgart (1979).
13. Bird, M., The equivalence problem for deterministic two-tape automata. J. Comp. System Sci. 7, 218-236 (1973).
14. Blattner, M., and Head, T., Single-valued a-transducers. J. Comp. System Sci. 15, 310-327 (1977). (See also, by the same authors, The decidability of equivalence for deterministic finite transducers. J. Comp. System Sci. 19, 45-49 (1979).)
15. Boasson, L., Courcelle, B., and Nivat, M., A new complexity measure for languages. Proc. Conf. on Theoretical Computer Science, Waterloo, Ontario, 130-138 (1977).
16. Bochmann, G.V., Semantic evaluation from left to right. Comm. ACM 19, 55-62 (1976).
17. Buda, A., Generalized$^{1.5}$ sequential machine maps. Inf. Proc. Letters 8, 38-40 (1979).
18. Chandra, A.K., Kozen, D.C., and Stockmeyer, L.J., Alternation. Research Report RC 7489, IBM, Yorktown Heights (1979).
19. Chirica, L.M., and Martin, D.V., An algebraic formulation of Knuthian semantics. Proc. 17th Ann. Symp. on Foundations of Computer Science, Houston, 127-136 (1976).
20. Courcelle, B., A representation of trees by languages. Theor. Comp. Sci. 6, 255-279 (1978); and Theor. Comp. Sci. 7, 25-55 (1978).
21. Culik, II, K., and Fris, J., The decidability of the equivalence problem for DOL-systems. Inf. and Control 35, 20-39 (1977).
22. Culik, II, K., and Salomaa, A., On the decidability of homomorphism equivalence for languages. J. Comp. System Sci. 17, 163-175 (1978).
23. Culik, II, K., and Salomaa, A., Test sets and checking words for homomorphism equivalence. Research Report CS-79-04, University of Waterloo (1979).

24. Damm, W., An algebraic extension of the Chomsky-hierarchy. Proc. 8th Symp. on Mathematical Foundations of Computer Science, Lecture Notes in Computer Science 74 (J. Bečvář, ed.), Springer-Verlag, 266-276 (1979).

25. Damm, W., The IO- and OI-hierarchies. Berich Nr. 41, Technische Hochschule Aachen, Informatik (1978).

26. Damm, W., Personal communication (1979).

27. Damm, W., and Fehr, E., On the power of self-application and higher type recursion. Proc. 5th International Colloquium on Automata, Lagnuages and Programming, Udine, Lecture Notes in Computer Science 62 (G. Ausiello and C. Böhm, eds.) (1978).

28. Damm. W., Fehr, E., and Indermark, K., Higher type recursion and self-application as control structures. In "Formal Descriptions of Programming Concepts" (E.J. Neuhold, ed.), North-Holland, Amsterdam, 461-489 (1978).

29. Dauchet, M., Transductions de forêts; bimorphisms de magmoides. Thèse, University of Lille (1977).

30. Duske, J., Parchmann, R., Sedello, M., and Specht, J., IO-macrolanguages and attributed translations. Inf. and Control 35, 87-105 (1977).

31. Duske, J., Parchmann, R., and Specht, J., Szilard languages of IO-grammars. Inf. and Control 40, 319-331 (1979).

32. Eilenberg, S., "Automata, Languages, and Machines." Academic Press, New York (1974).

33. Engelfriet, J., Simple program schemes and formal languages. Lecture Notes in Computer Science 20, Springer-Verlag (1974).

34. Engelfriet, J., Three hierarchies of transducers. Memorandum 217, Twente University of Technology (1978).

35. Engelfriet, J., Two-way automata and checking automata. In "Foundations of Computer Science III (J.W. de Bakker and J. van Leeuwen, eds.), Mathematical Centre Tracts 108, Part 1, 1-69 (1979).

36. Engelfriet, J., and Filè, G., The formal power of one-visit attribute grammars. Memorandum 286, Twente University of Technology (1979).

37. Engelfriet, J., and Filè, G., work in progress.

38. Engelfriet, J., Rozenberg, G., and Slutzki, G., Tree transducers, L systems and two-way machines. Memorandum 187, Twente University of Technology (1977) (also in Proc. 10th Ann. ACM Symp. on Theory of Computing, San Diego, 1978); to appear in J. Comp. Syst. Sci.

39. Engelfriet, J., and Meineche Schmidt, E., IO and OI. J. Comp. System Sci. 15, 328-353 (1977), and J. Comp. System Sci. 16, 67-99 (1978).

40. Engelfriet, J., Meineche Schmidt, E., and van Leeuwen, J., Stack machines and classes of nonnested macro-languages. Report RUU-CS-77-2, University of Utrecht (1977); to appear in J. ACM.

41. Engelfriet, J., and Skyum, S., The copying power of one-state tree transducers. DAIMI PB-91, University of Aarhus (1978).

42. Engelfriet, J., and Slutzki, G., Bounded nesting in macro grammars. Inf. and Control 42, 157-193 (1979).

43. Esik, Z., On decidability of injectivity of tree trans-
    formations. Troisième Colloque de Lille, Les arbres in
    algèbre et en programmation, 107-133 (1978).
44. Esik, Z., On functional tree transducers. Proc. 2nd Conf.
    on Fundamentals of Computation Theory (L. Budach, ed.),
    Akademi-Verlag, Berlin, 121-127 (1979).
45. Fischer, M.J., Grammars with macro-like productions. Ph.D.
    dissertation, Harvard University (1968). (See also 9th
    Conf. on Switching and Automata Theory, 131-142.)
46. Fischer, M.J., Two characterizations of the context-
    sensitive languages. IEEE Conf. Rec. 10th Ann. Symp. on
    Switching and Automata Theory, Waterloo, Ontario, 149-156
    (1969).
47. Ganzinger, H., Strukturelle Zusammenhänge zwischen funk-
    tionalen Sprachbeschreibungen und Ubersetzerbeschreibungen.
    Institut fur Informatik, University of München (1978).
48. Ginsburg, S., "Algebraic and Automat-Theoretic Properties
    of Formal Languages." North-Holland, Amsterdam (1975).
49. Goguem, J.A., Thatcher, J.W., Wagner, E.G., and Wright,
    J.B., Initial algebra semantics and continuous algebras.
    J. ACM 24, 68-95 (1977).
50. Greibach, S.A., Theory of program structures: schemes,
    semantics, verification. Lecture Notes in Computer Sci-
    ence 36, Springer-Verlag (1975).
51. Greibach, S.A., Hierarchy theorems for two-way fintie
    state transducers. Acta Informatica 11, 89-101 (1978).
52. Griffiths, T.V., The unsolvability of the equivalence
    problem for Λ-free nondeterministic generalized machines.
    J. ACM 15, 409-413 (1968).
53. Ibarra, O.H., Characterizations of some tape and time com-
    plexity classes of Turing machines in terms of multi-head
    and auxiliary stack automata. J. Comp. System Sci. 5,
    88-117 (1971).
54. Jazayeri, M., Ogden, W.F., and Rounds, W.C., The intrin-
    sically exponential complexity of the circularity problem
    for attribute grammars. Comm. ACM 18, 697-706 (1975).
55. Jespersen, P., Madsen, M., and Riis, H., New extended at-
    tribute translation system (NEATS). DAIMI, University of
    Aarhus (1978).
56. Jones, N.D., Lien, Y.E., and Laaser, W.T., New problems
    complete for nondeterministic log space. Math. Syst.
    Theory 10, 1-17 (1976).
57. Kamimura, T., and Slutzki, G., Dag-to-tree transductions.
    Technical Report no. 79/2, University of Delaware, Newark
    (1979).
58. Kennedy, K., and Warren, S.K., Automatic generation of ef-
    ficient evaluators for attribute grammars. Conf. Rec.
    3rd Symp. on Principles of Programming Languages, 32-49
    (1976).
59. Knuth, D.E., Semantics of context-free languages. Math.
    Syst. Theory 2, 127-145 (1968). Correction: Math. Syst.
    Theory 5, 95-96 (1971).
60. Ladner, R.E., Lipton, R.J., and Stockmeyer, L.J., Alter-
    nating pushdown automata. Proc. 19th Ann. Symp. on Foun-
    dations of Computer Science, Ann Arbor, 92-106 (1978).
61. Lewis, P.M., Rosenkrantz, P.J., and Stearns, R.E., Attri-
    buted translations. J. Comp. System Sci. 9, 409-439 (1974).

62. Lilin, E., Une généralisation des transducteurs d'états finis d'arbres: les S-transducteurs. Thèse de 3e cycle, University of Lille (1978).
63. Madsen, O.L., On defining semantics by means of extended attribute grammars. DAIMI IR-14, University of Aarhus (1979).
64. Maibaum, T.S.E., A generalized approach to formal languages. J. Comp. System Sci. 8, 409-439 (1974).
65. Maslov, A.N., The hierarchy of indexed languages of an arbitrary level. Soviet Math. Dokl. 15, 1170-1174 (1974).
66. Mayer, O., personal communication (1974).
67. Mayoh, B.H., Attribute grammars and mathematical semantics. DAIMI PB-80, Aarhus University (1978).
68. Mezei, J., and Wright, J.B., Algebraic automata and context-free sets. Inf. and Control 11, 3-29 (1967).
69. Nivat, M., On the interpretation of recursive program schemes. Symposia Math. 15, 255-281 (1975).
70. Nivat, M., Infinite words, infinite trees, infinite computations. In "Foundations of Computer Science III (J.W. de Bakker and J. van Leeuwen, eds.), Mathematical Centre Tracts 108, Part 2, 1-52 (1979).
71. Ogden, W.F., and Rounds, W.C., Composition of n transducers. 4th ACM Symp. on Theory of Computing, 198-206 (1972).
72. Parchmann, R., Grammatiken mit Attributschema und sweistufige Auswertung attributierter Grammatiken. Bericht Nr. 46, Technische Hochschule Aachen, Informatik (1978).
73. Perrault, C.R., Intercalation lemmas for tree transducer languages. J. Comp. System Sci. 13, 246-277 (1976).
74. Raiha, K.-J., and Saarinen, M., Developments in compiler writing systems. G.I.-6 Jahrestagung (E.J. Neuhold, ed.), Informatik-Fachberichte 5, 164-178, Springer-Verlag (1976).
75. Riis, H., and Skyum, S., personal communication (1979).
76. Rounds, W.C., Mappings and grammars on trees. Math. Syst. Theory 4, 257-287 (1970).
77. Ruzzo, W.L, Tree-size bounded alternation. Proc. 11th Ann. ACM Symp. on Theory of Computing, Atlanta, 352-359 (1979).
78. Schmidt, E. Meineche, Succinctness of descriptions of context-free, regular, and finite languages. DAIMI PB-84, Aarhus University (1978).
79. Schützenberger, M.P., Sur les relations rationnelles. In "Automata Theory and Formal Languages (H. Brakhage, ed.), 2nd G.I. Conference, Lecture Notes in Computer Science 33, 209-213, Springer-Verlag (1975).
80. Thatcher, J.W., Tree automata: an informal survey. In "Currents in the Theory of Computing (A.V. Aho, ed.), Prentice-Hall (1973).
81. van Leeuwen, J., Variations of a new machine model. 17th Ann. IEEE Symp. on Foundations of Computer Science, Houston, 228-235 (1976).
82. Wand, M., An algebraic formulation of the Chomsky hierarchy. In "Category Theory Applied to Computation and Control," Lecture Notes in Computer Science 25, 209-213, Springer-Verlag (1975).

83. Woods, W.A., Transition network grammars for natural lan-
    guage analysis. Comm. ACM 13, 591-606 (1970).
84. Zachar, Z., The solvability of the equivalence problem for
    deterministic frontier-to-root tree transducers. Acta
    Cybernetica 4, 167-177 (1978).

FORMAL LANGUAGE THEORY

THE INTERFACE BETWEEN LANGUAGE THEORY
AND COMPLEXITY THEORY[1]

Burkhard Monien
Ivan Hal Sudborough[2]

Fachbereich Mathematik/Informatik
Gesamthochschule Paderborn
Paderborn, West Germany

I.   INTRODUCTION

We wish to describe here some recent results in the interface between two fields in computer science: formal language
theory and computational complexity. The definition of these
two fields would be hard for anyone to state precisely, we believe, and we will not try to give such definitions here.
However, it does seem fair to assume that results concerning
the description of languages, whether by grammars, automata,
or other means, belong to the first area (and possibly the
second) and results concerning the number of steps, the amount
of memory, or the size of an algorithm required for a given
task belong to the second area (and possibly the first). Also,
it seems clear to us that certain long-standing concerns in
formal language theory, such as whether or not additional computing power is obtained when nondeterminism is added to a

---

[1]Preparation of this paper was supported in part by the
National Science Foundation under Grant No. MCS79-04012.
[2]On leave of absence from the Department of Electrical
Engineering and Computer Science, Northwestern University,
Evanston, Illinois, U.S.A.

287

class of automata, are also very much of concern in computational complexity research today. On the other hand, many of
the results concerning standard formal language theory classes,
such as the proof that the membership problem for context-free
languages is not more difficult than, say, boolean matrix multiplication, borrow their significance and often their techniques of proof from traditional computational complexity
theory [52]. Quite often, too, problems in computational complexity are described as language recognition problems and
traditional formal language theory classes (e.g., the context-
sensitive languages) are described as complexity classes. So,
we shall simply assume that the reader has a reasonable understanding of what these two areas might encompass and thereby
avoid any of these difficult definitional problems.

     We shall assume, in addition, that the reader is acquainted
with the traditional definitions of multitape Turing machines,
pushdown automata, as well as the standard families of phrase-
structure grammars: right-linear, linear, context-free, and
context-sensitive. Thus, we shall assume that the reader is
familiar with the fundamental definitions and results of formal language theory and computational complexity as described,
for instance, in [21]. Let M be a nondeterministic automaton (Turing machine, pushdown automaton, etc.) and let x be
a string over its input alphabet. We shall say that M accepts x if there is some accepting computation by M on input x. The language accepted by M, denoted by L(M), is
the set {x | M accepts x}. For x ∈ L(M), $\text{Time}_M(x)$ de-
notes the minimum number of steps used to accept x among all
the accepting computations of M on input x. Similarly, for

$x \in L(M)$, $Space_M(x)$ denotes the minimum number of distinct worktape cells visited by M in an accepting computation on x. It should be noted that for measuring the amount of space, the Turing machine is assumed to have a read-only input tape and a separate worktape. Furthermore, in the case of an auxiliary pushdown automaton, which is a multitape Turing machine with an added pushdown store, the space used on the pushdown store is not counted. In general, only the number of cells visited on the designated worktape are counted. By convention, we shall designate, for $x \notin L(M)$, that $Time_M(x) = \infty$ and $Space_M(x) = \infty$. For f a function from the nonnegative integers to the nonnegative integers, define the <u>language</u> <u>recognized</u> <u>by</u> M <u>within</u> <u>time</u> f, denoted by $LTIME_f(M)$, to be the set $\{x \mid Time_M(x) \le f(|x|)\}$, and the <u>language</u> <u>recognized</u> <u>by</u> M <u>within</u> <u>space</u> f, denoted by $LSPACE_f(M)$, to be the set $\{x \mid Space_M(x) \le f(|x|)\}$. We shall say that M <u>accepts</u> <u>within</u> <u>time</u> f or that M <u>accepts</u> <u>within</u> <u>space</u> f, if $L(M) = LTIME_f(M)$ or $L(M) = LSPACE_f(M)$, respectively.

Define:

$$DTIME(f) = \{L \mid L = L(M) = LTIME_f(M) \text{ for some deterministic Turing machine } M\}$$

$$NTIME(f) = \{L \mid L = L(M) = LTIME_f(M) \text{ for some nondeterministic Turing machine } M\}$$

$$DSPACE(f) = \{L \mid L = L(M) = LSPACE_f(M) \text{ for some deterministic Turing machine } M\}$$

$$NSPACE(f) = \{L \mid L = L(M) = LSPACE_f(M) \text{ for some nondeterministic Turing machine } M\}$$

$$2DPDASPACE(f) = \{L \mid L = L(M) = LSPACE_f(M) \text{ for some}$$
$$\text{deterministic auxiliary PDA } M\}$$
$$2NPDASPACE(f) = \{L \mid L = L(M) = LSPACE_f(M) \text{ for some}$$
$$\text{nondeterministic auxiliary PDA } M\}.$$

It should be noted that we have defined the complexity
classes above by the requirement that every string x in the
language has a computation that does not use more than space
or time $f(|x|)$. There is no restriction on the amount of
space or time used for words not in the language. Some define
classes by bounding the space or time of all computations [19,
20]. This variation in the definition will not make a difference, however, for most of the complexity classes considered
here. That is, if the bounding function is in some reasonable
sense constructible, then the amount of space can be marked
off in advance and the computation terminated whenever the
marked space is exceeded or a "clock" can be installed in parallel with the computation and the computation terminated
whenever the time bound is exceeded.

To make our notation less cumbersome we shall employ the
following abbreviations:

$$\mathbb{P} = \cup_{k \geq 1} DTIME(n^k)$$
$$\mathbb{NP} = \cup_{k \geq 1} NTIME(n^k)$$
$$\mathbb{PSPACE} = \cup_{k \geq 1} DSPACE(n^k).$$

(One should not be confused by the naming of complexity classes
in the form $DSPACE(f(n))$ and $DTIME(f(n))$ instead of
$DSPACE(f)$ and $DTIME(f)$, respectively. We shall use both
forms interchangeably. Thus for any $k \geq 1$, $DTIME(n^k)$ is the
complexity class $DTIME(f)$, where $f(n) = n^k$, for all n.)

For any function f from the nonnegative integers to the positive real numbers, we designate the following classes:

$$O(f) = \{g \mid \lim_{n \to \infty} \sup[g(n) \mid f(n)] < \infty\}$$

$$o(f) = \{g \mid \lim_{n \to \infty} \sup[g(n) \mid f(n)] = 0\}.$$

It follows from well-known "gap" theorems that there are functions f such that DTIME(f) and DSPACE(f) are identical to DTIME(r∘f) and DSPACE(r∘f), respectively, where r is any recursive function. (The notation r∘f denotes the composition of the functions r and f.) These "gaps," however, can be eliminated from the complexity class hierarchies by requiring that the function f that "names" the complexity class, e.g., DTIME(f) or DSPACE(f), be "honest" in some sense. Commonly used notions of honesty in this context are "time constructibility" [20,45] and "space constructibility" [41,45].

Definition. A function f on the nonnegative integers is time-constructible if there is a deterministic Turing machine M such that, for all x, $\text{Time}_M(x) = f(|x|)$ and $f \notin o(n)$. A function f is space-constructible if there is a deterministic Turing machine M such that (1) $\text{Space}_M(x) \leq f(|x|)$, (2) $\forall n$ there is a string x of length n such that $\text{Space}_M(x) = f(|x|)$. f is fully space-constructible if conditions (1) and (2) above can be replaced by the single condition: $\text{Space}_M(x) = f(|x|)$, for all input strings x.

For example, the function $f(n) = 2^n$ is time-constructible and fully space-constructible. Also, the function $h(n) = \log_2(\log_2 n)$, usually abbreviated by $h(n) = \log \log n$, is space-constructible but not fully space-constructible.

We describe in the following two sections: complete problems for several familiar complexity classes and formal language classes, separation results that indicate how much additional computing resource is needed to obtain a larger family of languages, and inclusion and characterization results that yield good bounds on the complexity of language classes. Section II gives complete problems and characterization theorems and Section III gives the separation results.

II. COMPLETE PROBLEMS AND CHARACTERIZATION THEOREMS

A large amount of research activity in formal language theory and computational complexity in the last few years has been concerned with identifying complete problems for various complexity classes and formal language classes. This work is important in two distinct ways. First, to find a complete language for a complexity class or formal language class is to show that a single problem, in some reasonable sense, represents the complexity of the whole class. Hence, the complexity of the class is better understood. Secondly, to identify various "natural" problems or languages as being complete for a class is to classify the complexity of these problems, in some reasonable sense. That is, many natural problems have been described which are complete for $\mathbb{NP}$ [26]. The complexity of these problems has been classified in the sense, for example, that they are in the class $\mathbb{P}$ if and only if $\mathbb{P} = \mathbb{NP}$ and they are in DSPACE(log n) iff $\mathbb{NP}$ = DSPACE(log n).

We shall now give various definitions of reductions and complete languages. Each of these notions has been previously described in the literature.

Definition. Let Σ and Δ be alphabets and let $f : \Sigma^* \to \Delta^*$ be a function. f is log space computable if there is a deterministic Turing machine with a two-way read-only input tape, a one-way output tape, and a two-way read-write worktape, which when started with $x \in \Sigma^*$ on its input tape will halt having written $f(x) \in \Delta^*$ on its output tape and having visited at most $\log_2(|x|)$ distinct tape squares on its worktape.

Definition. Let $A \subseteq \Sigma^*$ and $B \subseteq \Delta^*$ be arbitrary sets. A is log space reducible to B, denoted by $A \leq_{log} B$, if there is a log space computable function $f : \Sigma^* \to \Delta^*$ such that

$$\forall x \in \Sigma^* \; [x \in A \iff f(x) \in B].$$

A is homomorphism reducible to B, denoted by $A \leq_{hom} B$, if there is a homomorphism $h : \Sigma^* \to \Delta^*$ such that

$$\forall x \in \Sigma^* \; [x \in A \iff h(x) \in B].$$

Polynomial time (many-one) reductions can be defined in an analogous manner by stipulating that the function $f : \Sigma^* \to \Delta^*$, as described above, is computable within polynomial time by a deterministic Turing machine [26]. All of these three types of reductions are binary relations on languages. Considered as binary relations they are clearly reflexive and can be shown to be transitive [25]. In general, let $\leq$ be a binary relation on languages, such as the log space reducibility relation $\leq_{log}$ or the homomorphism reducibility relation $\leq_{hom}$,

and let $\mathcal{L}$ denote an artitrary family of languages. Define
CLOSURE$_<$($\mathcal{L}$) to be the set $\{L \mid L \leq L'$, for some $L' \in \mathcal{L}\}$.
If $\leq$ is reflexive, as the given reducibility relations are,
then clearly $\mathcal{L} \subseteq$ CLOSURE$_<$($\mathcal{L}$). We shall say that $\mathcal{L}$ is
closed under the relation $\leq$ if CLOSURE$_<$($\mathcal{L}$) $\subseteq \mathcal{L}$. A language L is complete for $\mathcal{L}$ with respect to $\leq$, or simply
complete for $\mathcal{L}$ when $\leq$ is understood, if (1) $L \in \mathcal{L}$, and
(2) $\mathcal{L} \subseteq$ CLOSURE$_<$($\{L\}$). A language L is hard for $\mathcal{L}$ with
respect to $\leq$, or simply hard for $\mathcal{L}$ when $\leq$ is understood,
if $\mathcal{L} \subseteq$ CLOSURE$_<$($\{L\}$).

It is known that the complexity classes $\mathbb{P}$, $\mathbb{NP}$, $\mathbb{PSPACE}$,
and $\cup_{k \geq 1}$DTIME(2^{n^k}), for example, are closed under all three
of the forms of reduction given [25]. The complexity classes
DSPACE(log n) and NSPACE(log n), for example, are also
closed under log space reductions and homomorphism reductions.
Finally, the following complexity classes and formal language
classes are closed under homomorphism reductions: the family
of context-free languages (CFL), the context-sensitive languages (LBA), the family of linear context-free languages
(LINEAR-CFL), the exponential time languages $\cup_k$DTIME(2^{kn}),
and the family of languages recognized by the two-way one-head
deterministic pushdown automata (2DPDAHEADS(1) or, simply,
2DPDA), and many, many others.

A homomorphism reduction is a special case of a log space
reduction; a log space reduction is a special case of a polynomial time reduction. A homomorphism reduction satisfies a
very special property, namely that the length of the image
f(x) of any string x is bounded by some fixed constant
$c \geq 1$ times the length of x. This is not true with the

other two types of reductions; a log space reduction and a
polynomial time reduction may map a string x into one of
length q($|x|$) for some fixed polynomial q.

We first describe three languages which are complete for
CFL, DCFL, and LINEAR-CFL, respectively, with respect to
some of the forms of reducibility mentioned. For any alphabet
Σ, let R_Σ be the regular set over the alphabet
$\Sigma \cup \{\#,], [\}$ which is denoted by the regular expression
$\Sigma^+([(\Sigma^* \#)^* \Sigma^*])^+$. That is, strings in R_Σ are of the form

$$w_0 [w_1^{(1)} \# w_2^{(1)} \# \ldots \# w_{n(1)}^{(1)}] [w_1^{(2)} \# \ldots \# w_{n(2)}^{(2)}] \ldots$$

$$[w_1^{(k)} \# w_2^{(k)} \# \ldots \# w_{n(k)}^{(k)}]$$

for some $k \geq 1$, where w_0 and, for $1 \leq i \leq k$ and
$1 \leq j \leq n(i)$, $w_j^{(i)}$ is a string in Σ^*. A string of the form
$[w_1^{(i)} \# w_2^{(i)} \# \ldots \# w_n^{(i)}]$ is called a <u>block</u> and each of the
strings $w_j^{(i)}$ in such a block is called a <u>choice</u> <u>string</u>.

Definition. Let B be a language over an alphabet Σ.
The language L(B) is the set of all strings in the regular
set R_Σ of the form

$$w_0 [w_1^{(1)} \# w_2^{(1)} \# \ldots w_{n(1)}^{(1)}] [w_1^{(2)} \# w_2^{(2)} \# \ldots \# w_{n(2)}^{(2)}] \ldots$$

$$[w_1^{(k)} \# w_2^{(k)} \# \ldots \# w_{n(k)}^{(k)}]$$

for which there exists a sequence of positive integers
$i_1, i_2, \ldots, i_k$, indexing a choice string in each of the k
blocks, such that the string $w_0 \, w_{i_1}^{(1)} \, w_{i_2}^{(2)} \ldots w_{i_k}^{(k)}$, formed
by the concatenation of the initial string and the indexed
choice strings in sequence, is in the set B.

The following describe results concerning languages of the form $L(B)$, for various sets B.

(1) Let D_2 be the (one-sided) Dyck language over two generators generated by the context-free grammar $S \to SS$, $S \to a_1 S \bar{a}_1$, $S \to a_2 S \bar{a}_2$, $S \to e$, then $L(D_2)$ is complete for CFL with respect to homomorphism reductions [16].

(2) Let Σ be the particular alphabet $\{a_1, a_2, \bar{a}_1, \bar{a}_2\}$. For this alphabet Σ, let R_Σ' be the regular subset of R_Σ denoted by the regular expression $\{a_1, a_2\}^+ ([\bar{a}_1 \{a_1, a_2\}* \# \bar{a}_2 \{a_1, a_2\}*])^+$. Then the language $L(D_2) \cap R_\Sigma'$ is complete for DCFL with respect to log space reductions [48].

(3) Let $P = \{ww^R \mid w \in \{a_1, a_2\}*\}$ be the set of even-length palindromes over $\{a_1, a_2\}$. Then $L(P)$ is in LINEAR-CFL and is complete for NSPACE(log n) $\supseteq$ LINEAR-CFL with respect to $\leq_{log}$ [47].

It follows, for example, that LINEAR-CFL $\subseteq$ DSPACE(log n) iff NSPACE(log n) = DSPACE(log n) and that CFL $\subseteq$ DTIME(T(n)) iff $L(D_2)$ is in DTIME(T(n)), for all T such that for any $c \geq 1$ there exists a $d \geq 1$ for which, for all n, $T(cn) \leq dT(n)$.

Next we describe complete problems for $\mathbb{P}$, $\mathbb{NP}$, and NSPACE(log n). We have, of course, already described a complete problem for NSPACE(log n), but now we wish to describe the proof of completeness, not just the complete set. We shall work with various forms of path systems [12]:

Definition. A path system is a four-tuple $P = (X, R, S, T)$, where (1) X is a finite set (of nodes); (2) $R \subseteq X \times X \times X$ is a three-place relation on X; (3) $S \subseteq X$ (the set of source nodes); (4) $T \subseteq X$ (the set of terminal nodes).

Definition. Let $P = (X,R,S,T)$ be a path system. A set of nodes Q is admissible if it can be obtained using finitely many applications of the following two steps:

(1) add a terminal node to Q;

(2) if $(x,y,z) \in R$ and y, z are in Q, then add x to Q.

A node x is admissible if it belongs to some admissible set. A path system $P = (X,R,S.T)$ is solvable if at least one source node is admissible.

Let SPS denote the set of encodings of solvable path systems. (We choose a particular encoding in [50]; in general, the type of encoding isn't so crucial. Most node-by-node enumerations, for example, are permissible encodings.) We wish to observe first that SPS in in $\mathbb{P}$. That is, we wish to describe a polynomial time algorithm which determines whether a path system $P = (X,R,S,T)$ is solvable. This is done by calculating the set of all admissible nodes by the iterative procedure $Q_0 = T$ and $Q_{n+1} = Q_n \cup \{x \mid \exists y, z \in Q_n$ such that $(x,y,z) \in R\}$, for $n \geq 0$. $\exists k \geq 0 \ [S \cap Q_k \neq \emptyset] \iff P$ is solvable. This property can be determined in polynomial time; in fact, P is solvable iff $S \cap Q_t \neq \emptyset$, where t is the number of nodes in P.

To see that $\mathbb{P} \subseteq \text{CLOSURE}_{\leq \log} (\{SPS\})$ we describe the following construction. Let us say that a Turing machine is in normal form if it is a single-tape Turing machine that reverses the direction of motion of its head when and only when the head scans a cell containing a blank symbol and it never prints this blank symbol. Thus, a normal form Turing machine has an easily computed and predictable head motion: all the

way across the input to the first blank to the right, all the
way back to the first blank to the left, and so on. By standard techniques it is shown that one can achieve this normal
form at the cost of squaring the time bound.

Let M be a normal form Turing machine that takes at most
$q(n)$ steps on input of length n, for some polynomial q,
and let $w = a_1 a_2 \ldots a_n$ be an input of length n. Construct
the path system $P(M,w) = (X,R,S,T)$, where:

(1) $X = \{<i,p,\sigma> \mid 0 \le i \le q(|w|)$, p is an internal
    state of M, and σ is a tape symbol of M$\}$.

(2) $R = \{(<i_1,p_1,\sigma_1>,<i_2,p_2,\sigma_2>,<i_3,p_3,\sigma_3>) \mid i_1 = i_2 + 1$
    and $i_3 = \text{PRE-SCAN}(i_1)$ or $\text{PRE-SCAN}(i_1)$ is un-
    defined; $\sigma_1 = \text{ORIGINAL}(\text{SCAN}(i_1))$ if $\text{PRE-SCAN}(i_1)$
    is undefined, $\text{NEXTSYMBOL}(p_3,\sigma_3)$ if $\text{PRE-SCAN}(i_1)$
    i_3 and $p_1 = \text{NEXTSTATE}(p_2,\sigma_2)$, where
    $\text{NEXTSTATE}(p_2,\sigma_2)$ is the next state of M when in
    state p_2 scanning σ_2, $\text{NEXTSYMBOL}(p_3,\sigma_3)$ is
    the symbol printed by M when in state p_3 scan-
    ning σ_3,   SCAN(i) is the square of the tape
    scanned at time i, ORIGINAL(j) is the original
    symbol on cell j of the tape, and PRE-SCAN(i) =
    $\max\{j < i \mid \text{SCAN}(j) = \text{SCAN}(i)\}$. Thus PRE-SCAN(i)
    is undefined if, at time i, M scans a cell for
    the first time.

(3) $S = \{<i,p_f,\sigma>\} \mid 0 \le i \le q(|w|)$, p_f is a final state,
    and σ is a tape symbol$\}$.

(4) $T = \{<0,p_0,a_1> \mid p_0$ is the initial state of M and
    a_1 is the first symbol of w$\}$.

The reader should observe that the three-place relation R of this path system is designed so that if $(<i_1,p_1,\sigma_1>,<i_2,p_2,\sigma_2>,<i_3,p_3,\sigma_3>) \in R$ and M at time i_2 is in state p_2 scanning the symbol σ_2 then at time $i_1 = i_2 + 1$, M will be in state p_1 scanning the symbol σ_1. The third component of the triple is to describe what the scanned symbol σ_1 at time $i_1 = i_2 + 1$ must be. If M scans a cell for the first time at step i_1, then the third component can be anything at all. On the other hand, if M scans a cell that has been scanned before, then i_3 is the last time that this cell was scanned and, therefore, the symbol σ_1 must be what was printed at time i_3 when in state p_3 scanning σ_3.

We will say that $<i,p,\sigma>$ is _realizable_ iff M at time i on input w is in state p and scans σ. It is then straighforward to prove by induction that $<i,p,\sigma>$ is realizable iff $<i,p,\sigma>$ is admissible. Then it follows that M accepts w within $q(|w|)$ steps iff $P(M,w)$ is solvable. Furthermore the reduction from w to $P(M,w)$, for any given M, is a log space reduction. Thus, $\mathbb{P} \subseteq CLOSURE_{\leq log}(\{SPS\})$. The following theorem has thereby been demonstrated:

Theorem. SPS is complete for $\mathbb{P}$ with respect to log space reductions.

As stated earlier, $\mathbb{P}$ is closed under log space reductions. It follows that a family C equals $\mathbb{P}$ iff (1) SPS is complete for C with respect to log space reductions, and (2) C is closed under log space reduction. It is known that $\mathbb{P}$ is identical to the set of languages (1) 2DPDASPACE(log n) [8], (2) 2NPDASPACE(log n), and (3) ASPACE(log n), where ASPACE(S(n)) is the family of languages recognized by alternating Turing machines within space $S(n)$ [7]. (An alternating Turing machine is essentially the extension of a nondeterministic Turing machine in which one has "existential" and "universal" states and (1) if in an accepting computation an existential state is entered, then at least one choice leads to an accepting state, (2) if in an accepting computation a universal state is entered, then all choices of moves must lead to an accepting state.)

That $\mathbb{P}$ = 2NPDASPACE(log n) shows clearly the connection between formal language theory and computational complexity theory. That is, pushdown automata define the class of context-free languages. If one now extends these one-way nondeterministic acceptors to allow two-way head motion and logarithm worktape space, one obtains a device that defines the complexity class $\mathbb{P}$. In fact, historically, an efficient algorithm for context-free languages was extended to yield an efficient algorithm for 2NPDA languages and this algorithm was in turn extended to yield a polynomial time algorithm for 2NPDASPACE(log n) [2,8].

How must the problem SPS be modified to yield a complete problem for $\mathbb{N}$P? This can be done by insisting that the set of admissible nodes used in showing the solvability of the path system be consistent in the sense defined below.

A path system $P = (X,R,S,T)$ is indexed if $X \subseteq \mathbb{N} \times Y$, for some set Y; that is, if all the nodes are pairs whose first component is a natural number. A set of nodes Q of an indexed path system $P = (X,R,S,T)$ is consistent if $(i,x) \in Q$ and $(i,y) \in Q$ implies $x = y$. That is, no two nodes in Q have the same first component. A path system $P = (X,R,S,T)$

is <u>solvable</u> <u>by</u> <u>a</u> <u>consistent</u> <u>set</u>, or <u>consistently</u> <u>solvable</u>, if there is a consistent admissible set which contains a source node. Let CSPS denote the set of encodings of consistently solvable path systems.

<u>Theorem</u>. CSPS is complete for ℕP with respect to log space reductions.

<u>Proof</u>. Let M be a nondeterministic normal form Turing machine and let g(n) be a polynomial. For any input word $w = a_1 a_2 \ldots a_n$ of length n, for $n \geq 1$, construct the same path system P(M,w) that was described earlier. P(M,w) is consistently solvable iff M accepts w in $g(|w|)$ steps.

To see that this is true we need only show that $\{(1,p_1,\sigma_1), (2,p_2,\sigma_2), \ldots, (i,p_i,\sigma_i)\}$ is a consistent admissible set iff $(1,p_1,\sigma_1), (2,p_2,\sigma_2), \ldots, (i,p_i,\sigma_i)$ represents the sequence of state-symbol pairs of a computation of i steps of M on input w.

It is straightforward to verify also that CSPS is in ℕP. One only needs to guess a set of nodes and then verify that it forms a consistent admissible set deterministically. □

The original construction of a complete language for ℕP was the set SATISFIABILITY of well-formed formulas in the propositional calculus that are satisfiable [10]. We show now that CSPS $\leq_{log}$ SATISFIABILITY. Let P = (X,R,S,T) be an indexed path system. Construct the well-formed formula w(P) which has the nodes X as variables and consists of the conjunction of the following clauses:

(1) If x is a node that is not terminal and
(x,y_1,z_1), (x,y_2,z_2), ..., (x,y_k,z_k) are all the
triples in R with x as first component, then
$(x \Rightarrow [(y_1 \wedge z_1) \vee (y_2 \wedge z_2) \vee ... \vee (y_k \wedge z_k)])$ is
a clause in w(P).

(2) $(s_1 \vee s_2 \vee ... \vee s_p)$ is a clause, if S =
$\{s_1,s_2,...,s_p\}$ is the set of source nodes.

(3) $(\bar{x} \vee \bar{y})$ is a clause, for all nodes x and y such
that $x = (i,x')$ and $y = (i,y')$, where $x' \neq y'$.

It follows that w(P) is satisfiable iff P is consistently
solvable. That is, the set of variables that are assigned the
value true form a consistent admissible set of nodes of the
path system. By (1) the set must be admissible, by (3) it
must be consistent, and by (2) it must contain a source node.

A large number of natural problems are known to be complete for NP with respect to log space reductions. Many of
these problems have been described, for example, in the recent
book by Garey and Johnson [15].

How must SPS be modified to yield a complete problem for
NSPACE(log n)? One only needs to restrict the triples
(x,y,z) in the three-place relation so that y = z. In other
words, instead of triples (x,y,y) we have pairs (x,y),
which may be thought of as edges in a directed graph. Thus,
the problem is whether or not there is a path in a directed
graph from a node in a given set of start nodes to a node in a
given set of terminal nodes. This problem is called the
graph accessibility problem and is denoted by GAP.

Theorem [40]. GAP is complete for NSPACE(log n) with
respect to log space reductions.

Proof. Let M be a nondeterministic Turing machine that uses at most log n worktape cells on input of length n. Let $w = a_1 a_2 \ldots a_n$ be an input word of length n.

Construct the graph G = (V,E) which has the configurations or instantaneous descriptions (IDs) of M on input w as nodes and has an edge from the ID x to the ID y when and only when $x \vdash_{\overline{M,w}} y$; that is, when and only when y is one of the finite number of IDs that can be entered in one step from x. Let the start node be the initial ID of M on input w and the terminal nodes be the accepting IDs. Then G ∈ GAP <=> M accepts w. □

A path system P = (X,R,S,T), such that X = {1,...,n}, for some n ≥ 1, has bandwidth k if for all (x,y,z) ∈ R it is true that $|x-y| \leq k$ and $|x-z| \leq k$. Let SPS(f(n)) and GAP(f(n)), for functions f ∈ 0(n), denote the solvable path system problem and graph accessibility problem, respectively, for path systems and graphs with bandwidth f(n), where n is the number of nodes of the path system or graph. It is known that, for every constructible function f ∈ 0(log n), $\{SPS(2^{cf(n)})\}_{c \geq 1}$ is complete for ASPACE(f(n)) with respect to log space reductions and $\{GAP(2^{cf(n)})\}_{c \geq 1}$ is complete for NSPACE(f(n)) with respect to log space reductions [37,50]. Furthermore, it is known that GAP(f(n)) ∈ DSPACE(log f(n) × log n) and SPS(f(n)) ∈ DSPACE(f(n) × log n), for f(n) ∈ 0(n) - 0(log n) [37,50]. Therefore, NSPACE(f(n)) ⊆ DSPACE(f(n) × log n) and ASPACE(f(n)) ⊆ $\cup_{k \geq 1} DSPACE(2^{kf(n)})$, for f(n) ∈ 0(log n). In particular, it follows that $NSPACE(\log n) \subseteq DSPACE((\log n)^2)$,

$NSPACE((\log \log n)) \subseteq DSPACE(\log n \log \log n)$, and

$ASPACE(\log \log n) \subseteq \cup_{k \geq 1} DSPACE((\log n)^k)$.

We can say that a language L_1 is $S(n)$-_space reducible_ to a language L_2, for $S(n) \not\in o(\log n)$, denoted by $L_1 \leq_{S(n)} L_2$, if there is an $S(n)$-space computable function f such that, for all x, $x \in L_1 <=> f(x) \in L_2$. It follows that $DSPACE(S(n)) = CLOSURE_{\leq S(n)}(DSPACE(\log n))$, $NSPACE(S(n)) = CLOSURE_{\leq S(n)}(NSPACE(\log n))$, $\cup_{k \geq 1} DTIME(2^{kS(n)}) = CLOSURE_{\leq S(n)}(\mathbb{P})$, and $\cup_{k \geq 1} NTIME(2^{kS(n)}) = CLOSURE_{\leq S(n)}(\mathbb{NP})$, for constructible $S(n) \not\in o(\log n)$. Thus, the following results can be shown, for example:

(1) $NSPACE(\log n) = DSPACE(\log n) <=> NSPACE(S(n)) = DSPACE(S(n))$, for all constructible $S(n) \not\in o(\log n)$.

(2) $NSPACE(S(n)) \subseteq DSPACE((S(n))^2)$, for all constructible $S(n) \not\in o(\log n)$.

(3) $\mathbb{P} = \mathbb{NP} <=> \cup_{k \geq 1} DTIME(2^{kS(n)}) = \cup_{k \geq 1} NTIME(2^{kS(n)})$ for all constructible $S(n) \not\in o(\log n)$.

(4) $\mathbb{NP} = DSPACE(\log n) <=> \cup_{k \geq 1} NTIME(2^{kS(n)}) = DSPACE(S(n))$ for all constructible $S(n) \not\in o(\log n)$.

Results are also known that show that $CLOSURE_{\leq \log}(CFL)$ and $CLOSURE_{\leq \log}(DCFL)$ are exactly the sets of languages recognized by nondeterministic and deterministic, respectively, $\log n$ tape-bounded auxiliary PDA within polynomial time [48]. Thus, $CFL \subseteq NSPACE(\log n)$ iff the addition of a pushdown store to a nondeterministic $\log n$ tape-bounded Turing machine does not add computing power for polynomial time-bounded computations. Recent results have shown that every deterministic context-free language can be recognized by a deterministic Turing machine in $(\log n)^2$ space and simultaneous polynomial time [13].

There are a large number of interesting open problems concerning the relationship between complexity classes and the complexity of formal languages. There are, of course the obvious problems of showing the separation of some of the familiar complexity classes. That is, to show that $\mathbb{P} \neq \mathbb{NP}$, NSPACE(log n) $\neq$ DSPACE(log n), CLOSURE$_{\leq \log}$(CFL) $\neq$ NSPACE(log n), or CLOSURE$_{\leq \log}$(DCFL) $\neq$ DSPACE(log n), for example. (We conjecture that these inequalities are all valid.) However, there are other interesting problems that we may suggest for research topics:

(1) Find relationships between the open problems. For example, is it true that CFL $\subseteq$ NSPACE(log n) implies 2NPDA $\subseteq$ NSPACE(n)? Is it true that NSPACE(log log n) = DSPACE(log log n) implies NSPACE(log n) = DSPACE(log n)?

(2) Find better upper bounds on the complexity of families of languages. For example, is it true that DCFL $\subseteq$ DSPACE(S(n)), for some $S(n) \in O((\log n)^2)$? Is CFL $\subseteq$ NSPACE(S(n)), for some $S(n) \in O((\log n)^2)$?

(3) Understand what makes a language or family of languages complex. For example, it is known that a large number of deterministic context-free languages are in DSPACE(log n), including the "one-sided" and "two-sided" Dyck languages over finitely many generators [29,38], and the bracketed context-free languages [24,30,31]. Find other interesting languages

in DCFL $\cap$ DSPACE(log n). For example, are the operator precedence languages in this intersection [48]?
Likewise, many subfamilies of CFL are known to be
complete for NSPACE(log n) with respect to log space
reductions, e.g., the nondeterministic one-counter
languages [14,34,46], LINEAR-CFL [47], and various
particular context-free languages [36,46]. Are the
following languages complete for NSPACE(log n) with
respect to log space reductions: (1) L(B), when
$B = \{0^n 1^n \mid n \geq 1\}$, and (2) the "unary knapsack problem," i.e., the language $\{0^{n_1} \# 0^{n_2} \# \ldots \# 0^{n_k} \#\# 0^m$
$\mid \quad m = \sum_{i=1}^{k} x_i n_i$ has a 0-1 valued solution
$(x_1, \ldots, x_n)\}$ [36].

III. SEPARATION AND CONTAINMENT RESULTS

In this section we shall attempt to outline known techniques for proving the non-containment of classes of languages.
That is, we shall exhibit known techniques for "separating" a
class C_1 from a class C_2. These techniques generally exhibit a language that is in, say, the class C_1 and not in
the class C_2; on the other hand, some are indirect methods
and show that for some class C_3, for which it is known that
$C_1 \neq C_3$, if $C_1 = C_2$, then $C_1 = C_3$.
The known separation theorems for complexity classes tend
to be good only when they describe separation of classes with
different size bounds on the same complexity measure. Thus,
for example, we know that NSPACE(log n) $\subsetneq$ NSPACE(log n log* n)
and DSPACE(log n) $\subsetneq$ DSPACE(log n log* n), where log* n is
the function defined by log* n = k, if k is the smallest

integer such that the composition of the logarithm function with itself k times applied to n is not larger than 1. However, we do not know that there is a language in DSPACE$(\log^{1+\delta}(n))$ - NSPACE$(\log n)$, for any $0 \leq \delta < 1$. In some quite restricted cases, on the other hand, we do have good separation results even for comparing different complexity measures on different computing models. We shall describe these results when we discuss "cardinality" or "counting" arguments for showing separation.

Of course, we are not only interested in results describing the separation of two classes C_1 and C_2, but also whether one class is contained in the other. Such containment results are often shown by step-by-step simulations, but the following known containments, some of which have been mentioned already in Section II, have been shown by algorithms that look at the whole computation graph and use "divide-and-conquer" or "dynamic programming" strategies:

(c1) NSPACE$(f(n)) \subseteq$ DSPACE$(f(n)^2)$, for $f \not\in o(\log n)$ [40].

(c2) NSPACE$(f(n)) \subseteq$ DSPACE$(f(n)$ log n), for

$f \in 0(\log n) - o(\log \log n)$ [37].

(c3) CFL $\subseteq$ DSPACE$((\log n)^2)$ [28].

(c4) 2DPDASPACE$(f(n))$ = 2NPDASPACE$(f(n))$ =

$\cup_{k \geq 1}$DTIME$(2^{kf(n)})$, for $f \not\in o(\log n)$ [8].

(c5) DTIME$(f(n)) \subseteq$ DSPACE$(f(n)/\log n)$, for

$f(n) \not\in o(n)$ [20].

We assume always that the functions occurring as time bounds are time-constructible and that the functions occurring as space bounds are fully space-constructible. (Some of the results stated above, however, are known for all bounding functions and not just constructible ones.)

Separation results can be obtained by the method of "diagonalization," "cardinality" or "counting" arguments, and by "translation" or "padding" techniques. Diagonalization, or "self-referencing argument," is a powerful technique that is often used in recursive function theory. It was, perhaps, first used by Cantor in showing that the set of real numbers in the range [0,1] is not denumerable. As an example, consider the set $D = \{x_i \mid x_i \notin L(T_i)\}$, where x_i refers to the i-th string of symbols over some foxed alphabet Σ with respect to some numbering and $L(T_i)$ refers to the language accepted by the i-th Turing machine with respect to some numbering of Turing machines. The set D is not recognized by any Turing machine. To see this, suppose that D were recognized by a Turing machine, say the j-th Turing machine T_j, i.e., $D = L(T_j)$. Then, $x_j \in L(T_j) <=> x_j \in D <=> x_j \notin L(T_j)$, which is a clear contradiction. Thus, D is not recursively enumerable. This method can be extended in a rather straightforward manner to describe sets that cannot be recognized by deterministic Turing machines in time $f(n)$ or within space $g(n)$. That is, one need only define the languages $D(f) = \{x_i \mid x_i \notin LTIME_f(T_i)\}$ and $D'(f) = \{x_i \mid x_i \notin LSPACE_f(T_i)\}$, then $D(f) \notin DTIME(f)$ and $D'(f) \notin DSPACE(f)$. Of ocurse, this technique leads only to good separation results if the set $D(f)$, or $D'(f)$, is accepted by a machine whose resources are bounded by a function growing not much faster than f. This is true in the case of deterministic Turing machines and the following results have been shown using this technique.

(s1) DSPACE(f) $\subsetneq$ DSPACE(g),   if f $\in$ o(g)   and

   f $\notin$ o(log log n)   [44,45].

(s2) DTIME(f) $\subsetneq$ DTIME(g(n)·log g(n)),   if f $\in$ o(g)   [18].

But if we consider classes which are not known to be closed under complement then the corresponding set D(f) is only accepted by a machine which uses much more powerful resources. So we know, for example, in the case of nondeterministic time bounded computations, only that for each L $\in$ NTIME(f)   the complement of L belongs to $\bigcup_d$ NTIME($d^{f(n)}$) and therefore the method of diagonalization gives us only the result NTIME(f) $\subsetneq$ NTIME(g) if g $\in$ 0($d^{f(n)}$) for all d $\in$ $\mathbb{N}$.

   Cardinality or counting arguments have also been used quite frequently in the literature to show separation. A well-known example of this technique is the so-called "uvwxy theorem" or "pumping lemma" for context-free languages [3]. We will explain this technique taking as an example the proof that the set L = $\{0^n 1^n \mid n \in \mathbb{N}\}$ is not accepted by an finite state automaton. Suppose that there exists a finite state automaton M accepting L. Then there must be two distinct natural numbers i and j such that M is in the same state after reading 0^i and 0^j. Since $0^i 1^i \in$ L, M must go from this state to a final state entered upon reading 1^i. Hence, M must also go to a final state under the string $0^j 1^i$, but this is a contradiction, since $0^j 1^i \notin$ L. Arguments of this kind have been used to show

   (s3) DCFL $\subsetneq$ CFL   [3].

   (s4) There are inherently ambiguous context-free

      languages   [3].

(s5) There are languages accepted by real-time (k+1)-
      tape Turing machines that cannot be accepted by
      any real-time k-tape Turing machine [1].

(s6) The language $L = \{0^i \mid i$ is a perfect cube$\}$ is not
      accepted by any one-way nondeterministic stack
      automaton [3].

(s7) NSPACE(f(n)) contains only regular sets for $f(n) \in$
      o(log log n) [45], and only regular sets can be
      recognized by single-tape Turing machines in
      time f(n), where $f(n) \in$ o(n log n) [17].

(s8) DSPACE(f) $\subsetneq$ DSPACE(g),

      NSPACE(f) $\subsetneq$ NSPACE(g),

      for $g \notin 0(f)$ and $f(n) \in 0(\log n)$ -
      o(log log n) [19].

Now let us explain how translations are used in order to
get stronger separation results. Let $L \subseteq \{0,1\}^*$ be some recursive language and let $w \in \{0,1\}^*$ be some word. Instead
of deciding whether $w \in L$, we consider a string of the form
$v = w10^k$, $k \in \mathbb{N}$, and we ask whether $v \in \{w10^{g(|w|)} \mid$
$w \in L\}$, where $g : \mathbb{N} \to \mathbb{N}$ is some strictly monotonic increasing function. An algorithm for deciding this question is de-
fined in the following way:

    1. Test whether $v = w10^{g(|w|)}$ for some $w \in \{0,1\}^*$.

    2. Test whether $w \in L$.

If we assume that the function g is easily computable by the
machine model which defines the complexity measure (e.g., g
is time constructible if we consider time-bounded computations,
g is fully tape constructible if we consider space-bounded
computations), then the amount of space or time needed to

decide whether $w \in L$ is essentially the same as the amount of space or time needed to decide whether $v = w10^{g(|w|)}$ and $w \in L$. However, since the input v is usually much longer than w and complexity is measured as a function of the length of the input, v is less complex than w.

Let us consider as an example nondeterministic time-bounded computations, and let g be any time-constructible strictly monotone increasing function. Let L be accepted by a nondeterministic Turing machine with the time bound $f(n)$. Set $T_g(L) = \{w10^{\hat{g}(|w|)} \mid w \in L\}$, where $\hat{g}(n) = g(n) - n - 1$. Then the machine accepting $T_g(L)$ needs at most $0(n) + 0(f(g^{-1}(n)))$ steps for its computation. Therefore we get:

$$L \in \mathrm{NTIME}(f) \Rightarrow T_g(L) \in \mathrm{NTIME}(\max\{n, fg^{-1}(n)\}).$$

Examples

$$g(n) = n^2 : L \in \mathrm{NTIME}(n^p) \Rightarrow T_g(L) \in \mathrm{NTIME}(n^{p/2}) \text{ if } p \geq 2$$

$$g(n) = 2^n : L \in \mathrm{NTIME}(d^n) \Rightarrow T_g(L) \in \mathrm{NTIME}(d^{\log_2 n})$$

$$\text{if } d \geq 2.$$

On the other hand, if there exists a machine M accepting $T_g(L)$ with the time bound $f(n)$, we can construct a machine accepting L by

1. Change the input $w \in \{0,1\}^*$ into $w10^{\hat{g}(|w|)}$.

2. Test whether $w10^{\hat{g}(|w|)} \in T_g(L)$.

This implies $T_g(L) \in \mathrm{NTIME}(f) \Rightarrow L \in \mathrm{NTIME}(f \circ g)$.

Analogous results hold for deterministic time-bounded Turing machines and for (deterministic or nondeterministic) space bounded machines (Turing machines, auxiliary pushdown

automata). In the case of space-bounded Turing machines this
technique only applies to machines with bound $f(n) \geq \log n$.

These connections allow us to carry over relationships
which hold for complexity classes defined by small functions
to complexity classes defined by arbitrarily large functions.
For example, this technique can be used to show the following
results:

(1) For any $\delta \geq 0$, NSPACE(log n) $\subseteq$ DSPACE((log n)$^{1+\delta}$) $\Rightarrow$
    NSPACE(f(n)) $\subseteq$ DSPACE(f(n)$^{1+\delta}$), for all f(n) $\notin$
    o(log n). (We know NSPACE(log n) $\subseteq$ DSPACE(log n)^2
    [40].)

(2) NTIME(n) $\subseteq$ DTIME(g(n)) $\Rightarrow$ NTIME(f(n)) $\subseteq$ DTIME(g(f(n))),
    for all f $\notin$ o(n). (We know only that NTIME(n) $\subseteq$
    $\underset{k \geq 1}{\cup}$ DTIME(2^{kn}).)

We can use this approach also to prove stronger separation
results. The transformations allow us to use an assumption
that equality exists between two families of languages to deduce the equality of other families of languages. If these
resulting classes are known to be unequal, then we know the
original classes were unequal also. Usually it is not sufficient to use such transformations once; rather, finitely many
applications of these transformational methods or even recursive, and hence a potentially unbounded number of, transformations may be required. That is, in the "recursive padding"
case the number of transformations depends upon the length of
the input and hence is unbounded. Results that are obtained
from nonrecursive padding are described first.

For each natural number i, let C_i be a family of languages and T_i be a mapping from strings over some finite alphabet Σ to strings over some finite alphabet Σ_i. Further suppose that $C_i \subseteq C_{i+1}$, for all $i \geq 1$. Let $C = \bigcup_{k>1} C_k$.

Then $C_k \subsetneqq C_{k+1}$ holds for all $k \in \mathbb{N}$ if the following four conditions hold:

(1) $C_k \neq C$ for all $k \in \mathbb{N}$.

(2) For every $L \in C$ there exists a $p \in \mathbb{N}$ such that
$$T_p(L) \in C_2.$$

(3) For all $k, p \in \mathbb{N}$ there exists a $j \in \mathbb{N}$ such that
$$T_p(L) \in C_k \Rightarrow L \in C_j.$$

(4) For all $j \in \mathbb{N}$ and for all $p \geq j + 1$,
$$T_p(L) \in C_j \Rightarrow T_{p-1}(L) \in C_{j+1}.$$

In order to prove this result let us assume that $C_r = C_{r+1}$ holds for some $r \in \mathbb{N}$. Choose $L \in C$ arbitrarily. Because of (2) there exists a $p \in \mathbb{N}$ such that

$$T_p(L) \in C_2 \subset C_{r+1} = C_r.$$

If $p > r$ then we can deduce because of (4):

$$T_p(L) \in C_r \Rightarrow T_{p-1}(L) \in C_{r+1} = C_r$$

$$\Rightarrow T_{p-2}(L) \in C_{r+1} = C_r$$

$$\vdots$$

$$\Rightarrow T_{r+1}(L) \in C_{r+1} = C_r.$$

Thus we get for every $L \in C$ that $T_p(L) \in C_r$ for some $p \leq r + 1$. Because of (3) there exists a $q \in \mathbb{N}$ such that

$L \in C_q$ for all $L \in C$ and this is a contradiction to (1). Therefore our assumption is false and $C_r \neq C_{r+1}$.

We can use this result if there is given a collection of classes C_i, $i \in \mathbb{N}$, $C_i \subset C_{i+1}$, and if

(i) we know that $C_k \neq \bigcup_i C_i$ for all $k \in \mathbb{N}$, and

(ii) we are able to define a collection T_k, $k \in \mathbb{N}$, of

mappings such that (2), (3), (4) hold.

In most cases it is sufficient to use transformations $T_k : \{0,1\}^* \to \{0,1\}^*$ defined by $T_k(w) = w10^{|w|^k}$. (Note that we considered transformations of this form already in connection with time-bounded machines.) This approach is called padding. Padding is sufficient whenever the model which describes the classes C_i is powerful enough. This is true in the case of time-bounded or space-bounded Turing machines and in the case of pushdown automata. In the case of finite-state automata with several two-way input heads, we have to define the translations in a different manner [22,24].

Let us consider again nondeterministic time-bounded Turing machines. Let $r \in \mathbb{N}$ be some fixed number and set $C_\kappa = $ NTIME(n^κ) for $\kappa \in I_r$, where $I_r = \{(s_0, s_1, \ldots, s_r) \mid s_0 \in \mathbb{N}, s_1, \ldots, s_r \in \{0,\ldots,9\}\}$, e.g., $(12,3,4,7)$ represents the rational number 12.347. Using I_r as the set of indices we have to change condition (4) into

(4') for all $p, j \in I_r$ such that $p \geq suc(j)$,

$$T_p(L) \in C_j \Rightarrow T_{dec(p)}(L) \in C_{suc(j)}$$

where the ordering and the predecessor function dec and the successor function suc are defined by embedding I_r into the set of rational numbers.

Note that $\mathbb{NP} = \underset{\kappa \in I_r}{\cup} C_\kappa$ and that for any two rational

numbers α, β with $\alpha < \beta$ there exist $r \in \mathbb{N}$ and $\kappa_1, \kappa_2 \in$

I_r such that $\alpha \leq \kappa_1 < \kappa_2 \leq \beta$ holds. If we are able to show

that for any $r \in \mathbb{N}$ and for any $\kappa \in I_r$, $C_\kappa \subsetneq C_{suc(\kappa)}$, then

we have also showed that for any two rational numbers α, β

with $\alpha < \beta$,

$$\text{NTIME}(n^\alpha) \subsetneq \text{NTIME}(n^\beta).$$

We use as transformations again the padding functions,

i.e., we set, for $\kappa \in I_r$, $T_\kappa(L) = \{w10^{\lfloor |w|^\kappa \rfloor} \mid w \in L\}$,

where $\lfloor x \rfloor$ denotes for any real number x the greatest inte-

ger not greater than x. We already showed that for any time-

constructible function g, $L \in \text{NTIME}(n^\kappa) \Rightarrow T_g(L) \in$

$\text{NTIME}(\max\{n, (g^{-1}(n))^\kappa\})$, $T_g(L) \in \text{NTIME}(n^\kappa) \Rightarrow L \in$

$\text{NTIME}((g(n))^\kappa)$. Since the function $g_\kappa(x) = \lfloor x^\kappa \rfloor$ is a time-

constructible function for any $\kappa \in I_r$ the conditions (2) and

(3) are fulfilled. It remains to show that (4') is fulfilled.

Assume that $T_p(L) \in C_j$, $p, j \in I_r$, and set $q = dec(p)$.

A machine accepting $T_q(L)$ operates in the following way:

1. It checks whether the input has the form $w10^{\lfloor |w|^q \rfloor}$

for some $w \in \{0,1\}^*$.

2. It changes the input into $w10^{\lfloor |w|^p \rfloor}$.

3. It checks whether $w10^{\lfloor |w|^p \rfloor} \in T_p(L)$.

If the input v does not have the form $w10^{\lfloor |w|^q \rfloor}$, then our

machine operates in linear time. Now let us assume that

$v = w10^{\lfloor |w|^q \rfloor}$ and set $v_1 = w10^{\lfloor |w|^p \rfloor}$. Then our machine

needs $0(|v|)$, $0(|v_1|)$, $0(|v_1|^j)$ steps in order to perform

1., 2., 3., respectively. Furthermore, $|v| \geq |w|^q$,

$|v_1| \leq 2|w|^{p \cdot j}$ and $p = q + \delta$, $\delta = 10^{-r}$. Therefore our machine operates within the time bound

$$O(|w|^{(q+\delta)\cdot j}) \le O(|w|^{q(j+\delta)}) \le O(|v|^{suc(j)})$$

and we have proved that (4') holds.

Note that we have proved the following result:

(s9) Assuming that $NTIME(n^k) \ne \mathbb{N}P$ for some k has been shown, $NTIME(n^\alpha) \subsetneq NTIME(n^\beta)$ holds for any two rational numbers α, β with $\alpha < \beta$ [11].

The following results have been proved also by means of this technique.

(s10) $NSPACE(n^p) \subsetneq NSPACE(n^q)$ for any rational numbers p,q such that $p < q$ [23].

(s11) $DTIME(f) \subsetneq DTIME(g(n)\cdot(\log g(n))^\varepsilon)$ for any $\varepsilon > 0$ if $f \in o(g)$ [43].

(s12) $2DPDAHEADS(k) \subsetneq 2DPDAHEADS(k+1)$
$2NPDAHEADS(k) \subsetneq 2NPDAHEADS(k+1)$ } for all $k \ge 1$ [22].

(s13) $DHEADS(k) \subsetneq DHEADS(k+1)$ for all $k \ge 1$ [34].

Assuming that $NHEADS(k) \ne NSPACE(\log n)$ has been shown, $NHEADS(k) \subsetneq NHEADS(k+1)$ for all $k \ge 1$ [34].

Here 2DPDAHEADS(k) (2NPDAHEADS(k), DHEADS(k), NHEADS(k), respectively) denote the classes of languages acceptable by deterministic (or nondeterministic) two-way k-head pushdown automata, or finite-state automata, respectively.

The recursive padding technique leads to stronger separation results in the case of space-bounded Turing machines, space-bounded auxiliary pushdown automata and nondeterministic time-bounded Turing machines. We will describe this method by considering again nondeterministic time-bounded Turing machines.

Let U be a universal Turing machine, that is, $L(U) =$ {ex | $e \in L_{pc}$, $x \in L(M_e)$}, where L_{pc} is the set of program encodings of nondeterministic Turing machines.

Because of [5], U can be constructed in such a way that for each $e \in L_{pc}$ there exists a $c_e \in \mathbb{N}$ such that $\text{Time}_U(\text{ex}) \leq c_e \cdot \text{TIME}_{M_e}(x)$ holds for any $x \in L(M_e)$. Furthermore, we use the recursion theorem. The recursion theorem can be stated in the following way: "For each nondeterministic Turing machine M there exists a $e_0 \in L_{pc}$ such that $L(M_{e_0}) = \{x \mid e_0 x \in L(M)\}$." e_0 can be chosen in wuch a way [41] that for some $c \in \mathbb{N}$, $\text{TIME}_{M_{e_0}}(x) \leq c \cdot \text{TIME}_M(e_0 x)$ holds for all $x \in L(M_{e_0})$.

Now suppose there exist two recursive functions f, g : $\mathbb{N} \rightarrow \mathbb{N}$, $f(n) \leq g(n)\ \forall n$, such that $\text{NTIME}(f) = \text{NTIME}(g)$. Let $\tilde{L} = \{x \in L(U) \mid \text{TIME}_U(x) \leq g(|x|)\}$. Since $\text{NTIME}(f) = \text{NTIME}(g)$, there exists a nondeterministic Turing machine U_1 such that $L(U_1) = \tilde{L}$ and $\text{TIME}_{U_1}(x) \leq f(|x|)$ holds for all $x \in L(U_1)$. Note that U_1 is a "fast" machine which operates on inputs x, where U needs $g(|x|)$ steps, faster than U does. The following construction allows us to use this acceleration unboundedly often.

Let L be any recursive language and let $h : \mathbb{N} \rightarrow \mathbb{N}$ be a time-constructible function such that $L \in \text{NTIME}(k)$.

Let M be a nondeterministic Turing machine accepting L within the time bound $h(n)$. Construct a Turing machine M' that operates as follows:

(i) Check whether the input string v has the form
$v = ex10^k$ with some $e \in L_{pc}$, $x \in \{0,1\}*$, $k \geq 0$.
Reject v if this is not true.

(ii) If $k \geq h(|x|)$ then operate on x according to the transition rules of M.

(iii) If $k < h(|x|)$ then operate on $ex10^{k+1}$ according to the transition rules of U_1.

M' needs only linear time to perform the operations described in (i), (ii). It needs $0(n) + f(n+1)$ steps in order to perform (iii). Therefore M' operates within the time bound $g(n)$ if we assume that $f(n+1) \in 0(g(n))$.

Because of the recursion theorem there exists a $e_0 \in L_{pc}$ such that $L(M_{e_0}) = \{x \mid e_0 x \in L(M')\}$ and $TIME_{M_{e_0}}(x) \leq c \cdot TIME_{M'}(e_0 x)$ for any $x \in L(M_{e_0})$. If $v = ex10^k$ and $k \geq h(|x|)$ then because of the construction of M', $v \in L(M')$ if and only if $x \in L$. By downward induction on k it is straightforward to show that $L(M_{e_0}) = \{x10^k \mid x \in L, \ k \geq 0\}$. This is clearly a contradiction since $L(M_{e_0}) \in NTIME(g)$ and L was an arbitrarily chosen recursive language.

Using this technique the following results have been proven:

(s14) $NTIME(f) \subsetneq NTIME(g)$, if $f \in o(g)$ and $f(n+1) \in 0(g(n))$ [43].

(s15) $DSPACE_2(f) \subsetneq DSPACE_2(g)$, $NSPACE_2(f) \subsetneq NSPACE_2(g)$, if $f \notin o(\log n)$ and $\lim_{n \to \infty} (g(n) - f(n+1)) = \infty$ [41].

(s16) $2DPDASPACE_2(f) \subsetneq 2DPDASPACE_2(g)$,

   $2NPDASPACE_2(f) \subsetneq 2NPDASPACE_2(g)$,

   if $f \notin o(\log n)$ and $\lim_{n \to \infty}(g(n) - f(n+1)) = \infty$ [49].

(s17) NHEADS(k) $\neq$ NLOG for all $k \in \mathbb{N}$ [42].

The subscript 2 in the notation of the SPACE-classes indicates that the defining machines have only one work tape and
only two work-tape symbols. There exist separation results
also for the classes defined by space-bounded machines using a
fixed number of work-tape symbols and a fixed number of worktape heads [41,42,49]. All the differences of classes in (s10)-
(s16) also contain languages over a one-letter alphabet
[35,41,42,49].

There are a lot of problems which are very interesting and
which are still unsolved:

(1) The separation result (s14) for nondeterministic time-
    bounded machines does not give us an answer if $f(n) =$
    2^{2^n} and $g(n) = n \cdot 2^{2^n}$. Find a proof that guarantees
    separation if for the defining functions f, g only
    $f \in o(g)$ holds. Especially in the case of determin-
    istic machines the present state of knowledge is quite
    unsatisfying.

(2) Considering multi-head automata, can we eliminate non-
    determinism or the pushdown tape at the cost of some
    extra heads? We know that 2NPDAHEADS(k) $\subseteq$
    2DPDAHEADS(3k+1) [33], but since NHEADS(2) contains
    some language which is complete for NSPACE($\log n$)
    [14,46], and 2DPDAHEADS(1) contains some language
    which is complete for $\mathbb{P}$ [14,34],

NHEADS(2) $\subseteq$ DHEADS(k) for some k would imply NSPACE(log n) = DSPACE(log n) and 2DPDAHEADS(1) $\subseteq$ NHEADS(k) for some k would imply $\mathbb{P}$ = NSPACE(log n). It would help to understand why $\mathbb{P} \neq$ NSPACE(log n) if one were to show that 2DPDAHEADS(1) - NHEADS(2) $\neq \emptyset$ or even 2DPDAHEADS(1) - NHEADS(k) $\neq \emptyset$ for some k > 2. For a similar reason it is interesting to compare NHEADS(2) and DHEADS(3).

(3) We can also ask whether we can save heads by using a more powerful model. We know that NHEADS(2k) $\subseteq$ 2NPDAHEADS(k) [50], and we know that there is a close relationship between the number of heads and the time used by a random access machine, i.e. [9,33],

2DPDAHEADS(k) $\subseteq$ RAMTIME(n^k) $\subseteq$ 2DPDAHEADS(k+1),

NHEADS(k) $\subseteq$ RAMTIME(n^k),

2NPDAHEADS(k) $\subseteq$ RAMTIME(n^{3k})

(we use a random-access machine whose only arithmetical operation is the successor function). Therefore, results of the type

DHEADS(k) $\subseteq$ NHEADS(k'), DHEADS(k) $\subseteq$ 2DPDAHEADS(k'), NHEADS(k') $\subseteq$ 2DPDAHEADS(k') with k' < k

would give us faster algorithms for the classes DHEADS(k) or NHEADS(k), respectively, than we know at this time. This would be of great practical importance since many of the well-known "dynamic programming algorithms" are just algorithms simulating the behavior of a multi-head finite-state automaton. For a similar reason it would be interesting to know whether 2NPDAHEADS(k) $\subseteq$ 2DPDAHEADS(k') for some k' < 3k.

REFERENCES

1. Aanderra, S.O., On k-tape versus (k-1)-tape real time computation. SIAM-AMS Colloquium on Applied Mathematics 7: Complexity of Computation (R. Karp, ed.), 75-96 (1974).

2. Aho, A.V., Hopcroft, J.E., and Ullman, J.D., Time and tape complexity of pushdown automaton languages. Info. and Control 13, 186-206 (1968).

3. Aho, A.V., and Ullman, J.D.,"The Theory of Parsing, Translation and Compiling, Vol. I, II." Prentice-Hall, Englewood Cliffs, N.J. (1972,1973).

4. Book, R.V., Translational lemmas, polynomial time, and log n)^j-space. Theoret. Comp. Sci. 1, 215-226 (1976).

5. Book, R.V., Greibach, S.A., Ibarra, O.H., and Wegbreit, B., Tape-bounded Turing acceptors and principal AFLs. J. Comput. Syst. Sci. 4, 622-625 (1970).

6. Book, R.V., Greibach, S.A., and Wegbreit, B, Time- and tape-bounded Turing acceptors and AFLs. J. Comput. Syst. Sci. 4, 606-621 (1970).

7. Chandra, A.K., and Stockmeyere, L.J., Alternation. Proc. 17th Ann. IEEE Symp. on Foundations of Computer Science, 98-108 (1976).

8. Cook, S.A., Characterizations of pushdown machines in terms of time-bounded computers. J. Assoc. Comput. Mach. 18, 4-18 (1971).

9. Cook, S.A., Linear time simulation of deterministic two-way pushdown automata. Proc. IFIP Congress, TA-2, North-Hollan, Amsterdam, 172-179 (1971).

10. Cook, S.A., The complexity of theorem proving procedures. Proc. 3rd Ann. ACM Symp. on Theory of Computing, 151-158 (1971).

11. Cook, S.A., A hierarchy of nondeterministic time complexity. J. Comput. Syst. Sci. 7, 343-353 (1973).

12. Cook, S.A., An observation on time-storage trade-off. J. Comput. Syst. Sci. 9, 308-316 (1974).

13. Cook, S.A., Deterministic CFLs are accepted simultaneously in polynomial time and log squared space. Proc. 11th Ann. ACM Symp. on Theory of Computing, 338-345 (1979).

14. Galil, Z., Some open problems in the theory of computation as questions about two-way deterministic pushdown automata languages. Math. Syst. Theory 10, 211-218 (1977).

15. Garey, M.R., and Johnson, D.S., "Computers and Intractability: A Guide to the Theory of NP-Completeness." W.H. Freeman, San Francisco (1979).

16. Greibach, S.A., The hardest context-free language. SIAM J. Comput. 2, 304-310 (1973).

17. Hartmanis, J., Computational complexity of one-tape Turing-machine computations. J. Assoc. Comput. Mach. 15, 325-329 (1968).

18. Hartmanis, J., and Stearns, R.E., On the computational complexity of algorithms. Trans. Amer. Math. Soc. 117, 285-306 (1965).

19. Hopcroft, J.E., and Ullman, J.D., Some results on tape bounded Turing machines. J. Assoc. Comput. Mach. 16, 168-174 (1969).

20. Hopcroft, J.W., Paul, W., and Valiant, L., On time versus space. J. Assoc. Comput. Mach. 24, 332-337 (1977)

21. Hofcroft, J.E., and Ullman, J.D., "Formal Languages and Their Relation to Automata." Addison-Wesley, Reading, Mass. (1969).
22. Ibarra, O.H., On two-way multihead automata. J. Comput. Syst. Sci. 7, 28-36 (1973).
23. Ibarra, O.H., A note concerning nondeterministic tape complexities. J. Assoc. Comput. Mach. 19, 608-612 (1972).
24. Igarashi, Y., Tape bounds for some subclasses of deterministic context-free languages. Info. and Control 37, 321-333 (1978).
25. Jones, N.D., Space bounded reducibility among combinatorial problems. J. Comput. Syst. Sci. 11, 62-85 (1975).
26. Karp, R.M., Reducibility among combinatorial problems. In "Complexity of Computer Computation" (R. Miller and J. Thatcher, eds.), Plenum Publishing Co., New York (1972).
27. Kozen, D., On parallelism in Turing machines. Proc. 17th Ann. Symp. on Foundations of Computer Science, 89-97 (1976).
28. Lewis, P.M., Stearns, R.E., and Hartmanis, J., Memory bounds for the recognition of context-free and context-sensitive languages. Proc. 6th Ann. IEEE Conf. on Switching Circuit Theory and Logical Design, 191-202 (1965).
29. Lipton, R.J, and Zalcstein, Y., Word problems solvable in log space. J. Assoc. Comput. Mach. 24, 522-526 (1977).
30. Lynch, N., Log space recognition and translation of parenthesis languages. J. Assoc. Comput. Mach. 24, 583-590 (1977).
31. Mehlhorn, K., Bracket languages are recognizable in logarithm space. Info. Processing Letters 5, 168-170 (1976).
32. Meyer, A.R., and Stockmeyer, L.J., Word problems requiring exponential time. Proc. 5th Ann. ACM Symp. on Theory of Computing, 1-9 (1973).
33. Monien, B., Characterizations of time bounded computations by limited primitive recursion. Lecture Notes in Comp. Sci. 14, 280-293, Springer-Verlag (1974).
34. Monien, B., Transformational methods and their application to complexity problems. Acta Informatica 6, 95-108; Corrigenda, Acta Informatica 8, 383-384 (1977).
35. Monien, B., Two-way multihead automata over a one-letter alphabet. Technical Report, Fachbereich 17, Gesamthochschule Paderborn, West Germany (1978). To appear in RAIRO.
36. Monien, B., Connections between the LBA problem and the knapsack problem. Technical Report, Fachbereich 17, Gesamthochschule Paderborn, West Germany (1979).
37. Monien, B., and Sudborough, I.H., On eliminating nondeterminism from Turing machines which use less than logarithm worktape space. Lecture Notes in Comp. Sci. 71, 431-445, Springer-Verlag (1979).
38. Ritchie, R.W., and Springsteel, F.N., Language recognition by marking automata. Info. and Control 20, 313-330 (1972).
39. Ruby, S., and Fischer, P.C., Translational methods and computational complexity. Proc. 6th Ann. IEEE Conf. on Switching Circuit Theory and Logical Design, 173-178 (1965).
40. Savitch, W.J., Relationships between nondeterministic and deterministic tape complexities. J. Comput. Syst. Sci. 4, 177-192 (1970).
41. Seiferas, J.I., Techniques for separating space complexity classes. J. Comput. Syst. Sci. 14, 73-99 (1977).

42. Seiferas, J.I., Relating refined space complexity classes. J. Comput. Syst. Sci. 14, 100-129 (1977).
43. Seiferas, J.I., Fischer, M.J., and Meyer, A.R., Separating nondeterministic time complexity classes. J. Assoc. Comput. Mach. 25, 146-167 (1978).
44. Sipser, M., Halting space bounded computations. Technical Report, University of California, Berkeley (1978).
45. Stearns, R.E., Hartmanis, J., and Lewis, P.M., II, Hierarchies of memory limited computations. Proc. 6th Ann. IEEE Conf. on Switching Circuit Theory and Logical Design, 179-190 (1965).
46. Sudborough, I.H., On tape bounded complexity classes and multihead finite automata. J. Comput. Syst. Sci. 10, 62-76 (1975).
47. Sudborough, I.H., A note on tape bounded complexity classes and linear context-free languages. J. Assoc. Comput. Mach. 22, 500-501 (1975).
48. Sudborough, I.H., On the tape complexity of deterministic context-free languages. J. Assoc. Comput. Mach. 25, 405-414 (1978).
49. Sudborough, I.H., Separating tape bounded auxiliary pushdown automata classes. Proc. 9th Ann. ACM Symp. on Theory of Computing, 208-217 (1977).
50. Sudborough, I.H., Some remarks on multihead automata. RAIRO Informatique Theorique/Theoretical Computer Science II, 181-195 (1977).
51. Sudborough, I.H., Relationship between low-level space bounded complexity classes on alternating and deterministic Turing machines. Technical Report, Fachbereich 17, Gesamthochschule Paderborn, West Germany (1979).
52. Valiant, L., General context-free recognition in less than cubic time. J. Comput. Syst. Sci. 10, 308-315 (1975).

Pattern Matching in Strings

Alfred V. Aho
Bell Laboratories
Murray Hill, New Jersey

I. INTRODUCTION

Being able to specify and match various patterns of strings and words is an essential part of computerized information processing activities such as text editing [26], data retrieval [36], bibliographic search [1], query processing [3], lexical analysis [27], and linguistic analysis [7]. This paper examines three basic classes of string patterns that are particularly useful in these activities and analyzes some of the time-space tradeoffs inherent in searching for these classes of patterns.

The three classes of patterns considered are (1) finite sets of strings, (2) regular expressions, and (3) regular expressions with back referencing. Efficient pattern matching algorithms for each of these classes are discussed. Several of these algorithms have the pleasing property of being both useful in practice and interesting in theory. It may appear that we have too many classes of patterns and too many algorithms but we will discuss some of the reasons why no single approach is ideal for all applications.

There are several issues that must be faced in designing pattern matching software. First there is the question of what class of patterns the user should be capable of specifying and what notation is necessary to describe a given pattern. A nonprocedural description of a pattern, such as a regular expression, may often be easier for a nonprogrammer to specify than a procedural description, such as a SNOBOL program [19]. In fact, several attempts have been made to clarify and axiomatize the description of

This paper was presented at the Symposium on Formal Language Theory, University of California, Santa Barbara, December 10-14, 1979, supported by NSF grant MCS79-04012.

SNOBOL-like patterns [18, 34]. However, there is a limit to how large a class of patterns can be specified simply in a nonprocedural manner.

The difficulty of constructing an efficient recognizer from a pattern specification must also be examined. For some applications such as text editing a restricted class of patterns from which an efficient recognizer can be constructed quickly is sufficient. For other applications such as textual search we may wish to allow more complex sets of patterns but we may then have to spend more time preprocessing the pattern to find an efficient recognizer for it. The problem is further complicated because some nonprocedural descriptions allow complex patterns to be described for which efficient recognizers do not exist or are hard to find. Finally the time-space tradeoffs in efficiently implementing the recognizer must be considered.

In this paper efficient algorithms for finding various subsets and supersets of regular expression patterns are of special interest. The simplest such question is finding a finite set of keywords in a text string, a problem for which several interesting and particularly effective algorithms have been recently found. Although regular expressions cannot describe all patterns that occur in information processing systems, it is shown that some modest generalizations of the string matching problem are NP-complete.

II. PATTERN-MATCHING PROBLEMS

For the applications considered here, a *pattern* is merely a set of strings. Each string in a pattern is said to be *matched* by the pattern. The input to a pattern-matching problem is a pair (p, x) where p is a specification of a pattern and x is an input string. There are many notations for specifying patterns, such as programs, grammars, and automata. For the applications considered here, various variants of the regular expression notation will be used.

The desired output of a pattern-matching algorithm also depends on the application. For example, if x is a sequence of lines of text (such as a dictionary, a program listing or a manuscript), then one useful output in editing and searching applications is all lines containing a substring matched by p. Another possible output is the leftmost longest substring of each line that p matches. A third possible output is all substrings matched by p, but here we have to be careful when p denotes the empty string. For the purposes of this paper, however, we will just consider the output to be "yes" if x contains a substring denoted by p, "no" otherwise.

We will measure the performance of a pattern-matching algorithm by the time and space taken to find a match measured as a function of the lengths of p and x. We will assume the pattern is given before the input string x. In this way an algorithm can construct from the pattern whatever kind of pattern-finding machine it needs before scanning any of the text string.

A. Regular Expressions

Much of formal language theory deals with methods for specifying patterns as we have defined them. For the classes of applications listed above regular expressions provide a convenient and easy-to-use notation for describing patterns. Classical automata theory defines a regular expression and the pattern it denotes as follows:

(1)   A character a by itself is a regular expression denoting the pattern $\{a\}$.

(2)   If r_1 and r_2 are regular expressions denoting patterns p_1 and p_2, respectively, then

    (a) $r_1 \mid r_2$ is a regular expression denoting $p_1 \cup p_2$.

    (b) $(r_1)(r_2)$ is a regular expression denoting the concatenation of p_1 and p_2, that is, the set of strings $\{xy \mid x \text{ is in } p_1 \text{ and } y \text{ is in } p_2\}$.

    (c) $(r_1)^*$ is a regular expression denoting $\bigcup_{i=0}^{\infty} p^i$ where p^i is the concatenation of p with itself i times. By convention p^0 is the empty string, which we denote by ϵ.

    (d) (r_1) is a regular expression denoting p_1.

Unnecessary parentheses in regular expressions can be avoided by adopting the convention that the Kleene closure operator * has the highest precedence, then concatenation, then $\mid$. All operators are left associative. For example, under this convention $(a \mid ((b)^*)(c))$ can be written as $a \mid b^*c$.

Regular expressions can be used to specify patterns that arise in many diverse applications such as shortest path problems, program testing, printed circuit board layout, graphics, and programming language compilation [2, 4, 22]. Here are some simple examples of regular expressions from text-editing applications.

(1)   The regular expression $(apple|blueberry)\text{-}(pie|tart)$ matches any of the four delicacies: *apple-pie, apple-tart, blueberry-pie, blueberry-tart*.

(2)   The regular expression *the* $(very,)^*$ *very old man* matches the strings *the very old man; the very, very old man; the very, very, very old man;* and so on.

In several applications, it is convenient to embellish the definition of regular expressions with various notational shortcuts. One simple extension is to introduce metacharacters that have specialized meanings. For example, in the definition above the symbols $\mid$, *, (, and) are metacharacters not considered to be part of the pattern alphabet. To include these symbols as targets for matches, we can introduce another metacharacter, say \, as an escape character. We can then use \| to denote the pattern { | }, * to denote {*}, and so on. \\ denotes {\}.

We can also introduce metacharacters to match various positions in a string. The metacharacters ˆ and $ will denote the left and right ends of a string. Thus *dous*$ will match *dous* only at the right end of a string.

One other convenient shorthand is a succinct notation for character classes. The symbol Σ will be used to denote the entire string alphabet. We can think of Σ as a "don't care" symbol that matches any symbol. We will use the regular expression [*abc*] to denote the set {*a*, *b*, *c*} and [¬*abc*] to denote $\Sigma - \{a, b, c\}$. Thus the regular expression

$$\hat{}[\neg aeiou]*a[\neg aeiou]*e[\neg aeiou]*i[\neg aeiou]*o[\neg aeiou]*u[\neg aeiou]*\$ \qquad (1)$$

will match all strings in which the five vowels appear in lexicographic order. For example, (1) matches the string "abstemious."

B. Regular Expressions with Back Referencing

All the extensions of the regular expression formalism discussed so far have been notational shorthands. One useful extension that increases the expressive power of regular expressions is *back referencing*. This extension allows complex patterns that cannot be specified by regular expressions alone. The back referencing concept was introduced in the first version of SNOBOL [11] and has appeared in Dennis Ritchie's implementation of the UNIX† pattern-matching program *grep* [25].

The following rules define the syntax of a *regular expression with back referencing* (rewbr for short). In these rules Σ is a finite alphabet and $N = \{v_1, v_2, \cdots\}$ is a set of variable names.

(1)   Each character a in Σ is a rewbr.

(2)   Each variable v_i in N a rewbr.

(3)   If r_1 and r_2 are rewbrs, then so are

    a) $r_1 \mid r_2$

    b) $(r_1)(r_2)$

    c) $(r_1)*$

    d) (r_1)

    e) $r_1.v_i$

---

† UNIX is a trademark of Bell Laboratories.

In rule 3(e), the dot is the back referencing operator. Its properties are similar to those of the conditional value assignment operator in SNOBOL4 [19]. As before, redundant parentheses can be avoided using the same precedences and associativities as with regular expressions. The back referencing operator is left associative and has the highest precedence of all operators.

The pattern denoted by a rewbr is more difficult to define than the pattern denoted by a regular expression because each rewbr can contain variables that may be assigned values by the back referencing operator. We shall define the pattern denoted by a rewbr r in terms of an intermediate quantity $V(r)$, *the value of r*. $V(r)$ will be a set of pairs of the form (s, α) where s is either null or a string in $(\Sigma \cup V)^*$ and α is an assignment of strings in $(\Sigma \cup V)^*$ to the variables in N. $V(r)$ is defined inductively as follows.

(1) $V(a) = \{(a, \alpha_0)\}$ where $\alpha_0(v) = v$ for all v in N.

(2) $V(v_i) = \{(v_i, \alpha_0)\}$.

(3)   Let r_1 and r_2 be rewbrs with values $V(r_1)$ and $V(r_2)$. Then,

   (a) $V(r_1 \mid r_2) = V(r_1) \cup V(r_2)$.

   (b) $V((r_1)(r_2))$ is the set of pairs $(s_1 s_2, \alpha)$ such that (s_1, α_1) is in $V(r_1)$, (t, α_2) is in $V(r_2)$, and s_2 is t with each v_i in t replaced by $\alpha_1(v_i)$. That is to say, the assignment of strings to variables given by α_1 determines the string with which to replace each variable in t. The assignment α for the string $s_1 s_2$ is defined: $\alpha(v) = \alpha_2(v)$ unless $\alpha_2(v) = v$, in which case $\alpha(v) = \alpha_1(v)$.

   (c) $V((r_1)^*) = \bigcup_{i=0}^{\infty} V(r_1^i)$. As before, $r^0 = \epsilon$ and $V(\epsilon) = \{(\epsilon, \alpha_0)\}$.

   (d) $V((r_1)) = V(r_1)$.

   (e) $V(r_1.v_i)$ is the set of pairs (s, α) such that for some α', (s, α') is in $V(r_1)$ and $\alpha(v_i) = s$ and for all $v \neq v_i$, $\alpha(v) = \alpha'(v)$.

The pattern denoted by a rewbr r is the set of strings s in Σ^* such that (s, α) is in $V(r)$ for some α. Some examples should help clarify this definition.

(1) $\Sigma^* \Sigma.v \Sigma^* v \Sigma^*$ denotes any string with at least one repeated character. To see this note that Σ^* matches any string of characters and that $\Sigma.v$ will match any single character and assign v the value of that character. The second variable v will then match a second occurrence of that character.

(2) $\Sigma^*.v \, v$ denotes any string of the form xx where x is any string of characters.

(3) $((\Sigma^*.v) \, v)^*$ denotes any string of the form $s_1 s_1 s_2 s_2 \cdots s_n s_n$ where each s_i is a string in Σ^*.

These examples illustrate some of the definitional power of rewbrs.

The pattern of example (1) can be denoted by an ordinary regular expression, but only by a considerably longer expression. The pattern in example (2) is not a regular or even context-free language so it cannot be expressed by a regular expression. Example (3) likewise cannot be expressed by a regular expression or context-free grammar. Regular expressions with back referencing but with one variable name and no alternation have been studied by Angluin [5].

III. MATCHING FINITE SETS OF KEYWORDS

This section considers the first of our three matching problems. We are given a pattern consisting of a finite set of keywords and an input string x. We wish to determine whether x has a substring that is a keyword in the pattern set.

A. The Knuth-Morris-Pratt Algorithm

A well-studied special case of this problem occurs when the pattern consists of exactly one nonempty keyword p. The straightforward way to look for a single keyword p in an input string x is by a program of the following form.

```
match(p, x)
begin
        let p = b₁b₂ · · · bₘ
        let x = a₁a₂ · · · aₙ
        i ← 1
        while i ≤ n−m+1 do
                if bⱼ = aᵢ₊ⱼ₋₁ for 1 ≤ j ≤ m
                then return "yes"
                else i ← i+1
        return "no"
end
```

The worst-case performance of this algorithm requires $mn - m^2 + m$ character comparisons. (Consider the case where $p = a^{m-1}b$ and $x = a^n$.) Knuth, Morris and Pratt discovered an elegant nonbacktracking algorithm that requires only $O(m+n)$ time [26]. The algorithm first constructs a table h from the keyword alone. Then the following procedure looks for the keyword in the input string.

```
match(p, x)
begin
        let p = b₁b₂ · · · bₘ
        let x = a₁a₂ · · · aₙ
        i ← 1
        j ← 1
        while i ≤ n and j ≤ m do
                begin
                        while j > 0 and aᵢ ≠ bⱼ do j ← h[j]
                        i ← i + 1
                        j ← j + 1
                end
        if j > m then return "yes"
        else return "no"
end
```

This algorithm can be pictured as aligning the keyword above the input string and comparing the keyword with the portion of the input string underneath. The key idea in the algorithm is that if we have matched the prefix $b_1b_2 \cdots b_{j-1}$ of the keyword with the substring $a_{i-j+1}a_{i-j+2} \cdots a_{i-1}$ of the text string and $a_i \neq b_j$, then we do not need to rescan $a_{i-j+1} \cdots a_{i-1}$ since we know this portion of the input string is equal to the prefix of the keyword we have just matched. Instead, in each iteration of the inner while-loop we slide the pattern $j - h[j]$ positions to the right and reset j to $h[j]$ until j becomes zero (in which case none of the pattern matches the current substring of the text string) or until $a_i = b_j$ (in which case $b_1 \cdots b_{j-1}b_j$ matches $a_{i-j+1} \cdots a_{i-1}a_i$). In the outer while-loop we resume the matching process by comparing a_{i+1} with b_{j+1}.

In order for this algorithm to work properly, the function h must have the property that $h[j]$ is the largest k less than j such that $b_1b_2 \cdots b_{k-1}$ is a suffix of $b_1b_2 \cdots b_{j-1}$ (i.e., $b_1 \cdots b_{k-1} = b_{j-k+1} \cdots b_{j-1}$) and $b_j \neq b_k$. If there is no such k, then $h[j] = 0$. The table h can be computed from the keyword by a program that is virtually identical to the matching program itself:

begin
    $i \leftarrow 1$
    $j \leftarrow 0$
    $h[1] \leftarrow 0$
    while $i < m$ **do**
        begin
            while $j > 0$ and $b_i \neq b_j$ **do** $j \leftarrow h[j]$
            $i \leftarrow i + 1$
            $j \leftarrow j + 1$
            if $b_i = b_j$ **then** $h[i] \leftarrow h[j]$
            else $h[i] \leftarrow j$
        end
end

It is not hard to show that in both programs the assignment statement $j \leftarrow h[j]$ in the inner loop is never executed more often than the statement $i \leftarrow i + 1$ in the outer loop. Consequently, the program to compute h runs in $O(m)$ time and the program match runs in $O(n)$ time.

The existence of an $O(m+n)$ string-matching algorithm follows from Cook's result that every two-way deterministic pushdown automaton (2DPDA) language can be recognized in linear time on a random access machine [9]. The language $\{y\#x \mid y \text{ is a substring of } x\}$ can be recognized by a 2DPDA. Knuth, in fact, traced through the simulation implied in Cook's result to derive the linear time pattern-matching algorithm.

Knuth, Morris and Pratt give a fascinating historical account of the development of this algorithm along with many further refinements and suggestions for efficient implementation [26]. The algorithm has been used in a few text editors since the early 1970's and some of the basic ideas were used by Gilbert in his work on comma-free codes in the early 1960's [17].

B. Multiple Keyword Patterns

Now consider the case where $p = \{y_1, y_2, \ldots, y_k\}$, a finite set of keywords rather than just one keyword. The straightforward way to look for multiple keywords in a string is to apply a single-keyword pattern-matching algorithm once for each keyword. In this section we shall outline a decidedly more efficient approach using ideas from finite automata theory and from the Knuth-Morris-Pratt algorithm. The language

$$L = \{y_1\#y_2\# \cdots \#y_k\#\#x \mid x = uy_iv \text{ for some } 1 \leq i \leq k\}$$

can be recognized by a 2DPDA, and consequently Cook's theorem implies that there is an $O(m+n)$ algorithm to do the matching, where m is the size of p (i.e., the sum of the lengths of the keywords) and n is the length of x.

An efficient way to do the pattern matching in $O(m+n)$ time is to first construct from the set of keywords a pattern-matching machine that will look for the keywords in parallel rather than one at a time. Various kinds of finite automaton models can be used for this purpose. Here we use a pattern-matching automaton A that consists of the following components:

(1) S, a finite set of states,

(2) Σ, a finite input alphabet,

(3) $g: S \times \Sigma \rightarrow S \cup \{\text{fail}\}$, a forward transition function,

(4) $h: S - \{s_0\} \rightarrow S$, a backward transition function,

(5) s_0, an initial state, and

(6) F, a set of accepting states.

The pattern-matching automaton A processes an input string x in the following manner:

```
match(A, x)
begin
        let x = a₁a₂ · · · aₙ
        state ← s₀
        i ← 1
        while i ≤ n do
                begin
                        while g[state, aᵢ] = fail do state ← h[state]
                        state ← g[state, aᵢ]
                        if state is in F then return "yes"
                end
        return "no"
end
```

The pattern-matching automaton starts off in the initial state scanning the first character of x. It then executes a sequence of moves. In one move on input symbol a_i the pattern-matching automaton makes zero or more backward transitions until it reaches a state for which $g[state, a_i] \neq$ fail. The pattern-matching automaton then makes a forward transition to state $g[state, a_i]$. If this state is an accepting state, the automaton halts and returns "yes"; otherwise, the automaton executes another move on the next input character a_{i+1}.

The forward and backward transition functions of the pattern-matching automata we construct will have the following two properties:

(1) $g[s_0, a] \neq$ fail, for all a in Σ.

(2)   If $h[s] = s'$, then the depth of s' is less than the depth of s, where the depth of a state s is the length of the shortest sequence of forward transitions from s_0 to s.

The first property guarantees that no backward transitions will occur in the initial state. The second property guarantees that the total number of backward transitions in processing an input string will be less than the total number of forward transitions. Since exactly one forward transition is made for each input character, less than $2n$ transitions of both kinds will be made in processing an input string of length n. Thus, the procedure match(A, x) can be implemented to run in $O(n)$ time.

We must now show that we can construct the forward and backward transition functions of a pattern-matching automaton from the set of keywords in $O(m)$ time. This can be done in the following manner.

(1)   First construct from p a trie in which the root is the initial state s_0. Each node of the trie is a state s that corresponds to a prefix $b_1 b_2 \cdots b_j$ of some keyword y in p. We define $g[s, b_{j+1}] = s'$ where s' corresponds to the prefix $b_1 \cdots b_j b_{j+1}$ of y. Each state corresponding to a complete keyword becomes an accepting state.

(2)   For state s_0 we define $g[s_0, a] = s_0$ for all a for which $g[s_0, a]$ was not defined in step (1).

(3) $g[s, a] =$ fail for all s and a for which $g[s, a]$ was not defined in steps (1) or (2).

These three steps define the forward transition function. Note that state s_0 has the property that $g[s_0, a] \neq$ *fail* for any a in Σ.

Before we define the backward transition function, we define a failure function f as follows:

(1)   For all states s of depth one, $f[s] = s_0$.

(2)   Assume f has been defined for all states of depth d. Let s_d be a state of depth d such that $g[s_d, a] = s'$. Then $f[s']$ is computed in the following way: Let $s = f[s_d]$. Let t be the value s after executing the following statement:

$$\textbf{while } g[s, a] = \text{fail } \textbf{do } s \leftarrow f[s]$$

Note that since $g[s_0, a] \neq$ fail, the while-loop will always terminate. Then $f[s'] = g[t, a]$.

The failure function has the following key property: if states s and t represent prefixes u and v of some keywords, then $f[s] = t$ if and only if v is the longest proper suffix of u that is also the prefix of some keyword in p.

The failure function itself can be used as the backward transition function. However, the failure function can cause some unnecessary backward transitions to occur. A more efficient backward transition function h that avoids these redundant backward transitions can be constructed from f as follows:

(1) $h[s] = s_0$ for all states s of depth one.

(2) Assume h has been defined for all states of depth d. Let s be a state of depth $d+1$. If the set of characters on which there is a forward non-fail transition in state $f[s]$ is a subset of the set of characters on which there is a forward non-fail transition in state s, then $h[s] = h[f[s]]$; otherwise, $h[s] = f[s]$.

It is not hard to construct the function h from the set of keywords in $O(m)$ time. See [1] for more details.

Example. Let $p = \{aaa, abaaa, ababaaa\}$. The forward transition function g, the failure function f, and the backward transition function h for this set of patterns are shown in Table I.

	g		f	h
	a	b		
0	1	0	-	-
1	2	4	0	0
2	3	fail	1	1
3	fail	fail	2	2
4	5	fail	0	0
5	6	8	1	0
6	7	fail	2	1
7	fail	fail	3	2
8	9	fail	4	0
9	10	fail	5	5
10	11	fail	6	1
11	fail	fail	7	2

Table I.

To illustrate the distinction between using f and h for the backward transition function consider the behavior of the pattern-matching automaton after having read the first six characters of the input string *ababaab*. If the automaton started from initial state 0, then it will have reached state 10. Using f for the backward transition function, on the last input character the pattern-matching automaton would make backward transitions to states 6, 2, and 1 before making a forward transition to state 4. Using h for the backward transition function, on the last input character the pattern matching character would make just one backward transition to state 1 before making the forward transition to state 4.

Aho and Corasick used this pattern-matching algorithm in a bibliographic search system in which a user could specify documents by prescribing Boolean combinations of keywords and phrases. This approach yielded a system whose cost was 4 to 12 times faster than an identical system using a straightforward string-matching algorithm [1]. This experience corroborates Knuth's remarks that knowledge of automata theory can be useful in practical problems [26].

There are several interesting theoretical aspects to this algorithm. If the pattern consists of only one keyword of length m, then $\log_\phi m$ backward transitions are necessary and sufficient in any one move [26]. Here $\phi = (1+\sqrt{5})/2$, the golden ratio. This bound is achieved when the pattern is a Fibonacci string defined as follows:

$$s_1 = b$$
$$s_2 = a$$
$$s_k = s_{k-1}s_{k-2}$$

If the pattern is a set of keywords the sum of whose lengths is m, then $O(m)$ backward transitions may be necessary in a single move. Galil, on the other hand, has shown that pattern matching can be done in real-time on a random access machine by continuing to read ahead at the same time failure transitions are being made [14].

C. The Boyer-Moore Algorithm

Boyer and Moore give an interesting algorithm that looks for a match of a single keyword $b_1 b_2 \cdots b_m$ in an input string $a_1 a_2 \cdots a_n$ by ignoring those portions of the input string that cannot possibly contribute to a match [6]. When the alphabet size is large, the algorithm determines whether a match occurs looking at only about n/m input string characters on the average. Boyer and Moore's approach is not readily modeled by conventional automata theory in that not all the input string is necessarily examined in determining a match.

The basic idea of the algorithm is to look for a match by sliding the keyword across the input string from left to right and by comparing characters in the keyword from right to left. Initially, we compare b_m with a_m. If a_m occurs nowhere in the keyword, then we can slide the keyword m characters to the right and try matching b_m with a_{2m}.

If a match occurs, we compare characters in the keyword with those in the text string from right to left until a match is verified or until a mismatch occurs. In case of a mismatch various strategies can be used to determine how far to shift the keyword to the right. The basic form of the Boyer-Moore algorithm is as follows:

```
match(p, x)
begin
        let p = b₁b₂ · · · bₘ
        let x = a₁a₂ · · · aₙ
        i ← m
        while i ≤ n do
                begin
                        j ← m
                        while j > 0 and aᵢ = bⱼ do
                                begin
                                        i ← i−1
                                        j ← j−1
                                end
                        if j = 0 then return "yes"
                        else i ← i + max(d₁[aᵢ], d₂[j])
                end
        return "no"
end
```

This algorithm uses two tables d_1 and d_2 to determine how far to slide the keyword to the right when $a_i \neq b_j$. Both tables can be computed in $O(m)$ time by preprocessing the keyword. The first table is indexed by characters; $d_1[a]$ is defined to be the largest j such that $a = b_j$ or m if a does not occur in the keyword.

There are several ways of defining the second table d_2 which is indexed by positions in the keyword. Knuth [26] suggested the definition

$$d_2[j] = \min \{s+m-j \mid s \geq 1 \text{ and } (s \geq j \text{ or } b_{j-s} \neq b_j) \\ \text{and } ((s \geq i \text{ or } b_{i-s} = b_i) \text{ for } j < i \leq m)\}$$

This table can be computed in $O(m)$ time using the following algorithm:

```
begin
    for i ← 1 to m do d₂[i] ← 2*m−i
    j ← m
    k ← m+1
    while j > 0 do
        begin
            f[j] ← k
            while k ≤ m and bⱼ ≠ bₖ do
                begin
                    d₂[k] ← min(d₂[k], m−j)
                    k ← f[k]
                end
            j ← j − 1
            k ← k − 1
        end
    for i ← 1 to k do d₂[i] ← min(d₂[k], m+k−i)
end
```

The function f computed by this algorithm is the failure function of Section 3.2 defined on the reversal of the keyword.

Boyer and Moore's original version of their algorithm had quadratic worst case behavior. However, for the version given above one can show the worse case behavior is linear in the length of the input string [13, 20, 26].

A question of theoretical interest that has not yet been fully resolved is optimum string pattern matching. Rivest has shown that the minimum number of input string characters that must be examined to determine a match is $n−m+1$ [33]. The minimum average number of characters that must be examined is not known. Nor is it known how to construct optimal average case algorithms.

Recently, Commentz-Walter has described an approach by which the ideas in the Boyer-Moore algorithm can be combined with those of Section 3.2 to look for patterns of finite sets of keywords in an input string in sublinear time on the average [8]. The basic idea is to construct a trie as described in Section 3.2 for the set of keywords reversed. Matching then proceeds as in the Boyer-Moore algorithm with the trie playing the role of the single keyword. For the details of this approach see [8].

IV. MATCHING REGULAR EXPRESSIONS

Consider now the case where we are given a regular expression r and an input string x and we wish to determine whether x contains a substring denoted by r. There are several approaches to answering this question.

A. Nondeterministic Finite Automata

One classical approach is to construct from the regular expression r a nondeterministic finite automaton (NDFA) M to do the pattern matching. The NDFA can take the form of an executable program [36] or a transition table that is interpreted by a simulator. The following recursive procedure can be used to construct M from r.

(1) If r is a single character a construct the machine

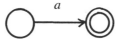

consisting of a transition on a from the initial state to the final state.

(2) If r is of the form $r_1 \mid r_2$, construct the machine

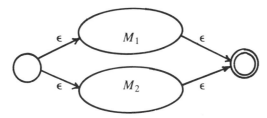

Here we have created a new initial state and a new final state. There is a transition on the empty string from the new initial state to the initial states of M_1 and M_2, the machines for r_1 and r_2. There is a transition on the empty string from the final state of M_1 and M_2 to the newly created final state.

(3) If r is of the form r_1r_2, construct the machine M

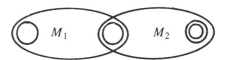

Here we have merged the final state of M_1, the machine for r_1, with the initial state of M_2, the machine for r_2. The initial state of M_1 becomes the initial state of M and the final state of M_2 becomes the final state of M.

(4) If r is of the form R_1*, construct the machine

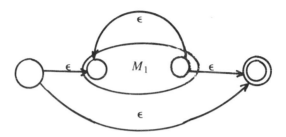

Here we have created a new initial state and a new final state. A transition on the empty string occurs between the new initial state and the initial state of M_1, between the final state of M_1 and the newly created final state, between the new initial state and the new final state, and between the old final state and the old initial state.

This construction of a NDFA M from a regular expression r has several useful properties.

(1)   The number of states in M is at most twice the length of r.

(2)   No state has more the two transitions to other states.

(3)   There are no transitions out of the final state.

These properties enable us to simulate the behavior of M on x efficiently. Let m be the length of r and n the length of x. In the simulation we maintain a queue of states M can be in after having read $a_1 \cdots a_{i-1}$. From this queue of states we can compute in $O(m)$ steps the set of states M can be in after having read a_i since each state on the queue has at most two out-transitions. In this way we can simulate the behavior of M on x in $O(mn)$ time and m space. Chapter 9 of [2] contains the details of the simulation.

B. Deterministic Finite Automata

Another classical approach to regular expression pattern matching is to construct from the regular expression a deterministic finite automaton (DFA) [29]. There are several ways of doing this. One way is to construct from the regular expression a nondeterministic finite automaton as above, eliminate the transitions on empty strings, and then use the Rabin and Scott [32] subset construction to convert the resulting nondeterministic finite automaton into a deterministic finite automaton that has at most one out-transition in each state. (See [2] or [22] for more details.)

A simpler and more direct way is to use the LR(0) parser construction technique to construct from the regular expression a deterministic finite automaton directly. Let t be the syntax tree [4] for the regular expression. Each state of the deterministic finite automaton corresponds to a set of leaves of the syntax tree that can be active at a given point in time in much the same way as each state of a DFA constructed from a NDFA using the subset construction corresponds to a set of nondeterministic states that can be active at a given point in time. For example, the syntax tree for the regular expression $\Sigma^*(abc \mid aba)$ is

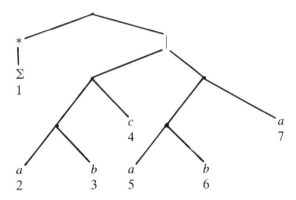

Initially, leaves 1, 2, and 5 are active so the initial state would be the set {1,2,5}. From the initial state there would be a transition on input character a to state {1,3,6}, the set of leaves that would be active after the DFA had read an a.

A DFA can be simulated efficiently by a program since it makes exactly one transition for each input character. Thus, once a DFA has been constructed from the regular expression, it can do the pattern matching in $O(n)$ steps. Note that neither the size of the input alphabet nor the length of the regular expression need affect the recognition speed. The main problem with using a DFA for pattern matching, however, is that the DFA may be time consuming to construct from the regular expression and that the transition function of a DFA may require a lot of storage. If the transition function is stored as a two-dimensional array, then the storage requirement will be the product of the alphabet size times the number of states. In many practical applications this can be excessive. Consequently, several interesting sparse matrix techniques have been developed to reduce the space requirements for the transition function. See [4, 10, 35] for descriptions of some of these techniques.

However, even the sparse matrix techniques cannot cope with an exponential number of states. For example, consider the regular expression consisting of Σ^*a followed by $m-1$ Σ's. This common regular expression denotes all strings in which the mth character from the right end is an a. Unfortunately the smallest deterministic finite automaton that recognizes this pattern has 2^m states.

C. Hybrid Deterministic-Nondeterministic Finite Automata

Given a regular expression of length m and an input string of length n, we can use a NDFA to do pattern matching in time $O(mn)$ and space $O(m)$. With a DFA we can do pattern matching in time $O(2^m + n)$ and space $O(2^m)$. Lower bounds and optimal algorithms for regular expression pattern matching are not known. It would be interesting to know more precise bounds on the difficulty of regular expression pattern matching. Fischer and Paterson [12] show that a single string pattern with don't care symbols (Σ's) can be matched in $O(n\log m\log\log m)$ time using the Schonhage-Strassen algorithm [2] for integer multiplication as a subroutine. It would also be interesting to know whether there exists a Boyer-Moore type algorithm for regular expression pattern matching.

The linear space requirements of the NDFA and the linear recognition speed of the DFA do suggest a hybrid deterministic-nondeterministic approach. In such a scheme we construct a NDFA from the regular expression. We then make the most frequently visited states of the NDFA into deterministic states by using the subset construction. In this way we can construct a finite automaton in which the most frequently visited states have at most one transition on any input character. These frequently visited states can be implemented as indexable arrays so that transitions from these states can be executed in constant time. Myers has discovered that in practice with this approach one can closely approximate the time efficiency of DFA's and the space efficiency of NDFA's in regular expression pattern matching [31]. The theoretical optimal average case behavior of these hybrid machines is still unknown.

V. MATCHING REGULAR EXPRESSIONS
WITH BACK REFERENCING

Variables make matching regular expressions with back referencing much more difficult that matching ordinary regular expressions. The most straightforward approach to matching a rewbr pattern r is to use backtracking to keep track of the possible substrings of the input string x that can be assigned to the variables in r. There are $O(n^2)$ possible substrings that can be assigned to any one variable in r, where n is the length of x. If there are k variables in r, then there are $O(n^{2k})$ possible assignments in all. Once an assignment of substrings to variables is fixed, the problem reduces to ordinary regular expression matching. Thus, rewbr matching can be done in at worst $O(n^{2k})$ time.

One might wish for a more efficient process. Unfortunately, the problem of determining whether a rewbr r matches an input string x is NP-complete. The following example illustrates a reduction from the vertex cover problem.

Let $E_1, E_2, \ldots, E_m$ be subsets of cardinality two of some finite set Σ. The vertex cover problem is to determine given a positive integer k whether there exists a subset Σ' of Σ of cardinality at most k such that Σ' contains at least one element in each E_i. We can think of the E_i's as being edges of a graph and Σ' as being a set of vertices such that each edge contains at least one node in Σ'. The vertex cover problem is a well-known NP-complete problem [2, 16, 23].

We can transform this problem into a matching problem for rewbrs as follows. Let $s, s_1, s_2, \ldots, s_m$ be strings consisting of the elements in Σ, $E_1, E_2, \ldots, E_m$, respectively. Let # be a new symbol not in Σ. For $1 \le i \le k$, let

$$x_i = \Sigma^* \, \Sigma.v_i \, \Sigma^*\#$$

For $1 \le i \le m$, let

$$y_i = \Sigma^* \, \Sigma.w_i \, \Sigma^*\#$$

For $1 \le i \le m$, let

$$z_i = w_i^* v_1^* v_2^* \cdots v_k^* w_i^* \#$$

Now, let r be the rewbr $x_1 \cdots x_k y_1 \cdots y_m z_1 \cdots z_m$.

We shall now construct an input string. Let t_0 be the string $s\#$ repeated $k+m$ times. For $1 \le i \le m$, let t_i be $s_i\#$. Let u be the input string $t_0 t_1 \cdots t_m$.

Consider what happens when we use r to match u. r matches u if and only if there exists an assignment of elements of Σ to the variables $v_1, \ldots, v_k$ such that for each i there exists a j such that v_j is in E_i, that is, if and only if the subset $\{v_1, \ldots, v_k\}$ of Σ is a vertex cover for $E_1, \ldots, E_m$.

This NP-completeness result strongly suggests that the time complexity for rewbr matching is inherently exponential in the worst case. Practical experience, on the other hand, reasonable performance for the rewbr patterns seen by the program grep. For example, on a DEC PDP-11/70 using the UNIX program grep to search Webster's second (with 2486813 characters in 234936 words) for those words in which no letter is repeated (of which *dermatoglyphics* is the longest) requires 9.7 min whereas to search for those words in which the letters are monotonically increasing (of which *egilops* is the longest) requires 3.8 min. The UNIX program *egrep* which simulates a DFA will find the latter pattern in 1.1 min.

VI. CONCLUSIONS

In this paper we have examined three classes of patterns that are basic to common text-processing applications. We have seen that there are several algorithms that can be used to search for these patterns. Knowledge of finite automata theory has proven useful in the design of several of these algorithms. Since no one algorithm seems to be ideal for all situations, it is necessary to examine the time and space requirements of the application at hand to determine the algorithm best suited for that situation.

Although we have limited our discussion to string-matching algorithms, we should point out that in many text-processing applications it is necessary to be able to look for patterns that combine both textual and numeric data. Some higher-level text-processing languages such as AWK [3] and POPLAR [30] have been developed for such applications recently. In such languages the algorithms described in this paper can be used to speed up the string matching process.

ACKNOWLEDGMENTS

The author would like to acknowledge many stimulating conversations on string pattern matching with Doug McIlroy, Lee McMahon, Dennis Ritchie, Tom Szymanski, and Ken Thompson. The author is also grateful to Ron Book for his helpful comments on the manuscript.

REFERENCES

1. Aho, A. V., and M. Corasick, "Efficient String Matching: An Aid to Bibliographic Search." *Comm. ACM* **18**:6 (June 1975), 333-340.

2. Aho, A. V., J. E. Hopcroft, and J. D. Ullman, *The Design and Analysis of Computer Algorithms,* Addison-Wesley, Reading, Mass., 1974.

3. Aho, A. V., B. W. Kernighan, and P. J. Weinberger, "AWK - A Pattern Matching and Scanning Language," *Software - Practice and Experience* **9**:4 (April 1979), 267-280.

4. Aho, A. V., and J. D. Ullman, *Principles of Compiler Design,* Addison-Wesley, Reading, Mass., 1977.

5. Angluin, D., "Finding Patterns Common to a Set of Strings," *Proc. 11th Annual ACM Symposium on Theory of Computing,* 1979, pp. 130-141.

6. Boyer, R. S., and J S. Moore, "A Fast String Searching Algorithm," *Comm. ACM* **20**:10 (October 1977), 262-272.

7. Cherry, L. L., and W. Vesterman, "Writing Tools - The STYLE and DICTION Programs," Bell Laboratories, Murray Hill, N.J., 1979.

8. Commentz-Walter, B., "A String Matching Algorithm Fast on the Average," *Proc. 6th International Colloquium on Automata, Languages and Programming,* Springer-Verlag, 1979, pp. 118-132.

9. Cook, S. A., "Linear Time Simulation of Deterministic Two-Way Pushdown Automata," *Proc. IFIP Congress* **71**, TA-2, North Holland, Amsterdam, pp. 172-179.

10. Even, S., D. I. Lichtenstein, and Y. Shiloach, "Remarks on Ziegler's Method for Matrix Compression," unpublished manuscript, 1977.

11. Farber, D. J., R. E. Griswold, and I. P. Polonsky, "SNOBOL, A String Manipulation Language," *J. ACM* **11**:1 (January 1964), 21-30.

12. Fischer, M. J., and M. S. Paterson, "String Matching and Other Products," *SIAM-AMS Proc.,* vol. 7, American Mathematical Society, Providence, R. I., 1974, pp. 113-125.

13. Galil, Z., "On Improving the Worst Case Running Time of the Boyer-Moore String Matching Algorithm," *Proc. 5th International Colloquium on Automata, Languages and Programming,* Springer-Verlag, 1978.

14. Galil, Z., "String Matching in Real Time," *J. ACM,* to appear.

15. Galil, Z., and J. Seiferas, "Saving Space in Fast String Matching," *Proc. 18th IEEE Symposium on Foundations of Computer Science,* (1977), pp. 179-188.

16. Garey, M. R., and D. S. Johnson, *Computers and Intractability: A Guide to the Theory of NP-Completeness,* Freeman, San Francisco, 1979.

17. Gilbert, E. N., "Synchronization of Binary Messages," *IRE Transactions on Information Theory,* IT-6 (1960), 470-477.

18. Gimpel, J. F., "A Theory of Discrete Patterns and Their Implementation in SNOBOL4," *Comm. ACM* **16**:2 (February 1973), 91-100.

19. Griswold, R. E., J. F. Poage, and I. P. Polonsky, *The SNOBOL4 Programming Language, second edition,* Prentice-Hall, Englewood Cliffs, N. J., 1971.

20. Guibas, L. J., and A. M. Odlyzko, "A New Proof of the Linearity of the Boyer-Moore String Searching Algorithm," *SIAM J. Computing,* to appear.

21. Guibas, L. J., and A. M. Odlyzko, "String Overlaps, Pattern Matching, and Nontransitive Games," *J. Combinatorial Theory, Series A,* to appear.

22. Hopcroft, J. E., and Ullman, J. D., *Introduction to Automata Theory, Languages, and Computation,* Addison-Wesley, Reading, Mass., 1979.

23. Karp, R. M., "Reducibility Among Combinatorial Problems," in R. E. Miller and J. W. Thatcher (eds.), *Complexity of Computer Computations,* Plenum Press, New York, pp. 85-103.

24. Karp, R. M., R. E. Miller, and A. L. Rosenberg, "Rapid Identification of Repeated Patterns in Strings, Trees, and Arrays," *Proc. 4th ACM Symposium on Theory of Computing, 1972, pp. 125-136.*

25. Kernighan, B. W., and M. D. McIlroy, (eds.), UNIX Programmer's Manual, seventh edition, Volume I, Bell Laboratories, Murray Hill, New Jersey, January, 1979.

26. Knuth, D. E., J. H. Morris, and V. R. Pratt, "Fast Pattern Matching in Strings," *SIAM J. Computing* **6**:2 (1977), 323-350.

27. Lesk, M. E., "LEX - A Lexical Analyzer Generator," CSTR 39, Bell Laboratories, Murray Hill, N.J., 1975.

28. Liu, K. C., and A. C. Fleck, "String Pattern Matching in Polynomial Time," *Proc. 6th Annual ACM Symposium on Principles of Programming Languages,* 1979, pp. 222-225.

29. McNaughton, R., and H. Yamada, "Regular Expressions and State Graphs for Automata," *IRE Trans. on Electronic Computers* **EC-9**:1, 39-47.

30. Morris, J. H., E. Schmidt, and P. Wadler, "Experience with an Applicative String Processing Language," *Proc. Seventh Annual ACM Symposium on Principles of Programming Languages,* 1980, pp. 32-46.

31. Myers, E., personal communication, 1977.

32. Rabin, M. O., and D. Scott, "Finite Automata and their Decision Problems," *IBM J. Research and Development* **3** (1959), 114-125.

33. Rivest, R. V., "On the Worst-Case Behavior of String-Searching Algorithms, *SIAM J. Computing* **6**:4 (December 1977), 669-674.

34. Steward, G. F., "An Algebraic Model for String Patterns," *Proc. 2nd Annual ACM Symposium on Principles of Programming Languages,* 1975, pp. 167-184.

35. Tarjan, R. E., and A. C. Yao, "Storing A Sparse Table," *Comm. ACM* **22**:11 (November 1979), 606-611.

36. Thompson, K., "Regular Expression Search Algorithm," *Comm. ACM* **11** (1968), 419-422.

37. Weiner, P., "Linear Pattern Matching Algorithm," *Proc. 14th IEEE Symposium on Switching and Automata Theory,* 1973, pp. 1-11.

Equations and Rewrite Rules

A Survey

Gérard Huet

IRIA and SRI International

Derek C. Oppen

Stanford University

1. Introduction

Equations — formulas of the form $M = N$ — occur frequently in mathematics, logic and computer science. In this paper, we survey in a uniform fashion the main results concerning equations, and the methods available for reasoning about them and computing with them.

Reasoning about equations may involve deciding if an equation "follows" or is a consequence of a given set of equations (axioms), or if an equation is "true" in a given theory.

Consider the following set of axioms for group theory:

$$x + 0 = x$$
$$x + -x = 0$$
$$(x + y) + z = x + (y + z).$$

Preparation of this paper was supported in part by the National Science Foundation under grants MCS78-02835 and MCS79-04012, and in part by the Air Force Office of Scientific Research under grant AFOSR-8752.

We might wish to know if another equation $0 + x = x$ is a consequence of these axioms, that is, is true in all groups. This is an example of "reasoning" about equations. As is well known, this equation can be shown to follow from the axioms solely by equational reasoning, that is, substituting arbitrary terms for variables and replacing "equals by equals".

When used in this manner, equations *state properties* that hold between objects.

Equations may also be used as *definitions*. For instance, a set of equations may define a particular group (we then speak of the group presented by the equations). The use of equations as definitions is well known in computer science since programs written in applicative languages, abstract interpreter definitions, and algebraic data type definitions are clearly of this nature. When these equations are regarded as oriented "rewrite rules", we may actually use them to *compute*. For instance, the following equations define the function *Append*:

$$Append(Null, x) = x$$
$$Append(Cons(x, y), z) = Cons(x, Append(y, z)).$$

We can use this definition to compute, say, $Append(Cons(A, Cons(B, Null)), Cons(C, Null))$ into $Cons(A, Cons(B, Cons(C, Null)))$.

Computing with equations and reasoning about equations are closely related. For instance, one method for reasoning about equations consists in "compiling" them into rewrite rules and using them to reduce expressions to canonical form. We shall show later how this method applies to the group axioms above, and how $0 + x = x$ can be proved by reducing both sides of the equality to the canonical form x.

However, reasoning about equations considered as definitions requires more than just equational reasoning. For instance, it is well known that *Append* is associative, but proving the theorem requires some kind of induction.

It is useful to start with a clear understanding of the various semantics one can associate with equations and with rewrite rules. We shall therefore first give various semantic definitions, and then consider their associated proof theories (if any). We shall develop these notions in the framework of traditional abstract algebra.

The survey attempts to be fairly comprehensive. However, for lack of space, we restrict ourselves to first-order equations. Further, we do not treat equations which define non-terminating computations; for them a more sophisticated model theory is required (continuous domains or algebras). Nor do we treat recent work on rewrite rules applied to equational congruence classes (we give an outline of this research in section 14).

2. Sorted Algebras

We assume we are given a set $\mathcal{S}$ of *sorts*, which are names for the various domains under consideration. We deal here only with simply sorted theories, in which these domains are disjoint.

Example: $\mathcal{S}^0 = \{\text{integer, boolean}\}$.

We now define a language Θ of *types*, obtained by composing sorts. We restrict ourselves to first-order theories, and assume that a type is just a finite sequence of sorts: $\Theta = \mathcal{S}^+$. We write $t = s_1 \times s_2 \times \cdots \times s_n \rightarrow s$ instead of $t = \langle s_1, s_2, \ldots, s_n, s \rangle$. A type denotes the type of operators (that is, mappings) with n arguments of sorts $s_1, s_2, \ldots, s_n$ and which return a value of sort s. When $n = 0$, we write $t = s$; in this case, t denotes a *constant* of sort s.

A *signature* over $\mathcal{S}$ consists of a set Σ of operators, together with a typing function $\tau{:}\Sigma \rightarrow \Theta$. For ease of notation, we assume that τ is given, and we use Σ to denote the signature.

If Σ is a signature over $\mathcal{S}$, we say that sort s in $\mathcal{S}$ is *strict* in Σ if and only if there exists an F in Σ such that $\tau(F) = s$ or $\tau(F) = s_1 \times s_2 \times \cdots \times s_n \rightarrow s$ and s_i is strict in Σ for each i. We say that the signature Σ is *sensible* if and only if, for every F in Σ such that $\tau(F) = s_1 \times s_2 \times \cdots \times s_n \rightarrow s$, if s is strict then so are all the s_i. We assume from now on that all signatures are sensible; this restriction is technical and will be motivated later. (Note that every signature can be extended to a sensible one by adding constant symbols.)

Example: Given $\mathcal{S}^0$ above, consider the signature $\Sigma^0 = \{0, S, +, TRUE, FALSE, \# \}$, with

$$\tau(0) = \text{integer}$$
$$\tau(S) = \text{integer} \rightarrow \text{integer}$$
$$\tau(+) = \text{integer} \times \text{integer} \rightarrow \text{integer}$$
$$\tau(TRUE) = \tau(FALSE) = \text{boolean}$$
$$\tau(\#) = \text{integer} \times \text{integer} \rightarrow \text{boolean}.$$

Note that every sort in $\mathcal{S}^0$ is strict in Σ^0.

A Σ-*algebra* or *algebra* is a pair $\langle \mathcal{A}, \mathcal{F} \rangle$ such that $\mathcal{A}$ is an $\mathcal{S}$-indexed family of sets and $\mathcal{F}$ is a Σ-indexed family of functions (the *fundamental operations* of the algebra), with:

$\mathcal{F}_F \in \mathcal{A}_s$ if $\tau(F) = s$, and

$\mathcal{F}_F \in \mathcal{A}_{s_1} \times \mathcal{A}_{s_2} \times \cdots \times \mathcal{A}_{s_n} \rightarrow \mathcal{A}_s$ if $\tau(F) = s_1 \times s_2 \times \cdots \times s_n \rightarrow s$.

$\mathcal{A}_s$ is called the *carrier* or *universe* of sort s in the algebra. We shall usually denote an algebra by its family of carriers if no ambiguity arises. For instance, we talk about the algebra $\mathcal{A}$ above, and use F to denote the corresponding operator $\mathcal{F}_F$. Note that $\mathcal{A}_s \neq \emptyset$ for any strict sort s.

Example: $\mathcal{A}^0$ is a Σ^0-algebra, with $\mathcal{A}^0_{integer} = \mathcal{N}$, $\mathcal{A}^0_{boolean} = \{\text{true, false}\}$, 0 is the integer 0, S is the successor function, $TRUE = $ true, $FALSE = $ false, $\neq(m, n)$ is true if $m \neq n$ and false otherwise.

We now define special types of algebras, whose carriers will consist of finite ordered trees, labelled with operators from Σ. These (free) Σ-algebras will be helpful in defining terms.

With every operator F in Σ we associate a tree consisting of one node labelled F. We now define recursively the family of sets of trees $\mathcal{T}(\Sigma)_s$, for $s \in \mathcal{S}$. If $\tau(C) = s$, then the tree with one node labelled C and no successors is an element of $\mathcal{T}(\Sigma)_s$. If $\tau(F) = s_1 \times s_2 \times \cdots \times s_n \rightarrow s$ and $M_i \in \mathcal{T}(\Sigma_i)_{s_i}$ for all $1 \leq i \leq n$, then the tree with one node labelled F and n successors $M_1, \ldots, M_n$ is an element of $\mathcal{T}(\Sigma)_s$. By abuse of notation, we will denote these terms by strings in the usual manner, as in, for example, C or $F(M_1, \ldots, M_n)$.

The corresponding algebra $\mathcal{T}(\Sigma)$ is called the *initial* algebra. We call $\mathcal{T}(\Sigma)_s$ the set of *ground terms* of sort s. For instance, $0 + S(0)$ is a ground term of sort integer, over Σ^0 above. Ground terms are called *words* in algebra and *abstract syntax trees* in computer science. Logicians use them implicitly by considering concrete syntax (strings) defined by a non-ambiguous grammar.

Note that $\mathcal{T}(\Sigma)_s \neq \emptyset$ if and only if s is strict.

Let us now consider an $\mathcal{S}$-indexed family of sets $\mathcal{V}$. Elements of $\mathcal{V}_s$ are called *variables* of sort s. We assume that the variables of distinct sorts are distinct and that no variable is a member of Σ. We denote by $\Sigma \cup \mathcal{V}$ the signature composed of Σ plus every $\mathcal{V}_s$ considered as a set of constants of sort s. The corresponding algebra $\mathcal{T}(\Sigma \cup \mathcal{V})$ (when restricted to a Σ-algebra) is called the *free* Σ-algebra *generated by* $\mathcal{V}$, and its carrier $\mathcal{T}(\Sigma \cup \mathcal{V})_s$ is the set of *terms* of sort s. This terminology is consistent with standard algebra books such as Cohn (27) where, in the case of only one sort, $\mathcal{T}(\Sigma \cup \mathcal{V})$ would be denoted $W_\Sigma(\mathcal{V})$. Compare also with $\mathcal{T}_{\Sigma(\mathcal{V})}$ in Goguen (53) and $M(\Sigma, \mathcal{V})$ in Nivat (127).

A completely formal development of term structures would require a careful definition of tree domains, and terms as mappings from these domains to $\Sigma \cup \mathcal{V}$ respecting the types. We shall not do this here, but rather will informally use *occurrences* — sequences of integers denoting an access path in a term, à la Dewey decimal notation. For M in $\mathcal{T}(\Sigma \cup \mathcal{V})$, we denote by $O(M)$ the set of such occurrences of M, and, for u in $O(M)$, we use M/u to denote the *subterm* of M at occurrence u. For example, with $M = 0 + S(0)$, we have $O(M) = \{\Lambda, 1, 2, 2 \cdot 1\}$, and $M/2 = S(0)$. We use $\mathcal{V}(M)$ to denote the set of variables occurring in M; that is, $x \in \mathcal{V}(M)$ if and only if $x \in \mathcal{V}$ and there exists a u in $O(M)$ such that $M/u = x$. Finally we define $M[u \leftarrow N]$ as the term M, in which we have replaced the subterm at occurrence u by N. (Occurrences were proposed by Gorn (56) and were subsequently used by Brainerd (14), Rosen (145) and Huet(73).)

We assume in the following that mappings between Σ-algebras are sort-preserving, and write $h:\mathcal{A} \rightarrow \mathcal{B}$ for a $\mathcal{S}$-indexed family of mappings $h_s:\mathcal{A}_s \rightarrow \mathcal{B}_s$.

Finally, if $\mathcal{A}$ and $\mathcal{B}$ are two algebras, we say that $h:\mathcal{A} \rightarrow \mathcal{B}$ is a Σ-*morphism* (or just *morphism*) if and only if, for all F in Σ, with $\tau(F) = s_1 \times s_2 \times \cdots \times s_n \rightarrow s$, we have $h_s(F_\mathcal{A}(a_1, \ldots, a_n)) = F_\mathcal{B}(h_{s_1}(a_1), \ldots, h_{s_n}(a_n))$.

Theorem. (The universal property for the free Σ-algebras)   Let $\mathcal{A}$ be any Σ-algebra. Any $\mathcal{A}$-assigment $\nu:\mathcal{V} \rightarrow \mathcal{A}$ can be extended in a unique way to a Σ-morphism from $\mathcal{T}(\Sigma \cup \mathcal{V})$ to $\mathcal{A}$.

We use ν to denote both the assignment and its extension.

Examples:

1. The *trivial* algebra is *Sort*, where $Sort_s = \{s\}$ and $F(s_1, \ldots, s_n) = s$ when $\tau(F) = s_1 \times s_2 \times \cdots \times s_n \rightarrow s$. The assignment τ defined by $\tau(x) = s$ if and only if $x \in \mathcal{V}_s$ extends in a unique way from $\mathcal{T}(\Sigma \cup \mathcal{V})$ to *Sort*. For instance, over Σ^0 above, with $n \in \mathcal{V}_{integer}$, we have $\tau(S(0) + n) = integer$.

2. Σ-endomorphisms from $\mathcal{T}(\Sigma \cup \mathcal{V})$ to itself are called *substitutions*. We shall generally be interested in the effect of such a substitution σ on a finite number of terms, and therefore assume that $\sigma(x) = x$ except on a finite set of variables $\mathfrak{D}(\sigma)$ which we call the *domain of* σ by abuse of notation. Such substitutions can then be represented by the finite set of pairs $\{\langle x, \sigma(x) \rangle \mid x \in \mathfrak{D}(\sigma)\}$. We say that σ is *ground* if and only if $\mathcal{V}(\sigma(x)) = \emptyset$ for any x in $\mathfrak{D}(\sigma)$.

One more definition is needed for the next section.

If $\mathcal{A}$ is an algebra, a sort-preserving relation $\sim$ on elements of $\mathcal{A}$ is called a Σ-*congruence over* $\mathcal{A}$ if and only if:

$$(\forall F \in \Sigma)\,(\forall a_1, b_1, \ldots, a_n, b_n \in \mathcal{A})$$
$$a_1 \sim b_1 \;\&\; \ldots \;\&\; a_n \sim b_n \Rightarrow F(a_1, \ldots, a_n) \sim F(b_1, \ldots, b_n).$$

3. Equations and Varieties

A Σ-*equation* or *equation* is a pair $M = N$ where M and N are members of $\mathcal{T}(\Sigma \cup \mathcal{V})_s$, that is, are formed from variables ranging over the elements of the universe and from symbols denoting the fundamental operations of the algebra. In equations, variables are (implicitly) universally quantified.

Let $\mathcal{A}$ be an algebra and $M = N$ be an equation. We say that $M = N$ is *valid in* $\mathcal{A}$ or that $\mathcal{A}$ is a *model of* $M = N$, and we write $\mathcal{A} \models M = N$, if and only if for every $\mathcal{A}$-assignment $\nu: \mathcal{V}(M) \cup \mathcal{V}(N) \to \mathcal{A}$ we have $\nu(M) = \nu(N)$; that is, M and N denote the same element of the carrier $\mathcal{A}_s$ no matter how the variables of M and N are interpreted as elements of $\mathcal{A}$. $\mathcal{A}$ is a *model* of a set of equations if every $\mathcal{A}$-assignment validates every equation in the set.

Examples:

$$\mathcal{A}^0 \models x + y = y + x$$
$$\mathcal{A}^0 \not\models 0 = S(x)$$
$$Sort \models M = N \text{ for every } M \text{ and } N \text{ of the same sort.}$$

It is apparent that the relation $=_{\mathcal{A}}$ on $\mathcal{T}(\Sigma \cup \mathcal{V})_s$, defined by $M =_{\mathcal{A}} N$ if and only if $\mathcal{A} \models M = N$, is a Σ-congruence, provided Σ is a sensible signature (or else provided that every carrier in the algebra is non-empty).

Now a set of Σ-equations may be thought of as defining a family of algebras, or some unique (up to an isomorphism) algebra. The *variety* or *equational class* $\mathcal{M}b(\Sigma, \mathcal{E})$ or simply $\mathcal{M}b(\mathcal{E})$ is the class of all models of $\mathcal{E}$. That is, $\mathcal{A} \in \mathcal{M}b(\mathcal{E})$ if and only if $\mathcal{A} \models E$ for every E in $\mathcal{E}$.

Note that $\mathcal{M}b(\mathcal{E})$ is never empty, since *Sort* is always in it.

Example: Let $\mathcal{E}^0 = \{x + 0 = x, x + S(y) = S(x + y)\}$. Define the Σ^0-algebra $\mathcal{A}^1$ by: $\mathcal{A}^1_{integer} = \mathcal{N}_{blue} \cup \mathcal{N}_{red}$, $\mathcal{A}^1_{boolean} = \{true, false\}$, $0 = 0_{blue}$, $S = Succ_{blue} \cup Succ_{red}$, $+ = \oplus$, with $n_{blue} \oplus m_{blue} = n_{blue} \oplus m_{red} = (n + m)_{blue}$, $n_{red} \oplus m_{blue} = n_{red} \oplus m_{red} = (n + m)_{red}$, $TRUE = true$, $FALSE = false$, and $\#(m, n)$ is false if m and n unpainted are the same and true otherwise. Then $\mathcal{A}^0$ and $\mathcal{A}^1$ are both models of $\mathcal{E}^0$. However $\mathcal{A}^0$ and $\mathcal{A}^1$ are not isomorphic, and $x + y = y + x$ is not valid in $\mathcal{A}^1$.

The *validity problem* in a class C of algebras is: given an equation E over $\mathcal{T}(\Sigma \cup \mathcal{V})_s$, decide whether or not $\mathcal{A} \models E$ for every algebra $\mathcal{A}$ in C. If so, we write $C \models E$. When $C = \{\mathcal{A}\}$ and E is a ground equation, then the validity problem is called the *word problem* for $\mathcal{A}$.

For instance, we shall consider the validity problem in the variety defined by $\mathcal{E}$: $\mathcal{M}b(\mathcal{E}) \models E$. There is an obvious relationship between this notion and the traditional notion of validity in first-order equational logic. The only difference is that $\mathcal{M}b(\mathcal{E})$ may contain more than the usual first-order models of $\mathcal{E}$, since we do not require the carriers of our algebras to be non-empty. $\mathcal{T}(\Sigma)_s$ coincides with the Herbrand universe of Σ of sort s whenever it is non-empty.

As in first-order logic, where semantic notions have an equivalent syntactic characterization through the completeness theorem, we have a proof theory corresponding to validity in a variety.

From now on, we use $\mathcal{T}$ instead of $\mathcal{T}(\Sigma \cup \mathcal{V})$ and $\mathcal{G}$ instead of $\mathcal{T}(\Sigma)$ when there is no ambiguity.

4. Proof Theory

The *equality* $=_{\mathcal{E}}$ generated by a set $\mathcal{E}$ of equations is the finest Σ-congruence over $\mathcal{T}$ containing all pairs $\langle \sigma(M), \sigma(N) \rangle$ for $M = N$ in $\mathcal{E}$ and σ an arbitrary substitution. In equational logic, $=_{\mathcal{E}}$ is called an *equational theory*, and $\mathcal{E}$ a *base* or a set of *axioms* for the theory.

The following is the well-known completeness theorem of Birkhoff (8):

Theorem. $\mathcal{M}(\mathcal{E}) \models M = N$ if and only if $M =_{\mathcal{E}} N$.

This theorem tells us that an equation $M = N$ is true in the variety defined by $\mathcal{E}$ if and only if it can be obtained from the equations in $\mathcal{E}$ by substitutions and by replacing equals by equals. That is, two terms are equivalent if and only if they can be shown equivalent in a finite number of proof steps. Whenever $\mathcal{E}$ is a recursive set of axioms, this gives us a semi-decision procedure for the validity problem in the variety. (The theorem assumes that $\mathcal{V}_s$ is a denumerable set, for every s in $\mathcal{S}$. However, in certain varieties, it is enough to consider finite sets of variables.)

Now we need the notions of satisfiability and consistency.

We say that $M = N$ is *satisfiable in* $\mathcal{A}$ if and only if there is an $\mathcal{A}$-assignment $\nu : \mathcal{V}(M) \cup \mathcal{V}(N) \rightarrow \mathcal{A}$ such that $\nu(M) = \nu(N)$. Equation $M = N$ is *satisfiable* (in the variety of $\mathcal{E}$) if and only if there is some algebra $\mathcal{A} \in \mathcal{M}(\mathcal{E})$ such that $M = N$ is satisfiable in $\mathcal{A}$.

Thus far, the satisfiability problem is vacuous: *Sort* validates any equation. However, one may be interested in knowing whether there exist non-trivial algebras validating some equations. In order to do this, we assume we have the distinguished sort **boolean**, and distinguished constants $TRUE$ and $FALSE$ of sort **boolean**. We call such signatures *signatures with booleans*. For example, Σ^0 is a signature with booleans.

Let Σ be a signature with booleans. The set of equations $\mathcal{E}$ is *consistent* if and only if $TRUE \neq_{\mathcal{E}} FALSE$. That is, if and only if $\mathcal{E}$ admits at least one model whose carrier of sort **boolean** is the genuine truth-values set {true, false}.

This condition refines in a nice way the usual notion in non-sorted equational logic, which defines $\mathcal{E}$ inconsistent if and only if $x =_{\mathcal{E}} y$ (recall that all variables are implicitly universally quantified). As before, inconsistency is recursively enumerable if $\mathcal{E}$ is recursive.

Examples: $\mathcal{E}^0$ is consistent, because $TRUE = FALSE$ is not valid in $\mathcal{A}^0$ (nor in $\mathcal{A}^1$ for that matter).

The equation $x + S(S(y)) = S(x + (y + S(0)))$ is valid in $\mathcal{M}(\mathcal{E}^0)$. Here is a proof: $x + S(S(y)) =_{\mathcal{E}^0} x + S(S(y+0)) =_{\mathcal{E}^0} x + S(y+S(0)) =_{\mathcal{E}^0} S(x + (y + S(0)))$. Similarly, $\mathcal{M}(\mathcal{E}^0) \models 0 + S(0) = S(0)$. More generally $\mathcal{M}(\mathcal{E}^0) \models 0 + M = M$ for every M of the form $S(S(\ldots S(0)\ldots))$. But $\mathcal{M}(\mathcal{E}^0) \not\models 0 + x = x$ since this equation is not valid in $\mathcal{A}^1$. In the same way, the commutativity of $+$ is not valid in $\mathcal{M}(\mathcal{E}^0)$, even though every ground instance of it is. We would like somehow to be able to restrict the notion of validity to the "standard model" $\mathcal{A}^0$. We consider this in the next section.

5. Initial Algebras and the Word Problem

The *initial* algebra $\mathfrak{I}(\Sigma, \mathcal{E})$ or simply $\mathfrak{I}(\mathcal{E})$ generated by a set of equations $\mathcal{E}$ is defined as the quotient of $\mathcal{G}$ by the congruence $=_{\mathcal{E}}$ restricted to ground terms. We leave it to the reader to check that this is indeed a Σ-algebra. (It is an initial object in the category whose objects are the Σ-models of $\mathcal{E}$ and the morphisms the Σ-morphisms; that is, there is a unique Σ-morphism from $\mathfrak{I}(\mathcal{E})$ to any algebra of $\mathcal{Mb}(\mathcal{E})$. See Goguen-Thatcher-Wagner (53) for details.)

Theorem. $\mathfrak{I}(\mathcal{E}) \models M = N$ if and only if for every ground substitution $\sigma : \mathcal{V} \to \mathcal{G}$, we have $\sigma(M) =_{\mathcal{E}} \sigma(N)$.

In other words, the validity problem over $\mathfrak{I}(\mathcal{E})$ is the same as the validity problem in the $\mathcal{E}$-variety of all its ground instances, and this captures the intuitive notion of standard model mentioned above. However, there is unfortunately no simple proof theory associated with this semantic notion, unlike the case for $\mathcal{Mb}(\mathcal{E})$ above. The situation is analogous to that in first-order Peano arithmetic on the one hand and the standard model $\mathcal{N}$ on the other.

Note that when M and N are ground terms, that is, for the word problem in the initial algebra, equational reasoning is complete. In other cases, $\mathfrak{I}(\mathcal{E}) \models M = N$ may be solved using induction schemas, for example on the structure of $\mathcal{G}$, but in general no induction schema will be strong enough to solve the validity problem in the initial algebra. The next section will give conditions under which this problem reduces to a problem of inconsistency.

Remarks: The set of equations valid in $\mathfrak{I}(\mathcal{E})$ is called $Induce(Th(\mathcal{E}))$ in Burstall-Goguen (77). $\mathcal{G}$ is $\mathfrak{I}(\emptyset)$ and $\mathcal{T}$ is $\mathfrak{I}(\Sigma \cup \mathcal{V}, \emptyset)$ restricted as a Σ-algebra.

Example: $\mathfrak{I}(\mathcal{E}^0)_{integer}$ is $\mathcal{N}$. However, $\mathfrak{I}(\mathcal{E}^0)$ is not $\mathcal{A}^0$ since its boolean carrier is more complicated — for instance, $0 \neq 0 \not=_{\mathcal{E}^0}$ *FALSE*. We can prove $\mathfrak{I}(\mathcal{E}^0) \models 0 + x = x$ by induction on the structure of $\mathcal{G}^0_{integer}$, which corresponds here to standard integer induction. Similarly, $\mathcal{I}(\mathcal{S}^0) \models x + y = y + x$ may be proved by a double induction argument.

Let us now briefly indicate the connection between our definitions and the word problem over finitely presented algebras.

We assume given a signature Σ and a variety defined by a set of equations $\mathcal{S}$. A *presentation* over this variety consists of a set C of constants (the *generators*) and a set $\mathcal{R}$ of ground equations (the *defining relations*) over $\mathcal{T}(\Sigma \cup C)$.

The algebra *presented* by $\langle C, \mathcal{R} \rangle$ is defined as $\mathcal{I}(\Sigma \cup C, \mathcal{S} \cup \mathcal{R})$. It is a $(\Sigma \cup C)$-algebra, and therefore also a Σ-algebra. The word problem for this presentation is as above — given a (ground) equation E over $\mathcal{T}(\Sigma \cup C)$, to determine whether or not $\mathcal{I}(\Sigma \cup C, \mathcal{S} \cup \mathcal{R}) \models E$. The presentation is said to be finite if C and $\mathcal{R}$ are, recursive if C and $\mathcal{R}$ are recursively enumerable.

The *uniform word problem* for the variety defined by axioms $\mathcal{S}$ is, given a finite presentation $\langle C, \mathcal{R} \rangle$ and an equation E over $\mathcal{T}(\Sigma \cup C)$, whether or not $\mathcal{I}(\Sigma \cup C, \mathcal{S} \cup \mathcal{R}) \models E$.

6. Unification

The equational systems we are describing in this survey manipulate the term structure $\mathcal{T}(\Sigma \cup \mathcal{V})$ or, more generally, $\mathcal{T}(\Sigma \cup \mathcal{V}, \mathcal{S})$, defined as $\mathcal{I}(\Sigma \cup \mathcal{V}, \mathcal{S})$ restricted to a Σ-algebra.

The *unification problem* is the satisfiability problem in this algebra. More precisely, let M and N be two terms in $\mathcal{T}(\Sigma \cup \mathcal{V})$. We say that M and N are $\mathcal{S}$-*unifiable* if and only if there exists a substitution $\sigma : \mathcal{V} \to \mathcal{T}(\Sigma \cup \mathcal{V})$ such that $\sigma(M) =_{\mathcal{S}} \sigma(N)$. We write $\mathcal{U}_{\mathcal{S}}(M, N)$ for the set of such substitutions, which we call $\mathcal{S}$-*unifiers*.

For instance, when $\mathcal{S}$ consists of Peano's axioms, the unification problem is precisely Hilbert's tenth problem, and so is undecidable (Matiyasevich 111). But if we keep only addition, the unification problem over integers without multiplication is decidable since it can be expressed as a formula of Presburger arithmetic, a decidable theory (Presburger 138). It has been announced by Szabó (157) that the following set has an undecidable unification problem:

$$x \times (y + z) = x \times y + x \times z$$
$$(x + y) \times z = x \times z + y \times z$$
$$x + (y + z) = (x + y) + z.$$

We are generally interested in finding not only whether two terms are unifiable, but also the set of all their unifiers. Of course we are not interested in the unifiers that can be obtained from others by composition — we are only interested in a basis from which we can generate all the solutions to a unification problem. This can best be explained by an ordering on substitutions, which is itself the extension of the instantiation ordering on terms. This is the purpose of the following definitions.

The *instantiation* or *subsumption* preorder $\preceq_\mathcal{E}$ is defined over $\mathcal{T}(\Sigma \cup \mathcal{V})$ by:

$M \preceq_\mathcal{E} N$ if and only if $\exists \sigma : \mathcal{V} \rightarrow \mathcal{T}(\Sigma \cup \mathcal{V})$ $N =_\mathcal{E} \sigma(M)$.

We now want to extend $\preceq_\mathcal{E}$ to substitutions. First let us recall that $\mathfrak{D}(\sigma) = \{x \in \mathcal{V} \mid \sigma(x) \neq x\}$. We also use the notation $\mathfrak{I}(\sigma)$ to denote $\bigcup_{x \in \mathfrak{D}(\sigma)} \mathcal{V}(\sigma(x))$, that is, the set of variables introduced by σ. Let V be any finite subset of $\mathcal{V}$. We define a preorder $\preceq_\mathcal{E} (V)$ on substitutions by:

$\sigma \preceq_\mathcal{E} \sigma'(V)$ if and only if $(\exists \rho)(\forall x \in V)$ $\sigma'(x) =_\mathcal{E} \rho(\sigma(x))$.

Now let M and N be two terms of the same sort, and $V = \mathcal{V}(M) \cup \mathcal{V}(N)$. Let W be any finite set of variables containing V, that is, $V \subseteq W \subset \mathcal{V}$. We say that a set of substitutions S is a *complete set of $\mathcal{E}$-unifiers* of M and N *away from* W if and only if

1. $(\forall \sigma \in S) \mathfrak{D}(\sigma) \subseteq V$ and $\mathfrak{I}(\sigma) \cap W = \emptyset$
2. $S \subseteq \mathcal{U}_\mathcal{E}(M, N)$
3. $(\forall \sigma \in \mathcal{U}_\mathcal{E}(M, N))(\exists \rho \in S) \rho \preceq_\mathcal{E} \sigma (V)$.

The first condition is technical, the second concerns soundness, and the third completeness. It can easily be shown that complete sets of unifiers always exist (take all $\mathcal{E}$-unifiers of M and N verifying 1).

The set S is said to be *minimal* if and only if it satisfies the additional condition

4. $(\forall \sigma, \sigma' \in S) \sigma \neq \sigma' \supset \sigma \npreceq_\mathcal{E} \sigma' (V)$.

Minimal complete sets of unifiers do not always exist. When they do, they are unique, up to the equivalence generated by $\preceq_{\mathcal{E}} (V)$.

Our definitions are consistent with the ones in Huet (72). Plotkin's definition of a complete set of unifiers, in Plotkin (136), is similar to our definition of a minimal CSU, modulo minor technical details. The necessity of considering a set W comes from the fact that terms M and N may come from a larger context, containing variables not in V, and we do not want to mix these with the "new" variables introduced by a unifier.

Examples:

1. When $\mathcal{E} = \emptyset$, it is well known that there exists a most general (that is, minimum) unifier. Algorithms to compute this unifier were proposed by Herbrand in 1930 in his thesis, Robinson (143), Baxter (5), Huet (72), Martelli and Montanari (110). All these algorithms are non-linear; a linear algorithm is given in Paterson and Wegman (131). The current state of the art on implementations is discussed in Martelli and Montanari (110). The equivalence $\equiv$ associated with $\preceq_\emptyset$ is variable renaming, and the corresponding ordering on $\mathcal{T}(\Sigma \cup \mathcal{V})/ \equiv$ completed with a maximum element defines a complete lattice. Unification corresponds to finding the least upper bound in this lattice. These issues are discussed in Plotkin (135), Reynolds (141) and Huet (72). Unification is one of the basic algorithms used in computational logic, and plays a central role in the inference rules of resolution (Robinson 143) and paramodulation (Robinson and Wos 142). We shall use it in the superposition algorithm in the next section.

2. Let $\mathcal{E}$ consist solely of the associativity axiom for some function symbol $\times$: $\mathcal{E} = \{(x \times y) \times z = x \times (y \times z)\}$. In this case there always exist minimal complete sets of unifiers, although the sets may be infinite. For instance with $M = x \times A$ and $N = A \times x$, with A some constant, $S = \{\{x \leftarrow A \times (A \times (\cdots \times (A \times A)\cdots))\}\} \cup \{\{x \leftarrow A\}\}$ is a minimal complete set of unifiers of M and N away from any W. An algorithm for generating such complete sets of unifiers is given in Plotkin (72). The unification problem reduces to the string equation problem, recently shown decidable by Makanin (107).

3. When $\mathcal{E}$ consists of the commutativity and associativity axioms for some function symbol $\times$: $\mathcal{E} = \{(x \times y) \times z = x \times (y \times z), x \times y = y \times x\}$ and $\Sigma = \{\times\}$, then the unification problem corresponds to solving equations in free abelian semigroups. There always exists a finite

minimal complete set of unifiers. Stickel (155) gives an algorithm to generate this set. His algorithm is correct over a more general problem: $\mathcal{E}$ may consist of commutative and associative laws for several function symbols, and Σ may contain other function symbols. But it remains an open problem to prove the termination of his algorithm when some of these other function symbols are of arity greater than 0.

4. Various other theories have been studied: commutativity (Siekmann 150); idempotence (Raulefs and Siekmann 140); commutativity, associativity and/or identity and/or idempotence (Stickel 156; Livesey and Siekmann 107). We shall see in section 12 a general method to generate a complete set of unifiers in a wide class of theories, which will include group theory. An abelian group theory unification algorithm is given by Lankford (94). However, his algorithm does not always terminate when extra function symbols are allowed (Stickel, private communication).

Unification has been studied for higher-order languages. An ω-order unification algorithm is given in Huet (71,72) and third-order unification is shown undecidable by Huet (70). Monadic second-order unification is decidable, as it is equivalent to associative unification, but it has recently been shown by Goldfarb (54) that polyadic second order unification is undecidable.

One-way unification (when unification is permitted in only one of the terms) is called *matching*. We say σ is an $\mathcal{E}$-*match* of M and N if and only if $\sigma(M) =_{\mathcal{E}} N$. A *complete set of $\mathcal{E}$-matches* of M and N *away from* W is defined as for unification, except that in 1 we replace $\mathfrak{D}(\sigma) \subseteq V$ by $\mathfrak{D}(\sigma) \subseteq \Upsilon(M) - \Upsilon(N)$. Such a set always exists when $\Upsilon(M) \cap \Upsilon(N) = \emptyset$.

7. Term Rewriting Systems

We are now ready to develop one of the main paradigms of computing with equations — using them as rewrite rules over terms. This paradigm is the basis for, on one hand, decision procedures based on canonical forms and, on the other hand, the construction of abstract interpreters for directed equations considered as a programming language.

A *term rewriting system* (over Σ) is a set of directed equations $\mathfrak{R} = \{\lambda_i \rightarrow \rho_i \mid i \in I\}$ such that, for all $\lambda \rightarrow \rho$ in $\mathfrak{R}$, $\Upsilon(\rho) \subseteq \Upsilon(\lambda)$.

The *reduction* relation $\rightarrow_{\mathfrak{R}}$ associated with $\mathfrak{R}$ is the finest relation over $\mathcal{T}$ containing $\mathfrak{R}$ and closed by substitution and replacement. That is,

$$M \rightarrow_{\mathfrak{R}} N \;\Rightarrow\; \sigma(M) \rightarrow_{\mathfrak{R}} \sigma(N) \tag{1}$$
$$M \rightarrow_{\mathfrak{R}} N \;\Rightarrow\; P[u \leftarrow M] \rightarrow_{\mathfrak{R}} P[u \leftarrow N]. \tag{2}$$

Equivalently, $\rightarrow_{\mathfrak{R}}$ is the finest relation containing all pairs $\sigma(\lambda), \sigma(\rho)$ such that $\lambda \rightarrow \rho \in \mathfrak{R}$ and closed under replacement (2).

Example: With $\mathfrak{R} = \{A \rightarrow B, F(B, x) \rightarrow G(x, x)\}$ we have $F(A, A) \rightarrow_{\mathfrak{R}} F(B, A) \rightarrow_{\mathfrak{R}} G(A, A)$.

From now on, we shall use $\rightarrow$ for $\rightarrow_{\mathfrak{R}}$. We use the standard notation $\rightarrow^+$ for the transitive closure of $\rightarrow$, $\rightarrow^*$ for its transitive-reflexive closure, and $\leftrightarrow$ for its symmetric closure. Note that $\leftrightarrow^*$ is the same as the $\mathfrak{R}$ equality $=_{\mathfrak{R}}$, when $\mathfrak{R}$ is considered a set of equations. Conversely, any set of equations $\mathcal{E}$ can be transformed into a term rewriting system $\mathfrak{R}$ over an extended signature Σ' in such a way that $\leftrightarrow^*$ is a conservative extension of $=_{\mathcal{E}}$. (Then, for all M, N in $\mathcal{T}(\Sigma \cup \mathcal{V})_s$, $M =_{\mathcal{E}} N$ if and only if $M \leftrightarrow^* N$.) The construction is as follows: for every $M = N$ in $\mathcal{E}$, choose nondeterministically one of the following:

1. if $\mathcal{V}(M) \subseteq \mathcal{V}(N)$, put $N \rightarrow M$ in $\mathfrak{R}$
2. if $\mathcal{V}(N) \subseteq \mathcal{V}(M)$, put $M \rightarrow N$ in $\mathfrak{R}$
3. with $\{x_1, \ldots, x_n\} = \mathcal{V}(M) \cap \mathcal{V}(N)$, introduce in Σ' a new operator H of the appropriate type, and put in $\mathfrak{R}$ the two rules $M \rightarrow P$ and $N \rightarrow P$ with $P = H(x_1, \ldots, x_n)$. (Note that this third possibility may force certain sorts to be strict in Σ' when they were not in Σ; it may then be necessary to add extra constants to Σ' for it to be sensible. Also certain Σ-algebras which were models may not be extendible as Σ'-algebras because the corresponding carriers are empty.)

The fundamental difference between equations and term rewriting rules is that equations denote equality (which is symmetric) whereas term rewriting systems treat equations directionally, as one-way replacements. Further, the only substitutions required for term rewriting rules are the ones found by pattern matching. The completeness of using rewrite rules to make deductions equationally is expressed by the following Church-Rosser property:

$\Re$ is *Church-Rosser* if and only if, for all M and N, $M =_{\Re} N$ if and only if there exists a P such that $M \to^{*} P$ and $N \to^{*} P$.

An equivalent characterization is "confluence". $\Re$ is *confluent* if and only if for all M, N, and P, $P \to^{*} M$ and $P \to^{*} N$ implies there is some Q such that $M \to^{*} Q$ and $N \to^{*} Q$.

We say that M is *irreducible* or *in normal form* (relative to $\Re$) if and only if there is no N such that $M \to N$; that is, no subterm of M is an instance of some lefthand side of a rule in $\Re$. We say that N is a $\Re$-*normal form of* M if and only if $M \to^{*} N$ and N is a normal form relative to $\Re$.

When $\Re$ is Church-Rosser the normal form of a term is unique, when it exists. A sufficient condition for the existence of such a canonical form is the termination of all rewritings:

$\Re$ is *nœtherian* or *finitely terminating* if and only if for no M is there an infinite chain of reductions issuing from M: $M = M_1 \to M_2 \to \dots$.

Let $M\downarrow$ be any normal form obtained from M by an arbitrary sequence of reductions.

When $\Re$ is a finite set of rules which is confluent and nœtherian, the equational theory $=_{\Re}$ is decidable, since now $M =_{\Re} N$ if and only if $M\downarrow = N\downarrow$. Actually, confluent and nœtherian rewrite rules provide a rather general method for solving the validity problem in decidable varieties.

The property of confluence is undecidable for arbitrary term rewriting systems, since a confluence test could be used to decide the equivalence, for instance, of recursive program schemas. The decidability of confluence for ground term rewriting systems is open. We shall now show that confluence is decidable for nœtherian systems.

The first step in the construction is showing that, for nœtherian systems, confluence is equivalent to "local confluence". $\Re$ is *locally confluent* if and only if for all M, N, and P, $P \to M$ and $P \to N$ implies there is some Q such that $M \to^{*} Q$ and $N \to^{*} Q$.

Newman Theorem. Let $\Re$ be a nœtherian term rewriting system. $\Re$ is confluent if and only if it is locally confluent.

This theorem was first proved by Newman (125); a simple proof appears in Huet (73). Various equivalent or related "diamond lemmas" have been proposed, for instance by Hindley (67); Knuth and Bendix (86); Nivat (126); Aho, Sethi and Ullman (2); and Lankford (91).

The second step consists in showing that local confluence of (finite) term rewriting systems is decidable. We show this now.

Superposition Algorithm.

Let $\lambda \to \rho$ and $\lambda' \to \rho'$ be two rules in $\mathfrak{R}$. We assume we have renamed variables appropriately, so that λ and λ' share no variables. Assume u is a non-variable occurrence in λ such that λ/u and λ' are unifiable, with minimal unifier σ (we assume of course that λ/u and λ' are of the same sort). We then say that the pair $\langle \sigma(\lambda[u \leftarrow \rho']), \sigma(\rho) \rangle$ of terms is *critical* in $\mathfrak{R}$.

Example: Consider $F(x, G(x, H(y))) \to K(x, y)$ and $G(A, z) \to L(z)$. We can superpose the first rule at occurrence 2 with the second one using the minimal unifier $\{x \leftarrow A, z \leftarrow H(y)\}$, obtaining the critical pair $\langle F(A, L(H(y))), K(A, y) \rangle$.

If $\mathfrak{R}$ is finite, there are only finitely many such critical pairs. They can be effectively computed using the standard unification algorithm.

Knuth-Bendix Theorem. $\mathfrak{R}$ is locally confluent if and only if $P\!\downarrow = Q\!\downarrow$ for every critical pair $\langle P, Q \rangle$ of $\mathfrak{R}$.

The original idea for this theorem is due to Knuth and Bendix (86), who combined it with Newman's theorem (see also Lankford (91)). The version of the theorem given above appears in Huet (73) and does not require termination.

Combining the Knuth-Bendix theorem and Newman's theorem gives us a decision procedure for the confluence of nœtherian term rewriting systems with a finite number of rules. When such a system $\mathfrak{R}$ satisfies the critical pair condition, it defines a canonical form for the corresponding equational theory $=_\mathfrak{R}$. We then say that $\mathfrak{R}$ is a *complete* or *canonical* term rewriting system.

There exist other sufficient criteria for the confluence of term rewriting systems that do not assume that every sequence of reductions terminates. Most of them rely on a sufficient condition for confluence: "strong confluence". $\mathfrak{R}$ is *strongly* confluent if and only if for all M, N, and P, $P \to M$ and $P \to N$ implies there is some Q such that $M \to^\epsilon Q$ and $N \to^\epsilon Q$, where $\to^\epsilon$ denotes the reflexive closure of $\to$.

Let us call term M linear if and only if every variable in M occurs only once. When $\mathfrak{R}$ is such that, for every $\lambda \to \rho$ in $\mathfrak{R}$, λ and ρ are linear, then $\mathfrak{R}$ is strongly confluent if for every critical pair $\langle P, Q \rangle$ of $\mathfrak{R}$, there exists an R such that $P \to^\epsilon R$ and $Q \to^\epsilon R$ (Huet 77). However the condition of linearity of ρ is not very natural. A more useful result requires only linearity of left hand sides of rules. Let us denote by $\nparallel$ the parallel reduction by rules of $\mathfrak{R}$ at disjoint occurrences.

Theorem. (Huet 73) If, for every $\lambda \to \rho$, λ is linear, and for every critical pair $\langle P, Q \rangle$ we have $P \nparallel Q$, then the relation $\nparallel$ is strongly confluent; and therefore $\mathfrak{R}$ is confluent.

This theorem extends the main theorem in (Rosen 145) which applies only to ground systems. It shows in particular that left-linear term rewriting systems with no critical pairs are confluent. Such recursive definitions are therefore determinate. They extend both the usual recursive schemes and the primitive recursive-like definitions.

8. Termination

In order to simplify the discussions and notation, we assume from now on that we are dealing with only one sort. We assume that Σ is finite, and that $\mathcal{G} \neq \emptyset$.

The main problem with the Knuth-Bendix confluence test is the proof of termination. Recall that $\mathfrak{R}$ is nœtherian if and only if there is no term M such that there exists an infinite sequence $M = M_1 \to M_2 \to \cdots$. Proving $\mathfrak{R}$ nœtherian is crucial, since without it local confluence does not tell us anything. For instance, the system $\mathfrak{R} = \{A \to B, A \to C, B \to A, B \to D\}$ is locally confluent, even though A has two distinct normal forms C and D.

It is undecidable whether an arbitrary term rewriting system is nœtherian. See Huet and Lankford (76) where it is shown however that this problem is decidable for ground systems.

We first remark that $\mathfrak{R}$ is nœtherian if and only if there is no ground term M having an infinite sequence of reductions (recall that we are assuming $\mathcal{G}$ is nonempty). That is, $\mathfrak{R}$ is nœtherian if and only if the relation $\to_{\mathfrak{R}}^{+}$ defines a well-founded partial ordering on $\mathcal{G}$. This suggests the following general method for proving $\mathfrak{R}$ nœtherian.

Let $\succ$ be any partial ordering relation (that is, transitive and irreflexive) on $\mathcal{G}$ such that:

(1) $\succ$ is well-founded; that is, there is no infinite sequence of ground terms $M_1 \succ M_2 \succ \cdots$.

(2) $M \rightarrow N \Rightarrow M \succ N$

Then (obviously) $\mathfrak{R}$ is nœtherian. Conversely, if $\mathfrak{R}$ is nœtherian, then the relation $\rightarrow^+$ satisfies (1) and (2).

Various refinements of this general scheme have been proposed. Let us present a few.

A. Well-founded Mapping Method

Let $\mathfrak{D}$ be any set given with a well-founded partial ordering $\succ_{\mathfrak{D}}$. The method consists in exhibiting a mapping $\varphi: \mathfrak{G} \rightarrow \mathfrak{D}$, and defining the relation $\succ$ by:

$M \succ N$ if and only if $\varphi(M) \succ_{\mathfrak{D}} \varphi(N)$.

Property (1) is obviously satisfied. The method then consists in showing (2). Conversely, if $\mathfrak{R}$ is nœtherian, consider $\mathfrak{G}$ for $\mathfrak{D}$, $\rightarrow^+$ for $\succ_{\mathfrak{D}}$, and the identity for φ. Also, if $\rightarrow$ is finitely branching (this is the case for instance whenever $\mathfrak{R}$ is finite), we may always show $\mathfrak{R}$ nœtherian by the method above, with $\mathfrak{D}$ being the set of natural numbers $\mathcal{N}$ with their usual ordering $>$, by defining $\varphi(M)$ to be the length of the longest sequence of reductions issuing from M (hint: use König's lemma).

However, the real crux of the matter comes with proving (2), and this is not very convenient, since it quantifies over all possible reductions $M \rightarrow N$. An important refinement consists in remarking that (2) is implied by (3) and (4) below:

(3) $M \succ N \Rightarrow F(\vec{P}, M, \vec{Q}) \succ F(\vec{P}, N, \vec{Q})$ for every operator F in Σ and sequences of ground terms $\vec{P}$ and $\vec{Q}$.

(4) $\sigma(\lambda) \succ \sigma(\rho)$ for every ground substitution σ and rule $\lambda \rightarrow \rho$ in $\mathfrak{R}$.

Condition (3) means that the relation $\succ$ is compatible with the Σ-algebra structure. This suggests refining the mapping method above into the following.

B. Increasing Interpretation Method

We take $\mathfrak{D}$ to be a Σ-algebra, and φ to be the unique Σ-homomorphism from $\mathcal{G}$ to $\mathfrak{D}$. Condition (3) is implied by the corresponding property in algebra $\mathfrak{D}$; that is, every operator of Σ corresponds in $\mathfrak{D}$ to a mapping strictly increasing in every argument:

(5) $(\forall x, y \in \mathfrak{D})(\forall \vec{u}, \vec{v} \in \vec{\mathfrak{D}}) x \succ_{\mathfrak{D}} y \Rightarrow F(\vec{u}, x, \vec{v}) \succ_{\mathfrak{D}} F(\vec{u}, y, \vec{v})$.

Given such an increasing interpretation of Σ, all we have to show is (4), or its stronger analogue in $\mathfrak{D}$; that is:

(6) $(\forall \lambda \to \rho \in \mathfrak{R}) \mathfrak{D} \models \lambda \succ_{\mathfrak{D}} \rho$.

Actually, (4) and (6) suggest rather different methods of proof: (4) suggests using structural induction in $\mathcal{G}$, whereas we must resort to nœtherian induction in $\mathfrak{D}$ to prove the stronger (6).

The increasing interpretation method has been proposed by Manna and Ness (109), and by Lankford (91) in the special case of polynomial interpretations over the integers.

Example: The ten group reductions shown in the Appendix can be shown to terminate using the following increasing interpretation over the set of integers greater than 1:

$$x + y = x \times (1 + 2 \times y)$$
$$I(x) = x^2$$
$$0 = 2.$$

However, the proof of (6) is not straightforward, since it involves showing for instance $(\forall x, y \in \mathcal{N}) x > 1$ and $y > 1$ implies $x^2 (1 + 2y)^2 > y^2 (1 + 2x^2)$. Actually sentences of the form of (6) are undecidable in general, for polynomial integer interpretations. This precludes practical use of this method, even assuming the human user guesses the right interpretation.

Of course, polynomial interpretations do not suffice in general, since they give a polynomial upper bound on the complexity of the computations by $\mathfrak{R}$, interpreted as a program computing over integers, whereas arbitrary recursive functions can be defined by term rewriting systems. This argument extends to primitive recursive complexity measures, as remarked by M. Stickel.

The increasing interpretation is completely general, however, since if $\mathfrak{R}$ is nœtherian then $\mathcal{G}$ itself as a Σ-algebra defines an increasing interpretation, taking $\rightarrow^+$ for $\succ_{\mathfrak{G}}$. But here we cannot restrict our-selves to total orderings, since for instance A and B must be unrelated in any increasing interpretation which shows the termination of $\mathfrak{R} = \{F(A) \rightarrow F(B), G(B) \rightarrow G(A)\}$. Therefore, even ordinal numbers are not general enough here!

Next let us show how condition (1) can be refined. We define in $\mathfrak{G}$ the *homeomorphic embedding* relation $\trianglelefteq$ by induction as follows:

$F(M_1, \ldots, M_n) \trianglelefteq N$ if and only if there exists in N a subterm $F(N_1, \ldots, N_n)$ and a permutation π of $(1, 2, \ldots, n)$ such that $M_i \trianglelefteq N_{\pi_i}$ for every $i, 1 \leq i \leq n$.

Kruskal's Theorem. For every infinite sequence M_1, M_2, ... of ground terms in $\mathfrak{G}$, there exist i and j, with $i < j$, such that $M_i \trianglelefteq M_j$.

See Kruskal (89) and Nash-Williams (121) for the proof of more general theorems (which do not require Σ to be finite). The theorem suggests replacing (1) by the (stronger) condition:

(7) $M \trianglelefteq N$ implies $\neg(M \succ N)$.

Finally, Dershowitz (33, 34) shows that (7) follows from (3) and:

(8) $F(\vec{P}, M, \vec{Q}) \succ M$.

All this justifies the following method.

C. Simplification Ordering Method

Let $\succ$ be any partial ordering on $\mathfrak{G}$ satisfying (3) and (8). (We then say that $\succ$ is a *simplification ordering*.) Then $\mathfrak{R}$ is noetherian if (4) is satisfied.

The method was first proposed by Dershowitz (33, 34). An important application is the following.

First recall that a partial ordering $\succ$ on a set $\mathcal{G}$ may be extended to a partial ordering $\gg$ on the set of multisets of $\mathcal{G}$, that is, of mappings $\mathcal{G} \rightarrow \mathcal{N}$, as follows: $S \gg S'$ if and only if $S \neq S' \,\&\, (\forall x \in \mathcal{G})\,[S'(x) > S(x) \Rightarrow (\exists y \succ x)\,S(y) > S'(y)]$.

Furthermore, the set of finite multisets of $\mathcal{G}$ is well founded by $\gg$ if and only if $\mathcal{G}$ is well-founded by $\succ$ (see Dershowitz and Manna (35)). The multiset ordering generalizes the lexicographic ordering, obtained when $\succ$ is a total ordering.

Next we define the *permutation equivalence* $\sim$ on $\mathcal{G}$ by: $M \sim N$ if and only if $M = F(M_1, \ldots, M_n)$, $N = F(N_1, \ldots, N_n)$, for some F in Σ, and there exists a permutation π of $1, 2, \ldots, n$ such that $M_i \sim N_{\pi_i}, 1 \leq i \leq n$.

We denote the permutation class $\widetilde{M}$ of $M = F(M_1, \ldots, M_n)$ by $F\{\widetilde{M}_1, \ldots, \widetilde{M}_n\}$. Let $\succ_\Sigma$ be any partial ordering on the operators of Σ. We define the *recursive path ordering* $\succ$ on $\mathcal{G}/\sim$ recursively as follows: $\widetilde{M} = F\{\widetilde{M}_1, \ldots, \widetilde{M}_n\} \succ \widetilde{N} = G\{\widetilde{N}_1, \ldots, \widetilde{N}_p\}$ if and only if:

    (a) either $F = G$ and $\{\widetilde{M}_1, \ldots, \widetilde{M}_n\} \gg \{\widetilde{N}_1, \ldots, \widetilde{N}_p\}$

    (b) or $F \succ_\Sigma G$ and $(\forall i \leq p)\, \widetilde{M} \succ \widetilde{N}_i$

    (c) or (otherwise) $(\exists j \leq n)\, \widetilde{M}_j \succeq \widetilde{N}$, where $\widetilde{M} \succeq \widetilde{N}$ if and only if $\widetilde{M} \succ \widetilde{N}$ or $\widetilde{M} = \widetilde{N}$.

The recursive path ordering generalizes the orderings defined in Plaisted (134), Itturiaga (80), and Dershowitz and Manna (35). Now defining $M \succ N$ as $\widetilde{M} \succ \widetilde{N}$, we get:

Theorem. $\succ$ is a simplification ordering.

For a proof, see Dershowitz (34) for a slightly more general formulation permitting infinite signatures that may contain varyadic operations.

This theorem gives a fairly general method for proving termination of $\mathcal{R}$:

D. Recursive Path Ordering Method

Guess some partial ordering $\succ_\Sigma$ and show (4) using the corresponding simplification ordering.

Of course, this method does not give us yet a completely mechanical way of checking (4) because of the quantification on every ground substitution. What we need here is to be able to define recursively an ordering $\succ$ on ground terms that "lifts" to an order $\succ$ over general terms, in the sense that $M \succ N$ implies $\sigma(M) \succ \sigma(N)$, for every ground substitution σ.

We are able to do this to a limited extent. First, the clause (c) in the definition above does not depend on the M_k's, for $k \neq j$, and we may therefore permit non-ground terms in these positions. Secondly, properties (3) and (8), which hold here because of the theorem above, quantify over all P's and Q's and we may again permit non-ground terms there, extending the recursive path ordering to non-ground terms. Actually, (3) is directly implied by the algorithm above, and (8) can be incorporated easily in the algorithm as follows. We construct the recursive path ordering $\succ$ on possibly non-ground terms, that is on $\mathcal{T}/\sim$. (We extend $\sim$ to include $x \sim x$ for every variable x.) We keep the three clauses (a), (b), and (c) above and we add one more clause:

(d) $\widetilde{M} \succ x$ if and only if $M \not\subseteq \Upsilon$ and $x \in \Upsilon(M)$.

It should be obvious to the reader that $M \succ N$ with the new definition implies that $\sigma(M) \succ \sigma(N)$ for every ground substitution σ with the old one (for (d), use a simple induction on M, and (8)). We call the new ordering the *generalized recursive path ordering*. All that precedes justifies the following:

E. Generalized Recursive Path Ordering Method

Let $\succ_\Sigma$ be some partial ordering on Σ, $\succ$ the generalized path ordering defined above. If for all $\lambda \to \rho$ in $\mathcal{R}$ we have $\lambda \succ \rho$, then $\mathcal{R}$ is nœtherian.

Example: (Disjunctive normal form)

$$\text{Let } \mathcal{R} = \left\{ \begin{array}{l} \neg(\neg(x)) \to x, \\ \neg(x \vee y) \to \neg(x) \wedge \neg(y), \\ \neg(x \wedge y) \to \neg(x) \vee \neg(y), \\ x \wedge (y \vee z) \to (x \wedge y) \vee (x \wedge z), \\ (y \vee z) \wedge x \to (y \wedge x) \vee (z \wedge x). \end{array} \right\}$$

We take $\neg \succ_\Sigma \wedge \succ_\Sigma \vee$. We leave it to the reader to show that for every $\lambda \to \rho$ in $\mathcal{R}$ we have $\lambda \succ \rho$, establishing the termination of $\mathcal{R}$. Note that what we have done here is to automate completely, inside the generalized recursive path algorithm, the proof exhibited by Dershowitz (34).

Other definitions of recursive orderings on general terms that lift simplification orderings (like the surface ordering) are given in Plaisted (133).

We conclude our discussion on simplification orderings by remarking that it has a semantic analogue, refining the increasing interpretation method, as follows.

F. Homeomorphic Interpretation Method

The method consists in choosing a Σ-algebra $\mathfrak{D}$ given with a partial ordering $\succ_{\mathfrak{D}}$ verifying the increasing condition (5) and the extra condition, for every operator F in Σ:

(9) $(\forall x \in \mathfrak{D})(\forall \overrightarrow{u}, \overrightarrow{v} \in \overrightarrow{\mathfrak{D}}) \, F(\overrightarrow{u}, x, \overrightarrow{v}) \succ_{\mathfrak{D}} x.$

Now $\mathfrak{R}$ is noetherian if (6) is satisfied. The justification of the method should be clear: taking φ to be the unique Σ-homomorphism from $\mathcal{G}$ to $\mathfrak{D}$, and ordering $\mathcal{G}$ by $M \succ N$ if and only if $\varphi(M) \succ_{\mathfrak{D}} \varphi(N)$, we get (2) by (5) and (6). But now (1) is a consequence of just (7), which follows from (6) and (9). That is, we do not need here $\succ_{\mathfrak{D}}$ to define a well-founded ordering on $\mathfrak{D}$.

This method may well provide a new practical approach to proofs of termination of term rewriting systems, taking algebras for which condition (6) is decidable. For instance, Dershowitz (33) proposes to use this method, taking for $\mathfrak{D}$ the reals with polynomial operators. He remarks that conditions (5), (9) and (6) are indeed decidable in this setting, using Tarski's decision method (Tarski 158). Furthermore, the existence of such polynomials of a bounded degree that decide the termination of $\mathfrak{R}$ is decidable. The practicality of this method depends of course on the availability of implementations of such decision procedures (Cohen 26, Collins 28). The use of interpretations over the reals was first proposed by Lankford (91).

We conclude this section by a generalization of simplification orderings to pre-orderings, that is, transitive and reflexive relations. Let $\succeq$ be a pre-ordering on $\mathcal{G}$ satisfying the simplification conditions:

(3') $M \succeq N \implies F(\overrightarrow{P}, M, \overrightarrow{Q}) \succeq F(\overrightarrow{P}, N, \overrightarrow{Q})$
(8') $F(\overrightarrow{P}, M, \overrightarrow{Q}) \succeq M.$

We then say that $\succeq$ is a *simplification pre-ordering*. Defining $M \succ N$ by $M \succeq N$ and not $N \succeq M$, we get:

G. Simplification pre-ordering method

Let $\succeq$ be a simplification pre-ordering. If (4) is satisfied, then $\mathfrak{R}$ is noetherian.

The correctness of this method is shown in Dershowitz (34) where it is stated that it may be used to prove the correctness of the recursive ordering described in Knuth and Bendix (86).

9. Compiling Canonical Forms

The Knuth-Bendix theorem of section 7 gives us conditions under which an equational theory admits a canonical form, as follows.

Let $\mathcal{E}$ be the (finite) set of equations given as basis (axioms) for the theory. If there exists a canonical term rewriting system $\mathcal{R}$ such that we have (denoting by $\mathcal{R}(M)$ the unique normal form of M obtained by applying to it an arbitrary number of reductions from $\mathcal{R}$):

(1) $(\forall M = N \in \mathcal{E})\ \mathcal{R}(M) = \mathcal{R}(N)$, and

(2) $(\forall \lambda \to \rho \in \mathcal{R})\ \lambda =_g \rho$,

then $\mathcal{R}(M)$ is a canonical form of M for the theory $=_g$, in the sense that

$$(\forall M, N \in \mathcal{T}(\Sigma \cup \mathcal{V}))\ M =_g N \text{ if and only if } \mathcal{R}(M) = \mathcal{R}(N).$$

Note that this gives us a decision procedure for the validity problem in $\mathcal{M}b(\mathcal{E})$, and therefore, as a corollary, a decision procedure for the word problem in $\mathcal{I}(\mathcal{E})$.

We saw in section 7 how to check local confluence with critical pairs, and in section 8 how to check $\mathcal{R}$ noetherian. Let us now give an algorithm that attempts to generate $\mathcal{R}$ satisfying (1) and (2) for a given $\mathcal{E}$.

Completion Algorithm.

$\mathcal{E}_i$ is a set of equations, $\mathcal{R}_i$ a term rewriting system, $i \in \mathcal{N}$. Initially let $\mathcal{E}_0 = \mathcal{E}$, $\mathcal{R}_i = \emptyset$ and $i = 0$.

1. If $\mathcal{E}_i = \emptyset$, stop with answer $\mathcal{R} = \mathcal{R}_i$. Otherwise, select $M = N$ in $\mathcal{E}_i$, and let $M{\downarrow}$ and $N{\downarrow}$ be normal forms for M and N respectively, using the current system $\mathcal{R}_i$. If $M{\downarrow} = N{\downarrow}$ then let $\mathcal{E}_{i+1} = \mathcal{E}_i - \{M = N\}$, $\mathcal{R}_{i+1} = \mathcal{R}_i$, increment i by 1 and go to 1. Otherwise go to 2.

2. Choose non-deterministically one of the following:

(a) if $\mathcal{V}(M{\downarrow}) \subset \mathcal{V}(N{\downarrow})$ then let $\lambda = N{\downarrow}, \rho = M{\downarrow}$.

(b) if $\mathcal{V}(N{\downarrow}) \subset \mathcal{V}(M{\downarrow})$ then let $\lambda = M{\downarrow}, \rho = N{\downarrow}$.

If neither (a) nor (b) applies, stop with failure.

Otherwise, let $\mathcal{E}'_i = \{\lambda' = \rho' \mid \lambda' \to \rho' \in \mathcal{R}_i,$ and λ' or ρ' contains an instance of λ as subterm$\}$. Then let $\mathcal{R}'_i = \mathcal{R}_i - \mathcal{E}'_i \cup \{\lambda \to \rho\}$ and go to 3.

3. If $\mathcal{R}'_i$ is not nœtherian, stop with failure. Otherwise, let $\mathcal{R}_{i+1} = \mathcal{R}'_i$, and $\mathcal{E}_{i+1} = (\mathcal{E}_i - \{M = N\}) \cup \mathcal{E}'_i \cup \{P = Q \mid \langle P, Q\rangle$ is a critical pair of $\mathcal{R}_{i+1}\}$. Increment i by 1 and go to 1.

The completion algorithm is due to Knuth and Bendix (86). Its correctness follows from the following facts: (i) At every iteration i, $=_{\mathcal{R}_i \cup \mathcal{E}_i}$ *equals* $=_{\mathcal{E}}$. (ii) Every $\mathcal{R}_i$ is nœtherian, and every $\lambda \to \rho$ in $\mathcal{R}_i$ is such that ρ is a normal form for $\mathcal{R}_i$ and λ is a normal form for $\mathcal{R}_i - \{\lambda \to \rho\}$. (iii) If the algorithm stops with success, $\mathcal{R}$ is locally confluent, and therefore (1) and (2) above are satisfied.

Note that the algorithm is non-deterministic because of the various choices. It may stop with success, stop with failure, or loop forever. But we were careful in its formulation, in that the only possibility of non-termination is by the global looping of the outer iteration, and this can be prevented by setting a bound on i.

Various optimizations of the algorithm are possible. For instance, we need to recompute only the critical pairs of $\mathcal{R}_{i+1}$ which could not be obtained as critical pairs of $\mathcal{R}_i$. We leave the details to the reader.

There are various cases of failure. When neither (a) nor (b) applies at step 2, this suggests starting the process over again with an augmented signature Σ' and an augmented set of equations $\mathcal{E}'$ as follows. Let $\{x_1, \ldots, x_n\} = \mathcal{V}(M{\downarrow}) \cap \mathcal{V}(N{\downarrow})$. Augment Σ with operator H of type $\tau(x_1) \times \cdots \times \tau(x_n) \to \tau(M)$, and augment $\mathcal{E}$ with the equation $H(x_1, \ldots, x_n) = M{\downarrow}$, for instance. As indicated above, some extra constants may be needed for the new signature to be sensible, in the multi-sorted case. But in any case, the new equational theory is a conservative extension of the old one; that is, for any terms P and Q over Σ, $P =_{\mathcal{E}'} Q$ if and only if $P =_{\mathcal{E}} Q$. Intuitively, the new equations are just definitions of the new symbols. These definitions are acceptable, since $M{\downarrow} =_{\mathcal{E}} N{\downarrow}$ implies that in any Σ-model of $\mathcal{E}$ the value of $M{\downarrow}$ does not depend on the assignments to variables other than the x_i's. When running the completion algorithm with $\mathcal{E}'$ the situation will be different, since the new equation will give rise to a new reduction $M{\downarrow} \to H(x_1, \ldots, x_n)$ and when $M = N$ is selected case (a) will apply. The new system may indeed converge, as shown in some examples in Knuth and Bendix (86). This modification can be taken into account in the algorithm, by replacing the "stop with failure" at step 2 by the following:

Let $\mathcal{E}_{i+1} = (\mathcal{E}_i - \{M = N\}) \cup \{M\downarrow = H(x_1,\ldots,x_n), N\downarrow = H(x_1,\ldots,x_n)\}$, $\mathcal{R}_{i+1} = \mathcal{R}_i$, increment i by 1 and go to 1.

The other case of failure comes from step 3, if we recognize $\mathcal{R}$ as non-nœtherian. This may actually come from three different causes:

1. We choose the wrong orientation of some rule at step 2; that is, some other choices may lead to a successfully terminating computation.

2. The nœtherian test used at step 3 is not general enough; that is, $\mathcal{R}'_i$ is indeed terminating but our test does not show it. Some more powerful test may be needed for successful completion.

3. Every choice at step 2 leads to a non-nœtherian $\mathcal{R}'_i$. This "unrecoverable" failure occurs for instance whenever a symmetric axiom such as commutativity is encountered. This is obviously the main pitfall of the whole method: it does not apply to theories with such permutative axioms. (However, see Section 14.)

The appendix contains a complete run of an implementation (by Jean-Marie Hullot) of the completion algorithm for the group axioms. The Knuth-Bendix ordering is used there for checking termination.

10. Decidability and Complexity of Word Problems

Word problems have been extensively studied in logic; some sources of results on decidability and undecidability are Tarski (159), McNulty (114) and Evans (45).

For example, when $\mathcal{E}$ is a standard set of axioms for group theory: $Group = \{x + 0 = x, x + (-x) = 0, (x + y) + z = x + (y + z)\}$, then certain word problems (and therefore the uniform word problem) are unsolvable. The word problem in the free group with ω generators, that is, $\mathcal{I}(\Sigma \cup \Upsilon, Group)$, is solvable. Dehn's algorithm (Dehn 32, Greenlinger 58) gives an algorithm for the word problem in a family of presentations of groups.

The computational complexity of several decidable word problems has been studied. The uniform word problem for abelian semigroups is solvable (see Malcev (108) and Emelichev (40)); Cardoza, Lipton and

Meyer (23) show that the problem is complete in exponential space under log-space transformability. See also Lipton and Zalcstein (105), and Meyer and Stockmeyer (115) for other results.

An extensively studied case is the uniform word problem for the case $\mathscr{E} = \emptyset$, that is, in the variety of all Σ-algebras. The problem is thus determining whether some ground equation follows from a given set of ground equations by substitutivity of equality, and so is also the decision problem for the quantifier-free theory of equality with uninterpreted function symbols. An example is determining whether $f(a) = a$ is a consequence of $\{f(f(f(a))) = a, f(f(f(f(f(a))))) = a\}$. Ackermann (1) showed that the problem was decidable, but did not give a practical algorithm.

The problem reduces to the problem of constructing the "congruence closure" of a relation on a graph. Let $G = (V,E)$ be a directed graph with labelled vertices, possibly with multiple edges. For a vertex v, let $\lambda(v)$ denote its label and $\delta(v)$ its outdegree, that is, the number of edges leaving v. The edges leaving a vertex are ordered. For $1 \leq i \leq \delta(v)$, let $v[i]$ denote the ith *successor* of v, that is, the vertex to which the ith edge of v points. A vertex u is a *predecessor* of v if $v = u[i]$ for some i. Since multiple edges are allowed, possibly $v[i] = v[j]$ for $i \neq j$. Let n be the number of vertices of G and m the number of edges of G. We assume that $n = O(m)$.

Let $\sim$ be a relation on V. Two vertices u and v are *congruent under* $\sim$ if $\lambda(u) = \lambda(v)$, $\delta(u) = \delta(v)$, and, for all i such that $1 \leq i \leq \delta(u)$, $u[i] \sim v[i]$. The relation $\sim$ is *closed under congruences* if, for all vertices u and v such that u and v are congruent under $\sim$, $u \sim v$. The *congruence closure* of $\sim$ is the finest equivalence relation that is closed under congruences and contains $\sim$.

The relation between the uniform word problem and congruence closure is given by the following theorem (see Shostak 149, or Nelson and Oppen 122):

Theorem. Let $\mathscr{E}$ be the set of defining equations of the algebra. Suppose that we wish to determine if $M = N$ follows from $\mathscr{E}$. Let G be a directed graph corresponding to the set of terms appearing in $\mathscr{E}$ and $M = N$, and let $\theta(P)$ be the vertex of G corresponding to the term P. Let $\sim$ be the congruence closure of $\{\langle \theta(U), \theta(V)\rangle\}$ for each equation $U = V$ appearing in $\mathscr{E}$. Then $M = N$ follows from $\mathscr{E}$ if and only if $\theta(M) \sim \theta(N)$.

Kozen (87) shows that the problem is in P (polynomial time),
Nelson and Oppen (122) show that it admits a $O(n^2)$ solution, and
Downey, Sethi and Tarjan (38) show that it admits a $O(n \log^2 n)$ solution. (The algorithms require linear space, and the times given apply
whether the algorithms are online or offline.) It is still open whether
the problem is solvable in linear time.

Canonical term rewriting systems may be used to solve word
problems over algebras, in cases where the completion algorithm of
section 7 terminates given the equations formed from the axioms of the
variety, plus the presentation of the algebra.

Furthermore, the completion algorithm may be used to solve
uniform word problems, if its termination can be established for all the
presentations involved. This is the case, for instance, for the variety of
all Σ-algebras, using a simple lexicographic ordering to show termination (Lankford, private communication). Here, the problems of super-
posing the lefthand sides and reducing terms both reduce to finding
common subexpressions in the set of equations. The latter problem is
the essential problem of congruence closure, and so can be implemented
in worst-case time $O(n \log^2 n)$ and space $O(n)$.

Bücken (17) has shown that the completion algorithm, when applied to the group axioms and any group presentation over which Dehn's
algorithm applies (Dehn 32, Greenlinger 58), terminates. That is, Dehn's
algorithm is subsumed by the completion algorithm, and the only con-
tent of its proof that is actually related to group theory can be phrased
as a proof of termination of the completion algorithm.

11. Separable Equational Theories

In this section, we assume Σ is a signature with booleans. Further,
we assume that Σ contains an operator $\#$, with $\tau(\#) = s \times s \rightarrow$ boolean.
We then say that $\mathcal{E}$ is s-*separable* if and only if

1. $x \# x = FALSE \in \mathcal{E}$ for $x \in \mathcal{V}_s$
2. for all M, N in $\mathcal{G}_s$, $M \neq_g N \Rightarrow M \# N =_g TRUE$.

Note that these conditions imply that, for all ground terms M
and N of sort s, if $M =_g N$ then $M \# N =_g FALSE$, and otherwise
$M \# N =_g TRUE$; and therefore that the word problem for sort s is

decidable. For consistent s-separable theories, the validity problem for terms of sort s in the initial algebra is equivalent to a consistency problem, as follows.

Theorem. Let $\mathcal{E}$ be a consistent s-separable set of equations, and M, N be two terms of type s. Then $\mathfrak{I}(\mathcal{E}) \models M = N$ if and only if $\mathcal{E} \cup \{M = N\}$ is consistent.

Proof:

$\Rightarrow$ obvious since, if $\mathcal{E}$ is consistent, $\mathfrak{I}(\mathcal{E}) \not\models TRUE = FALSE$.

$\Leftarrow$ Assume $\mathcal{E}' = \mathcal{E} \cup \{M = N\}$ is consistent, and let σ be any ground substitution. We have $\sigma(M) \sharp \sigma(N) =_{\mathcal{E}'} FALSE$ by condition 1 of s-separability. Further, if $\sigma(M) \neq_{\mathcal{E}} \sigma(N)$, then $\sigma(M) \sharp \sigma(N) =_{\mathcal{E}}$ $TRUE$ by condition 2, and hence $\sigma(M) \sharp \sigma(N) =_{\mathcal{E}'} TRUE$. This contradicts the consistency of $\mathcal{E}'$. Therefore, $\sigma(M) =_{\mathcal{E}} \sigma(N)$, and thus $\mathfrak{I}(\Sigma) \models M = N$. $\blacksquare$

More generally, let $\mathcal{E}'$ be any set of equations $\{M_i = N_i \mid i \in I\}$, and let $\mathcal{E}$ be consistent and $\tau(M_i)$-separable for every i. Then $\mathfrak{I}(\mathcal{E}) \models M_i = N_i$ for every i in I if and only if $\mathcal{E} \cup \mathcal{E}'$ is consistent.

This theorem is inspired by Guttag (63) and Musser (118, 119), and generalizes Goguen (49) (where a data type specification amounts to a theory s-separable for every sort s). It gives us a semi-decision procedure for the truth of sentences of the form $\exists \overrightarrow{x} M \neq N$ in $\mathfrak{I}(\mathcal{E})$. This is not very surprising, since for instance in arithmetic this corresponds to checking finitely refutable statements. It allows us to limit induction to a once and for all proof of s-separability, and allows us to obtain proofs by pure equational reasoning that normally require induction. However, its practical importance seems to be limited, since consistency is not even recursively enumerable. It may be most useful for decidable theories, for which consistency is decidable too. We shall see below how it can be used in conjunction with the Knuth-Bendix extension algorithm.

Example: Let $\mathcal{E}^1 = \mathcal{E}^0 \cup \{x \sharp x = FALSE, S(x) \sharp S(y) = x \sharp y,$ $0 \sharp S(x) = TRUE, S(x) \sharp 0 = TRUE\}$. It is easy to check, by induction on $\mathcal{T}(\Sigma^0)$, that $\mathcal{E}^1$ is integer-separable and consistent. Actually $\mathfrak{I}(\mathcal{E}^1) = \mathcal{A}^0$. We will describe later how to show that $+$ is associative and commutative in $\mathfrak{I}(\mathcal{E}^1)$, using the theorem above.

The theorem above is reminiscent of the traditional observation in first-order logic that a complete theory is maximally consistent. However, s-separable does not imply complete in the traditional sense. For instance, note that $\mathfrak{I}(\mathcal{E}^1) \models 0+x = x$. However $\mathcal{M}(\mathcal{E}^1) \not\models 0+x = x$, since, for instance, $\mathcal{A}^1 \in \mathcal{M}_{\Sigma^0}(\mathcal{E}^1)$.

When the completion algorithm terminates, it may be used to decide the consistency of a theory, and may therefore be used for solving the validity problem in the initial algebra of certain separable equational theories. It must be emphasized however that this new use of the completion algorithm is different in spirit from the its use in generating a canonical form for an equational theory. Generating a canonical term rewriting system is similar to compilation: you run the algorithm only once for the theory in which you are interested, even if it is very costly. The future proofs will consist uniquely in reductions to normal forms, and are thus fairly efficient (at least intuitively). On the other hand, each proof in $\mathfrak{I}(\mathcal{E})$ will require using the completion algorithm and its associated costs (such as proofs of termination) even if $\mathcal{E}$ itself is already completed. However, disproofs may be obtained even when the completion algorithm does not terminate: as soon as $TRUE = FALSE$ is generated as a critical pair, we know that the theory is inconsistent.

We give examples of such proofs in the Appendix. In a simple theory of list structures we show the associativity of the *Append* function, defined recursively. Then we introduce the recursive definition of the *Reverse* function, and show that it verifies $Reverse(Reverse(x)) = x$. Finally, we introduce an iterative (that is, recursive only in a terminal position) version of *Reverse*, called *Reviter*, and show the equivalence of the two programs. Note that none of these proofs actually uses the inequality axioms, since no superposition with them is ever possible.

12. A Meta-unification Algorithm

In this section, we show how we can do unification in theories that admit a canonical term rewriting system. More precisely, let $\mathfrak{R}$ be a (finite) canonical term rewriting system obtained by running the completion algorithm on the set of equations $\mathcal{E}$. We describe here a meta-unification algorithm which, given any such $\mathfrak{R}$ and a finite set of variables W, generates a complete set of $\mathcal{E}$-unifiers away from W. This algorithm is due to Fay (48), with improvements by Lankford. It combines in an elegant way ordinary unification and "narrowing", the process of effecting the minimum substitution to a normal form term so that the substituted term is not in normal form (Slagle 152).

More precisely, let M be in $\mathfrak{R}$-normal form, and V be a finite set of variables containing $\Upsilon(M)$. Let u be some non-variable occurrence in M such that the subterm M/u at u is unifiable with some lefthand side of a rule in $\mathfrak{R}$ using ordinary unification. In symbols, $M/u \not\in \Upsilon$, and $\mathcal{U}_\emptyset(M/u, \lambda) \neq \emptyset$ with $\lambda \to \rho \in \mathfrak{R}$. Assume $\lambda \to \rho$ has been renamed away from V; that is, $\Upsilon(\lambda) \cap V = \emptyset$. Let σ be the minimum unifier of M/u and λ, restricted to $\Upsilon(M)$. That is, σ is the minimum substitution such that $\sigma(M/u)$ is an instance of λ. We say that σ is a *narrowing substitution* of M away from V, and we write $NS(M, V)$ for the (finite) set of such substitutions.

We are now ready to describe a (non-deterministic) $\mathcal{E}$-unification algorithm. $\mathfrak{R}$ is assumed to be a canonical term rewriting system for $\mathcal{E}$, and we write $\mathfrak{R}(M)$ for the $\mathfrak{R}$-normal form of term M.

$\mathcal{E}$-unification algorithm.

The input consists of two terms M and N of the same type, and a finite set of variables W, with $\Upsilon(M) \cup \Upsilon(N) \subseteq W$. M_i and N_i are terms of the same sort, W_i is a set of variables, θ_i is a substitution. Variables σ and S denote respectively a substitution and a finite set of substitutions.

1. Initially let $M_0 = \mathfrak{R}(M), N_0 = \mathfrak{R}(N), W_0 = W, \theta_0 = \emptyset, i = 0$.

2. If $M_i = N_i$ then stop with answer θ_i. Otherwise let $S = NS(M_i, W_i) \cup NS(N_i, W_i)$, to which we add the minimum unifier of M_i and N_i if it exists. Select σ in S. Let $\theta_{i+1} = \sigma \circ \theta_i$. If for some x in W, $\theta_{i+1}(x)$ is not a normal form, stop with failure. Otherwise, let $M_{i+1} = \mathfrak{R}(\sigma(M_i)), N_{i+1} = \mathfrak{R}(\sigma(N_i)), W_{i+1} = W_i \cup \mathfrak{I}(\sigma)$, increment i by 1 and go to 2.

This algorithm can be viewed as non-deterministic, or equivalently as an algorithm enumerating a finitely-branching tree. This tree may be infinite, but if M and N are $\mathcal{E}$-unifiable, then there will be some successfully terminating execution sequence, that is, there will be a success node at a finite level in the tree. Actually, a stronger result holds, as follows. Let $V = \Upsilon(M) \cup \Upsilon(N)$, and let $\mathcal{U}_g(M,N,W)$ be the (possibly infinite) set of all answers θ_i, restricted to V; that is, $\mathcal{U}_g(M,N,W) = \{\{\langle x, \theta_i(x)\rangle \mid x \in V\} \mid$ the algorithm stops with answer $\theta_i\}$.

Theorem. $\mathcal{U}_g(M,N,W)$ is a complete set of $\mathcal{E}$-unifiers of M and N away from W.

For a proof, see Hullot (79) which expands Fay (48).

Various optimizations of the algorithm are possible. In general, however, the algorithm will not enumerate a minimal set of unifiers, even when such a set exists. This is the case for associativity, for instance, for which Plotkin's algorithm (Plotkin 136) is preferred. It is an interesting open problem to refine of the algorithm above in such a way that it indeed generates a minimal set whenever possible. (The "obvious" solution, consisting of throwing away solutions subsumed by others, is not satisfactory, since the result may not be complete for theories which do not admit minimal complete sets of unifiers.)

This algorithm gave the first known solution to unification in group theory, using for $\mathcal{R}$ the canonical set shown in the appendix.

13. Extensions and Combinations of Equational Theories

In previous sections we have discussed formalisms for describing and manipulating equational systems for different sorts of objects, and in particular have discussed methods for handling decision problems for particular equational theories. However, it is clear that in practice we want to "combine" equational theories, and in this section we discuss research presently being done on combinations of such theories. (See also Burstall and Goguen (21).)

It is also clear that in practice we wish to reason about formulas rather than just equations. We therefore wish to extend the language of equational calculi, in particular, to include boolean connectives and conditional expressions of the form if ... then ... else.

Consider the following axiomatization of the theory of arrays:

select(store$(a,i,e),j$) = if $i = j$ then e else select(a,j)
store$(a,i,$ select(a,i)) = a
store(store$(a,i,e),j,f$) =
    if $i = j$ then store(a,i,f) else store(store$(a,j,f),i,e$).

(The equality symbol appearing in the literal $i = j$ is equality in the theory of the array indices.) An obvious use of this axiomatization is to prove formulas such as $i \neq j \supset \text{select}(\text{store}(a, i, e), j) = \text{select}(a, j)$.

Consider the following (weak) axiomatization $\mathfrak{R}$ for the the reals under addition ("weak" because the axioms have other models, such as the integers under addition):

$$x + 0 = x$$
$$x + (-x) = 0$$
$$(x + y) + z = x + (y + z)$$
$$x + y = y + x$$
$$x \not< x$$
$$x < y \lor y < x \lor x = y$$
$$x < y \supset \neg(y < x)$$
$$x < y \land y < z \supset x < z$$
$$x < y \supset x + z < y + z$$
$$0 < 1.$$

Using these two theories, we may wish to prove the theorem $\text{select}(\text{store}(a, 0, e), 1) = \text{select}(a, 1)$; this is an example of a theorem in the "combination" of the two individual theories.

Some results are known on the decidability and complexity of combinations of theories such as these (Nelson and Oppen (122, 123), Oppen (129, 130)). As we shall see, equations between variables play a crucial role.

We assume that we have several quantifier-free theories formalized in classical first-order logic with equality, extended to include the three-argument conditional if-then-else. The symbols $=, \land, \lor, \neg, \supset, \forall, \exists$ and if-then-else are common to all theories; we call them the *logical symbols*. Each theory is characterized in the usual way by its set of *non-logical symbols* and *non-logical axioms*.

Let us give some examples. Define the quantifier-free theory $\mathcal{A}$ of arrays to have **store** and **select** as non-logical symbols and the axioms given above. Define the quantifier-free theory $\mathfrak{R}$ of reals under addition to $0, 1, +, <$ as non-logical symbols and axioms as given above. Define the theory $\mathcal{L}$ of list structure to have **car**, **cdr**, **cons** and **atom** as non-logical symbols and to have the following axiomatization:

$$car(cons(x, y)) = x$$
$$cdr(cons(x, y)) = y$$
$$\neg\ atom(x) \supset\ cons(car(x), cdr(x)) = x$$
$$\neg\ atom(cons(x, y)).$$

Finally, define the theory $\mathcal{S}$ whose non-logical symbols are all unin-terpreted function symbols. $\mathcal{S}$ has no axioms, so it is just the quantifier-free theory of equality.

A theory is *stably infinite* if, for all quantifier-free formulas F, if F has a model in the theory, then it has an infinite model. Note that any theory that has no finite models is stably infinite; therefore $\mathcal{B}$ is stably infinite. It is not difficult to prove that $\mathcal{S}, \mathcal{L}$ and $\mathcal{A}$ are stably infinite.

Let $\mathcal{T}_1, \mathcal{T}_2, \ldots, \mathcal{T}_k$ be k theories with no common non-logical sym-bols. Their *combination*, denoted $\bigcup_i(\mathcal{T}_i)$, is the theory whose set of non-logical symbols is the union of the sets of non-logical symbols of the $\mathcal{T}_i$, and whose set of axioms is the union of the sets of axioms of the $\mathcal{T}_i$. We do not consider combining theories which share non-logical symbols. The following theorem is proved by Nelson and Oppen (123).

Theorem. Let $\mathcal{T}_1, \mathcal{T}_2, \ldots, \mathcal{T}_k$ be k decidable and stably-infinite quantifier-free theories with no common non-logical symbols. Then $\bigcup_i(\mathcal{T}_i)$ is decidable.

The proof is constructive; a decision procedure for the union is described for determining the satisfiability of conjunctions of literals. The decision procedure "combines" the decision procedures for the in-dividual theories as follows.

Suppose we have just two theories $\mathcal{S}$ and $\mathcal{T}$ and wish to deter-mine if a quantifier-free conjunction F of literals in their combined language is satisfiable. We assume that $F \equiv F_{\mathcal{S}} \wedge F_{\mathcal{T}}$, where $F_{\mathcal{S}}$ is a conjunction of literals in the language of $\mathcal{S}$ and $F_{\mathcal{T}}$ is a conjunction of literals in the language of $\mathcal{T}$. (Any formula can be put in this form by introducing new variables; for instance, corresponding to the above formula $select(store(a, 0, e), 1) = select(a, 1)$ is the equivalent formula $select(store(a, x, e), y) = select(a, y) \wedge x = 0 \wedge y = 1$ in the required form.) The following algorithm determines whether F is satisfiable. The algorithm uses the variables $F_{\mathcal{S}}$ and $F_{\mathcal{T}}$ which contain conjunctions of literals.

Equality Propagation Procedure.

1. [Unsatisfiable?] If either $F_{\mathcal{T}}$ or $F_{\mathcal{T}'}$ is unsatisfiable, then F is unsatisfiable.

2. [Propagate equalities.] If either $F_{\mathcal{T}}$ or $F_{\mathcal{T}'}$ entails some equality between variables not entailed by the other, then add the equality as a new conjunct to the one that does not entail it. Go to step 1.

3. [Case split necessary?] If either $F_{\mathcal{T}}$ or $F_{\mathcal{T}'}$ entails a disjunction $u_1 = v_1 \vee \ldots \vee u_k = v_k$ of equalities between variables, without entailing any of the equalities alone, then apply the procedure recursively to the k formulas $F_{\mathcal{T}} \wedge F_{\mathcal{T}'} \wedge u_1 = v_1, \ldots, F_{\mathcal{T}} \wedge F_{\mathcal{T}'} \wedge u_k = v_k$. If any of these formulas are satisfiable, then F is satisfiable. Otherwise F is unsatisfiable.

4. If we reach this step, F is satisfiable.

The following theorems on the complexity of combinations of theories appear in Oppen (130).

Theorem. Let $\mathcal{T}_1, \mathcal{T}_2, \ldots, \mathcal{T}_k$ be as before. If the satisfiability problems for each of the $\mathcal{T}_i$ is in NP, then the satisfiability problem for $\bigcup_i (\mathcal{T}_i)$ is in NP and hence NP-complete. Otherwise the complexity of the satisfiability problem is dominated by the maximum of the complexities of the satisfiability problems for the $\mathcal{T}_i$.

Corollary. The satisfiability problem for $\mathcal{R} \cup \mathcal{S} \cup \mathcal{A} \cup \mathcal{L}$, that is, the quantifier-free theory of reals, arrays, list structure and uninterpreted function symbols under $+$, $\leq$, store, select, cons, car and cdr is NP-complete.

However, under certain conditions, a result on deterministic time is possible. A formula is *non-convex* if it entails a disjunction of equalities between variables without entailing any of the equalities alone; otherwise it is *convex*. Define a theory to be *convex* if every conjunction of literals in the language of the theory is convex; otherwise if is *non-convex*.

Some of the theories considered above are convex, others non-convex. The theories of equality with uninterpreted function symbols and of list structure under car, cdr and cons are convex (Nelson and Oppen 122). The theory of rationals under $+$ and $\leq$ is convex: the solution set of a conjunction of linear inequalities is a convex set; the solution set of a disjunction of equalities is a finite union of hyperplanes; and a convex set cannot be contained in a finite union of hyperplanes unless it is contained in one of them. The theories of integers under addition and of integers under successor are non-convex. For instance, the formula $1 \leq x \leq 2 \wedge y = 1 \wedge z = 2$ entails the disjunction $x = y \vee x = z$ without entailing either equality alone. The theory of arrays is non-convex. For instance, the formula $x = \text{select(store}(a, i, e), j) \wedge y = \text{select}(a, j)$ entails $i = j \vee x = y$. The theory of the reals under multiplication is not convex; for example, $xy = 0 \wedge z = 0$ entails the disjunction $x = z \vee y = z$. The theory of sets is also non-convex; for example, consider $\{a, b, c\} \cap \{c, d, e\} \neq \emptyset$.

Define the *DNF satisfiability problem* to be the problem of determining if a quantifier-free formula in disjunctive normal form is satisfiable.

Theorem. Let $\mathcal{T}_1, \mathcal{T}_2, \ldots, \mathcal{T}_k$ be decidable, convex, quantifier-free theories with no common non-logical symbols and with deterministic polynomial time DNF satisfiability problems. Then $\bigcup_i (\mathcal{T}_i)$ also has a deterministic polynomial time DNF satisfiability problem.

Thus, for instance, the theory $\mathcal{B} \cup \mathcal{E}$ has a polynomial time decision procedure for formulas in disjunctive normal form. This follows from Khachian (83) and Nelson and Oppen (122).

The critical notion in these results on combinations of sorted theories is that of equality between variables. In the equality-sharing decision procedure given above for combining decision procedures, the only information propagated between decision procedures is either an equality between variables or a disjunction of equalities between variables. And the complexity results show that the complexity of the combination is critically related to the "convexity" of the theories — whether or not conjunctions of literals can entail disjunctions of equalities.

These results can therefore be looked at as reducing the decision problem for non-equational theories to simpler decision problems of equational theories.

14. Further Results

For lack of space, a number of recent results are not described here. Let us indicate briefly a few promising directions.

The Knuth-Bendix characterization of confluence for nœtherian term-rewriting systems may be extended to congruence classes of terms under certain conditions. This has been done for commutativity (Lankford and Ballantyne 98), for commutativity and associativity (Lankford and Ballantyne 100, Peterson and Stickel 132), and in the general case for certain left-linear term rewriting systems (Huet 73). The completion algorithm can be extended to these cases, generating canonical systems for abelian groups, abelian rings, distributive lattices. Degano and Sirovich (31) use a complete set of such rewrite rules to show the decidability of equivalence for a new class of primitive recursive functions. Ballantyne and Lankford (4) show that this extension of the completion algorithm solves the uniform word problem for finitely presented commutative semigroups — it is conjectured that these methods extend to abelian groups and rings.

When term rewriting systems are not nœtherian, the problem arises of how to compute the normal forms of terms which have one. This problem of order of evaluation has well-known solutions for ordinary recursive definitions (Vuillemin 161, Downey and Sethi 36, Berry and Lévy 7), but is harder for more general term rewritings. Huet and Lévy (77) give a strong sequentiality criterion permitting efficient implementations of correct interpreters for term rewriting systems whose lefthand sides are linear, and which have no critical pairs. See also Hoffmann and O'Donnell (69) for related results.

15. Acknowledgments

We thank Ron Book, Bob Boyer, Nachum Dershowitz, Joe Goguen and Jean-Jacques Lévy for their many helpful comments. We especially thank Dallas Lankford for his lively and helpful correspondence.

16. Appendix

This appendix is an image of a computer session run on the Stanford Artificial Intelligence Laboratory KL-10. The program, developed by Jean-Marie Hullot at IRIA, is written in VLISP (developed at

Université de Vincennes by Patrick Greussay and Jérôme Chailloux).
The times given are for the program run interpretively.

We first give an example of the Knuth-Bendix completion algorithm compiling a canonical term rewriting system from the standard
set of three axioms for groups. User input is preceded by a question
mark. Comments are surrounded by square brackets.

```
? (kbini)
MODE ? auto
LIST OF OPERATORS ? (O + I)
WEIGHT OF O ? 1
WEIGHT OF + ? 0
WEIGHT OF I ? 0
MINIMUM WEIGHT OF A PURE WORD ? 1
LIST OF INFIX OPERATORS ? (+)
= READY
= ; time = 6 ms ;
```

[Now all the weights are set up, so that the termination will be proved
automatically, using the original Knuth-Bendix method.]

```
? (kb group)
```

R1 : O+X ⟶X	GIVEN
R2 : I(X)+X ⟶O	GIVEN
R3 : (X+Y)+Z ⟶X+(Y+Z)	GIVEN
R4 : I(X)+(X+Y) ⟶Y	FROM R3 AND R2
R5 : I(O)+X ⟶X	FROM R4 AND R1
R6 : I(I(X))+O ⟶X	FROM R4 AND R2
R7 : I(I(O))+X ⟶X	FROM R5 AND R4
R8 : I(O) ⟶O	FROM R7 AND R2

```
R5 DELETED
REWRITE RULES : R8 R1 FOR LEFT PART
R7 DELETED
REWRITE RULES : R8 R8 R1 FOR LEFT PART
```

R9 : I(I(I(X)))+X ⟶O	FROM R6 AND R4

R10 : I(I(X))+Y —⟶X+Y   FROM R4 AND R4
R6 REPLACED BY :
X+O = X
REWRITE RULES : R10 FOR LEFT PART
R9 DELETED
REWRITE RULES : R10 R2 FOR LEFT PART

R11 : X+O —⟶X   FROM R6

R12 : I(I(X)) —⟶X   FROM R11 AND R10
R10 DELETED
REWRITE RULES : R12 FOR LEFT PART

R13 : X+I(X) —⟶O   FROM R12 AND R2

R14 : X+(I(X)+Y) —⟶Y   FROM R12 AND R4

R15 : X+(Y+I(X+Y)) —⟶O   FROM R13 AND R3

R16 : X+I(Y+X) —⟶I(Y)   FROM R15 AND R4
R15 DELETED
REWRITE RULES : R16 R13 FOR LEFT PART

R17 : I(X+Y) —⟶I(Y)+I(X)   FROM R16 AND R4
R16 DELETED
REWRITE RULES : R17 R14 FOR LEFT PART

COMPLETE SET: CGROUP
R1 : O+X —⟶X
R2 : I(X)+X —⟶O
R3 : (X+Y)+Z —⟶X+(Y+Z)
R4 : I(X)+(X+Y) —⟶Y
R8 : I(O) —⟶O
R11 : X+O —⟶X
R12 : I(I(X)) —⟶X
R13 : X+I(X) —⟶O
R14 : X+(I(X)+Y) —⟶Y
R17 : I(X+Y) —⟶I(Y)+I(X)

9-Dec-79 21:19:43
= END
= ; time = 4790 ms ;

[The file PROOFS contains a simple axiomatization of list structures, simple recursive definitions of list manipulation programs, and lemmas proving their correctness. LISP is the axiomatization of list structures; note that it is list-separable.]

? (library proofs)
= PROOFS
= ; time = 41 ms ;
? (kbini)
MODE ? free
LIST OF INFIX OPERATORS ? (‡)
= READY
= ; time = 2 ms ;
? (kb lisp)

X‡X = FALSE   GIVEN
COMMAND ? y
R1 : X‡X —≫FALSE

CONS(X,Y)‡NULL = TRUE   GIVEN
COMMAND ? y
R2 : CONS(X,Y)‡NULL —≫TRUE

NULL‡CONS(X,Y) = TRUE   GIVEN
COMMAND ? y
R3 : NULL‡CONS(X,Y) —≫TRUE

CONS(X,Y)‡CONS(Z,U) = IF(X‡Z,TRUE,Y‡U)   GIVEN
COMMAND ? y
R4 : CONS(X,Y)‡CONS(Z,U) —≫IF(X‡Z,TRUE,Y‡U)

IF(TRUE,X,Y) = X   GIVEN
COMMAND ? y
R5 : IF(TRUE,X,Y) —≫X

IF(FALSE,X,Y) = Y   GIVEN
COMMAND ? y
R6 : IF(FALSE,X,Y) —≫Y

APPEND(NULL,X) = X   GIVEN
COMMAND ? y
R7 : APPEND(NULL,X) —≫X

APPEND(CONS(X,Y),Z) = CONS(X,APPEND(Y,Z))   GIVEN
COMMAND ? y
R8 : APPEND(CONS(X,Y),Z) —>CONS(X,APPEND(Y,Z))

COMPLETE SET: CLISP
R1 : X#X —>FALSE
R2 : CONS(X,Y)#NULL —>TRUE
R3 : NULL#CONS(X,Y) —>TRUE
R4 : CONS(X,Y)#CONS(Z,U) —>IF(X#Z,TRUE,Y#U)
R5 : IF(TRUE,X,Y) —>X
R6 : IF(FALSE,X,Y) —>Y
R7 : APPEND(NULL,X) —>X
R8 : APPEND(CONS(X,Y),Z) —>CONS(X,APPEND(Y,Z))

9-Dec-79 22:13:34
= END
= ; time = 905 ms ;
[Let's prove that APPEND is associative. PROOF1 contains the corresponding lemma.]
? (provelemma proof1)

APPEND(APPEND(X,Y),Z) = APPEND(X,APPEND(Y,Z))   GIVEN
COMMAND ? y
R9 : APPEND(APPEND(X,Y),Z) —>APPEND(X,APPEND(Y,Z))

COMPLETE SET: CPROOF1
R1 : X#X —>FALSE
R2 : CONS(X,Y)#NULL —>TRUE
R3 : NULL#CONS(X,Y) —>TRUE
R4 : CONS(X,Y)#CONS(Z,U) —>IF(X#Z,TRUE,Y#U)
R5 : IF(TRUE,X,Y) —>X
R6 : IF(FALSE,X,Y) —>Y
R7 : APPEND(NULL,X) —>X
R8 : APPEND(CONS(X,Y),Z) —>CONS(X,APPEND(Y,Z))
R9 : APPEND(APPEND(X,Y),Z) —>APPEND(X,APPEND(Y,Z))

9-Dec-79 22:16:09
= END
= ; time = 640 ms ;

[The resulting set is consistent, proving the lemma. Next we enrich our lisp theory with the recursive definition of the function REV, that reverses a list. We then prove that REV(REV(x))=x for every list x.]

? (kb clisp proof2)

R1 : X‡X ⟶FALSE

R2 : CONS(X,Y)‡NULL ⟶TRUE

R3 : NULL‡CONS(X,Y) ⟶TRUE

R4 : CONS(X,Y)‡CONS(Z,U) ⟶IF(X‡Z,TRUE,Y‡U)

R5 : IF(TRUE,X,Y) ⟶X

R6 : IF(FALSE,X,Y) ⟶Y

R7 : APPEND(NULL,X) ⟶X

R8 : APPEND(CONS(X,Y),Z) ⟶CONS(X,APPEND(Y,Z))

REV(NULL) = NULL   GIVEN

COMMAND ? y

R9 : REV(NULL) ⟶NULL

REV(CONS(X,Y)) = APPEND(REV(Y),CONS(X,NULL))   GIVEN

COMMAND ? y

R10 : REV(CONS(X,Y)) ⟶APPEND(REV(Y),CONS(X,NULL))

REV(REV(X)) = X   GIVEN

COMMAND ? y

R11 : REV(REV(X)) ⟶X

REV(APPEND(REV(X),CONS(Y,NULL))) = CONS(Y,X)

                                          FROM R11 AND R10

COMMAND ? y

R12 : REV(APPEND(REV(X),CONS(Y,NULL))) ⟶CONS(Y,X)

REV(APPEND(X,CONS(Y,NULL))) = CONS(Y,REV(X))

                                          FROM R12 AND R11

COMMAND ? y

R13 : REV(APPEND(X,CONS(Y,NULL))) ⟶CONS(Y,REV(X))

R12 DELETED

REWRITE RULES : R13 R11 FOR LEFT PART

COMPLETE SET: CPROOF2

R1 : X‡X ⟶FALSE

R2 : CONS(X,Y)‡NULL ⟶TRUE

R3 : NULL≠CONS(X,Y) —→TRUE
R4 : CONS(X,Y)≠CONS(Z,U) —→IF(X≠Z,TRUE,Y≠U)
R5 : IF(TRUE,X,Y) —→X
R6 : IF(FALSE,X,Y) —→Y
R7 : APPEND(NULL,X) —→X
R8 : APPEND(CONS(X,Y),Z) —→CONS(X,APPEND(Y,Z))
R9 : REV(NULL) —→NULL
R10 : REV(CONS(X,Y)) —→APPEND(REV(Y),CONS(X,NULL))
R11 : REV(REV(X)) —→X
R13 : REV(APPEND(X,CONS(Y,NULL))) —→CONS(Y,REV(X))

9-Dec-79 22:21:57
= END
= ; time = 2272 ms ;

[Complete and consistent! That is, REV(REV(x))=x in LISP. Notice
that the termination test has been left to the user, because the Knuth-
Bendix ordering could not be used on rule R10. The orientation of each
rule was given by the user after a COMMAND? ("y" means keep left
to right.) This recursive REVERSE is not very efficient. Let's write an
iterative version, called REVITER, and prove the equivalence of the two
programs: REV(x)=REVITER(x,NULL). We need the associativity
of APPEND, and the lemma REVITER(x,y)=APPEND(REV(x),y).
Note: this crucial lemma is not assumed; it is proved as well.]
? (kb cproof1 proof3)

R1 : X≠X —→FALSE
R2 : CONS(X,Y)≠NULL —→TRUE
R3 : NULL≠CONS(X,Y) —→TRUE
R4 : CONS(X,Y)≠CONS(Z,U) —→IF(X≠Z,TRUE,Y≠U)
R5 : IF(TRUE,X,Y) —→X
R6 : IF(FALSE,X,Y) —→Y
R7 : APPEND(NULL,X) —→X
R8 : APPEND(CONS(X,Y),Z) —→CONS(X,APPEND(Y,Z))
R9 : APPEND(APPEND(X,Y),Z) —→APPEND(X,APPEND(Y,Z))

REV(NULL) = NULL   GIVEN
COMMAND ? y
R10 : REV(NULL) —→NULL

REV(CONS(X,Y)) = APPEND(REV(Y),CONS(X,NULL))   GIVEN

COMMAND ? y
R11 : REV(CONS(X,Y)) —⟫APPEND(REV(Y),CONS(X,NULL))

REVITER(NULL,X) = X   GIVEN
COMMAND ? y
R12 : REVITER(NULL,X) —⟫X

REVITER(CONS(X,Y),Z) = REVITER(Y,CONS(X,Z))   GIVEN
COMMAND ? y
R13 : REVITER(CONS(X,Y),Z) —⟫REVITER(Y,CONS(X,Z))

APPEND(REV(X),Y) = REVITER(X,Y)   GIVEN
COMMAND ? y
R14 : APPEND(REV(X),Y) —⟫REVITER(X,Y)
R11 REPLACED BY :
REV(CONS(X,Y)) = REVITER(Y,CONS(X,NULL))
REWRITE RULES : R14 FOR RIGHT PART

REV(CONS(X,Y)) = REVITER(Y,CONS(X,NULL))   FROM R11
COMMAND ? y
R15 : REV(CONS(X,Y)) —⟫REVITER(Y,CONS(X,NULL))

REV(X) = REVITER(X,NULL)   GIVEN
COMMAND ? y
R16 : REV(X) —⟫REVITER(X,NULL)
R10 DELETED
REWRITE RULES : R16 R12 FOR LEFT PART
R14 REPLACED BY :
APPEND(REVITER(X,NULL),Y) = REVITER(X,Y)
REWRITE RULES : R16 FOR LEFT PART
R15 DELETED
REWRITE RULES : R16 R13 FOR LEFT PART

APPEND(REVITER(X,NULL),Y) = REVITER(X,Y)   FROM R14
COMMAND ? y
R17 : APPEND(REVITER(X,NULL),Y) —⟫REVITER(X,Y)

APPEND(REVITER(X,Y),Z) = REVITER(X,APPEND(Y,Z))
                                        FROM R17 AND R9
COMMAND ? y
R18 : APPEND(REVITER(X,Y),Z) —⟫REVITER(X,APPEND(Y,Z))

R17 DELETED
REWRITE RULES : R18 R7 FOR LEFT PART

COMPLETE SET: CPROOF3
R1 : X$X —>FALSE
R2 : CONS(X,Y)$NULL -->TRUE
R3 : NULL$CONS(X,Y) —>TRUE
R4 : CONS(X,Y)$CONS(Z,U) —>IF(X$Z,TRUE,Y$U)
R5 : IF(TRUE,X,Y) —>X
R6 : IF(FALSE,X,Y) —>Y
R7 : APPEND(NULL,X) —>X
R8 : APPEND(CONS(X,Y),Z) —>CONS(X,APPEND(Y,Z))
R9 : APPEND(APPEND(X,Y),Z) —>APPEND(X,APPEND(Y,Z))
R12 : REVITER(NULL,X) —>X
R13 : REVITER(CONS(X,Y),Z) —>REVITER(Y,CONS(X,Z))
R16 : REV(X) —>REVITER(X,NULL)
R18 : APPEND(REVITER(X,Y),Z) —>REVITER(X,APPEND(Y,Z))

9-Dec-79 22:36:34
= END
= ; time = 3358 ms ;

---

17. References

1. Ackermann W., *Solvable Cases of the Decision Problem*. North-Holland, Amsterdam, 1954.

2. Aho A., Sethi R. and Ullman J., *Code Optimization and Finite Church-Rosser Systems*. in Proceedings of Courant Computer Science Symposium 5, Ed. Rustin R., Prentice Hall (1972).

3. Aubin R., *Mechanizing Structural Induction*. Ph.D. thesis, U. of Edinburgh, Edinburgh 1976.

4. Ballantyne A.M. and Lankford D.S., *New Decision Algorithms for Finitely Presented Commutative Semigroups*. Report MTP-4, Department of Mathematics, Louisiana Tech. U., May 1979.

5. Baxter L. D., *An Efficient Unification Algorithm*. Technical Report CS-73-23, Dept. of Applied Analysis and Computer Science, U. of Waterloo, 1973.

6. Bergman G.M., *The Diamond Lemma for Ring Theory.* Advances in Math. 29 (1978), 178–218.

7. Berry G. and Lévy J.J., *Minimal and Optimal Computations of Recursive Programs.* JACM 26,1 (1979).

8. Birkhoff G., *On the Structure of Abstract Algebras.* Proc. Cambridge Phil. Soc. 31 (1935), 433–454.

9. Birkhoff G. and Lipson J.D., *Heterogeneous Algebras.* Journal of Combinatorial Theory 8 (1970), 115–133.

10. Boone W., *The Word Problem.* Ann. of Math. 2,70 (1959), 207–265.

11. Boyer R. and Moore J, *Proving Theorems About LISP Functions.* JACM 22 (1975), 129–144.

12. Boyer R. and Moore J, *A Lemma Driven Automatic Theorem Prover for Recursive Function Theory.* 5th International Joint Conference on Artificial Intelligence (1977), 511–519.

13. Boyer R. and Moore J, *A Computational Logic.* Academic Press, 1979.

14. Brainerd W.S., *Tree Generating Regular Systems.* Information and Control 14 (1969), 217–231.

15. Brand D., Darringer J. and Joyner J., *Completeness of Conditional Reductions.* Symposium on Automatic Deduction, 1979.

16. Brown T., *A Structured Design Method for Specialized Proof Procedures.* Ph.D. Thesis, California Inst. of Tech., Pasadena, California, 1975.

17. Bücken H., *Reduction Systems and Small Cancellation Theory.* Proc. Fourth Workshop on Automated Deduction, (1979), 53–59.

18. Burstall R.M., *Proving Properties of Programs by Structural Induction.* Computer J. 12 (1969), 41–48.

19. Burstall R.M., *Design Considerations for a Functional Programming Language.* Infotech State of the Art Conference, Copenhagen, 1977.

20. Burstall R.M. and Darlington J., *A Transformation System for Developing Recursive Programs.* JACM 24 (1977), 44–67.

21. Burstall R.M. and Goguen J.A., *Putting Theories Together to Make Specifications*. 5th International Joint Conference on Artificial Intelligence (1977), 1045–1058.

22. Cadiou J.M., *Recursive Definitions of Partial Functions and Their Computations*. PhD Thesis, Computer Science Department, Stanford U., 1972.

23. Cardoza E., Lipton R., and Meyer A., *Exponential Space Complete Problems for Petri Nets and Commutative Semigroups*. Proceedings of the Eighth ACM Symposium on Theory of Computing, May 1976, 50-54.

24. Church A., *The Calculi of Lambda-Conversion*. Princeton U. Press, Princeton N.J. (1941).

25. Church A. and Rosser J.B., *Some Properties of Conversion*. Transactions of AMS 39 (1936), 472–482.

26. Cohen P. J., *Decision Procedures for Real and p-adic Fields*. Comm. Pure and Appl. Math. 22 (1969), 131–151.

27. Cohn P.M., *Universal Algebra*. Harper and Row, New York, 1965.

28. Collins G., *Quantifier Elimination for Real Closed Fields by Cylindrical Algebraic Decomposition*. Proc. 2nd GI Conference on Automata and Formal Languages, Kaiserslauten, 1975. Lecture Notes in Computer Science, Springer-Verlag, to appear.

29. Colmerauer A., *Les grammaires de métamorphose*. Rapport interne, U. de Marseille-Luminy, 1975.

30. Courcelle B., *Infinite Trees in Normal Form and Recursive Equations Having a Unique Solution*. Rapport 7906, U. de Bordeaux 1, UER de Mathématiques et Informatique, Février 1979. To appear Math. Systems Theory.

31. Degano P. and Sirovich F., *On Solving the Equivalence Problem for a Sub-class of Primitive Recursive Functions*. Note Scientifiche S-79-18, Istituto di Scienze dell'Informazione, Pisa, Giugno 1979.

32. Dehn M., *Uber unendliche diskontinuierliche Gruppen*. Math. Ann. 71 (1911), 116–144.

33. Dershowitz N., *A Note on Simplification Orderings*. Information Processing Letters 9,5 (1979), 212–215.

34. Dershowitz N., *Orderings for Term-rewriting Systems*. Proc. 20th Symposium on Foundations of Computer Science (1979), 123–131. To appear Theoretical Computer Science.

35. Dershowitz N. and Manna Z., *Proving Termination with Multiset Orderings*. CACM 22 (1979), 465–476.

36. Downey P.J. and Sethi R., *Correct Computation Rules for Recursive Languages*. SIAM J. on Computing 5,3 (1976), 378–401.

37. Downey P. and Sethi R., *Assignment Commands with Array References*. JACM (1978), volume 25, no. 4.

38. Downey P., Sethi R. and Tarjan R. E., *Variations on the Common Subexpression Problem*. To appear JACM, 1980.

39. Ehrig H. and Rosen B.K., *Commutativity of Independent Transformations on Complex Objects*. IBM Research Report RC 6251, 1976.

40. Emelichev V. A., *Commutative Semigroups with One Defining Relation*. Shuya Gosudarstvennyi Pedagogicheskii Institut Uchenye Zapiski, vol. 6, 1958, 227-242.

41. Evans T., *The Word Problem for Abstract Algebras*. J. London Math. Soc. 26 (1951), 64–71.

42. Evans T., *Embeddability and the Word Problem*. J. London Math. soc. 28 (1953), 76–80.

43. Evans T., *On Multiplicative Systems Defined by Generators and Relations 1., Normal Form Theorems*. Proc. Cambridge Phil. Soc. 47 (1951), 637–649.

44. Evans T., *Some Solvable Word Problems*. Proc. Conf. on Decision Problems in Algebra, Oxford, 1976. To appear, North-Holland, Amsterdam.

45. Evans T., *Word Problems*. Bulletin of the AMS 84,5 (1978), 789–802.

46. Evans T., Mandelberg K. and Neff M.F., *Embedding Algebras with Solvable Word Problems in Simple Algebras. Some Boone-Higman Type Theorems*. Proc. Logic Colloq., U. of Bristol, 1973. North-Holland, Amsterdam, 1975, 259–277.

47. Fay M., *First-order Unification in an Equational Theory*. Master Thesis, U. of California at Santa Cruz. Tech. Report 78-5-002, May 1978.

48. Fay M., *First-order Unification in an Equational Theory*. 4th Workshop on Automated Deduction, Austin, Texas, Feb. 1979, 161–167.

49. Goguen J.A., *Proving Inductive Hypotheses Without Induction and Evaluating Expressions with Non-terminating Rules*. Unpublished manuscript, Oct. 1979.

50. Goguen J.A. and Tardo J.J., *An Introduction to OBJ, a Language for Writing and Testing Formal Algebraic Specifications*. Specifications of Reliable Sofware Conference, Boston, 1979.

51. Goguen J., Thatcher J., Wagner E. and Wright J., *Abstract Data Types as Initial Algebras and Correctness of Data Representations*. Conference on Computer Graphics, Pattern Recognition and Data Structure, May 1975, 89–93.

52. Goguen J.A., Thatcher J.W., Wagner E.G. and Wright J.B., *Initial Algebras Semantics and Continuous Algebras*. JACM 24 (1977), 68–95.

53. Goguen J.A., Thatcher J.W. and Wagner E.G., *An Initial Algebra Approach to the Specification, Correctness, and Implementation of Abstract Data Types*. "Current Trends in Programming Methodology", Vol 4, Ed. Yeh R., Prentice-Hall (1978), 80–149.

54. Goldfarb W., *The Undecidability of the Second-order Unification Problem*. Unpublished manuscript, July 1979.

55. Gorn S., *Handling the Growth by Definition of Mechanical Languages*. Proc. Spring Joint Computer Conf. (1967), 213–224.

56. Gorn S., *Explicit Definitions and Linguistic Dominoes*. "Systems and Computer Science", Eds Hart J. and Takasu S., U. of Toronto Press (1967), 77–115.

57. Gorn S., *On the Conclusive Validation of Symbol Manipulation Processes (How Do You Know It has To Work?)*. J. of the Franklin Institute, 296,6 (1973), 499–518.

58. Greenlinger M., *Dehn's Algorithm for the Word Problem*. Communications on Pure and Applied Mathematics, 13 (1960), 67–83.

59. Griesmer J.H. and Jenks R.D., *SCRATCHPAD/1. An Interactive Facility for Symbolic Mathematics.* Proceedings 2nd Symposium on Symbolic and Algebraic Manipulation, Ed. Petrick S., Los Angeles, March 1971.

60. Guard J.R., Oglesby F.C., Bennett J.H. and Settle L.G., *Semiautomated Mathematics.* JACM 16 (1969), 49–62.

61. Guttag J., *The Specification and Application to Programming of Abstract Data Types.* Ph. D. thesis, U. of Toronto, 1975.

62. Guttag J.V., *Abstract Data Types and the Development of Data Structures.* CACM 20 (1977), 397–404.

63. Guttag J.V. and Horning J.J., *The Algebraic Specification of Abstract Data Types.* Acta Informatica 10 (1978), 27–52.

64. Guttag J.V., Horowitz E. and Musser D., *The Design of Data Type Specifications.* "Current Trends in Programming Methodology", Vol 4, Data Structuring, Ed. Yeh R., Prentice Hall, 1978.

65. Guttag J.V., Horowitz E. and Musser D.R., *Abstract Data Types and Software Validation.* CACM 21 (1978), 1048–1064.

66. Hall P., *Some Word Problems.* J. London Math. Soc. 33 (1958), 482–496.

67. Hindley R., *An Abstract Form of the Church-Rosser Theorem I.* J. of Symbolic Logic 34,4 (1969), 545–560.

68. Hindley R., *An Abstract Form of the Church-Rosser Theorem II: Applications.* J. of Symbolic Logic 39,1 (1974), 1–21.

69. Hoffmann M. and O'Donnell M., *Interpreter Generation Using Tree Pattern Matching.* 6th ACM Conference on Principles of Programming Languages (1979).

70. Huet G., *The Undecidability of Unification in Third Order Logic.* Information and Control 22 (1973), 257–267.

71. Huet G., *A Unification Algorithm for Typed Lambda Calculus.* Theoretical Computer Science, 1,1 (1975), 27–57.

72. Huet G., *Résolution d'équations dans des langages d'ordre 1, 2, ..., ω.* Thèse d'Etat, Université de Paris VII, 1976.

73. Huet G., *Confluent Reductions: Abstract Properties and Applications to Term Rewriting Systems.* 18th IEEE Symposium on Foundations of Computer Science (1977), 30–45.

74. Huet G., *An Algorithm to Generate the Basis of Solutions to Homogenous Linear Diophantine Equations.* Information Processing Letters 7,3 (1978), 144–147.

75. Huet G. and Lang B., *Proving and Applying Program Transformations Expressed With 2nd Order Patterns.* Acta Informatica 11 (1978), 31–55.

76. Huet G. and Lankford D.S., *On the Uniform Halting Problem for Term Rewriting Systems.* Rapport Laboria 283, IRIA, Mars 1978.

77. Huet G. and Lévy J.J., *Call by Need Computations in Non-Ambiguous Linear Term Rewriting Systems.* Rapport Laboria 359, IRIA, Août 1979.

78. Hullot J.M., *Associative-Commutative Pattern Matching.* Fifth International Joint Conference on Artificial Intelligence, Tokyo, 1979.

79. Hullot J.M., *Canonical Forms and Unification.* Unpublished manuscript, 1980.

80. Iturriaga R., *Contributions to Mechanical Mathematics.* Ph. D. thesis, Carnegie-Mellon University, 1967.

81. Jeanrond H.J., *A Unique Termination Theorem for a Theory with Generalised Commutative Axioms.* Unpublished manuscript, July 1979.

82. Kamin S., *Some Definitions for Algebraic Data Type Specifications.* SIGPLAN Notices, Vol. 14, No. 3, March 1979.

83. Khachian, L., *Polynomial Algorithm for Linear Programming* Computing Center, Academy Sciences USSR, Moscow, 4 October 1978.

84. Kleene S.C., *Introduction to Metamathematics.* North-Holland, 1952.

85. Klop J.W., *A Counter Example to the Church-Rosser Property for Lambda-Calculus With Surjective Pairing.* Preprint 102, Dept. of Mathematics, U. of Utrecht, 1978.

86. Knuth D. and Bendix P., *Simple Word Problems in Universal Algebras.*"Computational Problems in Abstract Algebra". Ed. Leech J., Pergamon Press, 1970, 263–297.

87. Kozen D., *Complexity of Finitely Presented Algebras.* Ninth ACM Symposium on Theory of Computing, May 1977, 164-177.

88. Kozen D., *Finitely Presented Algebras and the Polynomial Time Hierarchy.* Report 77-303, Dept. of Computer Science, Cornell U., March 1977.

89. Kruskal J. B., *Well-quasi-ordering, the Tree Theorem and Vazsonyi's Conjecture.* Trans. Amer. Math. Soc. 95 (1960), 210–225.

90. Lankford D.S., *Canonical Algebraic Simplification.* Report ATP-25, Departments of Mathematics and Computer Sciences, University of Texas at Austin, May 1975.

91. Lankford D.S., *Canonical Inference.* Report ATP-32, Departments of Mathematics and Computer Sciences, University of Texas at Austin, Dec. 1975.

92. Lankford D.S., *A Finite Termination Algorithm.* Internal memo, Southwestern U., Georgetown, Texas, March 1976.

93. Lankford D.S., *On Deciding Word Problems by Rewrite Rules Simplifiers.* Unpublished Manuscript, Sept. 77.

94. Lankford D.S., *A Unification Algorithm for Abelian Group Theory.* Report MTP-1, Math. Dept., Louisiana Tech. U., Jan. 1979.

95. Lankford D.S., *Mechanical Theorem Proving in Field Theory.* Report MTP-2, Math. Dept., Louisiana Tech U., Jan. 1979.

96. Lankford D.S., *On Proving Term Rewriting Systems are nœtherian.* Report MTP-3, Math. Dept., Louisiana Tech U., May 1979.

97. Lankford D.S. *Some New Approaches to the Theory and Applications of Conditional Term Rewriting Systems.* Report MTP-6, Math. Dept., Lousiana Tech. U., Aug. 1979.

98. Lankford D.S. and Ballantyne A.M., *Decision Procedures for Simple Equational Theories With Commutative Axioms: Complete Sets of Commutative Reductions.* Report ATP-35, Departments of Mathematics and Computer Sciences, U. of Texas at Austin, March 1977.

99. Lankford D.S. and Ballantyne A.M., *Decision Procedures for Simple Equational Theories With Permutative Axioms: Complete Sets of Permutative Reductions.* Report ATP-37, Departments of Mathematics and Computer Sciences, U. of Texas at Austin, April 1977.

100. Lankford D.S. and Ballantyne A.M., *Decision Procedures for Simple Equational Theories With Commutative-Associative Axioms: Complete Sets of Commutative-Associative Reductions.* Report ATP-39, Departments of Mathematics and Computer Sciences, U. of Texas at Austin, Aug. 1977.

101. Lankford D.S. and Ballantyne A.M., *The Refutation Completeness of Blocked Permutative Narrowing and Resolution.* Fourth Conference on Automated Deduction, Austin, Feb. 1979, 53–59.

102. Lankford D.S. and Musser D., *On Semi-Deciding First Order Validity and Invalidity.* Unpublished Manuscript, March 1978.

103. Lévy J.J., *Réductions correctes et optimales dans le lambda-calcul.* Thèse d'Etat, U. de Paris VII, Jan. 1978.

104. Lipton R. and Snyder L., *On the Halting of Tree Replacement Systems.* Conference on Theoretical Computer Science, U. of Waterloo, Aug. 1977, 43–46.

105. Lipton R. J. and Zalcstein Y., *Word Problems Solvable in Logspace.* Technical Report no. 48, Department of Computer Science, SUNY at StonyBrook, 1975.

106. Livesey M. and Siekmann J., *Unification of Sets.* Internal Report 3/76, Institut fur Informatik I, U. Karlsruhe, 1977.

107. Makanin G.S., *The Problem of Solvability of Equations in a Free Semigroup.* Akad. Nauk. SSSR, TOM 233,2 (1977).

108. Malcev A. I., *On Homomorphisms of Finite Groups.* Ivano Gosudarstvenni Pedagogicheski Institut Uchenye Zapiski, vol. 18, 1958, pp. 49-60.

109. Manna Z. and Ness S., *On the Termination of Markov Algorithms.* Third Hawaii International Conference on System Sciences, Jan. 1970, 789–792.

110. Martelli A. and Montanari U., *An Efficient Unification Algorithm.* Unpublished manuscript, 1979.

111. Matiyasevich Y., *Diophantine Representation of Recursively Enumerable Predicates*. Proceedings of the Second Scandinavian Logic Symposium, North-Holland, 1970.

112. McCarthy J., *Recursive Fuctions of Symbolic Expressions and Their Computations by Machine, Part I*. CACM 3,4 (1960), 184–195.

113. McCarthy J., *A Basis For a Mathematical Theory of Computation*. Computer Programming and Formal Systems, Eds. Brafford P. and Hirschberg, North-Holland (1963), 33–70.

114. McNulty G., *The Decision Problem for Equational Bases of Algebras*. Annals of Mathematical Logic, 11 (1976), 193-259.

115. Meyer A. R. and Stockmeyer L., *Word Problems Requiring Exponential Time*. Fifth ACM Symposium on Theory of Computing, April 1973, 1–9.

116. Moses J., *Algebraic Simplification, a Guide For the Perplexed*. The Macsyma Papers, 1970, 32–54.

117. Musser D. L., *A Data Type Verification System Based on Rewrite Rules*. 6th Texas Conf. on Computing Systems, Austin, Nov. 1978.

118. Musser D. L., *Convergent Sets of Rewrite Rules for Abstract Data Types*. Unpublished Manuscript, Information Sciences Institute, Jan. 1979.

119. Musser D. L., *On Proving Inductive Properties of Abstract Data Types*. Seventh ACM Symposium on Principles of Programming Languages, Jan. 1980.

120. Musser D. L., *Abstract Data Type Specification in the AFFIRM system*. To appear, IEEE Transactions on Software Engineering.

121. Nash-Williams C. St. J. A., *On Well-quasi-ordering Finite Trees*. Proc. Cambridge Phil. Soc. 59 (1963), 833–835.

122. Nelson C. G. and Oppen D. C., *Fast Decision Algorithms Based on Congruence Closure*. Stanford CS Report No. STAN-CS-77-646, 1977. To appear JACM.

123. Nelson C. G. and Oppen D. C., *Simplification by Cooperating Decision Procedures*. To appear CACM.

124. Nevins A., *A Human Oriented Logic For Automatic Theorem Proving.* JACM 21,4 (1974), 606–621.

125. Newman M.H.A., *On Theories With a Combinatorial Definition of "Equivalence".* Annals of Math. 43,2 (1942), 223–243.

126. Nivat M., *Congruences parfaites et quasi-parfaites.* Séminaire Dubreuil, 7, 1971–72. (Preliminary Version in Proc. Second Annual ACM Symposium on Theory of Computing, 1970, 221-225.)

127. Nivat M., *On the Interpretation of Recursive Polyadic Program Schemes.* Symposia Mathematica Vol. XV, Istituto Nazionale di Alta Matematica, Italy, 1975, 225–281.

128. O'Donnell M., *Computing in Systems Described by Equations.* Lecture Notes in Computer Science 58, Springer Verlag, 1977.

129. Oppen D. C., *Reasoning About Recursively Defined Data Structures.* Fifth ACM Symposium on Principles of Programming Languages, January 1978. To appear JACM.

130. Oppen D. C., *Convexity, Complexity, and Combinations of Theories.* Fourth Symposium on Automated Deduction, Austin, 1979. To appear Theoretical Computer Science.

131. Paterson M.S. and Wegman M.N., *Linear Unification.* J. of Computer and Systems Sciences 16 (1978), 158–167.

132. Peterson G.E. and Stickel M.E., *Complete Sets of Reductions for Equational Theories With Complete Unification Algorithms.* Tech. Report, Dept. of Computer Science, U. of Arizona, Tucson, Sept. 1977.

133. Plaisted D., *Well-Founded Orderings for Proving Termination of Systems of Rewrite Rules.* Dept. of Computer Science Report 78–932, U. of Illinois at Urbana- Champaign, July 1978.

134. Plaisted D., *A Recursively Defined Ordering for Proving Termination of Term Rewriting Systems.* Dept. of Computer Science Report 78–943, U. of Illinois at Urbana-Champaign, Sept. 1978.

135. Plotkin G., *Lattice-Theoretic Properties of Subsumption.* Memo MIP–R–77, U. of Edinburgh, 1970.

136. Plotkin G., *Building-in Equational Theories.* Machine Intelligence 7 (1972), 73–90.

137. Post E., *Recursive Unsolvability of a Problem of Thue*. J. Symbolic Logic 12(1947), 1–11.

138. Presburger M., *Uber die Vollstandigkeit eines gewissen Systems der Arithmetik ganzer Zahlen, in welchem die Addition als einzige Operation hervortritt*. Comptes-Rendus du 1er Congrès des Mathématiciens des Pays Slaves, 1929.

139. Raoult J.C. and Vuillemin J., *Operational and Semantic Equivalence Between Recursive Programs*. 10th ACM Symposium on Theory of Computing, San Diego, 1978.

140. Raulefs P. and Siekmann J., *Unification of Idempotent Functions*. Unpublished manuscript, 1978.

141. Reynolds J., *Transformational Systems and the Algebraic Structure of Atomic Formulas*. Machine Intelligence 5 (1970), 135–152.

142. Robinson G. A. and Wos L. T., *Paramodulation and Theorem Proving in First-order Theories with Equality*. Machine Intelligence 4, American Elsevier, 1969, 135–150.

143. Robinson J.A., *A Machine-Oriented Logic Based on the Resolution Principle*. JACM 12 (1965), 32–41.

144. Rosen B.K., *Subtree Replacement Systems*. PhD Thesis, Harvard U., 1971.

145. Rosen B.K., *Tree-Manipulation Systems and Church-Rosser Theorems*. JACM 20 (1973), 160–187.

146. Scott D., *Outline of a Mathematical Theory of Computation*. Monograph PRG–2, Oxford U. Press, 1970.

147. Seidenberg A., *A New Decision Method For Elementary Algebra and Geometry*. Ann. of Math., Ser. 2, 60 (1954), 365–374.

148. Sethi R., *Testing for the Church-Rosser Property*. JACM 21 (1974), 671–679. Erratum JACM 22 (1975), 424.

149. Shostak R., *An Algorithm for Reasoning about Equality*. CACM, 583-585, July 1978.

150. Siekmann J., *Unification of Commutative Terms*. Unpublished manuscript, 1978.

151. Siekmann J., *Unification and Matching Problems*. Ph. D. thesis, Memo CSM-4-78, University of Essex, 1978.

152. Slagle J.R., *Automated Theorem-Proving for Theories with Simplifiers, Commutativity and Associativity*. JACM 21 (1974), 622–642.

153. Staples J., *Church-Rosser Theorems for Replacement Systems*. Algebra and Logic, ed. Crossley J., Lecture Notes in Math., Springer Verlag 1975, 291–307.

154. Staples J., *A Class of Replacement Systems with Simple Optimality Theory*. To appear, Bull. of the Australian Math. Soc.

155. Stickel M.E., *A Complete Unification Algorithm for Associative-Commutative Functions*. 4th International Joint Conference on Artificial Intelligence, Tbilisi, 1975.

156. Stickel M.E., *Unification Algorithms for Artificial Intelligence Languages*. Ph. D. thesis, Carnegie-Mellon University, 1976.

157. Szabó P., *The Undecidability of the D_A-Unification Problem*. Unpublished manuscript, 1979.

158. Tarski A., *A Decision Method for Elementary Algebra and Geometry*. U. of California Press, Berkeley, 1951.

159. Tarski A., *Equational Logic*. Contributions to Mathematical Logic, ed. Schütte et al, North-Holland, 1968.

160. Thatcher J., Wagner E. and Wright J., *Data Type Specifications: Parameterization and the Power of Specification Techniques*. Tenth ACM Symposium on Theory of Computing, May 1978.

161. Vuillemin J., *Correct and Optimal Implementation of Recursion in a Simple Programming Language*. J. of Computer and System Sciences 9,3 (1974),332–354.

162. Wadsworth C.P., *Semantics and Pragmatics of the λ-calculus*. PhD Thesis, Oxford U., 1971.

163. Wand M., *First Order Identities as a Defining Language*. Indiana U. Tech. Report 29, 1976.

164. Wand M., *Final Algebra Semantics and Data Type Extensions*. JCSS, vol. 19, no. 1, Aug. 1979.

165. Winker S., *Dynamic Demodulation*. Internal memo, Dept. of Computer Science, Northern Illinois U., 1975.

166. Zilles S., *Data Algebra: A Specification Technique for Data Structures*. Ph. D. thesis, MIT, 1978.

APPLICATION OF FORMAL LANGUAGE THEORY
TO PROBLEMS OF SECURITY
AND SYNCHRONIZATION[1]

Joffroy Beauquier[2]
Maurice Nivat[3]

LA 248 "Informatique Théorique et Programmation"
Universités Paris VI et Paris VII
Paris, France

INTRODUCTION

This paper is composed of two distinct parts: the first
one, on security problems, is Beauquier's work; the second, on
synchronization, is Nivat's. The reason why these two pieces
of work are presented here under the same title is that we believe they both exemplify the same fruitful method: given
some system, be it a security system or a system of concurrent
processes, one may first look at the set of all its possible
behaviors. On a properly defined alphabet, whose elements represent the elementary actions which the components of the system are allowed to perform, such a set of behaviors is a
language which may be expected to have properties previously
studied and known. A singular fact, which may be not so singular if one really thinks about it, is that many actual systems thus considered lead to sets of behavior which are
rational (regular) or algebraic (context-free): in what

[1] Preparation of this paper was supported in part by the
National Science Foundation under Grant No. MCS79-04012.
[2] Université de Picardie, Amiens, France.
[3] Université Paris VII, Paris, France.

follows Beauquier deals mainly with behaviors which happen to
be elements of a standard language (intersection of the Dyck
set with a rational language) of a very special type (which
implies decidability of the inclusion problem). Nivat, in
Section II, is more interested in rational languages or at
least in their "extension to infinity," that is, to their adherences where for any ordinary language L the adherence
Adh(L) is defined as the set of all infinite words such that
all of their left factors are left factors of words in L.

Both authors had been interested by such parts of language
theory for different reasons, of a mainly theoretical nature:
both of them experienced that some results they had obtained
beforehand were readily applicable to the practical situation
thus considered here and that, on the contrary, the consideration of this practical situation leads to new problems of
theoretical interest.

This paper is divided into two parts, Part I having been
written by the first author and Part II by the second. We believe that both parts argue effectively for the use of language theory in the study of challenging new problems raised
in the development of "information systems."

I.   PROBLEMS OF SECURITY

A.   Generalities

Today's computers manipulate structured objects which are supposed to carry some information. Such objects are trees, processes, tapes, memory cells, etc. For each type of object, there exists a finite set of distinct ways in which it can be manipulated. Each type of manipulation is called an access (an access may be reading a value, sorting a set of values or calling an editor process). The security system is the finite set of rules which delimit the accesses that can be made during the progress of computation. We intend here to show how the use of formal language theory allows one to analyze completely the behavior of a concrete security system. The security systems we are considering belong to the family of capability-based security systems (cf. [6,14,16,19]).

The notion of capability was introduced by Dennis and Van Horn [8] in order to formalize a general addressing mechanism for all the objects which occur in an operating system. An access capability may be considered as a ticket, with an object name and several access modalities for this object. If another object does not have such a capability of accessing a given object, it cannot physically address this object.

In the following, we shall consider a capability as a pair (x,m) , where x is an object of the system and m an access modality to this object. In this model of security systems, the security policy may be defined by:

(1) A finite set of permanent capabilities. These capabilities are distributed between the objects at the beginning of computation and cannot be revoked during the progress of the computation.

(2) A finite set of rules which specify how new capabilities can be created and transferred from one object to another and also how capabilities can be revoked.

This model has been proposed by Linden [19] and is closely related to systems studied in [5,7,14]. The model is defined by three rules.

Rule 1. Transmission of capabilities as parameters.

Let x, y and z be objects in the system. Suppose that x has, at a given time, a capability (y,m) (that means an access right to y according to the access modality m) and a capability (z,t). Then, if x has an access to y, x can possibly pass to y the capability (z,t) as parameter, and y can use this capability until y gives the control back to x. Then its capability (z,t) is revoked.

Example. Before the call the control is to user A.

	User A	Editor
	Editor, call	File Y, read
Available	Dictionary, read	
capabilities	File X, read	
	File Y, write	

After the call of Editor by User A, the control is to Editor.

User A	Editor
Editor, call	File Y, read
Dictionary, read	Dictionary, read
File X, read	File X, read
File Y, write	

Then, for example, the Editor can read the Dictionary. After the return from Editor to user A, the control is to user A.

User A	Editor
Editor, call	File Y, read
Dictionary, read	
File X, read	
File Y, write	

Now, the Editor control cannot read the Dictionary.

Rule 2. Create a new object.

Let x be an object in the system. Then x can create a new object y. If the created object y can itself call another object, it receives as permanent capabilities the set of permanent capabilities of its creator x. It also receives as parameters the set of capabilities that the creator possesses as parameters, at the time of the creation. The creator x receives as permanent capabilities all the possible capabilities, related to the created object.

Rule 3. Reading a segment.

Let s be an object of a special type that we call capability segment. Suppose that, at a given time, s contains a capability (y,m) written in it. Then, if the object x has a capability (s,read) for reading the capability segment s, x can use the capability (y,m) for performing an access to object y.

Some remarks. Rule 2 is exactly the same as in "Take and Grant" systems [15]. Rule 1 seems to be akin to the rule "Grant." Nevertheless, it is quite different. In our model, the given capability is revoked at the return time, whereas Jones, Lipton and Snyder do not use revocation (although they mention it as a possible extension).

This difference has an important consequence. The "Take and Grant" systems of Jones, et al., are related, in our formalism, to regular sets and linear algorithms, whereas our systems are related to context-free languages and exponential algorithms.

We say that any security system defined by both a finite set of permanent capabilities, and also the rules of capabilities transmission 1, 2, 3, is a P.P.C.S.-system (Permanent, Parameter, Create, Segment).

The problems. We are interested in two problems concerning security systems: the "safety" problem and the "compatibility" problem.

The "safety" problem. Each user of a security system needs to know: What information of mine can be accessed by others? What information of others can be accessed by me? The question here is: Is it true that the object x can access the object y? The "safety" problem has been raised in its full generality by the work of Harrison, Ruzzo and Ullman [11]. They show that what can be called the "uniform safety problem" is undecidable. In our interpretation their result says that, given an arbitrary set of rules and an initial repartition of permanent capabilities, it is undecidable whether or not x will obtain a capability for y. This is a uniform problem in the sense that rules are arbitrary.

Let us note that, in a special case (which corresponds to rational constraints), Jones, Lipton and Snyder [15] have shown that the "safety" problem is decidable by a linear algorithm.

The "compatibility" problem. Real capability based security systems sometimes allow a user to define its own security sub-system. This sub-system must be compatible with the main system. In particular, there must not exist progressions of computations authorized in the security sub-system and unauthorized in the main security system. This problem is usually treated by testing carefully the security sub-system. Another example is given when a program, tested in a given security system, is used in another security system (cf. the "Trojan Horse" problem in [3]).

Usually, the program is completely tested in the new security system, although it has been already tested in the first one. The ability to decide the compatibility of the two security systems avoids all these tests. We shall show that the "safety" and "compatibility" problems are effectively decidable for P.P.C.A.-systems.

B.   The Main Construction

Initially, we will consider P.P.C.S.-systems in which the rules "Create" and "Read a capability-segment" are never used. We will examine afterwards the modifications involved by the use of these two rules. Now we focus on the problem of the transmission of capabilities as parameters and of their restitution at the time of the return.

Let S be a P.P.C.S.-system. To each computation allowed
by S, we associate the sequence $(x_1,m_1)(x_2,m_2) \cdots (x_k,m_k)$
of capabilities used during the computation, and we call this
sequence the track of the computation. Then the system S
may be described by the set of its behaviors, that is, by a
formal language.

Let $D_n'^*$ be the restricted Dyck set over an alphabet with
n types of parentheses ($D_n'^*$ is the set of well parenthesized
words). The idea is to build a finite automaton A, recognizing a regular set K, a homomorphism ϕ and an integer n,
such that the set of computation tracks of S is exactly the
set $\phi(D_n'^* \cap K)$.

Let X be the set of objects in system S (X may be considered as a finite alphabet, since the rule "Create" is never
used) and let M be the set of all pairs (x,m), where
$x \in X$ and m is an access modality to the object x. In
fact, M is the set of capabilities in the system S.

We call protection domain any subset of M. We shall
build a finite automaton whose states are protection domains.
The arrows of the finite automaton are labelled by a letter
over an alphabet Y. Y is the union of a non-barred alphabet
Z and of a barred alphabet $\bar{Z}$, in bijection with Z, where
$Z = M \times P(M)$ ($P(M)$ is the set of protection domains). Then
a letter of Y may be considered as a pair, made up of a capability and a protection domain. We set Cardinal (Z) = n.

We will consider non-barred letters as opening parentheses
and barred letters as closing parentheses.

The use of an arrow labelled by a non-barred letter $y = ((x,m), D)$ means that a call of the object x, according to the access modality m, has been performed in the protection domain D.

The use of a barred letter $\bar{y} = (\overline{(x,m)}, D)$ means that a return instruction from x has been performed and that the control comes back to the object having called x.

In the two cases, the state of the automaton from which the arrow comes indicates the protection domain before the call or the return; the state at which the arrow arrives indicates the protection domain after the call or the return.

We will present now a precise version of the algorithm, allowing us to associate a formal language to a P.P.C.S.-system. We suppose that any object x in the system has an initial set of permanent capabilities (that means a permanent protection domain) P_x. P_x is possibly empty. We suppose also that the start point of the system is given by a particular object x_0.

<u>Initialization step</u>. Let $P_{x_0} = \{y_1, y_2, \ldots, y_k\}$. We create an automaton state labelled by P_{x_0} and, from this state, we create k different hanging arrows, labelled respectively by (y_1, P_{x_0}), (y_2, P_{x_0}), $\ldots$, (y_k, P_{x_0}).

<u>General step</u>. At a step of the construction, the automaton has hanging arrows.

I. For each hanging arrow we perform the following. Let $((x,m), D)$ be the label of the hanging arrow, which comes then from the state D. With our capabilities transmission rules, the protection domain after the call of x is given

by (1) the permanent protection domain of x, P_x, and (2)
the set of capabilities possibly passed as parameters, D.

Let $D' = D \cup P_x = \{z_1, z_2, \ldots, z_p\}$. Two cases are to be
considered.

(a) x is an object able to call other objects. There
two new sub-cases are to be considered.

(i) D' is the label of an automaton state already
built. Then we direct the hanging arrow labelled
by $((x,m),\ D)$ to this state.

(ii) D' does not appear in the automaton already built.
Then we create a new state labelled by D' and we
direct the hanging arrow to this new state. In
the two sub-cases, from the automaton state D',
we create $Card(D') = p$ new hanging arrows labelled by (z_1, D'), (z_2, D'), $\ldots$, (z_p, D') (if
they do not already exist).

(b) x is an object unable to call other objects (for example, a file). Then we create a particular new state,
that we name trivial state associated with x (if
such a state does not already exist). The hanging
arrow labelled by $y = ((x,m),\ D)$ is directed to this
state.

II. Each time that in I we create an arrow labelled by y
from a state D to a state D', we create an arrow labelled
by y from the state D' to the state D. With this construction we are guaranteed to find again, after a return, the
protection domain of the corresponding call. So, the problem
of parameter restitution is effectively solved.

End test. We perform the general step while there exist hanging arrows. Since M and Y are finite, the construction always ends.

Example. The initial distribution of permanent capabilities is given as a matrix:

	Editor = x_1	File X = x_2	Dictionary = x_3
User A	Call	Read, Write	
Editor			Read

At the beginning of the computation, user A has the control.

Now, we consider that any state in the finite automaton is terminal. The initial state is the state built in the initialization step.

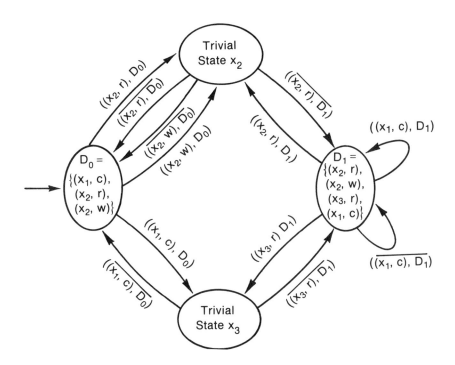

Let $\bar{M}$ be an alphabet in bijection with M and let ϕ be the homomorphism $\phi : Y^* \to (M \cup \bar{M})^*$ determined by defining

$$\phi((x,m), D) = (x,m) \quad \text{if} \quad ((x,m), D) \in Z,$$

$$\phi((x,m), D) = (\overline{x,m}) \quad \text{if} \quad ((\overline{x,m}), D) \in \bar{Z}.$$

It follows from the construction that the tracks of the allowed computations in the system S are the words of the language $\phi(D'^*_n \cap K)$.

We will now solve the "safety" and "compatibility" problems.

The "safety" problem. Is it true that the object x can access the object y, according to the access modality m? With our formalism, the question is: Does there exist a word w in $\phi(D'^*_q \cap K)$, an access modality to x, m', and words w_1 and w_2 such that $w = w_1(x,m')(y,m)w_2$? We will show that the answer to the question is the same as to the following one: Do there exist two protection domains D' and D such that $((x,m'), D')((y,m), D)$ is a transition of the regular set K? Clearly, if the answer is negative for the second question, it is also negative for the first one.

Now, suppose that $((x,m'), D')((y,m), D)$ is a transition of K. Following point I of the construction there exists a word

$$((x_0,m_0), D_0((x_1,m_1), D_1) \cdots ((x_k,m_k), D_k)$$

in Z^* (that is, a word without barred letters) that leads from the initial state to the state labelled by D'.

Then, by point II of the construction, the word

$$f = ((x_0,m_0),\ D_0)((x_1,m_1),\ D_1) \cdots$$
$$\cdots\ ((x_k,m_k),\ D_k)((x,m'),\ D')((y,m),\ D)(\overline{(y,m),\ D}) \cdots$$
$$\cdots\ (\overline{(x,m'),\ D'})(\overline{(x_k,m_k),\ D_k}) \cdots (\overline{(x_0,m_0),\ D_0})$$

is a word of K and also a word well parenthesized. Then

$$\phi(f) = (x_0,m_0)(x_1,m_1) \cdots (x,m')(y,m)(\overline{y,m})(\overline{x,m'}) \cdots$$
$$\cdots\ (\overline{x_0,m_0})$$

is the track of a possible computation in S. During this
computation the object x accesses the object y according
to the access modality m.

Now the "safety" problem is equivalent to the determination
of the transitions of K and is consequently decidable.

The "compatibility" problem. Let S_1 and S_2 be two
P.P.C.S.-systems. We suppose that the sets of objects in S_1
and S_2 are equal. We may associate two formal languages,
$\phi(D_n'^* \cap K_1)$ and $\phi(D_n'^* \cap K_2)$ to S_1 and S_2. Then, S_1 is
compatible with S_2 if and only if $\phi(D_1'^* \cap K_1) \subset \phi(D_n'^* \cap K_2)$.

For arbitrary regular sets K_1 and K_2, this inclusion
is not decidable. But we shall show that, for the particular
regular sets we handle, the inclusion can be decided.

We say that a regular set K (resp., finite automaton A)
is a security regular set (resp., security finite automaton)
if it can be associated to a P.P.C.S.-system S by the previous construction.

We first give some definitions and lemmas.

Definition. Let L be a language over an alphabet Z. We say that a word w of Z* is completable in L if and only if there exists a word w' of Z* such that ww' ∈ L.

Definition. Let A be a finite automaton with a transition function δ. A state T of A is reachable from the initial state T_0 of A if there exists a word w such that $\delta(T_0, w) = T$.

Lemma 1. Let A be a security finite automaton recognizing a security regular set K. Then any state of A is reachable from the initial state by a word w completable in $D_n'^* \cap K$.

Proof. By point I of the main construction, for any state of A, labelled by T, there exists a word

$$((x_0, m_0), T_0)((x_1, m_1), T_1) \cdots ((x_k, m_k), T)$$

in Z* that leads from the initial state T_0 to the state labelled by T.

By point II of the construction, the word

$$((x_0, m_0), T_0)((x_1, m_1), T_1) \cdots$$
$$((x_k, m_k), T)(\overline{(x_k, m_k)}, T) \cdots (\overline{(x_0, m_0)}, T_0)$$

is a word in K and also a word in $D_n'^*$. □

Lemma 2. Let K_1 and K_2 be two security regular sets, over the alphabet Y (Card(Y) = n). Then, there exists a word w in K_1 but not in K_2, if and only if there exists a word completable in $D_n'^* \cap K_1$, that is in K_1 but is not in K_2.

Proof. Let w be a word in $K_1 \cap \mathcal{C}(K_2)$ ($\mathcal{C}(K_2)$ is the complementary of K_2). We can choose w minimal in $K_1 \cap \mathcal{C}(K_2)$. Let A_1 and A_2 be the security finite automata recognizing K_1 and K_2. Recall that A_1 and A_2 are deterministic. We set $w = w'y$ ($w' \in Y^*$, $y \in Y$). By hypothesis of minimality, w' belongs to $K_1 \cap K_2$. Let $T_0, T_1, \ldots, T_r$ be the sequence of A_1 states when it reads w and $T_0'T_1' \ldots T_r'$ the corresponding sequence in A_2.

The hypothesis of minimality of w involves

$$T_0 \subseteq T_0', \quad T_1 \subseteq T_1', \quad \ldots, \quad T_{r-1} \subseteq T_{r-1}'.$$

(We recall that T_i is, in fact, a protection domain, that means a set of capabilities). y is of the form $y = ((x,m), T)$ and, since $w \in K \cap \mathcal{C}(K_2)$, $(x,m) \in T_r$ and $(x,m) \notin T_r'$.

By Lemma 1, there exists a word v completable in $D_n'^* \cap K_1$ by u such that $\delta_1(T_0, v) = T_{r-1}$ (δ_1 is the transition function of A_1). Let f be the word $f = vyyu$. Clearly $f \in D_n'^* \cap K_1$ and $f \notin D_n'^* \cap K_2$, since $(x,m) \in T_r'$ and v is minimal. Then $v \in K_1$ and $v \notin K_2$. $\square$

Lemma 3. Let K_1 and K_2 be two security regular sets over Y ($\text{Card}(Y) = n$), associated with two security finite automata A_1 and A_2 and to a canonical homomorphism ϕ. Then $\phi(D_n'^* \cap K_1) \subset \phi(D_n'^* \cap K_2)$ implies $K_1 \subset K_2$.

Proof. Let us suppose that $K_1 \cap \mathcal{C}(K_2) \neq \emptyset$ and let v be a minimal word in $K_1 \cap \mathcal{C}(K_2)$, completable in $D_n'^* \cap K_1$. By Lemma 2, such a word exists.

We set $v = v'y$ $(v' \in Y^*,$ $y = ((x,m), T) \in Y)$ and $f = v'yu$, according to the notations of Lemma 2. By Lemma 2, $f \in D_n'^* \cap K_1$ and $f \notin D_n'^* \cap K_2$.

Since v is minimal, $v' \in K_2$. Let T_0, V_1, V_2, ..., V_r be the sequence of A_1 states reading v'.

Let us suppose that there exists $g \in D_n'^* \cap K_2$ such that $\phi(g) = \phi(f)$. We set

$$g = ((x_0,m_0), T_0)((x_1,m_1), T_1') \cdots$$
$$((x_{r-1},m_{r-1}), T_{r-1}')((x,m), T')g'$$

and

$$v' = ((x_0,m_0), T_0)((x_1,m_1), V_1) \cdots$$
$$((x_{r-1},m_{r-1}), V_{r-1}).$$

Since A_2 is deterministic, and since v' and g are recognized by A_2,

$$T_1' = V_1, \ldots, T_{r-1}' = V_{r-1}.$$

Then, δ_2 being the transition function of A_2,

$$\delta_2(T_0, v') = T'.$$

But, since $v'y = v$ does not belong to K_2,

$$(x,m) \notin T'.$$

Then there is a contradiction in assuming that a word g and, in particular, a letter $((x,m), T')$ exists. In consequence,

$$\phi(f) \in \phi(D_n'^* \cap K_1) \cap \mathcal{C}(\phi(D_n'^* \cap K_2)). \quad \square$$

Theorem. Let S_1 and S_2 be two P.P.C.S.-systems having the same set of objects. Then the compatibility of S_1 with respect to S_2 is decidable.

Proof. The security regular sets K_1 and K_2 related to S_1 and S_2 can be effectively built. By Lemma 3, the compatibility of S_1 with respect to S_2 is equivalent to the inclusion $K_1 \subset K_2$, that is decidable by a classical algorithm.
□

Now, we will extend our results to P.P.C.S.-systems which use the rules "Create" and "Read a capability segment." These extensions are only slight modifications and the basic idea of the main construction remains unchanged.

The rule "Create" is used. Then, a P.P.C.S.-system must be described by a formal language over a non-bounded alphabet, since, at each time, a new object can be possibly created in the system.

The compatibility problem. We consider now two P.P.C.S.-systems S_1 and S_2 and let $\hat{L}_1$ and $\hat{L}_2$ be the languages over non-bounded alphabets that describe their behaviors.

Let L_1 and L_2 be the languages associated to S_1 and S_2 when the rule "Create" is never used. We will prove

Lemma 4. $\hat{L}_1 \subset \hat{L}_2$ if and only if $L_1 \subset L_2$.

Proof. Only the sufficient condition is to be proved. First, we recall how the rule "Create" can be used. At each step of the progress of a computation, the object having the control can possibly create a new object which receives a new name and whose access modalities depend on its nature. For example, a user can create a file F with three access modalities, $(F, read)$, $(F, write)$ and $(F, sort)$.

If the created object can itself call other objects, it receives as permanent capabilities the set of permanent capabilities that the creator has as parameters at the time of the creation. The creator receives as permanent capabilities all the possible capabilities related to the created object. After the creation, the creator can give its capabilities for the created object as parameters to any other object for which it has a capability.

Remark. So, if an object has a capability for a created object of which it is not the creator, this object has necessarily a capability for the creator of the created object.

Now, we note L_1-L_2, the set $L_1 \cap \mathcal{C}(L_2)$. Suppose that $\hat{L}_1$-$\hat{L}_2 \neq \emptyset$, and let w be a word in L_1-L_2. Since $w \in L_1$ and $w \in L_2$, w contains a leftmost transition $(x,m)(x',m')$, which represents a call authorized in the security system S_1 and unauthorized in S_2.

Several cases are to be considered.

I. x and x' are objects which exist in the systems S_1 and S_2 at the beginning of the computation. We shall say that x and x' are initial objects (initial objects are in opposition with created objects). Let w be the word

$$w = (x_0,m_0)(x_1,m_1) \cdots (x_{k-1},m_{k-1})(x,m)(x',m') \cdots ,$$

where $(x_i,m_i) \in M \cup \bar{M}$ for $i = 1, 2, \ldots, k-1$.

Let $D_0, D_1, \ldots, D_{k-1}, D_k, D_{k+1}$ be the sequence of protection domains of the computation related to w in S_1 and $D_0', D_1', \ldots, D_{k-1}', D_k', D_{k+1}'$ the corresponding sequence in S_2. Since $w \in \hat{L}_1$-$\hat{L}_2$, $(x',m') \in D_{k+1}$ and $(x',m') \notin D_{k+1}'$, and, by hypothesis, for $i = 1, 2, \ldots, k$, $(x_i,m_i) \in D_i$ and

$(x_i, m_i) \in D_i'$. Let $i_1, i_2, \ldots, i_q$ be the integers such that $x_{i_1}, x_{i_2}, \ldots, x_{i_q}$ are the created objects. Let z_{i_j} be the initial creator of x_{i_j}. From a previous remark, it turns out that, since $(x_{i_j}, m_{i_j}) \in D_{i_j} \cap D_{i_j}'$, there exists a capability (z_{i_j}, m_{i_j}') in $D_{i_j} \cap D_{i_j}'$.

Then we replace in w each letter (x_{i_j}, m_{i_j}) by (z_{i_j}, m_{i_j}') (and each letter $(\overline{x_{i_j}, m_{i_j}})$ by $(\overline{z_{i_j}, m_{i_j}'})$).

We obtain a word $\overline{w}$ which does belong to L_1:

$$\overline{w} = (y_0, n_0)(y_1, n_1) \cdots (y_{k-1}, n_{k-1})(x, m)(x', m') \cdots .$$

The protection domain in which x calls x' is always D_{k+1} in S_1 and D_{k+1}' in S_2. Since $(x', m') \notin D_{k+1}'$, $\overline{w} \notin L_2$.
Thus, $L_1 - L_2 \neq \emptyset$

II. x is an initial object and x' is a created object. Since x cannot call x' in S_2, x is not the creator of x'. Let y be the creator of x'. Then x received the capability (x', m') as parameter, from y, in S_1 and not in S_2. Let w be

$$w = (x_0, m_0)(x_1, m_1) \cdots (x_{k-1}, m_{k-1})(x, m)(x', m') \cdots .$$

Then, there exists $j \in [0, k-1]$ such that $(x_j, m_j) = (y, n)$ for any access modality n. We suppose that for $\ell \geq j$, $x_\ell \neq y$. Let $D_0, D_1, \ldots, D_{k-1}, D_k, D_{k+1}; D_0', D_1', \ldots, D_{k-1}', D_k', D_{k+1}'$ by the sequences of protection domains as above. Then, for $k-1 \geq \ell \geq j$, $(x', m') \in D_1$. That implies that, for $k-1 \geq \ell \geq j$, $(x_\ell, m_\ell) \neq (\overline{y, n})$. Since y is the creator of x', $(x', m') \in D_j'$. Since $(x_\ell, m_\ell) \neq (\overline{y, n})$ for $\ell \in [j, k-1]$, $(x', m') \in D_j' \cap D_{j+1}' \cap \ldots \cap D_{k+1}'$. There is a contradiction with our hypothesis: $(x', m') \notin D_{k+1}'$, so that this case never appears.

III. x is a created object. Let w be the word

$$w = (x_0,m_0)(x_1,m_1) \cdots (x_{k-1},m_{k-1})(x,m)(x',m') \cdots$$

and let D_0, D_1, ..., D_{k-1}, D_k, D_{k+1}; D_0', D_1', ..., D_{k-1}', D_k', D_{k+1}' be the sequences of protection domains as above. Let (z,n) be the leftmost occurrence of a letter, such that

(i) z is an initial object,

(ii) (z,n) is to the left of (x,m) in w,

(iii) if $(z,n) = (x_r,m_r)$ then (x',m') belongs to
$$D_r \cap D_{r+1} \cap \cdots \cap D_{k+1}.$$

Informally, z is the initial object which has given to x the capability (x',m') as parameter, in the system S_1. Clearly, (x',m') does not belong to D_r'. Elsewhere, x would have received a capability for x' in S_2. So that there exists a word

$$w' = (x_0,m_0)(x_1,m_1) \cdots (x_{r-1},m_{r-1})(z,n)(x',m') \cdots$$

in $\hat{L}_1 - \hat{L}_2$, where z is an initial object. If x' is an initial object, we are in the case I, already treated. If x' is a created object, we are in the case II, already treated. This subcase never appears. So, $L_1 - L_2 \neq \emptyset$. □

Then, in this case, the compatibility problem is decidable.

The "safety" problem. This problem only concerns the initial set of objects of a system.

The rule "Read a capability-segment" is used. The use of this rule modifies the construction of the finite automaton since the management of the capability segments must be done. Now the states of the finite automaton are triples. The first element is always a protection domain.

The two other elements are vectors whose length is the number r (the capability-segments are supposed to be ordered from 1 to r) of capability segments in S (this number is supposed to be fixed). The elements of the first vector are symbols 0 or 1. The ith element indicates whether the object having control can or not read the ith capability segment. The elements of the second vector are protection domains. The ith element indicates the set of capabilities possibly written in the ith capability-segment. The treatment of hanging arrows in the point I of the main construction is modified in this way:

Let ((x,m), D) be the label of the hanging arrow, which comes from the state (D,V_1,V_2). The protection domain after the call of x is constituted by

1. the permanent protection domain of x, P_x,

2. the set of capabilities possibly passed as parameters, D,

3. the set of capabilities possibly read in capability-segments.

Let

$$D' = D \cup P_x \cup \left(\bigcup_{\{i \mid V_1(i)=1\}} V_2(i) \right).$$

The sequel of point I is without change. The point II has to be completely modified.

II'. Each time that, in I, we create an arrow labelled by $y = ((x,m), D)$ from a state (D,V_1,V_2) to a state (D',V_1',V_2'), we create, if necessary, a state (D,V_1',V_2') and an arrow labelled by y from (D',V_1',V_2') to (D,V_1',V_2').

Then, for each $(x,m) \in D$, we create a hanging arrow labelled

by $((x,m), D)$ from the state (D,V_1',V_2').

Since the number of capability-segments is finite there is

a finite number of triples (D,V_1,V_2) and the construction

finally stops.

The problems of "safety" and "compatibility" may be at-

tacked then in the same way as above.

C.   Problems

The first class of problems concerns extension and modi-

fication of capabilities transmission rules, in order to ob-

tain more precise models of security systems. The question is

to determine in what cases a result of decidability can be

obtained.

It seems to us that, in many cases, provided that the

rules are context independent, a positive decidability result

holds.

The second class of problems concerns the optimization of

a given P.P.C.S.-system, according to some complexity measure

(for example, the accuracy measure of Jones [14]). Rather

than performing the optimization step by step, as it is usu-

ally done, it seems to use more convenient for P.P.C.S.-

systems, to use our construction and to work on the finite

automaton it gives. From the finite automaton, it is easy to

obtain all initial districutions of permanent capabilities,

related to the same formal language. In this finite set, it

suffices then to choose the initial distribution which is the

best one for the desired criterion.

II. SYNCHRONIZATION OF CONCURRENT PROCESSES

The phenomena of deadlock and starvation which may appear when several concurrent processes are running simultaneously have been discovered long ago [9,10,12] and extensively studied every since. One way of approach to this problem is the use of expressions describing the set of possible behaviors of the processes: the "path expressions" of Campbell, Haberman, Lauer [4,17,18] are such expressions defining rational (regular) set of finite behaviors. Such sets of behaviors are also used by Milne and Milner [22] where they appear as the set of branches of a tree and recently in Lynch and Fischer [20].

Deadlocks and starvations appear when one looks at the possibility for a system of processes to be activated forever and one is then led to consider also the set of infinite behaviors which are limits of finite behaviors, as was first clearly pointed out by Redziejowski [26]. The present author has studied for other purposes such limits of sequences of finite words in $A^{\infty} = A* \cup A^{\omega}$, the set of all finite and infinite words on an alphabet A with its natural topological structure of complete metric space [1,23].

In what follows we apply the results on adherences and centers of languages, to be found in [1], to the study of deadlock and starvation of systems of concurrent processes with a special emphasis on the case of rational processes for which the natural questions one may ask happen to be decidable. Since these decidability results were, for most of them, already known from the theory of safe Petri nets (see Lauer, et

al.), we believe that the techniques employed below which make
use only of ordinary finite automata are conceptually quite
economical and simple.

On the other hand, we can raise problems for nonrational
processes which appear to be difficult and could be of some
interest to both language theorists and those interested in
the synchronization of concurrent processes.

The author acknowledges with pleasure the help of several
people with whom he had fruitful discussions in preparing this
paper: André Arnold, Luc Boasson, Peter Lauer, Ugo Montanari,
Gérard Roucairol and Gilles Ruggiu.

A.   Processes and Their Behaviors

A _process_ p is a device which performs actions: all the
actions which all the processes we shall consider are able to
perform are taken in a set A of atomic instantaneous actions.

A _finite_ _behavior_ of p is a word in A^*, f =
f(1) ... f(n), where f(i) is the action performed by p at
time i.

An _infinite_ _behavior_ of p is an infinite word in A^ω,
u = u(1)u(2) ... u(n) ..., where u(i) is the action performed by p at time i.

We denote by $B_n(p)$ the set of finite behaviors of length
n of the process p and by B(p) the union of all $B_n(p)$,
$n \in \mathbb{N}$. We denote $B_\omega(p)$ the set of all infinite behaviors of
p.

1. An initial segment of a behavior is a behavior. We
prefer to call an initial segment a _left_ _factor_: we define
for all f = f(1) ... f(n) $\in A^n$ its set of left factors

FG(f) as the set of words F[i] = f(1) ... f(i) for

$0 \leq i \leq n$ (by definition, f[0] is the empty word ε). For

u = u(1)u(2) ... u(n) ... in A , we define

FG(u) = {u[n] | n $\in$ $\mathbb{N}$} with u[n] = u(1) ... u(n).

The first assumption can be written as follows:

for all f $\in$ B(p), FG(f) $\subseteq$ B(p),

and

for all u $\in$ B$_\omega$(p), FG(u) $\subseteq$ B(p).

For all L $\subseteq$ A* (resp., L $\subseteq$ A$^\omega$), letting

FG(L) = $\cup$ {FG(f) | f $\in$ L},

(resp.,

FG(l) = $\cup$ {FG(u) | u $\in$ L}),

we can also express the first assumption by the inclusion

FG(B(p) $\cup$ B$_\omega$(p)) $\subseteq$ B(p).

2. We suppose that A contains an action e called the
empty action: intuitively saying that p performs e at
time n is equivalent to saying p does nothing at time n.
The second assumption is that the process p can be delayed
at any instant for a finite amount of time or forever. This
assumption is expressed by the two conditions:

(a) for all f, g $\in$ A*, fg $\in$ B(p) => feg $\in$ B(p)

and fe$^\omega$ $\in$ B$_\omega$(p) (fg is the ordinary product in A,

e$^\omega$ is the infinite word all of whose letters are equal

to e and fe$^\omega$ is the infinite word u such that

u[|f|] = f and for all n > |f|, u(n) = e);

(b) for all $f \in A^*$, $u \in A^\omega$, $fu \in B_\omega(p)$ => $feu \in B_\omega(p)$

and $fe^\omega \in B_\omega(p)$ (we extend the product in A^* by

defining for all $f \in A^*$, $u \in A^\omega$ the product fu as

the infinite word v such that $v[|f|] = f$ and for

all $n > |f|$, $v(n) = u(n - |f|)$).

3. If for all $n \in \mathbb{N}$, $u[n]$ is a behavior of p , then
the infinite word u is an infinite behavior of p . This
means that if p behaves properly from time 1 to time n
for all n , then it behaves properly forever.

We can write this third assumption differently: we define
the <u>adherence of a language</u> $L \subset A^*$ as in [1]:

$$Adh(L) = \{u \in A^\omega \mid FG(u) \subset FG(L)\}.$$

Then our third assumption is that

$$B_\omega(p) \supset Adh(B(p)).$$

A process p is said to be <u>coherent</u> if it satisfies the
first assumption, <u>delayable</u> if it satisfies the second assumption, and <u>normal</u> if it satisfies the third assumption.

<u>Example</u>. We consider a process which can read and write
in a memory cell alternatively, the first action being to read.

If we define its set of behaviors by

$$B(p) = (e^* \underline{read}\ e^*\ \underline{write})^* (e^*\ \underline{read}\ e^* \cup e^*)$$

and

$$B_\omega(p) = (e^*\ \underline{read}\ e^*\ \underline{write})^\omega \cup B(p)e^\omega,$$

then p is coherent, delayable and normal.

To prove this we use the obvious relations

$$FG(LL') = FG(L) \cup LFG(L'), \quad \text{if} \quad L, L' \subset A^* \quad \text{or}$$
$$L \subset A^*, \quad L' \subset A^\omega,$$

and

$$FG(L^*) = L^*FG(L).$$

Then we can compute

$$FG(B(p)) = FG((e^* \underline{read} \ e^* \ \underline{write})^*) \cup$$
$$(e^* \underline{read} \ e^* \ \underline{write})^*FG(e^* \underline{read} \ e^* \cup e^*).$$

Since $FG((e^* \underline{read} \ e^* \ \underline{write})^*) =$
$(e^* \underline{read} \ e^* \ \underline{write})^*FG(e^* \underline{read} \ e^* \ \underline{write}) =$
$(e^* \underline{read} \ e^* \ \underline{write})^*(e^* \underline{read} \ e^* \cup e^*)$ and
$FG(e^* \underline{read} \ e^* \cup e^*) = e^* \underline{read} \ e^* \cup e^*$, we do have
$FG(B(p)) = B(p)$.

Also define for $L \subset A^* \setminus \{\varepsilon\}$ the set L^ω as the set of
all infinite words $u = \ell_1 \ell_2 \ldots \ell_n \ldots$ which are infinite
products of words in L. We thus have

$$FG(L^\omega) = L^*FG(L)$$

and verify easily that $FG(B_\omega(p)) \subset B(p)$.

The fact that p is delayable is obvious.

The fact that p is normal can be proved in the following
way. Suppose for all n, $u[n] \in B(p)$. If there exists a
largest $n \in \mathbb{N}$ such that $u(n) \in \{\underline{read}, \underline{write}\}$, then we have
$u = u[n]e^\omega$ and, since $u[n] \in B(p)$, $u \in B(p)e^\omega \subset B_\omega(p)$.
Otherwise, for all n such that $u(n) = \underline{read}$ (resp., $\underline{write}$)
there exists $n' > n$ such that $u(n') = \underline{write}$ (resp., $\underline{read}$)

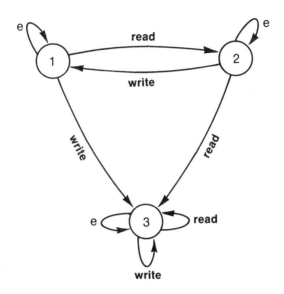

and $\forall n"$, $n < n" < n'$, $u(n") = e$; thus, u is an infinite

product of words in $e^* \underline{read} \ e^* \underline{write}$ and thus belongs to

$B_\omega(p)$.

A convenient way of representing the behaviors of p is

the above-illustrated automaton. The set of finite behaviors

$B(p)$ is the set of all f's such that $\lambda(①,f) \neq ③$ and

the set of infinite behaviors of p is the set

$$B_\omega(p) = \{u \in A^\omega \mid \forall n \in \mathbb{N}, \ \lambda(①,u[n]) \neq ③ \}.$$

B. Synchronization of Processes

We are now given a vector $\vec{p}$ of processes $\vec{p} =$

$<p_1,\ldots,p_h>$. Each of the p_i is given by its set of behav-

iors $B(p_i) \cup B_\omega(p_i)$. Suppose first these processes are inde-

pendent, that is, each of them may perform at any time n the

action it wishes to perform. In this case we can easily de-

scribe the behaviors of $\vec{p}$ in the following way:

Every h-tuple of words of length n, $\vec{f} = <f_1,\ldots,f_h>$ where $f_i \in B(p_i)$, is a possible behavior of $\vec{p}$ from time 1 up to time n and every h-tuple of infinite words $\vec{u} = <u_1,\ldots,u_h>$ where $u_i \in B_\omega(p)$ is a possible infinite behavior of $\vec{p}$.

We define the homogeneous product

$$B(p_1) \otimes B(p_2) \otimes \ldots \otimes B(p_h)$$

as the union for all n of

$$B_n(p_1) \times B_n(p_2) \times \ldots \times B_n(p_h),$$

that is, the set of h-tuples $<f_1,\ldots,f_h>$ with $|f_1| = |f_2| = \ldots = |f_h|$ and $f_i \in B(p_i)$. We write $B(\vec{p}) = B(p_1) \bigcirc \ldots \bigcirc B(p_h)$ and $B_\omega(\vec{p}) = B_\omega(p_1) \times B_\omega(p_2) \times \ldots \times B_\omega(p_h)$.

An obvious fact is that the h-tuple $\vec{f} = <f_1,\ldots,f_h>$ in $B(\vec{p})$ can be considered as a word in $(A^{(h)})*$ where $A^{(h)}$ is the cartesian product of h copies of A. Conversely, $\vec{f} = \vec{f}(1) \ldots \vec{f}(n)$ where $\vec{f}(i) \in A^{(h)}$ defines an h-tuple of words in $(A^n)^{(h)}$, namely $<f_1,\ldots,f_h>$ with $f_i = f_i(1) \ldots f_i(n)$.

In a similar way we have a clear isomorphism between $(A^{(h)})^\omega$ and $(A^\omega)^{(h)}$.

We shall freely use these isomorphisms, writing, for example,

$$B(p_1) \otimes \ldots \otimes B(p_h) = (B(p_1) \times \ldots \times B(p_h)) \cap (A^{(h)})*.$$

Now a synchronization condition is introduced as a subset $\bar{S}$ of $A^{(h)}$ which represents the forbidden simultaneous actions of $p_1 \ldots p_h$. (We call vector of actions any h-tuple

$\vec{a} = <a_1, \ldots, a_h>$, $a_i \in A$.)   The whole idea of synchronizing

concurrent programs is to forbid for example the simultaneous

use by two programs of a common resource. We denote by S

the complement of $\bar{S}$ in $A^{(h)}$ and we define $B(\vec{p}, S)$, the

set of synchronized finite behaviors of the system $(\vec{p}, S)$, as

$B(\vec{p}, S) = B(\vec{p}) \cap S*$, and $B_\omega(\vec{p}, S)$, the set of synchronized

infinite behaviors of $(\vec{p}, S)$, as $B_\omega(\vec{p}, S) = B_\omega(\vec{p}) \cap S^\omega$.   A

behavior is synchronized if and only if at each time n the

vector $\vec{a}$ of actions performed by $\vec{p}$ is not forbidden.   One

can make immediately some remarks and raise some questions.

If for all $i = 1, \ldots, h$ the process p_i is normal,

then $(\vec{p}, S)$ is normal.   This means that

$$\forall n, \quad \vec{u}[n] \in B(\vec{p}, S) \implies \vec{u} \in B_\omega(\vec{p}, S).$$

p_i being normal, $\forall n$, $u_i[n] \in B(p_i) \implies u_i \in B_\omega(p_i)$ and thus

$\forall n$, $\vec{u}[n] \in B(\vec{p})$ and $\vec{u} \in B_\omega(\vec{p})$.   But also $\forall n$, $\vec{u}[n] \in S*$

$\implies \vec{u} \in S^\omega$.

One can thus define an   S-deadlock of $\vec{p}$ as an element f

of $B(\vec{p}, S)$ such that

$$\forall \vec{s} \in S, \quad \vec{f}\vec{s} \notin B(\vec{p}, S).$$

We can state that an infinite behavior $\vec{u}$ of $\vec{p}$ is a syn-

chronized behavior of $(\vec{p}, S)$ if and only if none of its left

factors $\vec{u}[n]$ is an   S-deadlock of $\vec{p}$.   In other words,   if

p avoids all deadlocks in one of its infinite behaviors, then

it behaves properly forever.   Then we have the following ques-

tions given $\vec{p}$ and S:

   (i) are there S-deadlocks of $\vec{p}$?

   (ii) is $B_\omega(\vec{p}, S)$ empty?

  (iii) does there exist a strategy to avoid all deadlocks?

Example. Suppose two processes p_1 and p_2 can read and write in the same memory cell as the process p described in the example above, with the restriction that they cannot both write at the same time nor can one read when the other writes.

Then $B(p_1) \cup B_\omega(p_1)$ and $B(p_2) \cup B_\omega(p_2)$ are both described by the automaton drawn above. The synchronization condition S is given by

$$S = \{<\underline{read},\underline{read}>, <\underline{read},\ e>, <e,\ \underline{read}>,$$
$$<\underline{write},\ e>, <e,\ \underline{write}>\}.$$

(We could have added $<e,e>$ but we forbid it, for $<e,e>$ means that both processes do nothing and we wish that at every instant of time one of them be active.)

Anticipating what follows, we shall describe $B(\vec{p})$ for $\vec{p} = <p_1,p_2>$ by the following automaton.

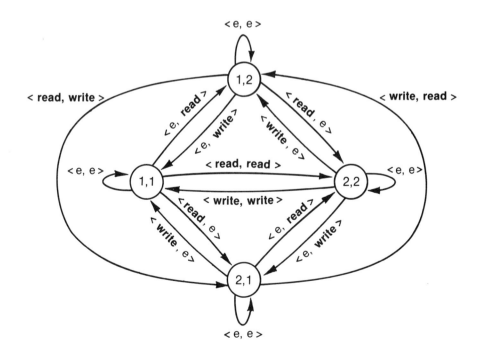

There is a missing state, say q_s, the sink state: all the missing arrows should go to the sink state and also all the arrows coming out of the sink state should return to it.

Then $B(\vec{p})$ is the set of words in $(A^{(2)})*$ which carry the state $(1,1)$ onto one of the states $(1,1)$, $(1,2)$, $(2,1)$, $(2,2)$ and $B_\omega(\vec{p})$ is the set of all words in $(A^{(2)})^\omega$ such that for no n does $\vec{u}[n]$ carry $(1,1)$ into the sink state.

To describe $B(p,S)$ one simply deletes the arrows labeled by elements of S. All missing arrows go to a sink state q_s which is not drawn. Then $B(\vec{p},S)$ is the set of words $\vec{f}$ carrying $(1,1)$ into $(1,1)$, $(1,2)$, $(2,1)$ or $(2,2)$, and $B_\omega(\vec{p},S)$ is the set of infinite words $\vec{u}$ such that for no n does $\vec{u}[n]$ carry $(1,1)$ into q_s. We immediately check that $(\vec{p},S)$ has the property that every finite behavior $\vec{f}' \in B(\vec{p},S)$ can be extended in an infinite behavior $\vec{u}' \in B_\omega(\vec{p},S)$. A system with this property is called adequate by P. Lauer, et al., in [18].

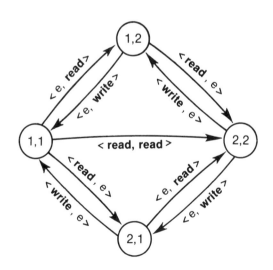

C. Control of Processes and
Systems of Processes

In order to describe the set $B_\omega(\vec{p},S)$ for some system $(\vec{p},S)$, the best one can do is to describe some mechanism which, having retained some information m_n on the beahvior of the system up to time n, tells which actions $\vec{s} \in S$ the system may perform at time $n + 1$, in order to avoid future deadlocks.

We define such a mechanism as a control

$$c = \langle M, m_0, \phi, \psi \rangle$$

where M is a set of states, $m_0 \in M$ is an initial state, ϕ maps M into the set of subsets of S, ψ maps the set $\{(m,\vec{s}) \mid m \in M, \vec{s} \in \phi(m)\}$ into M.

A control defines a set of finite and infinite behaviors:

$$B(c) = \{\vec{f} = \vec{f}(1) \ \ldots \ \vec{f}(n) \mid m_1, \ldots, m_n \in M,$$
$$\forall i = 1, \ldots, n, \ \vec{f}(i) \in \phi(m_{i-1}) \ \text{ and }$$
$$m_i = \psi(m_{i-1}, \vec{f}(i))\},$$

and

$$B_\omega(c) = \{\vec{u} \in S^\omega \mid m_1, \ldots, m_n, \ldots \in M,$$
$$\forall i \in N_+, \ \vec{u}(i) \in \phi(m_{i-1}) \ \text{ and }$$
$$m_i = \psi(m_{i-1}, \vec{u}(i))\}.$$

The control c is said to be a full control of $(\vec{p},S)$ iff $B_\omega(\vec{p},S) = B_\omega(c)$ and $(\vec{p},S)$ is said to be fully controlled if and only if there exists such a control c. We have

Property 1. Every coherent and normal systems $(\vec{p},S)$ is fully controlled.

$\underline{\text{Proof.}}$ We recall that a normal system $(\vec{p},S)$ satisfies

$$B_\omega(\vec{p},S) \supset \text{Adh}(B(\vec{p},S)).$$

If it is coherent the system $(\vec{p},S)$ satisfies

$$FG(B_\omega(\vec{p},S) \cup B(\vec{p},S)) \subset B(\vec{p},S).$$

Whence for a normal and coherent system one has

$$B_\omega(\vec{p},S) \subset \text{Adh}(FG(B_\omega(\vec{p},S))) \subset \text{Adh}(B(\vec{p},S))$$

whence $B_\omega(\vec{p},S) = \text{Adh}(B(\vec{p},S))$. Then one can build the following control c:

$$M = B(p,S), \quad m_0 = \varepsilon,$$
$$\phi(\vec{f}) = \{\vec{s} \in S \mid \vec{f}\vec{s} \in B(\vec{p},S)\} \quad \text{for all } \vec{f} \in B(\vec{p},S),$$
$$\psi(\vec{f},\vec{s}) = \vec{f}\vec{s} \quad \text{for all } \vec{f} \in B(\vec{p},S), \quad \vec{s} \in S$$

such that $\vec{f}\vec{s} \in B(\vec{p},S)$. Clearly $B(c) = B(p,S)$ and

$$B_\omega(c) = \text{Adh}(B(c)) = \text{Adh}(B(\vec{p},S)) = B_\omega(\vec{p},S). \quad \square$$

Let us define a $\underline{\text{safe}}$ control c in the following way: define $\psi(m,\vec{f})$ inductively as $\psi(m,\vec{\varepsilon}) = m$ for all m ($\vec{\varepsilon}$ is the empty word of $(A^{(h)})*)$ and $\psi(m,\vec{s}\vec{f}) = \psi(\psi(m,\vec{s}),\vec{f})$; a state m is accessible from m_0 if and only if there exists an $\vec{f}$ such that $\psi(m_0,\vec{f}) = m$. We may assume that all the states are accessible from m_0: if they are not then we delete all the nonaccessible states in c, obtaining a reduced $\bar{c}$ such that $B(\bar{c}) = B(c)$ and $B_\omega(\bar{c}) = B_\omega(c)$. Assuming that c is thus reduced, we say that c is safe if and only if for all $m \in M$, $\phi(m) \neq \emptyset$.

If c is a safe control, then we have

$$B(c) = FG(B_\omega(c)).$$

The containment $FG(B_\omega(c)) \subseteq B(c)$ is satisfied for all c. Consider thus $\vec{f} \in B(c)$. Since $\psi(m_0, f) \neq \emptyset$ there exists $\vec{s}_1$ such that $\vec{f s}_1 \in B(c)$, since $\psi(m_0, \vec{f s}_1) \neq \emptyset$ there exists $\vec{s}_2$ such that $\vec{f s}_1 \vec{s}_2 \in B(c)$ and so on. By a repeated application of this argument one can find an infinite sequence

$$\vec{s}_1, \vec{s}_2, \ldots, \vec{s}_n, \ldots \quad \text{such that for all} \quad n$$
$$\vec{f s}_1 \vec{s}_2 \ldots \vec{s}_n \in B(c) \quad \text{whence}$$
$$\vec{f s}_1 \vec{s}_2 \ldots \vec{s}_n \ldots \in B_\omega(c).$$

One can prove the following:

<u>Property 2</u>. If c is a full control of $(\vec{p}, S)$ then there exists a safe control $\underline{c}$ of $(\vec{p}, S)$.

<u>Proof</u>. We may assume that c is reduced (all states accessible from m_0). We build $\underline{c}$ in the following way: let N_0 be the subset of M given by

$$N_0 = \{m \in M \mid \phi(m) = \emptyset\};$$

define $N_{\ell+1}$ inductively as

$$N_{\ell+1} = N_\ell \cup \{m \in M \mid \forall \vec{s} \in \phi(m)\psi, \quad \psi(m, \vec{s}) \in N_1\}.$$

Consider the union $N = \bigcup_{\ell \in \mathbb{N}} N_\ell$. The control $\underline{c}$ is the following: $\underline{M} = M \setminus N$, $\underline{m}_0 = m_0$ (we shall see that $\underline{M} \neq \emptyset \Rightarrow m_0 \in \underline{M}$), $\underline{\phi}(m) = \{\vec{s} \in S \mid \psi(m, \vec{s}) \in \bar{M}\}$, and $\underline{\psi}(m, \vec{s}) = \psi(m, \vec{s})$ for all $m \in \underline{M}$ and $\vec{s} \in \underline{\phi}(m)$.

We first prove that $\underline{c}$ is safe. Suppose indeed $\underline{\phi}(m) = \emptyset$ for some $m \in \underline{M}$. This means $\forall \vec{s} \in S$, $\psi(m, \vec{s}) \in N$. Since

$\{\psi(m,\vec{s}) \mid s \in S\}$ is finite there exists an integer ℓ such that $\forall \vec{s} \in S$, $\psi(m,\vec{s}) \in N_\ell$. But this implies $m \in N_{\ell+1}$ whence $m \in N$ contrary to the assumption $m \in \underline{M}$. We now prove that $\forall \vec{f} \in S^*$, $\psi(m_0,f) \in N$ if and only if $\vec{f}S^* \cap B(c)$ is finite. Indeed, $\psi(m_0,\vec{f}) \in N_0 \iff \vec{f}S^* \cap B(c) = \emptyset$ and by induction

$$\psi(m_0,\vec{f}) \in N_{\ell+1} \iff \forall \vec{s}, \quad \psi(m_0,\vec{fs}) \in N_\ell$$
$$\iff \forall \vec{s}, \quad \{\vec{g} \mid \vec{fsg} \in B(c)\} \subset S^\ell$$
$$\iff \{\vec{g} \mid \vec{fg} \in B(c)\} \subset S^{\ell+1}.$$

For the safe control thus built we have

$$B(\underline{c}) = \{\vec{f} \in S^* \mid \vec{f}S \cap B(c) \text{ is infinite}\}.$$

One proves easily that then $Adh(B(\underline{c})) = Adh(B(c))$ and thus $B_\omega(\underline{c}) = B_\omega(\vec{p},S)$ which prove that $\underline{c}$ fully controls $(\vec{p},S)$. For any language $L \subset S^*$ we can define the center of L denoted $\underline{L}$ as the set of all $\vec{f}$ such that $\vec{f}S^* \cap L$ is infinite. Using Koenig's lemma it is easy to prove that

$$\underline{L} = FG(Adh(L)) \quad (see~[1]),$$

$$Adh(\underline{L}) = Adh(L),$$

and

$$\forall L, L', \quad Adh(L) = Adh(L') \iff \underline{L} = \underline{L}'.$$

The problem of constructing a safe full control of $(\vec{p},S)$ is exactly the same as to construct the center $B(\vec{p},S)$. The construction given above which is not effective if M is infinite is effective in the case of a finite control c, where c is said to be finite if and only if M is a finite set:

then the increasing sequence of subsets of the finite set M,

N_0, N_1, ..., N_1, ... is sationary and one can compute the

union $N = \bigcup\limits_{\ell \in \mathbb{N}} N_\ell$. $\square$

D. Product of Processes

Suppose the processes P_1, ..., P_k are all fully controlled by c_1, ..., c_k, respectively. (The definition of a
control given above for a system $(\vec{p}, S)$ is valid for a single
process p which may be considered as the system (p, A).)
We can show the following

Property 3. If for all $i = 1$, ..., k, P_i is a fully
controlled process, and if $S \subset A^{(k)}$ is a synchronization
condition, then the system $(\vec{p}, S)$ is fully controlled.

Proof. Take $c_i = <Q_i, m_i^0, \phi_i, \psi_i>$. One first builds the
product c of the c_i's thus defined:

$$\vec{M} = M_1 \times M_2 \times \ldots \times M_k,$$
$$\vec{m}^0 = <m_1^0, \ldots, m_k^0>,$$
$$\vec{\phi}(<m_1, \ldots, m_k>) = \phi(m_1) \times \phi(m_2) \times \ldots \times \phi(m_k),$$

and

$$\vec{\psi}(<m_1, \ldots, m_k>, <a_1, \ldots, a_k>) = <\psi_1(m_1, a_1), \ldots, \psi_k(m_k, a_k)>.$$

Clearly $\vec{c}$ is such that

$$B(\vec{c}) = B(c_1) \otimes B(c_2) \otimes \ldots \otimes B(c_k) = B(\vec{p})$$

and

$$B_\omega(\vec{c}) = B_\omega(c_1) \times \ldots \times B_\omega(c_k) = B_\omega(\vec{p}).$$

From $\vec{c}$ we can then build $\vec{c}_S$ which is defined by the same
$\vec{M}$, the same $\vec{m}^0$:

$$\vec{\phi}_S(<m_1,\ldots,m_k>) = (\phi(m_1) \times \ldots \times \phi(m_k)) \cap S$$

and

$\vec{\psi}_S$ is the restriction of $\vec{\psi}$ to

$$\{(\vec{m},\vec{s}) \mid \vec{m} \in \vec{M}, \quad \vec{s} \in \vec{\phi}_S(m)\}.$$

The control $\vec{c}_S$ may or may not be reduced. Whether it is reduced or not one has

$$B(\vec{c}_S) = B(\vec{p},S)$$
$$B_\omega(\vec{c}_S) = B_\omega(\vec{p},S). \quad \square$$

This very general construction is mainly useful when the c_i's, $i \in [k]$, are all finite. Then clearly $\vec{c}$ and $\vec{c}_S$ are also both finite and we get the theorem:

Theorem 1. If the processes $p_1, \ldots, p_k$ are all fully controlled by finite controls $c_1, \ldots, c_k$, and if $S \subset A^{(k)}$ is any synchronization condition, then the system $(\vec{p},S)$ can be fully controlled by a safe finite control.

Proof. One applies Property 3 to get the finite full control $\vec{c}_S$, and then applies, after reduction of $\vec{c}_S$, Property 2 to get the desired finite safe full control $\underline{\vec{c}}_S$ of $(\vec{p},S)$. $\quad \square$

E.   Rational Processes

A process p is said to be __rational__ if and only if its set of finite behaviors $B(p)$ is a rational language in A^*. We assume, as in Part A, that p is coherent, delayable and normal. We thus prove

Property 4. A rational process p is safely finitely controlled.

Proof. Suppose $B(p)$ is recognized by the finite automaton

$$\mathcal{a} = <Q, q_0, \lambda, Q_f>.$$

The fact that p is coherent implies that

$$\forall f, g \in A^*, \quad \lambda(q_0, fg) \in Q_f \Rightarrow \lambda(q_0, f) \in Q_f.$$

Then p is controlled by $c = <M, m_0, \phi, \psi>$,

$$M = Q_f, \quad m_0 = q_0 \in Q_f,$$
$$\phi(q) = \{a \in A \mid \lambda(q, a) \in Q_f\} \quad \text{for all} \quad q \in Q_f,$$

and

$$\psi(q, a) = \lambda(q, a).$$

One has $B(c) = \{f \in A^* \mid \lambda(q_0, f) \in Q_f\} = B(p)$ and $B_\omega(c) = \text{Adh}(B(c)) = B_\omega(p)$ since $B(p) = \text{Adh}(B(c))$ by the normality of p. $\square$

Remark. All the processes described in a language such as COSY [18] are rational processes and thus safely finitely controlled. In COSY the sets of finite behaviors are given by rational expressions rather than by finite automata but MacNaughton-Yamada's algorithm allows us to build these finite controls.

In the case of rational processes we can answer all the questions raised in Section B as concerns deadlocks:

Theorem 2. The problems of deciding whether

(a) there exist S-deadlocks of $\vec{p}$,

(b) $B_\omega(\vec{p}, S)$ is empty,

(c) there exists a strategy to avoid deadlocks,

are all solvable if $\vec{p} = <p_1, \ldots, p_k>$ is a vector of rational processes and $S \subset A^{(k)}$ is any synchronization condition.

Proof. We build the finite controls $c_1, \ldots, c_k$ for $p_1, \ldots, p_k$ and the product $\vec{c}$ as in Proposition 3. Then there exists an S-deadlock of $\vec{p}$ if and only if there exists an $\vec{f} \in (A^{(k)})*$ such that

$$\phi(\psi(m_0, \vec{f})) = \emptyset,$$

and $B_\omega(\vec{p}, S) \neq \emptyset$ if and only if the subset N of M built as in Proposition 2 is different from M. Both conditions are clearly decidable.

The strategy to avoid all deadlocks is exactly given by the finite control $\vec{c}_S$ built in Theorem 1. □

Remark. The nonrational case raises difficult questions. See [24].

F.   Starvation and Fairness

The synchronized infinite behavior $\vec{u}$ of $(\vec{p}, S)$ induces starvation of p_i if and only if there exists $n_0 \in \mathbb{N}$ such that

$$\forall n, \quad n > n_0 \Rightarrow u_i(n) = e.$$

(Intuitively, p_i starves if, after a while, it does nothing forever.) Classical problems in the theory of synchronization are the following:

(a) Is there a possibility of starvation, in other words, does there exist $\vec{u} \in B_\omega(\vec{p}, S)$ and $i \in [k]$ such that $\vec{u}$ induces starvation of p_i?

(b) Is there a possibility of non-starvation (fairness), i.e., a word $\vec{u} \in B_\omega(\vec{p}, S)$ which induces no starvation?

(c) Is there a strategy to avoid all starvation phenomena?

The last problem can be rephrased in the following way: let $F(\vec{p},S)$ be the set of all $\vec{u} \in B_\omega(\vec{p},S)$ such that $\vec{u}$ induces no starvation ($\forall n \in \mathbb{N}$, $\forall i \in [k]$, $n_i > n$, $u_i(n_i) \neq e$). How can one describe $F(\vec{p},S)$?

We can give partial answers to these problems, at least in the case of rational processes $p_1, \ldots, p_k$. We prove, under the assumption that $p_1, \ldots, p_k$ are rational processes and $S \subset A^{(k)}$ is any synchronization condition the following properties.

Property 5. There exists $\vec{u} \in B_\omega(\vec{p},S)$ which induces starvation of p_i if and only if there exists in any reduced finite full control $\vec{c}_S$ of $(\vec{p},S)$ a loop of the form $(m,\vec{f})$ such that

$$\psi(m,\vec{f}) = m \quad \text{and} \quad f_i \in e^*.$$

Proof. If such a loop exists, and $\vec{g}$ is a word such that $\psi(m_0,g) = m$ then $\vec{g}(\vec{f})^\omega \in B_\omega(\vec{p},S)$ induces starvation of p_i. Conversely if $\vec{u} \in B_\omega(\vec{p},S)$ induces starvation of p_i then for all $n > n_0$, $u_i(n) = e$. The sequence of all $\psi(m_0,\vec{u}[n])$, $n > n_0$, all of whose elements belong to the finite set $\vec{M}$ of states of $\vec{c}_S$ contains repetition: thus there exist n_1, n_2 such that $n_1 < n_2$ and

$$\psi(m_0, u[n_1]) = \psi(m_0, \vec{u}[n_2]).$$

Clearly the word $\vec{f} = u(n_1 + 1) u(n_1 + 2) \ldots u(n_2)$ and the state $m = \psi(m_0, \vec{u}[n_1])$ are such that

$$\psi(m,\vec{f}) = m \quad \text{and} \quad f_i \in e^*. \quad \square$$

Property 6. There exists a possibility of non-starvation, that is, $\vec{u} \in B_\omega(\vec{p},S)$ such that

$$\forall i \in [k], \quad \forall n \in \mathbb{N}, \quad n' > n, \quad u_i(n') \neq e$$

if and only if there exists a fair loop in $\vec{c}_S$ that is a pair $(m,\vec{f})$ such that $\psi(m,f) = m$ and $\forall i \in [k], \quad f_i \not\in e^\star$.

Proof. It is very similar to the above one.

If $\vec{c}_S$ is reduced there exists $\vec{g}$ such that $\psi(m_0,\vec{g}) = m$ and thus $\vec{g}(\vec{f})^\omega \in B_\omega(\vec{p},S)$ is clearly a fair behavior.

Conversely, suppose $\vec{u}$ is a fair behavior: consider n_1^1 such that $u_1(n_1^1) \neq e$, $n_2^1 > n_1^1$ such that $u_2(n_2^1) \neq e$ and so on until $n_k^1 > n_{k-1}^1$ such that $u_k(n_k^1) \neq e$. Then there exists $n_1^2 > n_k^1 > n_{k-1}^1 > \ldots > n_1^1$ such that $u_1(n_1^2) \neq e$ and for all $i \in [k]$, $n_k^2 > n_{k-1}^2 > \ldots > n_1^2$ such that $u_i(m_i^2) \neq e$. We can thus build a double indexed sequence n_i^ℓ, $i \in [k]$, $\ell \in \mathbb{N}_+$, such that $i < i'$ and $\ell = \ell' \Rightarrow n_i^\ell < n_{i'}^{\ell'}$, $\ell < \ell' \Rightarrow u_i^\ell < u_{i'}^{\ell'}$, for all ℓ the word $\vec{u}(n_1^\ell) \ldots \vec{u}(n_1^{\ell+1}-1)$ $= \vec{g}(\ell)$ is fair, that is, satisfies $\forall i \in [k]$, $g(\ell)_i \not\in e^\star$. It suffices to consider the sequence of states $\psi(m_0, \vec{u}[n_1^\ell])$, $\ell \in \mathbb{N}_+$, which certainly contains a repetition to find a fair loop in $\vec{c}_S$. $\square$

One may be even more precise: suppose all the p_i's are rational and consider $\vec{\underline{c}}_S$ the finite safe full control of $(\vec{p},S)$ whose existence follows from Theorem 1. All states $m \in M$ are accessible from M_0 and for all $m \in M$, $\phi(m) \neq \emptyset$. Then there exists a possibility of non-starvation if and only if for all $m \in M$ and $i \in [k]$ there exists a word $\vec{f}$ such that $f_i \not\in e^\star$ and $\psi(m,\vec{f}) \in M$.

On the contrary one can describe those $\underline{c}_S$ for which there exists no possibility of non-starvation: M is the non-disjoint union of M_0, M_1, ..., M_k and we have $m_0 \in M_0$, and for all $m \in M_0$ and sufficiently large n,

$$|\vec{f}| = n \implies \psi(m,\vec{f}) \in M_i \quad i \neq 0,$$

and for all $m \in M_i$, $\vec{s} \in \phi(m)$, $s_i = e$. Given $\underline{\vec{c}}_S$ one can easily build M_1, ..., M_k as

$$M_i = \{m \in M \mid \vec{s} \in \phi(m) \implies s_i = e\}$$

and define $M_0 = M \setminus \bigcup_{i \in [k]} M_i$.

Then there exists a possibility of non-starvation if and only if M_0 is nonempty and such that

$$\forall m \in M_0, \quad \forall i \in [k], \quad \exists \vec{f} \text{ such that } \psi(m,\vec{f}) \in M_0 \text{ and }$$

$$f_i \notin e^*.$$

Property 7. In general there does not exist a control c such that $F(\vec{p},S) = B_\omega(c)$.

But one can decide whether this is the case. (If there exists a c such that $F(\vec{p},S) = B_\omega(c)$ then the system $(\vec{p},S)$ is said to be fairly controlled.)

Proof. For all control c, $B_\omega(c)$ is an adherence, i.e., satisfies

$$B_\omega(c) = \text{Adh}(FG(B_\omega(c))).$$

The simple following example shows that in the rational case, $F(\vec{p},S)$ is not an adherence.

Take $\vec{p} = \langle p_1, p_2 \rangle$.

$B(p_1) = (a_1 \cup e)*, \quad B_\omega(p_1) = (a_1 \cup e)^\omega,$

$B(p_2) = (a_2 \cup e)*, \quad B_\omega(p_2) = a_2 \cup e)^\omega.$

Also,

$S \subset \{a_1, a_2, e\} \times \{a_1, a_2, e\}$

is given by

$S = \{\langle a_1, a_2 \rangle, \ \langle a_1, e \rangle, \ \langle e, a_2 \rangle\}.$

Then

$B(\vec{p}, S) = S*, \quad B_\omega(\vec{p}, S) = S^\omega,$

$F(\vec{p}, S) = \{\vec{u} \in S^\omega \mid \forall n \in \mathbb{N}, \ n_1', n_2' > n \quad \text{imply}$

$\qquad u_1(n_1') = a_1 \quad \text{and} \quad u_2(n_2') = a_2\}.$

Clearly $FG(F(\vec{p}, S)) \supset \langle a_1, e \rangle *$. If $F(\vec{p}, S)$ were an adherence, then $\langle a_1, e \rangle^\omega$ would belong to $F(\vec{p}, S)$ since all the left factors of $\langle a_1, e \rangle^\omega$ belong to $FG(F(\vec{p}, S))$. $\square$

<u>Remark</u>. We can go further in the analysis of the full safe control $\underline{c}_S$ already considered in the above remark.

The set of states is $M = M_0 \cup M_1 \cup \ldots \cup M_k$ such that $m_0 \in M_0$ and for all $i \in [k], \ m \in M_i, \ \vec{s} \in \phi(m) \Rightarrow s_i = e$ and $\psi(m, \vec{s}) \in M_i$. Obviously all the infinite behaviors $\vec{u}$ which fall in one $M_i, \ i > 0$, induce starvation of the corresponding p_i.

Thus certainly the fair infinite behaviors are such that

$\forall n \in \mathbb{N}_+, \quad \psi(m_0, \vec{u}[n]) \in M_0.$

Let us build c^0 the safe control such that

$$B_\omega(c^0) = \text{Adh}\{\vec{f} \mid \psi(m_0,\vec{f}) \in M_0\}.$$

(We first restrict $\vec{c}_S$ to M_0 and then make it safe as in the proof of Property 2, by retaining only those states $\bar{M}_0 \subset M_0$ such that

$$\forall m \in \bar{M}_0, \quad \forall i \in [k], \quad \vec{f} \in (A^{(k)})* \quad \text{implies}$$
$$\psi(m,\vec{f}) \in \bar{M}_0 \quad \text{and} \quad f_i \notin e*).$$

The set $F(\vec{p},S)$ is an adherence if and only if

$$F(\vec{p},S) = B_\omega(c^0).$$

Indeed, we have $F(\vec{p},S) \subset B_\omega(c^0)$ and $B(c^0) \subset FG(F(\vec{p},S))$. (This last inclusion follows from the fact that $B(c^0) \subset FG(B_\omega(\vec{p},S))$ by construction.) Suppose for some $\vec{f} \in B(c^0)$, $\psi(m_0,\vec{f}) = m \in \bar{M}_0$, every extension $\vec{f}\vec{u}$ of $\vec{f}$ induces some starvation. Then for all $\vec{u}$ such that $\vec{f}\vec{u} \in B_\omega(\vec{p},S)$, there exists an $i \in [k]$ such that for some sufficiently large n, $\psi(m, \vec{u}[n]) \in M_i$. This implies precisely that $m \notin \bar{M}_0$.

We can now give an easy criterion to determine whether $F(\vec{p},S) = B_\omega(c^0)$. This is the case if and only if every loop in c^0 is a fair loop, that is, $\forall m \in \bar{M}_0$, $\vec{f} \in (A^{(k)})*$,

$$\psi(m,\vec{f}) = m \implies \forall i \in [k], \quad f_i \notin e*. \quad \square$$

Remark.

1. We remark first that according to Properties 5, 6 and 7, the three problems of determining whether

   (a) there exists a possibility of starvation,

   (b) there exists a possibility of non-starvation,

(c) the system $(\vec{p},S)$ is fairly controlled (in which case
   it is finitely fairly controlled)

are all decidable.

2. In our discussion we have distinguished several cases

(d) no starvation at all is possible: $F(\vec{p},S) = B_{\omega}(\vec{p},S)$,

(e) no possibility of non-starvation: $F(\vec{p},S) = \emptyset$,

(f) the immediate case in which we were able to partition
   $B_{\omega}(\vec{p},S)$ in two sets:

   (i) the set of infinite behaviors which contain a left
       factor $\vec{f}$ such that every extension of $\vec{f}$ is
       unfair: we call such a behavior an essentially
       unfair behavior;

   (ii) the set of infinite behaviors u such that for
        all n there exists v such that $u[n]v$ is
        fair: these behaviors are accidentally unfair.
        Some schedule to make sure that all processes are
        activated after time n would suffice to ensure
        the fairness of the corresponding behavior.

We believe that this distinction between (i) and (ii) is
important.

G. Conclusion

As we have seen, the problem of controlling a system
$(\vec{p},S)$ amounts to finding the center of $B(\vec{p},S)$: from what
precedes, the center of a rational language is a rational language, and given an automaton $\mathcal{A}$ recognizing the rational
language L, it is rather easy to construct the automaton $\underline{\mathcal{A}}$
recognizing the center $\underline{L}$ of L. We also know that the center $\underline{L}$ of an algebraic (context-free) language L is

algebraic, but then the algorithm mapping L onto $\underline{L}$ is not
so simple [23]. This will deal with the case of rational processes exchanging messages via a pushdown store [25]. But
processes exchanging messages will rather use either a finite
collection of specialized buffers (whose behavior is analogous
to the behavior of a counter, or equivalently a one-symbol
pushdown store) or FIFO buffers (these messages are then taken
at the top of the FIFO and stored at the bottom of the same
FIFO). Whence the problem of describing the center of a language recognized by either a multi-counter machine or a FIFO
automaton (which is exactly the same as a pda but for the fact
that the pushdown is replaced by a FIFO queue [2,27]). In
both cases nothing is known and the problem appears to be
difficult [25].

REFERENCES

1. Boasson, L., and Nivat, M., Adherences of languages.
   Report 79-13, Laboratoire d'Informatique Théorique et
   Programmation, Paris (1979).
2. Book, R., Greibach, S., and Wrathall, C., Comparisons and
   reset machines. Lecture Notes in Computer Science 62,
   Springer Verlag (1978).
3. Branstad, D.K., Privacy and protection in operating systems. Computer 6, 43-46 (1973).
4. Campbell, R.H., and Haberman, A.N., The specification of
   process synchronization by path expressions. Lecture Notes
   in Computer Science 16, Springer Verlag (1974).
5. Cohen, E., and Jefferson, D., Protection in the hydra
   operating system principles. ACM Operating Systems Review
   9, 5, 141-160 (1975).
6. Denning, P.J., Fault-tolerant operating systems. Computing Surveys 8, 4 (1976).
7. Denning, P.J., and Graham, G.S., Protection--principles
   and practice. Proc. AFIPS, SJCC 40, 417-429 (1972).
8. Dennis, J., and Van Horn, E., Programming semantics for
   multiprogrammed computations. CACM 9, 143-155 (1966).
9. Dijkstra, E.W., Cooperating sequential processes. In
   "Programming Languages" (F. Genuys, ed.), Academic Press,
   New York (1968).
10. Haberman, A.N., Synchronization of communicating processes.
    Comm. Assoc. Comp. Mach. 14, 171-176 (1972).

11. Harrison, M.A., Ruzzo, W.L., and Ullman, J.D., On protec-
    tion in operating systems. Operating Systems Rev. 9, 5,
    14-24 (1975).
12. Hoare, C.A.R., Towards a theory of parallel programming.
    In "Operating System Techniques," Academic Press, New York
    (1972).
13. Hoare, C.A.R., Communicating sequential processes. Comm.
    Assoc. Comp. Mach. 21, 666-677 (1978).
14. Jones, A.K., Protection in Programmed Systems. Ph.D.
    thesis, Carnegie-Mellon Univ., Pittsburgh, Pa. (1973).
15. Jones, A.K., Lipton, R.J., and Snyder, L, A linear algo-
    rithm for deciding subject-object security. Proc. 17th
    Ann. FOCS Conf., Houston, 33-41 (1976).
16. Jones, A.K., and Wulf, W.A., Towards the design of secure
    systems. Software--Practice and Experience 5, 321-336
    (1975).
17. Lauer, P.E., and Campbell, R.H., Formal semantics of a
    class of high level primitives for coordinating concurrent
    processes. Acta Informatica 5, 297-332 (1975).
18. Lauer, P.E., Torrigiani, P.R., and Shields, M.W., COSY, a
    system specification language based on paths and processes.
    Acta Informatica 12, 109-158 (1979).
19. Linden, T.A., Operating system structures to support secur-
    ity and reliable software. ACM Computing Surveys 8, 4,
    409-445 (1976).
20. Lynch, N.A., and Fischer, M.J., The behavior and implemen-
    tation of distributed systems. Lecture Notes in Computer
    Science 70, Springer Verlag (1979).
21. Mazurkiewics, A., Proving properties of processes. Report
    ICS-PAS 134, Polish Academy of Sciences, Varsovie (1973).
22. Milne, G., and Milner, R., Concurrent processes and their
    syntax. J. Assoc. Comp. Mach. 26, 302-321 (1979). Also
    Report CSR-2-77, University of Edinburgh.
23. Nivat, M., Sur les ensembles de mots infinis engendrés par
    une grammaire algébrique. RAIRO Informatique Théorique
    12, 259-278 (1978).
24. Nivat, M., De la synchronization des processus. To appear
    in Revue Technique Thomson-CSF.
25. Nivat, M., Concurrent producer-consumers, a case study.
    In preparation.
26. Redziejowski, R.R., The theory of general events and its
    application to parallel programming. Technical Paper
    TP 18-220, IBM Nordic Laboratory (1972).
27. Vauquelin, B., and Franchi-Zannettacci, P., Automates à
    file. Rapport 7904, Laboratoire associé 226, Bordeaux
    (1979)